ICONS OF R&B AND SOUL

Recent Titles in Greenwood Icons

Icons of Horror and the Supernatural: An Encyclopedia of Our Worst Nightmares
Edited by S.T. Joshi

Icons of Business: An Encyclopedia of Mavericks, Movers, and Shakers
Edited by Kateri Drexler

Icons of Hip Hop: An Encyclopedia of the Movement, Music, and Culture
Edited by Mickey Hess

Icons of Evolution: An Encyclopedia of People, Evidence, and Controversies
Edited by Brian Regal

Icons of Rock: An Encyclopedia of the Legends Who Changed Music Forever
Edited by Scott Schinder and Andy Schwartz

ICONS OF R&B AND SOUL

An Encyclopedia of the Artists Who Revolutionized Rhythm

VOLUME 1

Bob Gulla

Greenwood Icons

GREENWOOD PRESS
Westport, Connecticut • London

Library of Congress Cataloging-in-Publication Data

Gulla, Bob.
 Icons of R&B and soul: an encyclopedia of the artists who revolutionized rhythm / Bob Gulla.
    p. cm.—(Greenwood icons)
 Includes bibliographical references and index.
 ISBN 978-0-313-34044-4 (set: alk. paper)—ISBN 978-0-313-34045-1 (vol. 1: alk. paper)—ISBN 978-0-313-34046-8 (vol. 2: alk. paper)
 1. African Americans—Music—History and criticism. 2. Rhythm and blues music—United States—History and criticism. 3. Soul music—United States—History and criticism. 4. Rhythm and blues musicians—United States. 5. Soul musicians—United States. I. Title.
 ML3479.G85 2008
 781.643092′396073—dc22
 [B]   2007040518

British Library Cataloguing in Publication Data is available.

Copyright © 2008 by Bob Gulla

All rights reserved. No portion of this book may be reproduced, by any process or technique, without the express written consent of the publisher.

Library of Congress Catalog Card Number: 2007040518
ISBN: 978-0-313-34044-4 (set)
      978-0-313-34045-1 (vol. 1)
      978-0-313-34046-8 (vol. 2)

First published in 2008

Greenwood Press, 88 Post Road West, Westport, CT 06881
An imprint of Greenwood Publishing Group, Inc.
www.greenwood.com

Printed in the United States of America

The paper used in this book complies with the Permanent Paper Standard issued by the National Information Standards Organization (Z39.48–1984).

10 9 8 7 6 5 4 3 2 1

Contents

List of Photos	vii
Preface	ix

Volume One

R&B and Soul Timeline	xvii
Ray Charles	1
Little Richard	27
Fats Domino	47
Ruth Brown	69
LaVern Baker	91
Sam Cooke	107
Jackie Wilson	129
Etta James	147
Ike and Tina Turner	167
The Isley Brothers	191
James Brown, *by Andy Schwartz*	211
Curtis Mayfield	233

Volume Two

Smokey Robinson and The Miracles	249
The Temptations	267
The Supremes	289
Stevie Wonder, *by Jesse Jarnow*	309
Marvin Gaye	329
Dusty Springfield	355
Aretha Franklin	377

Otis Redding	395
Sly and the Family Stone	417
George Clinton	439
Kenny Gamble, Leon Huff, and Thom Bell	459
Prince, *by Jesse Jarnow*	481
Bibliography	501
Index	511

Photos

Ray Charles (page 1). 1973. Courtesty of Photofest.

Richard Wayne Penniman; aka Little Richard (page 27). ca. 1950s. Courtesy of Photofest.

Fats Domino (as himself) (page 47). In Roy Lockwoods's 1957 film, *Jamboree*. Courtesy of Warner Bros./Photofest.

Ruth Brown (page 69). Performing at Michael's Pub in New York City, 1988. Courtesy of Photofest.

LaVern Baker (page 91). ca. 1950s. Courtesy of Photofest.

Sam Cooke (page 107). ca. 1960s. Courtesy of Photofest.

Jackie Wilson (page 129). ca. 1960. Courtesy of Photofest.

Etta James (page 147). ca. 1970. Michael Ochs Archives/Getty Images.

Ike and Tina Turner (page 167). ca. 1960s. Courtesy of Photofest.

The Isley Brothers (page 191). ca. 1973. Courtesy of Photofest.

James Brown (page 211). Undated picture. Courtesy of Photofest.

Curtis Mayfield (page 233). Undated picture. AP Photo/Curtom Records.

Smokey Robinson and The Miracles (page 249). Courtesy of Photofest.

The Temptations (page 267). Shown from the left: Eddie Kendricks, David Ruffin, Otis Williams, Melvin Franklin, and Paul Williams. Courtesy of Photofest.

The Supremes (page 289). Late 1960s. Shown from left: Mary Wilson, Florence Ballard, and Diana Ross. Pictorial Press Ltd./Alamy.

Stevie Wonder (page 309). ca. 1970s. Courtesy of Photofest.

Marvin Gaye (page 329). 1974. Courtesy of Photofest.

Dusty Springfield (page 355). 1969. AP Photo.

Aretha Franklin (page 377). Undated picture. Pictorial Press Ltd./Alamy.

Otis Redding (page 395). 1967. Courtesy of Photofest.

Sly and the Family Stone (page 417). 1969. Shown clockwise from top: Larry Graham, Freddie Stone, Gregg Errico, Sly Stone, Rose Stone, Cynthia Robinson, and Jerry Martini. Courtesy of Photofest.

George Clinton (page 439). Performs with Parliament-Funkadelic, c. late 1970s. Courtesy of Photofest.

Gamble & Huff (page 459). Leon Huff and Kenny Gamble pose for this 1970 photo. Michael Ochs Archives/Getty Images.

Prince (page 481). Starring as The Kid in Albert Magnoli's 1984 film, *Purple Rain*. Courtesy of Photofest.

Preface

We are inundated with information. On the Web, in the bookstores, over the airwaves, our daily lives are saturated with data—new, old, reliable, not so reliable. We possess so much information at our fingertips that we as a people feel compelled to collate it as a community into encyclopedic Web pages (i.e., Wikipedia) so as not to lose track of all the knowledge we're amassing as a culture.

So it comes as a bit of a surprise when we stumble collectively on an idea that is more or less unexplored. Not that we haven't read about the personalities collected herein or that the R&B and soul genres are under-represented in the marketplace of ideas. It just hasn't been collected, packaged, and presented like the collection now in your hands.

There is a handful of books on the market right now that address the racial, political, and social repercussions of R&B and Soul. In the late 1940s, and through the 1950s and 1960s, the seminal acts were remarkable in that they functioned as both "uniters" and dividers. Influential performers like Ruth Brown and Fats Domino brought young black and white audiences together (when venues allowed it), but they also caused racial tension among the older guard. Many older Americans saw these talented artists, and their fame, wealth, and power as a source of resentment, deepening the racial divide. This divisiveness has provided fertile turf for sociologically minded authors, in particular Peter Guralnick, Nelson George, and Craig Werner, all of whom have written eloquently on the subject.

While the *Icons* series understands that the racial ramification is central to the story of soul and R&B, it also understands it is not the only tale to tell. The artists themselves—many who've made such an incredible impact on pop and popular culture—had imposing obstacles to overcome. Sam Cooke's storied transition from sacred to secular, Otis Redding's brief but soaring career as R&B's great hope, and Etta James's endless battles with the demons of drug addiction. Some of these stories have been told in cradle-to-grave biographies or autobiographies. Many have been compiled in encyclopedic fashion; their stories told hastily with only the most salient details.

A few of the artists presented here have been written about prodigiously, like James Brown and Little Richard. David Ritz, a reputable author specializing in R&B and Soul artists, has written biographies and ghost-written with a handful of artists included in these pages: Aretha Franklin, Ray Charles, Marvin Gaye, and Etta James to name a few. His work was helpful throughout the research process. Another author, R&B scholar Rick Coleman, recently dusted off the remarkable story of the legendary Fats Domino. His book *Blue Monday: Fats Domino and the Lost Dawn of Rock and Roll*, added insight and information to the Fat Man saga.

An equal handful, however, don't have many words at all dedicated to their lives and work. George Clinton, the Isley Brothers, LaVern Baker, and Stevie Wonder, for example, have had luminous careers, but minimal coverage. Digging up the information to execute these stories required consulting a variety of sources, then piecing those sources together as an archaeologist would piece together bones.

The result is a chronological excursion through R&B and soul, as envisioned through the eyes of its most significant contributors, from its incipient hit makers through its controversial popularization in the 1950s, its world domination in the 1960s, and its ultimate demise at the hands of disco and dance music, unofficially known as the R&B death knell, in the late 1970s.

Because the original, classic wave of R&B and soul suffered a miserable extinction at the hands of disco, I've ended this set with the last true soul legend, Prince, the one man brave enough to soldier on in soul despite the poor odds. Sure, there were many popular artists throughout the 1980s that also mined the genre, but none qualify as legends along the lines of the chosen few presented here. Much of the latest generation's so-called neo-soul music is fleeting, ephemeral, and so many of the artists responsible for it have been so derivative, it was hard to rationalize including anyone after Prince. Michael Jackson, arguably, was the only other consideration, but ultimately he ranks as a pop artist, despite his important early work for Motown with his brothers in the Jackson 5.

Anyone interested in the major personalities of the genres should find the work featured here useful, whether it be for student research or just to enhance one's appreciation of the idiom's most accomplished purveyors. Appended to each essay is a complementary sidebar, an element designed to add color and dimension to the subject's life story, whether it be the history of a studio, an instrument, or an executive integral to the star's life and work. Further Reading and Selected Discography suggestions can also be found at the end of each essay. These are not definitive, but good jumping-off points for lengthier explorations.

More complete, but still not definitive is the ending Bibliography, and complete listening section, which taken together provide a good indication of the breadth of sources used in executing these essays. A timeline is also included; it takes a look at the years through the prism of R&B and soul music's epic moments.

To execute the various essays included in this book, I consulted both traditional and new media sources, from books and magazines to Web sites, blogs, and Internet video sites. I traced the path of each subject's career in a linear way, beginning with childhood, family life, and musical beginnings, and then ending with either their death or the present day. Along the way, each one's salient moments receive coverage; peak and post-peak activities are pointed out. Most subjects experienced down periods of creativity and artistic misguidance at one time or another, resulting in unanimously maligned work. Critics recognize these phases, so when this happens, I make sure to say so. I did not intend to cast these artists in nothing but a positive light. On the other hand, editorializing is kept to a minimum.

Incidentally, the artists are represented chronologically, in part because so much of what happened throughout the history of R&B had so much to do with what came before it, or its antecedents. This kind of evolution is critical to the study of popular music. Having a foundation is an integral part of any study, especially in the arts, not only for critics looking for antecedents and precedents, but for casual listeners looking to optimize their appreciation and enjoyment of the music they already love.

DEFINING MOMENT

"Rhythm and blues" was a term used to describe a number of postwar American popular music forms, like boogie-woogie, 12-bar blues, and jump blues. All of these forms possessed a backbeat, an element that would later become fundamental to rock and roll. Where Delta blues is often seen as music of resignation, R&B, despite its common name, is actually more antithetical to it. It is seen as dance music, erotic music, escapist music, and spiritual music. It also expressed hope, pride, defiance, solidarity, and rebirth. These qualities can be found in all the best R&B, from early examples like Duke Ellington's "Black, Brown, and Beige" to Chuck Berry's "Brown-Eyed Handsome Man," the Impressions' "Keep on Pushing," Sam Cooke's "A Change Is Gonna Come," and John Coltrane's "A Love Supreme."

The early center of rhythm and blues was Los Angeles, which hosted a number of small independent labels that arose after the war. Specialty, Duke/Peacock, King/Federal, Chess, Sun, Modern, RPM, Vee-Jay, and Atlantic all formed to take advantage of, among other audiences, the new population of urban blacks. Their success foreshadowed the later rise of Motown a decade later, the most successful of all black-owned businesses.

The major labels at the time had been slipping in their attention on what had been going on in popular music. Most had applied their efforts to bland big band and vocal pop. In 1948, RCA Victor began marketing black music under the name "Blues and Rhythm," a term that replaced the original "race music," a moniker deemed offensive in traditional, conservative postwar America. At the time, a *Billboard* journalist named Jerry Wexler was editing the charts for his magazine and he simply reversed the words. The term was used then in the chart listings from 1949 onward and the charts in question encompassed a number of contemporary forms that emerged around that time. *Billboard* even called it the "Harlem Hit Parade" in 1949.

Based on the exciting progress it saw with acts like Wynonie Harris and Roy Brown, Atlantic Records, an independent label owned by Ahmet Ertegun, Herb Abramson, and later Wexler, began assembling a roster of artists of its own in 1947. They signed Ruth Brown and LaVern Baker, along with Tiny Grimes, Sticks McGhee, and the Clovers. Atlantic's grouping of these like-minded artists proved instrumental in shifting R&B as an art form over to a wider audience. Suddenly, a movement was born. As the sound evolved Atlantic and others, including Specialty, Modern, and RPM began ramping up their output. Ray Charles, Chuck Willis, Fats Domino, Hank Ballard, Clyde McPhatter, Jackie Wilson, and others bridged the gap between blues, big band, R&B, and rock and roll.

When Billy Haley and rock and roll surged in 1954, R&B also gained traction, as an Afro-American companion to the predominantly white sounds of rock.

A few years later, by the early 1960s, rock and roll had nearly completely usurped R&B and the genre in its narrowest sense waned. Rock and roll dominated record sales, and many of the genre's biggest sellers had already passed their peak creative years. An offshoot of R&B, soul music, took its place at center stage thanks to the able hands of Charles, Sam Cooke, and the acts of Berry Gordy's Detroit label, Motown.

Soul music redefined R&B and brought it into the 1970s and beyond. Many of the greatest soul performers of the age—Cooke, Curtis Mayfield, Smokey Robinson—radically reinterpreted R&B and turned it into popular music, in many cases for both whites and blacks. R&B on its own rarely sold to white audiences; white record stores did not carry it, white radio stations did not play it (rather, they played whitewashed versions of R&B tunes), and the white-owned television stations did not invite R&B acts to perform. Early on, due to segregated booking policies, black acts were not even booked to play at the better hotels and casinos. But soul music, with its ability to attract white audiences, changed all that. The demand had become too great to ignore.

By the 1970s, R&B had again returned to favor as a term, only with different connotations. It was used as an umbrella phrase to describe the various splinters of R&B, soul, disco, and funk.

SUBJECT MATTERS

Part of the fun and a good source of deliberation involved in putting this *Icons* project together had to do with deciding which artists would make the

Preface

final list. In many instances, of course, the choices were what we'd refer to as no-brainers: Ray Charles, James Brown, Aretha Franklin, Otis Redding, Sam Cooke. These are names synonymous with the topic. Elsewhere, though, shades of gray arose.

One feverish debate had to do with whether Fats Domino and Little Richard were considered "R&B" or "rock and roll." In many sources, they are referred to as nothing short of "rock and roll royalty." But in others, they are described as seminal R&B artists. So which is it? Well, the short answer is they were, in fact, both. They played rock and roll before the term was invented, when all musicians in that rhythmic style were referred to as R&B acts. Fats and Little Richard were front and center during the bumpy transition from R&B to rock and roll between the years of 1949 and 1954. But because rock and roll stemmed from R&B, it hadn't emerged as a distinct art form. And so, during the transition, artists like LaVern Baker, Jackie Wilson, Domino, and Little Richard all resided at the intersection of the two. This is why there is so much confusion.

Clearly, Little Richard and Fats Domino, with their piano pounding techniques and rollicking rhythms, represented the future of rock and roll style. But their music, written by legends like "Bumps" Blackwell and Dave Bartholomew, was pure R&B. Fats Domino, Bartholomew's early charge, articulated the confusion in an interview: "When we played a slow number they called it 'Rhythm & Blues.' When we played a fast number, they called it 'rock and roll.'" In case you were wondering, Chuck Berry also received serious consideration. But because his instrument of choice was the guitar rather than the more conventional, R&B-accepted piano, he fit more squarely into rock and roll, which truly came of age when he, Billy Haley, and Ike Turner began making their guitars featured instruments within their bands.

I also felt that the incredible story of blue-eyed soul queen Dusty Springfield, a white woman from Britain, was more significant than say, Roberta Flack, Mary Wells, Martha Reeves, or a number of other women who made brief but important contributions to the soul canon of the 1960s. Springfield's masterful *In Memphis* is reason enough for inclusion in this book. But Dusty also served as a soul ambassador to many outside the States, not to mention she had a riveting tale to tell.

I also made the 11th-hour decision to write on the life and times of LaVern Baker, a woman often called the "first female rock and roller," and an essential artist whose contributions to popular music have been tragically overlooked. She became one of seven women presented in this set. My only regret is that I had to omit the most excellent Drifters, with Clyde McPhatter and, later, Ben E. King. They remain the first act on my virtual waiting list.

These decisions are all arguable, of course, and have provided fodder for lively debate. Please don't feel, though, that the results of my decisions, the topics of my essays, have not been thought through thoroughly.

I also had to draw a couple of other lines: Motown is well represented here with essays on the Supremes, the Temptations, Smokey Robinson and the

Miracles, Stevie Wonder, and Marvin Gaye. The label dominated the 1960s soul scene and helped define the genre. Because they were so well represented, I had to exclude deserving acts like the Four Tops, Martha Reeves and the Vandellas, and the Jackson 5.

And speaking of Motown, attentive readers might pick up on the fact that there is no chapter on Berry Gordy himself, but there is one on Kenny Gamble, Leon Huff, and Thom Bell, the men responsible for creating the Sounds of Phildelphia. Just as Gordy created the Motown Sound, Gamble, Huff, and Bell created Philly soul. The reason for this is simple. The Motown story is told here from many different angles, through the artists that are represented with essays. But the Philly soul story—with its brilliant bands—the O'Jays, Harold Melvin and the Blue Notes, the Spinners, and others—was not. Telling that story through the eyes of the men who popularized it provided me with an easy way out. Besides, I feel Philly soul at its best is one of the genre's picture perfect offshoots.

And speaking of groups, another line was drawn concerning which ones to include. There were many vocal and instrumental acts throughout the classic R&B and soul period running from the mid-1950s to the mid-1970s and I did include a handful: the Temptations, Sly and the Family Stone, George Clinton's Parliament-Funkadelic, and the Isley Brothers. But there were so many more excellent and important bands we did not have the space to include, especially from the decade of the 1970s when soul turned to funk and slick pop in the hands of War; Kool and the Gang; Earth, Wind and Fire; and the Commodores. Chic, led by Bernard Edwards and Nile Rodgers, dominated the late 1970s with its funk-R&B fusion.

IN CLOSING

There is a tremendous amount to be learned from these life stories. An important aspect of presenting this collection is discovering the common elements from the lives and careers of these artists. For example, many if not all had to overcome a daunting and mean-spirited racial climate. In the South this meant dealing with Jim Crow laws and intimidating, bigoted law enforcement officials. Because entertainers kept late hours and did so much traveling, they frequented risky and unsavory areas populated by police and trouble.

Also, most of the men and women in these pages dealt with unscrupulous businessmen. Some of the artists, Ruth Brown, for example, Sam Cooke, and Ray Charles, were able to fight the inequity of the system and gain some respect, not to mention financial justice, by starting their own business, or taking their profiteering bosses to task. Most were not.

Virtually all of these legends had their indulgences—a symptom of fame and circumstance—from money to sex and drugs, and most coped with addictions of one form or another. But back when these artists were active, media coverage and press scrutiny was only a fraction of what it is today, so the private lives of these musicians remained, for the most part, private. For example, when Etta James disappeared for a couple of years, few but those who knew her personally had any idea of her whereabouts. It was only until she told her own story in her book *Rage to Survive* that we found out the hell she'd gone through. And what a story it is. That she is alive today is a miracle.

I also delved deeper into the critically important role music played in integration. In many cities and towns across America music served as something that united white with black, men with women, young with old. Often, because of racial conflicts, that unity never materialized. In the worst of times, audiences were segregated with white fans in the ground-level seats and blacks looking on from the balcony. In the best of times, generally in the North, these important acts would play to sophisticated, open-minded multiracial audiences. Still, music united as much as it divided.

In the 1950s, many labels set a precedent by featuring white and black collaborations, with white urbanites establishing the companies and black artists making products for them to sell. This partnership continued through the 1960s. These labels—Stax, Atlantic, Curtis Mayfield's Curtom, Ray Charles's Tangerine, and others—were at the forefront of a social revolution. Without the integrative foundation established by these collaborations, racial barriers would have stayed up longer, and remained stronger.

In the 1960s, the music itself played a revolutionary role in the civil rights movement. Artists like Sam Cooke, Curtis Mayfield, Sly Stone, the Temptations, Stevie Wonder, Marvin Gaye, and others wrote eloquently of racial inequality and the turbulent socio-cultural climate. Their albums made massive national impact and helped pave the way for better race relations if not outright civil rights legislation.

And last—perhaps best of all—is that the story of a good number of these brilliant artists embodies the archetypal narrative arc that runs from rags to riches. It is a distinctly American concept, and the tremendous success, creative accomplishment, and social impact of these performers have remained a template for aspiring young black artists ever since. In Detroit in the 1950s for example, every teenager on every street corner, inspired by the work of the Drifters, Hank Ballard, Ruth Brown, Clyde McPhatter, Jackie Wilson, and Billy Ward, wanted to be a pop star. It is a testament to the life and work of these pioneers.

R&B and Soul Timeline

1940   In response to jazz and its unemotional big band sound, musicians looking for something new begin branching out into a more passionate, blues and gospel-derived sounds.

1942   Louis Jordan, nicknamed "The King of the Juke Box," begins reaching a mass audience, scoring 57 R&B hits during the period from 1942 to 1951. His influence is far-reaching and his music bridges the gap between big band and original R&B and even rock and roll. In 1946 his "Choo Choo Ch'Boogie" by Louis Jordan and His Tympany Five becomes the biggest hit ever in the increasingly popular jump blues style that later leads to rock and roll. His biggest hit is "Saturday Night Fish Fry."

1945   Saul, Joe, and Jules Bihari form Modern Records in 1945 in Los Angeles. They have a keen ear for talent and record artists in many genres including B.B. King, Jesse Belvin, and Johnny Guitar Watson.

1945   Lew Chudd forms Imperial Records. Soon after Art Rupe forms Specialty Records, also in Los Angeles, to record rhythm and blues. Each label will focus intently on New Orleans R&B for the next 10 years.

1945   "The Honeydripper" by Joe Liggins is number 1 on the black music charts for a record 18 weeks. The sexually suggestive term is an early indicator for the new direction of R&B music.

1946   Aladdin Records signs Amos Milburn in 1946. His first session includes the great "Down the Road Apiece" and he notches 19 consecutive Top 10 hits between 1946 and 1954.

1947   Ahmet Ertegun and Herb Abramson found Atlantic. The label does a great deal to introduce black music—jazz, soul, and R&B—to a wider audience.

1948	The phrase "rhythm and blues" is coined by *Billboard* reporter Jerry Wexler. The term replaces the negative "Race Records" chart a year later and signifies the new shift in black music. Wexler would join Atlantic Records in 1953.
1948	Wynonie Harris's version of "Good Rockin' Tonight" tops the R&B charts and gives rise to the popularization of that word in connotation with the music. Harris is often considered the first rock singer.
1949	Atlantic records Stick McGhee's "Drinkin' Wine Spo-Dee-O-Doe."
1949	The electric guitar and the saxophone gain prominence, and become centerpieces of the new R&B sound.
1949	Memphis radio station WDIA hires the first black disc jockey, Paul Williams, and changes its format to R&B.
1949	Beginning in 1949, Ruth Weston, aka Ruth Brown, a Dinah Washington and Sarah Vaughan fan from Portsmouth, Virginia, has an incredible string of groundbreaking successes in R&B. Atlantic Records would come to be known as "The House That Ruth Built."
1950	Fats Domino records "The Fat Man" with Dave Bartholomew in a back room at Cosimo Matassa's music store, giving way to a full rock and roll sound.
1950	Atlantic Records scores its first number 1 with Ruth Brown's "Teardrops from My Eyes," the biggest R&B hit for a female artist for the next 40 years.
1951	Jukeboxes that play 45 rpm singles are invented.
1951	Sam Phillips records "Rocket 88" with Ike Turner's band and singer Jackie Brenston. Phillips sells it to Chess Records of Chicago where the distorted rocker tops the charts, boosting the profile of rock and roll as a dangerous and devilish music.
1951	Alan Freed kicks off his *Moondog Show* in Cleveland, an R&B radio show that becomes a hit with young black fans.
1952	Ray Charles had begun recording in 1949, but signs with Atlantic in 1952. From there he enjoys an unprecedented chart run, first in R&B through the 1950s and then with pop crossovers beginning in the early 1960s.
1952	Billy Haley and the Saddlemen, a country swing band, records "Rock the Joint," the first white rock song. Haley would change the band's name to the Comets and record "Crazy Man Crazy" next, a "rock" song that would reach number 13 on the pop charts.
1952	In New Orleans, a naive 17-year-old named Lloyd Price enters Cosimo Matassa's studio and shouts "Lawdy Miss Clawdy" with Fats Domino on piano.

R&B and Soul Timeline

1952	Sam Phillips quits the radio business and starts Sun Records with the money he made from selling "Rocket 88" to Chess.
1952	Fats Domino's "Goin' Home" is the first R&B song to hit the pop charts, reaching number 30.
1952	Alan Freed's first live rock and roll concert, also known as the *Moondog Coronation*, opens in Cleveland.
1953	Freed hosts the first integrated show with Billy Haley and the Comets playing with the Dominoes, who saw their star vocalist Clyde McPhatter leave the band, replaced by Jackie Wilson.
1954	The R&B charts feature immensely popular acts and cannot be denied, selling 15 million total records in 1953. It becomes so popular though, that white artists begin to cover black artists songs, stealing ideas, sales, and ultimately, money.
1954	Alan Freed moves to New York City, helms a new radio program at WINS, and begins hosting popular rock and roll parties in the East.
1954	15-year-old Jamesetta Hawkins (Etta James) meets Johnny Otis in San Francisco and the talent scout convinces her to make a recording. The result is "Roll with Me Henry," a response to Hank Ballard's "Work with Me Annie." The song is a hit and Etta embarks on a landmark career in R&B.
1955	Elvis records "That's All Right, Mama," but realizes he needs a drummer to approximate real rock and roll.
1955	"Rock Around the Clock," a song from the film The *Blackboard Jungle*, hits number 1 and remains on the list for 38 weeks.
1955	In the fall of this year, Little Richard cuts "Tutti Frutti" for Specialty, also in Cosimo Matassa's studio.
1955	Chuck Berry and Bo Diddley introduce a more guitar-oriented and electric-blues-derived sound to popular music.
1955	Concert sites all over the country ban rock and roll shows by acts like Fats Domino and Little Richard in an attempt to clean up youth culture. Many refer to it in racist terms as "jungle music."
1956	Television hosts Ed Sullivan of *The Ed Sullivan Show* and Steve Allen of *The Steve Allen Show* begin presenting white rock and roll acts like Bill Haley, Jerry Lee Lewis, and Elvis Presley. It would be years before black acts were invited.
1956	The Platters, a black vocal group, reach Top 10 on the pop chart with "Only You" and "The Great Pretender." It's the first time white record buyers prefer original versions to the covers produced by white artists.
1957	A local, Philadelphia-based television show, *American Bandstand*, goes national via ABC-TV and attempts to promote a white, more wholesome side to popular music.

1957	Detroit's Jackie Wilson, a former boxer and a member of Billy Ward's Dominoes, goes solo. He hits it big thanks to three Berry Gordy tunes: "Reet Petite," "To Be Loved" and "Lonely Teardrops." He is called "The Black Elvis" for his sexy image and singing style.
1957	The Stax studio is opened in Memphis by Jim Stewart and Estelle Axton.
1957	Little Richard quits the music business while on a blockbuster tour in Australia, claiming he had been warned of his own damnation in a spiritual vision.
1957	At the urging of Robert "Bumps" Blackwell, Sam Cooke gives into the temptation of singing pop music and walks away from a successful career in gospel.
1958	Curtis Mayfield and his vocal group the Impressions, originally with Jerry Butler, meld the singing styles of doo-wop with more sophisticated and "soulful" emotions.
1959	Ray Charles hits the mainstream with the improvised R&B jam, "What'd I Say."
1959	Berry Gordy, a former boxer and autoworker, starts Tamla-Motown Records. In 10 years it would become the most successful black-owned and operated company in American history with 600 million records sold.
1959	The Isley Brothers venture to New York City and find a record label to release "Shout."
1960	Gordy notches his first number 1 R&B hit with the Miracles' "Shop Around."
1960	Aretha Franklin begins singing on the gospel circuit.
1960	Ray Charles has four hits in the *Billboard* Hot 100 simultaneously: "Georgia on my Mind," "Ruby," "Hard Hearted Hannah," and "Come Rain or Come Shine."
1960	The Temptations form from two Detroit vocal groups and sign to Motown.
1961	Etta James records "At Last," her signature tune, a number 2 R&B hit and a Top 25 pop hit.
1961	Sam Cooke smoothes the edges of R&B and begins the evolution of soul music. Ben E. King, the former Drifter, has a number 1 R&B hit with another soul song, "Stand by Me," his first release as a solo artist.
1961	Gordy has his first pop number 1 hit with the Marvelettes' "Please Mr. Postman."
1962	Booker T. and the MGs enjoy their first hit with the Southern soul instrumental "Green Onions."
1962	Ray Charles surprises the pop music world by tackling country music and the pop charts with the spectacularly successful album *Modern Sounds in Country & Western Music*.

R&B and Soul Timeline

1962	R&B legends begin to fade as Fats Domino, Clyde McPhatter, and LaVern Baker notch their final major hits after a decade in the spotlight.
1962	Little Richard tours with the Beatles and plays the Star Club in Hamburg with the then unknown Fab Four.
1963	Motown defines state of the art R&B with huge successes by Martha and the Vandellas, Marvin Gaye, the Miracles, Mary Wells, and "Fingerprints," the debut hit from 12-year-old prodigy "Little" Stevie Wonder.
1963	James Brown issues the epic *Live at the Apollo*, now considered one of the greatest live albums ever recorded. Brown is the first R&B artist to hit the Top 5 on the album charts.
1964	Motown's dominance continues, even as the Beatles arrive from England, with its biggest hits to date by the Temptations, Four Tops, and its newest group the Supremes, who score three number 1's in the second half of this year.
1964	Inexplicably, Billboard eliminates their Rhythm & Blues charts, explaining they've become indistinguishable from the Pop charts. They realize the gravity of their error and reinstate them one year later, when R&B becomes more popular than ever.
1964	Sam Cooke is shot and killed by a woman at a hotel on December 10. His murder is shrouded in mystery and is never satisfactorily solved.
1964	The Temptations begin a string of hit making with "The Way You Do the Things You Do" and "My Girl." David Ruffin emerges as the group's talented lead singer.
1965	Southern soul rises with breakthroughs from Wilson Pickett, Otis Redding, Solomon Burke, and Joe Tex scoring hits that penetrate the pop market.
1965	James Brown goes from soul to more jarring funk with his aptly titled "Papa's Got a Brand New Bag."
1966	Southern soul music gets its first Pop number 1 with Percy Sledge's "When a Man Loves a Woman."
1966	Ike and Tina Turner are tapped to open a tour for the Rolling Stones and enjoy international exposure because of it.
1967	Otis Redding plays the Monterey Pop Festival and wins over a white rock audience with his spectacular presentation and passionate singing.
1967	Sly and the Family Stone sign with Epic/CBS and manager David Kapralik. Over the course of five years they would redefine soul music and along with James Brown invent funk, culminating with the powerful *There's a Riot Goin' On* in 1971.
1967	After a few false starts singing jazz and standards, Aretha Franklin goes to Muscle Shoals and returns with her first real

	soul work. It kicks off her reception as the most acclaimed and successful female singer in pop history.
1967	Tammi Terrell, on the verge of stardom thanks to her fine work with Marvin Gaye, collapses on stage, in Marvin's arms, at Hamden-Sydney College in Virginia in 1967. She is diagnosed as having a brain tumor and undergoes six operations in two years. Her health deteriorates and she dies in 1970 at 24.
1967	Dusty Springfield, a British soul sensation, flies to Memphis at the behest of Atlantic's Jerry Wexler to record at the Muscle Shoals studio. The result is *In Memphis*, Springfield's masterpiece and one of soul's great 1960s recordings.
1967	Otis Redding, 26, dies in a plane crash December 10, just three days after sitting down with Steve Cropper to record his biggest hit, "Dock of the Bay."
1967	George Clinton's soul vocal group the Parliaments has its first hit, "(I Wanna) Testify." But Clinton has trouble with his label, the first of many label entanglements he'd have, and decides to form Funkadelic, a "smokescreen" featuring the Parliament backing band. Clinton revolutionizes R&B and funk with his free-for-all approach to recording musicians and his colorful, carnival live presentation.
1968	Florence Ballard, founding member of the Supremes, is dismissed from the group for her chronic depression and alcoholism, replaced by Cindy Birdsong. After the dismissal, Ballard separates from her husband and goes on welfare after losing a lawsuit for back royalties against Motown Records. She dies of a heart attack at the age of 32 in 1976. Her story is one of pop's greatest tragedies.
1968	Following the assassination of civil rights leader Martin Luther King Jr., soul music usurps the grittier R&B market of Southern soul and roars to the forefront of society, appealing to both black and white audiences.
1968	Motown responds to the growing influence of deep soul and the psychedelic soul of Sly and the Family Stone by pushing its own artists toward a less pop-friendly style, resulting in major hits by Marvin Gaye and the Temptations.
1968	The divisive David Ruffin misses a Temptations gig to watch his girlfriend sing and the band considers it to be the last straw. They dismiss him and hire Dennis Edwards. On several occasions Ruffin attempts to force his way back into the band by jumping on stage during performances.
1968	Norman Whitfield works with the Temptations, paving the way for elongated soul jams, now coined "pyschedelic soul."

R&B and Soul Timeline

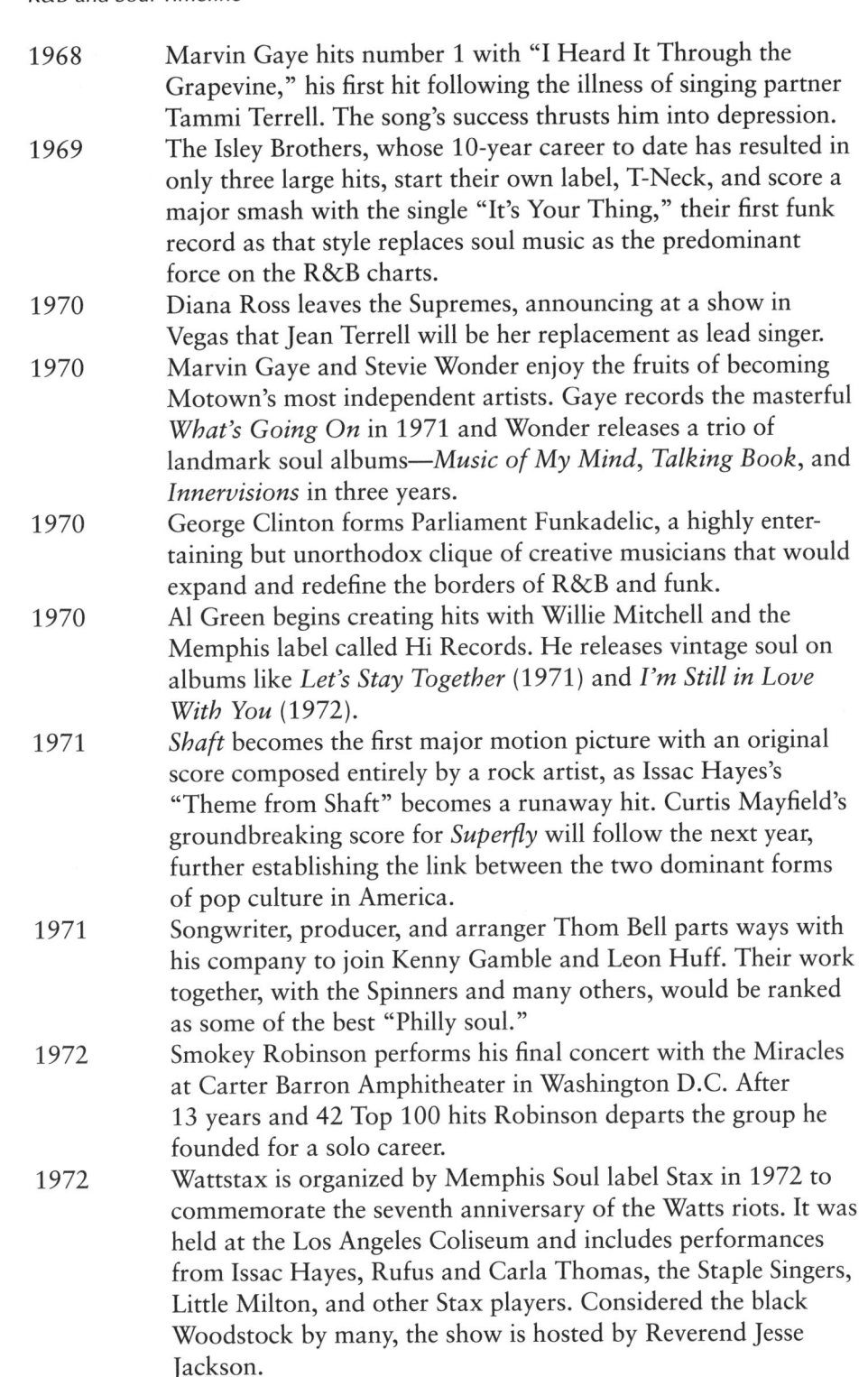

1968	Marvin Gaye hits number 1 with "I Heard It Through the Grapevine," his first hit following the illness of singing partner Tammi Terrell. The song's success thrusts him into depression.
1969	The Isley Brothers, whose 10-year career to date has resulted in only three large hits, start their own label, T-Neck, and score a major smash with the single "It's Your Thing," their first funk record as that style replaces soul music as the predominant force on the R&B charts.
1970	Diana Ross leaves the Supremes, announcing at a show in Vegas that Jean Terrell will be her replacement as lead singer.
1970	Marvin Gaye and Stevie Wonder enjoy the fruits of becoming Motown's most independent artists. Gaye records the masterful *What's Going On* in 1971 and Wonder releases a trio of landmark soul albums—*Music of My Mind*, *Talking Book*, and *Innervisions* in three years.
1970	George Clinton forms Parliament Funkadelic, a highly entertaining but unorthodox clique of creative musicians that would expand and redefine the borders of R&B and funk.
1970	Al Green begins creating hits with Willie Mitchell and the Memphis label called Hi Records. He releases vintage soul on albums like *Let's Stay Together* (1971) and *I'm Still in Love With You* (1972).
1971	*Shaft* becomes the first major motion picture with an original score composed entirely by a rock artist, as Issac Hayes's "Theme from Shaft" becomes a runaway hit. Curtis Mayfield's groundbreaking score for *Superfly* will follow the next year, further establishing the link between the two dominant forms of pop culture in America.
1971	Songwriter, producer, and arranger Thom Bell parts ways with his company to join Kenny Gamble and Leon Huff. Their work together, with the Spinners and many others, would be ranked as some of the best "Philly soul."
1972	Smokey Robinson performs his final concert with the Miracles at Carter Barron Amphitheater in Washington D.C. After 13 years and 42 Top 100 hits Robinson departs the group he founded for a solo career.
1972	Wattstax is organized by Memphis Soul label Stax in 1972 to commemorate the seventh anniversary of the Watts riots. It was held at the Los Angeles Coliseum and includes performances from Issac Hayes, Rufus and Carla Thomas, the Staple Singers, Little Milton, and other Stax players. Considered the black Woodstock by many, the show is hosted by Reverend Jesse Jackson.

1972	Motown's Berry Gordy moves his operations to Los Angeles and requires that most of his stable of artists and staff move with him. The move distracts from the label's focus and begins its decline.
1975	R&B girl group LaBelle (Sarah Dash, Nona Hendryx, and Patti LaBelle) sign with Epic, and record *Nightbirds* under the guidance of New Orleans legend Allen Toussaint. Their first single, a song about a New Orleans prostitute called "Lady Marmalade," goes on to become one of the first mainstream hits of the disco era.
1975	The Isley Brothers release *The Heat Is On*, and their tune "Fight the Power" becomes a rallying cry for future generations, paving the way for the embracing of the group by the hip-hop community. This relationship paves the way for lead singer Ronnie Isley to assume the role of "Mr. Bigg" in 1990s R&B videos.
1979	Al Green is injured while performing and he interprets this as a sign from on high that he is to stop singing his soul music from the stage. He leaves music to concentrate his energy on being a pastor of his own small church, preaching the gospel around the country, and singing gospel music.
1983	Prince rekindles soul music with the dazzling *1999* in 1983 and *Purple Rain* in 1984.

Courtesy of Photofest.

Ray Charles

THE GENIUS OF SOUL

Superlatives come easily when describing the life's work of Ray Charles Robinson, so great were his contributions to popular music. Primarily, and perhaps most important, Brother Ray served as the chief architect of soul music. By fusing the sound of gospel with rhythm and blues on tunes like "This Little Girl of Mine" and "Hallelujah I Love Her So," Charles created a remarkable new sound, one that captured the rebel exuberance of rock and roll as well as the fervent spirit of the Southern church. This pioneering hybrid quickly became a cornerstone of popular music.

Several other innovations followed. As a gifted student of modern popular music and a versatile talent with virtually no stylistic limitations, Charles also helped to bring jazz to a mainstream audience. Influenced by performers like Nat King Cole and Charles Brown, he began his professional music career as an imitator of Cole, while eking out a living on the Florida jazz circuit.

Cole was one of the scene's hottest performers, and in pursuing a livelihood as an artist it was Charles's intention to "give the people what they wanted." He did, and he eventually got what he wanted in return: a thriving career.

As a singer, Ray Charles was a force of nature, a performer with gifts as unique and impressive as anyone in the art form. Only Elvis Presley and Billie Holiday could measure up to him in terms of sheer power and passion. It can ooze Southern-comfort molasses one minute and bowl you over like a country preacher the next. His interpretive instincts as a vocalist were extraordinary as well, especially in his way with a ballad. Few singers could turn a song into something as inimitable and personal as Ray Charles could. He knew it, too. "I can sing my ass off," he'd been known to say.

As a composer and arranger, too, Charles was second only to the great Duke Ellington. Charles's fluency in a wide range of styles, also unrivaled, made it possible for him to mix and match all kinds of sounds, from jazz and big band to pop and country, and every hybrid in between, many of which never existed before Ray came along.

As reported by the many who worked with him and for him, Charles the songwriter and melodicist was an utter perfectionist, a man who heard the notes in his head exactly as he wanted them and he left it to his annotators to script them. While he employed the great arrangers of his day to collaborate—Quincy Jones, Marty Paitch, Gerald Wilson—Charles knew what he wanted, even from them. "Writing for Ray is different," said one of his collaborators, Benny Carter. "He basically has the song mapped out in his mind, so you're giving him what he wants."

Perhaps most unexpectedly and miraculously, though, was the work Charles did in country music. Forever the métier of white artists (with few exceptions), Charles astonished his colleagues and fans with his milestone 1962 recording, *Modern Sounds in Country & Western*. By risking alienation of his R&B supporters, he challenged music fans on both sides of the ever-widening racial divide. He dared bring two incredibly disparate groups together with a single, remarkable sound and it worked. In an era in which R&B/soul albums rarely scored high on the charts, *Modern Sounds* topped the national list, knocking *West Side Story* out of the top slot in June 1962. The record's lead single, "I Can't Stop Loving You," sold over a million copies in just a few weeks. The record was so successful it spawned a series of C&W follow-ups, by Charles and by others seeking to replicate the success on both sides of that same racial divide. Charles's visionary approach to popular music now included that most unlikely of bedfellows: "hillbilly."

Never before had any one artist been accepted in so many fields of endeavor. His blurring of styles was so convincing that popular music never again had the same clear distinctions. Jazz and big band melded with pop. Country merged with soul. R&B sounded great spiced with jazz and big-band orchestration. In the prime of his career, Ray Charles became the beacon of popular music, a quasar, in which, despite being surrounded by the cheesy pop groups of the 1950s and the roots of rock and roll, he shone a light across the musical landscape that guided many artists on his trail. The funny thing was, these fusions were natural for him. He'd grown up in an environment where there were no distinctions between musical categories, and his own artistry ultimately reflected that generous, unflinching, and innovative vision.

A mosaic of influences, Charles parlayed his diverse musical background into an equally diverse career. The country folk, gospel, and blues of his childhood formed the bedrock of his abilities, while his formal classical and jazz smoothed the edges. Combine that with the so-called race music of the 1950s, and you've got the sublime artistry of Ray Charles, an artist whose canon represents both everything that came before and nothing that was heard before. One only need know that his nickname in the music industry was simply, "The Genius."

Did his blindness make him more sensitive, and therefore more attuned to making music? It's impossible to tell. But one thing is certain: his music also bridged the gap between audiences and helped, at the very height of racism in America, to dismantle racial barriers.

THE EARLY YEARS

"Before I begin, let me say right and now that I'm a country boy!" Ray Charles exclaims in his as-told-to autobiography with author David Ritz, *Brother Ray*. And so he was. Born healthy on September 23, 1930, in Albany, Georgia, Charles grew up in abject poverty. He was the child of a railroad worker named Bailey Robinson and Aretha Williams, a smart, sensible, hard-working woman who brought her son Ray up with Bailey Robinson's first wife, Mary Jane. Soon after birth, Aretha moved her family to the north Florida town of Greenville, a racially segregated village about 30 miles from the Georgia border. It was in Greenville that Ray would spend his childhood.

By all counts, Ray was a happy boy, content to grow up without a dad, loved intensely by his mother and Mary Jane. His brother George, younger by a year, served as a capable companion for the first few years. The two would help out with chores, make mischief in the woods, and feel the warmth of a closely knit community of characters. It was early on that Ray discovered music as well.

"I was born with music inside of me," Ray told Ritz. "That's the only explanation I know of, since none of my relatives could sing or play an instrument. Music was one of my parts. Like my ribs, my liver, my kidneys, my heart. Like my blood . . . And from the moment I learned that there were piano keys to be mashed, I started mashing 'em, trying to make sounds out of feelings" (David Ritz, *Brother Ray*, Da Capo, p. 8).

Besides the gospel music of his Baptist church, Charles first heard real boogie-woogie piano emanating from a place called the Red Wing Café, where an impressive but unheralded man named Wylie Pitman ("Mr. Pit"), the proprietor, introduced Ray to the instrument. Soon, Ray opted to work at his piano skills rather than play with his friends. He was also exposed to blues and big band sounds on Pitman's busy jukebox, a critical café fixture that gave Charles his first keyhole view of the outside world. In addition to those sounds, Charles was inundated with the hillbilly vibes of the Deep South as well as the country music transmitted from Tennessee radio station WSM, home of the *Grand Ole Opry* and other traditional country music programs. Throw jazz on top of that, an art form he'd learn later at school, and you have the chief components in Charles's own music.

Two cataclysmic events shaped Charles's earliest boyhood. The first was the death of his brother. When it happened, Ray was five and George just four. The two of them were in and around a washtub, goofing and splashing about. George climbed in the tub, a large, wooden half-barrel kind of a thing, head first; Ray laughed at him as he pretended to swim, flailing his arms about. Unfortunately, George wasn't pretending; he was struggling, gasping for air, drowning. When Ray recognized this, he froze momentarily, and by the time he panicked and screamed for his mother it was too late. George was dead. "I can see it all too vividly," he told Ritz. "It shines in my head . . . It was a powerful thing to have witnessed. . . . Turned out to be one of the last things I would ever see" (Ritz, p. 13).

Just months after his brother's drowning death, Ray's eyes started tearing. But the substance oozing out of them was thick, not like regular tears. In fact, sometimes the substance would be so thick he'd have to pry them open in the morning. Doctors were stumped, as young Ray, nearly six at the time, lost his sight gradually. In fact, it took two years for him to completely lose his sight to the debilitating disorder, a disease some speculated to be glaucoma. He was seven when he went totally blind. It would be the second cataclysmic event of his young life.

Not that Ray let a lack of vision hinder his childhood. Thanks to a mother who encouraged him to do as much as a normal child in terms of work and play, and his own indefatigable spirit, the boy managed to lead a reasonably well-adjusted life, despite the fact that he was the only blind person in all of Greenville. "Even though I couldn't see much," he told Ritz, "I wasn't afraid of running around. I knew every inch of Greenville and didn't lose my confidence about finding my way; I went wherever I wanted to go."

His approach to living had nothing to do with his physical handicap. "Folk underestimate the blind. . . . The blind don't have to live in fear and the blind don't have to tremble in the dark" (Ritz, p. 301).

While many of the kids his age played games requiring sight, Ray didn't despair. He retained a close circle of friends and a generous array of hobbies. He still raised hell on occasion, just like other kids, and he still spent time at the café listening to all kinds of music. At home, his mother made him responsible for doing all the chores of a typical child. When he'd sneak out for a little mischief with friends, or steal away for an adventure, he heard about it on his return. Aretha was a loving mother, but also a stern disciplinarian who focused on instilling her son with a strong sense of morality and virtue.

She also knew deep in her heart that her blind son needed special educational resources that he'd never get in Greenville. So, when Ray was eight, she made the tough decision to send him away to a school for the blind. At the time, Ray had never been out of Greenville, no less on a train he had to take to get there, and he'd certainly never been further than a stone's throw from his mother. St. Augustine, where the State School for the Blind was located, was 160 miles from home. It may as well have been across the ocean for all Ray knew. He was shocked and devastated.

MUSIC SCHOOL

The move away from home agonized Ray. The transition was a painful one. "With all these people around, I was still alone," he said, of his first few months in the environment. "And I hurt. Deep down inside, I hurt bad." He withdrew from his fellow students, and the lack of interaction made him feel isolated. But time passed and the hurt eased. Slowly young Ray became himself again and his personality emerged. Throughout his life Ray showed tremendous resilience, and soon he adjusted to his new environment.

One of the first things Ray learned at school was Braille. A quick study, it only took him a week or two to get it down. Primarily, his musical education involved classical, Chopin, Strauss waltzes. But that didn't put him off. He took to the program. He was an eager student, regardless of what they were teaching him. Even though "the gutbucket music" of his youth wasn't tolerated in the halls of the school, he did begin to understand how to formalize his lifelong appreciation of music.

Charles was a good, attentive student with obvious gifts. He began reading and composing music early on that first year. During school hours, he listened and learned; and his teachers, recognizing his aptitude and excitement, challenged him to meet his considerable potential. After hours, though, the learning didn't stop. In fact, that was when Charles's informal learning kicked in. After the teachers went home for the night, he and the other students found an empty room on the sly and let loose, digging into all the feel-good music they couldn't play during class time; improvisational jazz, boogie-woogie, and blues.

It was at this time, too, that Charles widened his view to include the masters, with an intense appreciation for the work of players like Art Tatum ("Tatum was God") and Artie Shaw ("I loved his sweet sound"), two musicians to whom Charles professed unceasing respect. He also listened intently to the *Grand Ole Opry* on Saturday night radio, a show that fostered his admiration for country and western artists like Hank Snow, Jimmie Rodgers, Roy Acuff, and Hank Williams, among others.

At the same time, the voracious student deepened his appreciation for big bands, both white and black. On the black side, the work of bandleaders like Ellington, Basie, Millinder, and Buddy Johnson had always electrified him. The work of white bandleaders like Tommy Dorsey, Glenn Miller, Gene Krupa, and Shaw, while they didn't "swing" quite as much as Ray liked, also held his interest.

Yet through all the music of Ray's youth, all the big band sounds of the 1940s, all the blues, boogie, and jazz, one voice and one piano stood out above all the rest: Nat King Cole's. "He influenced me above all others," he admits. "Musically, I walked in his footsteps until I found a stride of my own.... That was my first program—to become a junior Nat Cole" (Ritz, p. 44).

Cole, who began as a jazz piano player, led a trio at the time Charles first followed him. He could play bop. He had pop hits as well. "If he wanted to," says Ray, "he could turn out the blackest blues you'd care to hear." But beyond his versatility, Charles admired him for other reasons. He was a truly great pianist who could accompany his own vocals with genius fills and tasty flourishes. He also—and this is critically important—proved he could appeal to both black and white audiences. Which meant that he was not relegated to certain venues and played only on select radio stations. Cole gained exposure nationally and internationally, across the great racial divide. And he made lots of money doing it, a result not lost on the enterprising Charles.

After three years at St. Augustine, Ray, now ten years old, began venturing away from the school and learning his way around the city, much the same way he did in Greenville. He'd take long walks without a dog or a cane (two objects he felt symbolized weakness), and eventually grew confident enough to walk through town as fast or faster than folks with sight. "Man, I moved, I set my own rhythm," he said.

One of the first things Charles looked for when he went off-campus was, not surprisingly, piano gigs. Now that the world felt more welcoming and he began setting out on his own, he was ready to take on responsibilities outside the classroom. He'd play piano at tea parties around town, all "proper" tunes and pop hits of the day, that essentially amounted to Charles's first paying music jobs.

GROWING UP

Ray's mother Aretha died when Ray was 15. Though he wasn't sure, he estimated her age to be 31 or 32. The doctor told relatives she had died when her "stomach blew up with gas and choked her heart." That may have been an unscientific way of explaining a heart attack, a common cause of death at the time.

Losing his only parent stunned Ray. He was frozen with grief. "I was a zombie," he recalls. "I had real trouble, and all I kept thinking was why . . . I didn't have even a chance to tell her goodbye."

The months following Aretha's death were critical for Ray. He grew firmer in his independence. He understood the importance of his convictions, and he realized he was now in complete control of his own future. "I was going to make up my own mind," he said.

His first significant decision came immediately. Should he return to school, where he'd attend for his ninth year? Or should he strike out on his own, venture into the world, a place he knew very little about? He realized at some point he needed to pursue a livelihood, establish himself in a career. He also understood the importance of money. "I wasn't about to get a tin cup, a cane, and find myself a street corner." Not only did he not want a cane, he didn't want any help. In fact, Ray frequently liked to point out his "three nos": no dog, no cane, no guitar.

So he headed to Jacksonville, Florida's largest city, to make a life for himself. Initially, he stayed with friends of the family, the Thompsons, who Ray explains, "treated him like a son." They shared their meals with him, made him feel comfortable in their home, but also made sure he didn't go too crazy in his new surroundings.

It didn't take long for Ray to secure a few gigs, mostly speculative gigs that didn't guarantee him any cash until he proved himself. This he did quickly, and the local music community began to hear about the young blind pianist. Depending on what the situation required, Ray could play just about anything, from the classical of his schooling to the country and hillbilly of his youth. But he mainly focused on boogie-woogie solo piano gigs and a part-time job filling in during the big band boom of the period.

Not that he had enough gigs to suit him. Sure, there was work, but there was also competition, and most of that competition could play the lights out, just like Ray. Everywhere he went, he was pushed by someone nearly as good, and Ray had to stay in peak form just to get the kind of gigs that would pay enough to support himself.

One day, a bandleader named Tiny York invited Ray to play outside of Jacksonville, mainly down in Orlando. Ray accepted the gig and the chance to see what was happening outside Jacksonville. Unfortunately, the job fell through, and Ray was left holding what was left of the bag in an unfamiliar city. These would be his most difficult days. He was just 16.

"I'm not sure what kept me going. There wasn't a lot of hope for a brighter future. I suppose I didn't have choice. The idea of selling pencils wasn't too appealing" (Ritz, p. 76).

Ray's support system had disappeared. There was no one to take care of him, feed him when he was hungry, make him feel loved. He was renting a room from a woman for a few dollars a week, but still had trouble paying up.

The competition for gigs grew even stiffer when the war ended. Soldiers returning from World War II, looking to make a living, flooded the market with talent, and Ray was forced to compete.

Eventually, Ray met another bandleader, this one named Joe Anderson. When Anderson found out Ray could write, he petitioned him to spice up his own "stock" arrangements. This was a key moment in the young musician's career: writing was a new arena for him and relished the opportunity to take advantage of his ability. He also saw it as a way of increasing his value as a musician.

When Orlando dried up, Ray traveled to Tampa. He'd been refining his chops in big bands and combos, reveling in the sounds of the great jazz of the day, from monstrous instrumentalists like Lionel Hampton and Charlie Christian to bandleaders like Tommy Dorsey and Chick Webb. His appreciation for Nat Cole deepened as well, and the combos he played with found Ray imitating Cole's credible but sweet approach to singing and playing.

While in Tampa, Ray also joined with an all-white band called the Florida Playboys in 1948. They were essentially a country cover band, playing all the popular hits of the day. Ray, pounding out hot, hillbilly piano, enjoyed the gig and was paid reasonably well. He even learned how to yodel!

Three years removed from the death of his mother, against all odds, Ray had managed to eke out a living as a working musician. He'd gigged around Florida, learned the ins and outs of the state's biggest cities, played enough to build his piano chops, his entertainment moves, and his songwriting/arranging abilities. Now 18 and more restless than ever, it was time to fly the coop. He told a friend to look at a map for him and tell him where the furthest point in the United States was from Florida. The answer would be his next destination.

GOIN' WEST

Ray boarded a bus to Seattle, the furthest place from where he was standing in Florida. Ray, still 18, knew nothing about his destination, other than it would take five days to get there. He had no knowledge of the music scene, the job opportunities, the weather. He simply wanted a fresh start. "I was starting to think of myself as a man. I had moved to a new part of the world," he told Ritz, of arriving in his new home. "And as far as I was concerned I was my own boss" (Ritz, p. 97).

The first thing he did as his own boss was assemble a trio. They called it the McSon Trio and it featured Gosady McGee, a friend from Florida, on guitar, and Milt Garred on bass. The name came from the "Mc" in McGee and the "Son" from Charles last name, Robinson. (Ray later dropped the Robinson and stuck with "Charles" because he didn't want confusion with the popular boxer Sugar Ray Robinson.)

Charles insisted that the McSon Trio was leaderless, and their remuneration reflected that. They were each paid $25 a night and the work was steady.

They got a little radio airplay, too, which led to the band, and Ray's, first recording sessions.

Jack Lauderdale, a music enthusiast with a recording company, approached Ray with the opportunity. "A record! Man, that was the ultimate!" he said (Ritz, p. 100). "I had been listening to records my whole life . . . and here I was, actually about to make one." It was 1949.

Ray's first recording was "Confession Blues," a laid-back Nat Cole–style tune that he wrote back in Florida. From there the recordings would become more frequent. His follow-up, "Baby Let Me Hold Your Hand," was a hit on the black music charts and the first record that earned Charles national attention. The success allowed Charles and Lauderdale, his first record executive, the luxury of a bigger band. "Kissa Me Baby," for example, features Ray singing/shouting in front of a nine-piece outfit.

THE HABIT

Making records wasn't the only thing Ray started doing in Seattle. He also began taking heroin, a drug habit he'd have for the next 17 years. "No one made me do it," he states. "I hooked myself" (Ritz, *Genius & Soul* liner notes, p. 13).

Constantly around musicians and the high life, Ray had been exposed to marijuana and cocaine early on, but hadn't seen heroin until Seattle, when some of the cats he was accompanying were doing it. Always curious, Ray bugged them to give him a taste. He was so persistent, his bandmates, initially reluctant because he was so young, finally gave in. He liked it enough to start using regularly.

"Once I started I had no reason to stop," he admits. "I didn't have to get high every day. . . . I didn't have enough money to do that anyway. . . . All my bread wasn't going for dope." A "nervy kid," Ray was also intrigued by the secrecy and illicit nature of heroin and drugs in general. Coming of age, Ray often says he became a man in Seattle, trying every new experience that came his way. If that involved mind-altering experiences, too, well, so be it.

At the time, Ray was earning decent enough money to support his drug habit, as well as his paramour Louise (mother of his first child, Evelyn, born in 1950), buy a new piano, and keep his band happy. There were so many changes going on in Ray's life—musically, professionally, creatively, socially—that his residency in Seattle proved to be a blur, a watershed period in Ray's life that would be eventually lead him to much bigger and more lucrative pursuits.

It wasn't long before Ray felt he'd outgrown Seattle. Encouraged by Lauderdale and motivated to take his act to the next level, Ray moved to Los Angeles in 1950. In Seattle, he'd brushed up on all different types of musical vernacular, from bebop to R&B, from blues to swingin' boogie-woogie.

He did this mainly to make sure he'd be prepared for virtually any situation. That is, regardless of the offer, regardless of the venue, Ray was poised to knock 'em dead.

LOWELL AND LOS ANGELES

In the City of Angels, Ray encountered the same warm reception he enjoyed in Seattle. Soon Lauderdale hooked him up with another one of his artists, hot blues act Lowell Fulsom. In the spring of 1950, Ray headed out on the road with Fulsom, who'd had a hit, "Every Day I Have the Blues," at the time and was drawing substantial crowds every night. He didn't know it yet, but Ray Charles would be on the road for the better part of the next three decades.

Having played piano and written charts for Fulsom early on, it didn't take long for Ray to become musical director for the band. Not only that, Fulsom gave Charles the thumbs-up to perform a few of his own numbers every night. Fulsom tells Ritz what he brought to the table. "Ray gave the band a snap it never had before," he says. "He could write arrangements in his head, just calling out the notes to one of the cats who'd write them down. Ray heard it all in his head" (Ritz, *Genius & Soul* liner notes, p. 14).

Ray's stint with Fulsom, a breathless couple of years, took him around the country a handful of times. (Occasionally he'd lay over in Los Angeles and hit the studio for a few recording sessions.) But his travels helped him garner real exposure in the industry. At the time, he was beginning to distance himself from his Nat Cole/Charles Brown pop-jazz style. He was ready to make a move. "I thought it'd be nice if people began to recognize me, if they tell me I sounded like Ray Charles" (Ritz, p. 128).

His affiliation with Fulsom earned him a slot at the Billy Shaw Agency in New York City, where he'd sink or swim nationally as a solo artist and band-leader. "I hate the idea of falling on my ass and making a fool of myself so much that I knew I'd find a way to avoid it" (Ritz, p. 133). Around the same time, Jack Lauderdale's recording operation was foundering, its owner convinced he had to shut it down. One man's misfortune is another man's opportunity. Enter Ahmet Ertegun and Herb Abramson of Atlantic Records.

ATLANTIC CROSSING

"I'd call it one of the happiest relationships of my life," says Ray (Ritz, *Genius & Soul* liner notes, p. 15). Ahmet, Herb, and later Jerry Wexler would all scout songs for Ray and run them by him. They set him up with the very best session players when Ray decided to lay down a few tracks, and they respected his freedom as an artist. Never, in his time with Atlantic, did he feel compelled to compromise his considerable artistic integrity.

Touring, though, proved to be troublesome. Shaw forced Ray to tour with pick-up bands. That is, bands hastily assembled on the road in each city so as to avoid the high cost of supporting a nine-piece band on the road. Obviously, that philosophy ran counter to Ray's demand for excellence. How could he expect his pick-up outfits to swing and groove after only a few hours together? The slipshod arrangement didn't last long and when Ray returned from a tour, he insisted on assembling a band, a killer band full of bop and post-bop musicians. So he went down to Texas and assembled the best group he could find, seven pieces of pure talent: four horns, a piano, a bass guitar, and a drummer. "Hard-core jazz musicians can play anything," says Ray (Ritz, *Genius & Soul* liner notes, p. 15).

The sound of Ray's new band embodied everything Ray ever wanted in a band: simplicity, grit, soul, power, and precision. "Finally, I was shaping my own musical environment from top to bottom," says Ray (Ritz, p. 148).

And it took the music industry by storm. "I remember hearing 'Come Back Baby' for the first time," says Aretha Franklin. "I was 12 or 13. Other than my father's voice in church, this was the most soulful thing I'd ever heard" (Ritz, *Genius & Soul* liner notes, p. 15).

It was during this time, 1953–1955, that Ray began shaping his own sound. Not that he was aware of his innovations. He often admits he had no idea that he'd be recognized with such major creative achievements later on. "In my mind I was just bringing out more of me," he says (Ritz, p. 148). More of him meant allowing his gospel upbringing to seep into his boogie-woogie, R&B, and jazzy sounds. He'd take lines from gospel tunes, the structure and chords of gospel tunes, the *feel* from gospel tunes and turn them into modern R&B.

For example, Clara Ward's "This Little Light of Mine" became Charles's "This Little Girl of Mine," and the gospel standard "Talkin' 'Bout Jesus" became "Talkin' 'Bout You." He also merged the secular and the religious on "Hallelujah I Love Her So."

Of course, the fusion didn't please everyone. Big Bill Broonzy said, "He's mixing the blues with spirituals. I know that's wrong . . . He should be singing in a church" (Clarke, *The Penguin Encyclopedia of Popular Music*, p. 225).

Charles said, "I got letters accusing me of bastardizing God's work. . . . Many folk saw my music as sacrilegious. They said I was taking church songs and making people dance to them in bars and nightclubs" (Ritz, p. 151). "Some preachers got on my ass," Charles remembered, "said I was doing the devil's work. Bullshit. I was keeping the spirit but changing the story so it related to the real world. I'm a realist, and as a realist, I figure that the music I knew, the churchy music I grew up on, was something I could draw on and adapt" (Ritz, *Genius & Soul* liner notes, p. 15).

Of course, none of the religious reactions really bothered Ray. The fact was, Ray did not fear God; he believed in the God that accepted all people. Ray's God didn't consider transgressions as reasons for banishing his worshipers to hell. Ray's God appreciated honesty and sincerity and heart, soul, and truth. And that's what Ray was serving up.

Encouraged, rather than daunted, by the outcry, he accelerated his productivity; the songs came pouring out of him. It would, in retrospect, serve as the most fruitful writing period of his career.

CROSSOVER HIT MACHINE

"I Got a Woman" in 1954 would be Ray's first song, the first of many, to hit number one on the R&B charts. It would also be the year he married a woman named Della Beatrice, "B" as Ray affectionately referred to her, when he was 25. She was a quiet, reserved girl, a singer, who just a year after they met gave birth to Ray Jr., Ray's first son.

The marriage lasted over a dozen years, enduring many difficulties along the way. B had the distinct displeasure of being married to Ray while his career was in full swing. Charles was on the road most of the time, with all its attendant temptations—which he often succumbed to—not to mention his fierce drug habit. Charles insisted that his attempt to make his marriage work was in earnest. But even he admitted it was a trying relationship, especially for his wife. "I'm surprised we managed that long," he says. "I give her a great deal of credit for putting up with me and my strange ways. . . . She was worried, I'm certain, and the hurt must have been painful and long-lasting" (Ritz, p. 160).

His long-lasting turbulence on the homefront didn't disrupt his momentum as an artist. His gospel conversions like "This Little Girl of Mine" and "Hallelujah I Love Her So" charted high. They also sold particularly well to a white audience, unusual for a black recording artist. It was about this time that the term "crossover" came to be a part of Ray's work. One of the ways he managed to hold onto a white audience was by taking cornball material like "My Bonnie" and "Swanee River," stuff Ray learned as a kid, and added heavy doses of funk and gospel. It was white material given the R&B treatment. While he jokingly admits he couldn't actually "see" the growing number of white faces at his show, he did understand that if he opened his show up to appeal to both white and black races, he'd make a heck of a lot more money. This he did, and that he made.

THE RAELETTS

This was also about the time that Ray made another significant creative decision. Now that his band was in place, he decided to add backing singers. The decision was based on his days as a boy in the church. He tried it first on "This Little Light of Mine," asking his two sax players Fathead Newman and Donald Wilkerson to sing behind him with a girl named Mary Ann Fisher.

Being partial to women, though, it didn't take long for Charles to eliminate the men and hire all girls to sing behind him.

One night, Ray went to see Lionel Hampton. Chuck Willis was opening, and Willis had three girls backing him, a group that called itself the Cookies. After the show, Ray approached the girls with an offer, and soon, after working out a deal, he had them singing with him in the studio. "Drown in My Own Tears," recorded in 1955, was the first time Ray used an all-girl backing trio, now called the Raeletts. "I liked that male/female friction, and once I had it I never let it go" (Ritz, p. 169). Ray's masculine soulfulness and the girls' feminine sound complemented each other magically and soon many acts in popular music, including Elvis Presley, brought women in to sing backing vocals.

"WHAT'D I SAY"

Ray enjoyed a watershed moment in 1959 with the epic jam "What'd I Say." But it had more to do with serendipity than anything the normally prepared Charles had planned out. Here's how it happened. One night, about 10 minutes to closing after playing a 4-hour gig, Ray admitted he was out of material. He had played his entire repertoire with that band. But the owner, eager to keep his audience drinking, forced Ray to fill that last ten minutes up, even though that would have meant repeating himself. Thinking quickly, he told his band to follow him. He pounded out some chords on his electrified piano and the band entered behind him, in improvisational fashion. The tune was playful and rockin' in a soulful way. It had sexual overtones (of course!), a robust rhythm, and the Raeletts singing with Ray in a kind of call-and-response banter. At first, the impromptu experiment seemed playful enough. But the audience, intoxicated by the piece's exuberant feel and passionate repartee, responded wildly. "Then I could feel the whole room bouncing and shaking and carrying on something fierce" (Ritz, p. 169).

At that moment, Ray knew he had inadvertently come up with something special. Over the next few nights he refined the jam, adding lyrics and tightening up the arrangement. At the first opportunity, they booked studio time in New York to get the recording on wax. Recorded in February 1959 and produced by Ahmet Ertegun and Jerry Wexler, the song was a revelation when it was released in June the same year. With Ray on electric piano, and the horn section of Hank Crawford, Fathead Newman, and Marcus Belgrave, "What'd I Say" became Ray's biggest hit to date, not to mention the fact that it inadvertently began a run on electric pianos, an instrument many in the industry teased Ray for playing. The record also sold well to both black and white audiences. In fact, it was the first record to bring the mass market to Ray Charles.

Of course, as with so many of his accomplishments, "What'd I Say" dogged him with troubles. Given the sexual connotations of Ray's repartee with the

Raeletts, some radio stations actually banned the song. This upset Ray; he considered this treatment racist and unfair. After the song was released, several white acts covered it, and those versions received airplay. On the other hand, the controversy also pleased him. Not only did the song earn him notoriety, but the white version exposure led to further royalties and his own version made it onto additional stations as well.

From here, Ray's ideas, and hits, kept flowing. Following "What'd I Say" in 1959, Charles released "I Believe to My Soul," a pained ballad that exists in startling contrast to the ebullience of the earlier track. "I Believe to My Soul" is a stark lament, notable for its abject depression and utter despondence. The mood swing from his previous hit was wide, the style shift significant, and because of that Ray had again expanded his creative continuum.

Now that he'd sufficiently proven himself as a singles artist, Charles began thinking more conceptually, in terms of album-length projects. He conceived the idea of singing ballads with a string section. He recruited arranger Ralph Burns to assist on his renditions of tunes like "Come Rain or Come Shine," "Am I Blue," and "Don't Let the Sun Catch You Cryin'," all chestnuts from his past, and all songs that Ray sang with every ounce of blues in his body. Few could interpret a song with as much passion and pain as Ray Charles, and this is the first time he presented it on a full side of an album.

For the same recording, Ray decided that a side's worth of big band brass would make for a great juxtaposition of those lushly arranged string tunes. In music's early days, you had artists who'd sing R&B, artists who played jazz, and artists who'd sing standards. It was virtually unheard of for an artist to combine those concepts, not only because it made little marketing sense, but also because few were even capable of it. "I was in heaven in both situations. I wanted to sing pretty things with lots of fiddles around me, and I wanted to sing bright things with the brass kicking my ass" (Ritz, *Genius & Soul* liner notes, p. 19).

When Atlantic released this album of dual purpose in the fall of 1959, they decided to call it *The Genius of Ray Charles*. But the title didn't sit right with Ray. "I'd never have used the word in regard to myself. I think I'm pretty good at what I do, but I never considered myself a genius" (Ritz, p. 195). The name stuck then, and remains one of his monikers.

Genius placed Charles at the forefront of recording artists. His courageous choices and inspired performances were widely hailed. In fact, he turned the music business on its head with his versatility, proving that an extraordinary talent could sing anything, provided the songs were good. Few artists were as daring as Charles and no one could acquit himself in so many areas as well.

THE OTHER SIDE OF THE ATLANTIC

Ray finished his last session for Atlantic in the summer of 1959. While had been doing well on the label and enjoyed a solid relationship with its brass,

Ray was after all a businessman interested in making money at least the equivalent of all the hard work he was doing. When Sam Clark, president of ABC Records, and Sid Feller, ABC's head of A&R, approached him with an enticing contract, Charles didn't hesitate.

In the fall of 1969, Clark offered Charles an artist-friendly contract that included a big advance, a more attractive royalty rate, as well as complete creative freedom and ownership of all his masters, the latter being an unprecedented perk for an artist, especially at a black artist, at the time. With a preliminary contract in hand, Charles returned to Atlantic with it in hopes that owner Ahmet Ertegun would match its terms, or at least compromise Ray's existing contract with them. But Ertegun passed on the option, admitting that ABC's terms were "too rich for his blood," and so let his premier artist go.

When Charles got to ABC, nothing changed with him creatively. Though ABC originally signed Charles to fill an R&B gap in their roster, Charles was headed in a different direction—in fact, many different directions. Not that he told his new home much about what he was thinking. But had the label been perceptive, they would have noticed Ray's recent forays into string ballads, big band, pop standards, and country, and not expected much in the way of R&B. Whatever the case, Charles had unlimited creative freedom and was eager to tackle the many diverse projects in his head.

One of his first orders of business at ABC was to form a publishing company, a concern called Tangerine, after his favorite fruit. Atlantic owned the work he did while on that label, but according to the terms of his new deal, ownership of his music would revert back to him at the conclusion of his contract. Even though he was writing less original music than in his Atlantic days, this enhancement proved to be a shrewd move; publishing revenues would become significant in his life.

Ray's first few singles for ABC were among his most successful, both creatively and commercially. He added the brawny baritone sax of Leroy "Hog" Cooper, a recruitment that enabled Hank Crawford to switch back to alto sax, his first instrument. This change increased Charles's permanent group to eight pieces and shored up his musical intentions.

He also began work with singer/songwriter/bluesman Percy Mayfield. Charles's collaborations with Mayfield were casual and effective. Mayfield would write songs for Charles and then they'd work together to try out possible arrangements. One of the first projects they partnered on was "Hit the Road Jack" in 1961. The song, which turned heartbreak into something of a comedy skit, hit number one in the early fall of that year. Other tunes they worked out together included Mayfield compositions "Hide 'Nor Hair" and "At the Club." These singles would be some of his last small band performances.

Still restless and intent on expanding his repertoire, Charles decided that despite his progress with his eight-piece and Percy Mayfield in particular, he wanted to form a real big band. He had wanted to integrate his smaller band into a big band in the studio, but after some contemplation decided to scrap everything and start again. One of the reasons Charles opted to put this band together was because he was on solid ground financially. "I put my big band together when I thought I could afford it. I had no magic formula, no scheme for it to make me money. I wanted music in my ears that only a big band could provide" (Ritz, p. 208).

He realized the change would be expensive and would create much work for him. He had to find material, charts, and musicians all at once. But when he encountered Quincy Jones, who was in the process of disbanding his own ensemble, part of his problem was solved. Jones gave Charles whatever material he wanted and Charles also wrote some tunes of his own.

It was around this time, his early years with ABC, that Ray began recording more concept albums. In 1960 he released *Genius Hits the Road*, with each song based loosely on a different state ("Moonlight in Vermont," "Georgia on My Mind"). In January of 1961, he issued *Dedicated to You*, featuring a collection of songs dedicated to different women ("Hardhearted Hannah," "Stella by Starlight").

"Georgia on My Mind," in particular, altered the direction of Ray's career. A Hoagy Carmichael chestnut from the 1930s South, the song took on vibrant new life 30 years later with a little of Charles's singular polish. Not only did he personalize the song and make it his own, he proved he could do virtually any song from any period, from any style, and succeed with it. This revelation would serve as the beginning of Ray's retirement from songwriting and his ascension as an interpreter.

Immediately following that, Charles issued *Genius + Soul = Jazz* for Impulse, the new ABC jazz subsidiary. With the help of arrangers Ralph Burns and Quincy Jones, who also assembled the Count Basie Big Band for the recording date, Ray took this opportunity to revisit more songs from his childhood, from all those days he'd keep his ear next to Mr. Pitman's jukebox, songs like "Stompin' Room Only" and "One Mint Julep." "I've Got News for You" is a storming blues with a fiery arrangement, and an apex for Ray. His output, on Hammond B3 organ for a change, was joyously funky, and a continuation of his innovative big band work he did near the end of his Atlantic tenure.

Six months after this, Ray, impassioned by the success of so many of his experiments, entered the studio for yet another one. This one would be a collection of duets with singer Betty Carter. When Charles first heard Carter, she was singing with Lionel Hampton's band in Philadelphia. "She's got that old feeling—that raw feeling—that destroys me" (Ritz, p. 222).

To many, Ray's work with Betty Carter was a match made in heaven, and it still rivals great singing duets like Ella Fitzgerald and Louis Armstrong or Dinah Washington and Brook Benton in terms of compatibility. "It was a free jazz voice; she had this floating quality that haunted me" (Ritz, *Genius & Soul* liner notes, p. 22).

Their duets were intoxicating, with Ray his charming, good-humored, romantic self and Betty coming off sweet and genuine. The standard to emerge from that coupling was, of course, "Baby, It's Cold Outside," in early 1962, a coy, irresistible Frank Loesser track that now doubles as a classic pop ballad and a Christmas tune.

All of this incredible chart success landed Ray on firm financial footing. Thanks to a favorable contract and some nonpareil material, he was ready to enjoy the fruits of his labor.

COUNTRY COOKIN'

Beyond the big band jazz, beyond the sexy duets, and his other concept albums, Ray Charles's most successful concept was his most unexpected one: country music. This, as Charles is quick to admit, was more by accident than design. "I didn't plan on making a killing on the country stuff. I just wanted to try my hand at hillbilly music. After all, the *Grand Ole Opry* had been performing inside my head since I was a kid in the country" (Ritz, p. 222).

At first, ABC was understandably skeptical about the project. Executives at the label were worried that the project wouldn't make sense to his fans, and they warned him that it might harm his career more than help. But Ray had a vision for the project and he was determined to see it through. The process of production was simple. Ray's A&R man, Sid Feller, initially suspicious but ultimately cooperative with his star, researched country music and presented him with 250 tunes from which to choose. Of the songs he picked, only one, "Bye Bye Love," was familiar to him. When making those selections Charles said he aimed for meaningful lyrics. "[You] gotta believe the story. See, I'm the actor and lyrics are the script. Lousy script, lousy performance. So these country songs spoke to me" (Ritz, *Genius & Soul* liner notes, p. 22).

His determination to see this project through was country music's gain. The resulting album, *Modern Sounds in Country & Western Music* took what was at the time a Southern means of musical expression confined to a niche audience and blew it up into a national attraction, almost single-handedly giving it mass appeal. "He did more for country music than any other living human being, because when he did that album, already Ray Charles was, you know, a household word," said Willie Nelson on *60 Minutes* in 1994. "Here's Ray Charles doing country songs, introducing those songs to millions and millions of people who, otherwise, would have never had a chance to hear them" (Ed Bradley, *60 Minutes*, CBS Television, December 2004).

As proof of how accidental his country music success happened to be, Feller placed "I Can't Stop Loving You," as the fifth song on the second side of the album, believing it was one of the weakest tracks. Released in February 1962, it became a number one pop sensation, remaining atop the charts for five weeks, and a worldwide smash. Though the song had a pop feel with white backing voices, R&B fans didn't turn their noses up at it either. The song remained number one on the R&B chart for four months. Three weeks after the single's release it had sold 300,000 copies. A month in, that figure had increased to 700,000. Retailers were likening it to the mania surrounding early Elvis Presley 45s. *Modern Sounds in Country & Western Music*, which knocked *West Side Story* soundtrack out of the number one slot on the album chart, has become the most famous and successful LP of Ray Charles's entire career.

Virtually no one in the record business saw this incredible, genre-busting event coming. That is, no one but Ray. Only *he* had remembered the endless hours he spent listening to hillbilly music as a kid on jukeboxes and on the radio. Only he could draw from the time he spent playing piano in a hillbilly band early on. And few even took seriously the fact that he followed up the gospel funk free-for-all of "What'd I Say" with a cover of country star Hank Snow's "I'm Movin' On," complete with steel guitar and train sounds.

"I was only interested in two things: being true to myself and being true to the music. I only wanted to take country songs and sing them my way" (Ritz, p. 223).

Besides, Ray considered hillbilly music and "black music" nearly identical. "You got the same goddamn thing exactly!" Still, Charles's transformation, if only temporary, changed the way he was perceived and also changed the way the public perceived country music. He wasn't the first black person to sing country, and he certainly wasn't the first pop singer to try his hand at country music (Bing Crosby sang lots of country, too). But he was responsible for bringing more attention than anyone to country music, country songs, and country artists. Here he was, an artist in the early 1960s that many in the press still referred to as a "blind, Negro pianist," bring the music of the Southern white working class to a national audience. The irony may have been lost on Ray, but the result certainly wasn't. Ray enjoyed the money, he enjoyed the fame, and he most assuredly appreciated the flexibility this unexpected superstardom afforded him.

Six months after releasing *Modern Sounds*, Ray followed up with *Modern Sounds of Country and Western Music Volume 2*, an album that did almost as well as the first. This one-two punch established Ray as a superstar and a mega-draw on the concert circuit, but that, according to the artist, didn't change him much. "I've always been a loner, and a lot of money and fame didn't change that. . . . Folks say I'm private to the point of being antisocial, and I won't argue" (Ritz, p. 227). But Charles goes on to explain that his behavior is largely due to his inability to live his life without interruption. Fans began to recognize Charles in public and he was the first to admit he didn't like those situations. "I withdraw into my little shell . . . I'm not relaxed with more than three or four people in a room, and if I don't know those people well, I'm really uncomfortable" (Ritz, p. 227).

Royalties came rolling in. He commanded top dollar on tour and Ray finally started making the kind of money his genius and strong work ethic deserved. When the cash started flowing, though, he remained a man of simple means. He was content to let his account remain untouched with ABC. Rather than pocketing his royalties and spending freely, he invested them and lived off the proceeds of touring.

STUDIO CITY

In 1962, Ray decided to centralize his business operations in Los Angeles. Since the Atlantic deal, Ray had been forced to work frequently out of New York City, even though he was living in California. So rather than make that trek, he moved everything out West. He bought property in a working-class neighborhood in LA. He assisted in the design of the building, a modest, two-story structure which would house both his business offices and his recording studio, which he called RPM Studios. At the same time, he built a new home for himself in the tony View Park section of the city.

Charles loved his recording studio, he says, "as much as the first car he ever bought." It allowed him the freedom to come and go, make music anytime he pleased, without being tied down to studio time or someone else's schedule. "When you own the joint, you rock when you want to rock and roll when you want to roll" (Ritz, p. 249).

Ray developed incredible facility in the studio, given his limitations. Renowned producer Tom Dowd helped Ray set up his gear, beginning with a three-track machine. That would later become a 24-track console. Generally speaking, he liked to "track" every instrument in a song before his vocals and piano. That way he had a song finished and he could do, and redo, his own parts as often as he liked.

> After he took over in the booth, a new era started. Now he sat in the booth at the console, balancing and mixing the orchestra and chorus, who were out in the studio playing. . . . After some stops for adjustments or changes were made, a finished take was approved after listening to a playback. . . . Then the fun began—Ray would set up mics in the studio for his voice and piano. While an assistant started the tape machines rolling, he would sing and play. . . . Ray would listen to the combined tape playback—the original orchestra and chorus plus his just completed vocal and piano. After his approval of the completed take, the basic recording was finished. (Sid Feller, *The Complete Country & Western Recordings 1959–1986*, liner notes, pp. 9–10)

Feller's contributions, in addition to being Ray's early producer and right-hand man in the studio, was to follow Charles's creative ideas and get them on paper, write the scores, something he started in 1959 and continued up through his passing in 2004. "Ray's main contribution to me was allowing me to be a part of his musical life" (Feller, p. 10).

With the independence the studio afforded him, Ray decided not to renew his contract with ABC-Paramount after two three-year stints on the label. Instead he signed with his own company, Tangerine, in early 1966.

INDULGENCES

"I don't like to conclude a day without female companionship," says Ray (Ritz, p. 232). With a lion-sized sexual appetite, Ray frequently indulged in relationships, whether for one night, a few months, or, infrequently, even longer. In his line of work, Ray was surrounded by women, and he rarely turned down an opportunity to meet someone new. He believed this indulgence was wholesome. "There's a certain male drive which keeps us wanting more and more women" (Ritz, p. 231).

"[He's] the most independent man I've ever seen in my life. The only time where he ever appeared to have any kind of handicap was when a beautiful woman was in the room," said Jones. "Then he started walking into walls and so forth. 'Can I help you Mr. Charles?'" Jones says the sympathetic women would say. "He'd get real blind, you know, when the pretty girls were around" (Quincy Jones, *60 Minutes*, December 2004).

Occasionally, Ray would settle down into a relationship with his lady friends. He married Eileen Williams in 1951. Then, after splitting up the next year he had a child, Evelyn, with Louise Mitchell. Margie Hendrix, a Raelett, had Ray's child, Charles Wayne, in 1959. All of this womanizing, though, unsettled Ray momentarily. Eager for something more permanent and comfortable, he met Della Beatrice Howard Robinson, "B" for short, in 1954 and they were married the following year.

Ray's intentions with B were true enough for the first few years, but B had the misfortune of marrying Ray just as his career was taking off and the demands of touring increased. Ray was customarily gone nine or ten months of every year. With all the temptations of the road ever present, Ray never stopped having affairs or doing heroin. This took a toll on the relationship. B was home constantly, and Ray only visited between tours and recording dates. But, inexplicably, they held on for a 22 years, or at least B did. "The pressures on us both were very heavy, and yet we endured them for a long spell" (Ritz, p. 160). Perhaps most damaging and humiliating of all, according to Ray himself, were those paternity suits filed against him. But B bit her lip and stayed steadfastly by her husband's side.

He'd go on to have three sons with B: David Robinson, Ray Charles Robinson, and Robert Robinson. Though Charles was only married twice, he had a total of 12 children by 7 different women. Of the few criticisms levied at Charles, this high-profile indulgence was the one that occurred to the most people. He never denied paternity, and never failed to take care of his offspring. He did endure two suits brought on by female acquaintances, but not due to confusion over paternity. Ray admitted paternity. He simply refused extravagant bankrolling. "I wasn't denying I was the father. I was just denying I was the Bank of America" (Ritz, p. 236).

Still, he admitted, "I carry the sins and the silliness of my generation" (Ritz, p. 238).

Another passion Charles had was heroin. He was addicted for seventeen years, beginning in the late 1940s and culminating in his arrest in Boston 1964. The arrest was his third.

During his lifetime, Charles was frank about his drug usage. He'd talk frequently about how he enjoyed drugs but always managed to stay in control. Charles never gave the impression of being strung out or incapacitated. He used drugs moderately to feed his addiction, but never appeared to let it take over his art. "I never lost myself, even after I shot up. I made my gigs. I sang my songs. I never wanted to lose control. I didn't see the point" (Ritz, p. 181).

"Some of the biggest records that I've ever had is during the time when I was using drugs," said Charles (*60 Minutes*, December 2004). "You see, but that ain't to say that it was the drugs that created the big records."

He often bristled when asked about his drug troubles. He said, "I've known times where I've felt terrible, but once I get to the stage and the band starts with the music, I don't know why but it's like you have pain and take an aspirin, and you don't feel it no more" (Bernstein, *Washington Post*, June 11, 2004).

In addition to Boston, he was arrested in Philadelphia in 1958, in Indianapolis in 1961. But while the first two were rather inconsequential, sort of minor warnings of his drug use, the Boston arrest at Logan Airport was the one that forced Ray to kick.

When federal agents apprehended Charles, the artist confessed readily. Though he was angry at being caught, he said he had always been ready to confess should the time come. "I sure as hell didn't want to go to jail. But I saw the bust as my own doing" (Ritz, p. 253). He was charged with possession of marijuana and heroin.

But because the case was held up in court, Ray wasn't sentenced until a year later. He stopped touring for the first time in 20 years and took stock of his life. In the summer of 1965, worried about the hold that drugs had on him, he checked himself into St. Francis hospital outside of Los Angeles for treatment.

Even in kicking drugs, Ray did things his way. He refused assistance, sedatives, or other means of easing the pain of coming off addiction. He describes his cleansing as rejecting the poison in his body. "The poison churned inside me until everything was loosened. . . . Everything about me stunk" (Ritz, p. 257).

AFTER THE FALL

When he emerged from treatment, his musical style seemed to have changed. The year he spent off the road seemed to have quieted him. His independence from his former label, ABC-Paramount, had eased his mind and the A&R pressures he felt, however subtle they might have had. Having his own studio at his disposal also helped settle him. In addition to being free from drugs, Ray was now in complete control, musically, creatively, and financially.

This freedom allowed him to choose to record any kind of music he pleased. Not that he didn't do that in the past. But his move away from record executives allowed him to make decisions without any other considerations at all. He had grown more sedate, and chose over the recording sessions to follow to lay down fewer free-wheeling blues numbers, sticking instead to popular songs and standards, often with string arrangements that seemed more suitable for easy listening airplay.

By early 1966, Ray had ostensibly entered into a new phase of his career, one that would last throughout the rest of his life. Major innovations no longer interested him, though he always kept a keen eye out for great songs. He'd write very little of his own material from the second half of the 1960s on, but he refined his abilities as an interpreter.

The music climate of the time didn't make it easy on him, or any other black artist who'd been on the scene for a while. Rock and roll had swept aside virtually all the rest of popular music. The British Invasion, and the Beatles in particular, dominated the charts and captivated the imagination of the record-buying public. Rock and roll also led to the Motown and Girl Group sounds, with acts like the Shirelles, the Supremes, and Smokey Robinson and the Miracles. These sounds would replace to doo-wop, blues, and R&B as representative "black music." The popularity of these styles suppressed, or at least temporarily displaced, the music of Ray Charles. The irony? Ray Charles had served as a beacon for both of those movements.

Marvin Gaye and the rest of the Motown sound adored Ray, even while they were co-opting his audience. "Everyone at Motown idolized Ray," said Gaye. "He had both the commercial success and the raw feeling we were all looking for" (Ritz, *Genius & Soul* liner notes, p. 30).

But as the Motown sound evolved, so did the notion of soul music, which saw black artists reaching forward to a new sound, and reaching back for the type of feelings that R&B artists of the 1950s had established. In addition, the late 1960s was in political and social turmoil. This upheaval began to infiltrate the sound of many artists, and music and life became more closely intertwined than it had ever been, as the music of the era served as the soundtrack to the violence and unrest.

Charles had aligned himself with Dr. Martin Luther King Jr. in the early 1960s in the South, when he played a benefit in Alabama for King's cause. At the time, segregation in the South was a dire social and cultural issue and Charles only wanted the rights the country's white citizens already possessed. "All we wanted was what was legitimately ours to begin with" (Ritz, p. 275). But Charles never became overtly political. Positive by nature, Charles liked King's positive thinking. Racial turmoil, by his own admission, made no sense to Ray. "The riots in the big cities in the sixties might have pointed out the lousy living conditions, but I couldn't understand folk burning down their own neighborhoods" (Ritz, p. 275).

Charles didn't ignore the music of the 1960s. Some of it, in particular the structure-less free jazz and the heavier psychedelic stuff, annoyed him because it didn't follow what he perceived to be the hard, fast rules of songwriting and arranging. But he became a fan, and interpreter, of the Beatles, adopting "Eleanor Rigby" and "Yesterday" into his canon.

At the same time, Ray started spending more time traveling around the world. His music had found its way across the globe, to Europe, South America, Japan, and Australia, and Ray brought his music to as many fans as he could. He added continental singers like Edith Piaf to his list of influences and he widened his circle of associates, friends, and collaborators to include artists from around the world. He worked with French singer Nicoletta, Israeli composer David Ben-Gurion, and many others around the world. In doing so, he opened up to styles beyond the blues, jazz, R&B, and country of his youth and his universal appeal grew in conjunction with his repertoire.

Not that the late 1960s proved to be hit-less for Charles. Along with his Beatles' interpretations, he also sang a few film themes. "In the Heat of the Night," scored by Quincy Jones, hit the charts in 1967 and was the most successful of these.

THE 1970s

Ray's record sales sharply decreased in the 1970s for a variety of reasons. The climate had changed dramatically, and Ray's place in popular music had changed right along with it. His response to the shifting tides of the business was to move to the center. Rather than test styles and experiment compulsively with genres as he'd done throughout the previous decade, he chose material directed at a more mature, middle-of-the-road audience.

Critics derided Charles's choice, but Ray ordinarily paid little attention to what people said about him, especially critics.

In 1973, he released a long overdue political statement, in album form, called *A Message from the People*. Two years later he released *Renaissance*. Many of the songs, what he called "message songs" on these projects contained an unexpected edginess, as if Ray had finally had enough, and needed to get a few things off his chest. He had never made a message album before and the result brought a significant contemporary feel to his work for the first time in a decade.

Both of these recordings featured timely, relevant material, including Stevie Wonder's "Livin' in the City" and Randy Newman's "Sail Away." But the real surprise here, and the song from the period that endures to this day, is Ray's reading of "America the Beautiful." "Some of the verses were just too white for me, so I cut them out and sang the verses about the beauty of the country and the bravery of the soldiers" (Ritz, *Genius & Soul* liner notes, p. 35). A little country church backbeat propels the tune, and it would go on to become one Ray's most memorable performances, alongside "Georgia on My Mind" and "What'd I Say." The timing of the song was notable. When many black acts were still troubled by the civil rights upheaval and the social climate of the country, Ray chose a song that professed his national pride. "A black magazine wrote that I was selling out by singing 'America.' . . . So my attitude on *Message* was like a mama chastising a baby. 'You may be a pain in the ass, you may be bad, but child, you belong to me.'" And he added. "No one will tell me what to play. To me, that's the spirit of America" (Ritz, pp. 289–90).

Around this time, in 1975, his wife of twelve years, B, filed for legal separation, and Ray accommodated her a few months later with official divorce papers. The two had lived separate lives virtually since meeting and even frequent visits to a marriage counselor couldn't bring them back together. Remembering the good times he had with B, Ray was wistful about the divorce. "The collapse of a marriage . . . is a sad and hurtful thing. And all I can do . . . is recall those happy good years when we were both singers kicking around Texas very young and starry-eyed in love" (Ritz, p. 285).

THE ACCOLADES

From the late 1970s on, the remainder of Ray's career consisted mainly of encores and victory laps. He showed up in the John Belushi–Dan Aykroyd film *The Blues Brothers* (1980), followed a few years later by his very emotional involvement in the famine relief recording "We Are the World" (1985). His brief cameo in the song was poignant and powerful, and a reminder that Charles's fusion of styles included more soul than any performer before or since.

Over the years, he appeared in many television commercials, most of which he produced himself. The best known of those were for Coca-Cola (one with Aretha Franklin), Olympia Beer, the Scotch recording tape company, and California Raisins.

In 1987 he received the coveted Lifetime Achievement Award at the Grammys. Over the course of his career he won 14 Grammy awards in all, including the aforementioned Lifetime Achievement and the President's Merit Award. His latest Grammy came in 1993 for Best R&B Vocal Performance for "A Song for You."

Charles is also one of the original inductees into the Rock and Roll Hall of Fame and a recipient of the Presidential Medal for the Arts, France's Legion of Honor, and the Kennedy Center Honors. He has been inducted into numerous other music Halls of Fame, including those for Rock and Roll, Jazz, and Rhythm and Blues, a testament to his enormous influence.

In May 2002 he performed at the Coliseum in Rome, the first musical performance there in 2,000 years.

He has received eight honorary doctorates, the most recent in 2003 from Dillard University in New Orleans. Later that summer, he performed his 10,000th career concert at the Greek Theater in Los Angeles.

In 2003, he headlined the White House Correspondents Dinner in Washington, D.C., at which President and Mrs. Bush, Colin Powell, and Condoleeza Rice were in attendance. Astonishingly, and perhaps tellingly, he has performed at the request of the past seven presidents.

Charles died on June 10, 2004. His last album was *Genius Loves Company*, a duets album released posthumously that same year. Ironically, it would become the best-selling album of his career. His duet partners include B.B. King, Elton John, James Taylor, Norah Jones, Van Morrison, Willie Nelson, and other stars. Because Ray was so sick during the recording process, the quality is spotty, but many of his strengths still managed to shine through.

Last Album Blues

Ray Charles's last album was *Genius Loves Company*, a duets album released posthumously in August 2004. The album was recorded between July 2003 and 2004. Ironically, it would attain incredible commercial heights. The disc, recorded shortly before Charles died at the age of 73, sold an astounding 202,000 copies in its first week out, making it the best-selling duets album since SoundScan began tracking sales in 1991, according to *Billboard*.

It has since shipped more than 2 million copies in the United States and more than 3 million copies worldwide. To date, it has received gold, silver and platinum certifications across North America, Europe, and beyond. *Genius Loves Company*, Ray's 250th recording is, without a doubt, one of the best-selling recordings of his six-decade career.

The Grammy organization handed Charles a debt of gratitude when the disc went on to win eight Grammy Awards that year, including Album of the Year and Record of the Year for a duet with Norah Jones. *Genius* beat competition from many popular contemporary artists, including Alicia Keys, Usher, Kanye West, and Green Day for the evening's top accolade.

In 2004, a biopic directed by Taylor Hackford came out to great acclaim. Actor Jamie Foxx portrayed Ray skillfully and earned an Oscar for his efforts.

During a career that spanned 58 years, Charles starred on over 250 albums, many of them top sellers in a variety of musical genres, and had a dozen chart-topping R&B hits. His influence continues to be inestimable. His best-known and most successful students include Van Morrison, Joe Cocker, Steve Winwood, and, of course, the Beatles.

Throughout his six-decade career, Charles earned comparisons to major singers in all fields, from Frank Sinatra to James Brown. Such versatility helped him connect with an audience of fragmented tastes, while still forging a distinctive legacy by the force of his own persona.

In the afterword of his autobiographical book, *Brother Ray*, co-writer David Ritz talked about the perils and candor of interviewing Charles. Ritz's job was to interview him, and fashion the recordings into a coherent first-person narrative. In order to cover adequate ground with intelligence and depth, the conversation had to be smart and the questions tough.

> I began tentatively by saying, "Now if this question is too tough . . . "
> "How . . . can a question be too tough? The truth is the truth."
> And the truth came pouring out. That his life had been tough. That his life had been blessed. . . . That he had been gutsy in traveling the long dark road, blind and alone. That he had been a junkie. That being a junkie never stopped him from working day and night, touring, recording, succeeding. That he had given up junk only when faced with prison. That every day he still drank lots of gin and smoked lots of pot and worked just as tirelessly. That he had a huge appetite for women. . . . That he wasn't even certain of how many children he had fathered. That he was unrepentant about it all. That he was more than confident; he was cocky; he knew his own powers—as a man, a musician, a lover, an entrepreneur who had outsmarted a ruthless industry, maintained ownership of his product and stashed away millions.
> I never met anyone braver. He had no fears. He walked through the world like a lion. (Ritz, p. 320)

SELECTED DISCOGRAPHY

Genius & Soul: The 50th Anniversary Collection (Rhino, 1997)

The Complete Country & Western Recordings 1959–1986 (Rhino, 1998)

Modern Sounds in Country & Western Music, Volume 1 & 2 (Rhino, 1998)

Standards (Rhino, 1998)

FURTHER READING

Charles, Ray and David Ritz. *Brother Ray: Ray Charles Own Story*. New York: Da Capo, 2004.

Lydon, Michael. *Ray Charles: Man and Music*. London: Routledge, 2004.

Werner, Craig. *A Change Is Gonna Come: Music, Race, and the Soul of America*. New York: Plume, 1999.

Courtesy of Photofest.

Little Richard

THE QUASAR OF ROCK

In 1956, the year that Elvis was said to have launched rock and roll, Presley covered four Little Richard songs. Bill Haley covered "Rip It Up," and the Everly Brothers, Gene Vincent, Carl Perkins, and Jerry Lee Lewis, the forefathers of rock and roll, all covered Little Richard's material. When the kings of rock all paid tribute to one man, well, that must make *him* the king.

In fact, many experts refer to Richard Penniman as "the architect of rock and roll," which makes good sense. In the early 1950s, a handful of R&B acts were accelerating in the same stylistic direction as Little Richard, including Hank Ballard, Lloyd Price, Ike Turner, and Jackie Wilson. Richard just happened to arrive at his destination—the intersection of rock and roll and R&B—first. And he did it the fastest as well, with a lightning vocal delivery, furious piano pounding, and an ecstasy-inducing, high-voltage show.

Richard recorded for RCA-Victor, Elvis's eventual record label, back in 1951, five years before the King. When he released "Tutti Frutti" in 1956, it became a worldwide hit, a true phenomenon, even faster than Elvis's "Heartbreak Hotel," which also caught on quickly that same year but not with the same fury of Little Richard. The fact that Elvis was white, and therefore more palatable to television and most radio stations, made his road a whole lot easier to travel than Little Richard's way.

It was his tenure at Specialty Records that enabled Little Richard to assume the role of rock and roll architect. Working at Cosimo Matassa's now legendary J&M Studio in New Orleans with producer Robert "Bumps" Blackwell and some of the Crescent City's finest musicians, Little Richard laid down a spectacular series of rock and roll recordings, including "Rip It Up," "Slippin' and Slidin'," "Lucille," "Jenny Jenny," and "Keep A-Knockin'," in addition to the songs previously mentioned. He also appeared in rock and roll–themed movies such as *Don't Knock the Rock* and *The Girl Can't Help It* (both from 1956).

"I was the first black artist whose records the white kids were starting to buy," he said in *Rolling Stone*.

> And the parents were really bitter about me. We played places where they told us not to come back, because the kids got so wild. They were tearing up the streets and throwing bottles and jumping off the theater balconies at shows. At that time, the white kids had to be up in the balcony; they were "white spectators." But then they'd leap over the balcony to get downstairs where the black kids were. (David Dalton, "Little Richard, Child of God," *Rolling Stone*, May 28, 1970)

Little Richard became both the fantasy and the nightmare of rock and roll. With his outrageous get-ups and notorious pancake makeup, and his reputation for outrageous sexual activity, he embodied the grotesque, nightmarish image that disturbed the placid and conservative 1950s, the exact ghoul of a person a parent would never want their daughter to meet, let alone lay eyes on.

On the other hand, he represented pure, exhilarating freedom. He said and sang and performed anything he pleased; he resembled a true force of nature that could not be denied.

THE EARLY YEARS

Richard Penniman came into this world in 1935, 1 of 12 children born to Leva Mae and Charles "Bud" Penniman, They lived in Macon, Georgia, where

Bud worked as a mason, a part-time bootlegger, and bar proprietor. They married early, and Leva Mae, a firm, but soft-spoken woman, had her first child just prior to turning 16.

Bud Penniman made a decent living in construction and brought the kids up with just what they needed, no more, no less. They didn't have to work, and were provided for every day. They dressed respectably, ate well enough, and led a normal middle-class existence.

Richard May Penniman was their third child and the family's most mischievous one. He was, he explains, born slightly deformed. His right leg was shorter than his left, he had a relatively large head and, he says, one big eye and one little eye. He walked with short steps to compensate for the size difference of his legs; a physical quirk that led people to believe he had feminine characteristics.

Because of his physical handicaps, his mother let him get away with a lot. He managed to escape chores and other household responsibilities. He did some nasty things at home, including pushing old cars down a hill and defecating in a preserve jar and putting it on the shelf or giving it as a present. His mother, a spiritual woman, often thought her son was possessed by the devil himself.

At school, his outrageous behavior earned him a wide circle of friends, many of whom called him "Big Head." He had a knack for making people laugh; being the center of attention came naturally. He'd do anything he could to get people's attention, whether making them laugh, make them mad, or get them to cry. Whatever it took, he'd do it, and then he'd run away laughing. But mostly Richard wanted to play with girls. "See, I felt like a girl. I used to play house with my cousins and I'd say, 'I'm the momma!' . . . The boys wouldn't play with me after I started saying stuff like that" (Charles White, *The Life and Times of Little Richard: The Quasar of Rock*, New York: Harmony Books, 1984, p. 9).

Richard identified much more with his mother than his father. He idolized Leva Mae. He watched her intently as she got ready in the morning, dressing and applying makeup. When she wasn't at home, he'd sneak into her bedroom and do the same to his own face, apply makeup, and splash himself with her rosewater.

He had real crushes on boys at an early age, but he also flirted with older women, who liked him because he was so different. He had homosexual affairs as a young teen, though he kept his liaisons secret. Still, his friends knew he was different. The girls loved him because he was *like* them, but the boys were relentless and threatening. Richard endured a torrent of nasty nicknames, including "sissy," "faggot," and "freak." It got to the point where he hated to be around guys.

The problem extended to his father, with whom he had a marginal relationship. His father, one of seven boys himself, criticized him for his personal idiosyncrasies. He said he was only half a son to him, a slight referring to his effeminate nature.

Part of Richard's personality was his voice. He was always hollering and singing around the house and with his friends. As a child he was surrounded by music; the women would do the wash and break out into song, mainly spiritual numbers from church. Richard himself sang in the church as well, and was recruited to sing in the children's choir, a group called Little Tots. But as he grew older, his voice became louder, more obstreperous. When it did, the women in the church began to shush him, told him to stop his hollering. It didn't stop him from singing though. Nothing stopped him from singing.

He loved being in church. He wanted to be a preacher even as a young boy. He admired the men in his own church that preached and carried on. Many of his family members—uncles and cousins, mainly—were integral in their churches and he looked up to them. When he was about 10 he began acting the part of the healer around town. As part prank, part real-life desire, he'd approach ailing people, sing or chant some prayers, and touch them. Often, Richard said they'd tell him how good they felt, and would hand him some money.

MAKIN' IT IN MACON

"There was a warmth and friendliness about life in Macon, a community spirit commonly found in the poorer parts of towns and cities" (White, p. 18). The city itself was fertile musical ground in the 1930s and 1940s, with the sounds of gospel, blues, and R&B emanating from everywhere. Downtown Macon was saturated with live music clubs and a vibrant nightlife. Musicians also had numerous opportunities to play at the area's many military bases. Local personalities included DJ Hamp Swain and local black entrepreneur Clint Brantley, a club owner and booker. The city's rich musical traditions would not only spawn Little Richard, but two other giants of popular music: Otis Redding and James Brown.

Early on, Richard got a job with Brantley at the Macon City Auditorium selling Coca-Cola. He loved the job not for the money, but for all the great performers he got to see without paying: Cab Calloway, Hot Lips Page, Cootie Williams, and his favorite singer, Sister Rosetta Tharpe. One night before a show, Richard met Tharpe, and he sang a couple of her songs for her. She asked him that night, in front of everybody, if he'd join her on stage for a duet, which he did. It was the best thing that had happened to him in his young life.

But troubles at home with his family forced Richard out of the house. He wasn't doing well in school, and his association with the more outrageous, often gay personalities in and around Macon made life difficult. His father disapproved vehemently of his lifestyle and his presence at home was a source of stress for both of his parents.

That's when, in 1948, Richard decided to join up with something called Dr. Hudson's Medicine Show. Dr. Hudson needed help selling snake oil and various other odd jobs on the road. A pianist accompanied the show and

Richard occasionally sang with him as well. While he was traveling with Hudson, he met Ethel Wynnes, a club owner in Fitzgerald, Georgia. She took pity on him, fed him, and took him in.

One night, a singer, I.A. Harris, flaked out on his band at Wynnes's club and she decided to replace him with Richard, billed, because of his young age and diminutive stature, as "Little Richard." Then a 14-year-old boy, Richard was flamboyant and frisky, loud, and occasionally abrasive. The band he stepped in with didn't care for his style at all, and neither did the women in the audience, who felt an odd sort of repulsion for such an outrageous and effeminate guy. They almost didn't care about the fact that he could sing the roof off the place, something he did that night. Despite their feelings about the bizarre Richard, they liked him enough to take him on the road. It was his first big break, and a turning point in his life.

From here, he bounced around various touring and minstrel shows, vaudeville revue packages where he'd sing a few songs amid a cavalcade of comedy sketches and female impersonators. He toured with several different caravans and began making a name for himself. For one of the shows, he assumed the character of a woman named Princess LaVonne.

At this point his stage act was attracting the attention of area gays. He began to get more lucrative offers from bigger shows, which put him in front of larger audiences. For a show called the Broadway Follies he found himself, as a cross-dresser, in Atlanta frequently. At the time, the city was a hotbed of talent, experiencing a golden era of good vibrations and a fertile entertainment scene. Nightlife teemed on Auburn Avenue, and Little Richard sang as an opening act for many of the city's biggest names, including B.B. King and Jimmy Witherspoon.

One of the acts he opened for frequently was a lurid artist named Billy Wright, a curly-haired, loud dressing, gospel-blues shouter. Wright's outrageous stage act had a profound influence on Richard. He studied his antics and his image. He even began wearing the same makeup: Pancake 31. In 1951, Wright put him in touch with a local Atlanta radio station that often did recording work for RCA-Victor. One of the station's DJs, Zenas Sears, a white program host of a popular R&B program, helped Richard secure a contract with the label, and Richard cut his first recordings. One of those songs, "Every Hour," produced a local hit.

Back home, the Penniman family was thrilled to hear Richard's music on the radio. His father, especially, saw it as his son's first glimpse of legitimate progress and he got behind Richard's efforts for the first time. Back in Macon, he started attracting larger audiences. With a career in gear and his parents at last supporting him, things were looking up.

To beef up his act, Richard picked up the piano, thanks to another gay Macon personality called SQ Rita, or Esquerita. He used to pound on his piano at home, but never truly learned to play until he developed a relationship with the flamboyant SQ.

Richard returned to the recording studio in Atlanta for RCA-Victor in early 1952 to cut some follow-up sides. Unfortunately, the four songs he cut were rather unimpressive, and none made an impact at radio. He went back to Macon, a little disappointed, and started gigging around clubs again, this time fronting the Percy Welch Orchestra.

In February of that year, tragedy struck the Pennimans. Bud, Richard's father, was shot outside his bar, the Tip In Inn. A man named Frank Tanner killed him, though the reasons weren't clear. His sister happened to be at the Inn earlier that night, and said that all had been calm. Bud had played Richard's music on the jukebox, and the two had shared a couple of dances. Tanner would be charged with the murder, but later released.

The loss destroyed the family mentally as well as financially. With no money coming in, Richard, at 19, became the clan's principal breadwinner. Unfortunately, about the same time, he was released from his contract with RCA due to lack of interest. He picked up a job washing dishes to bring money in quickly.

Enter Clint Brantley.

Brantley was the successful entrepreneur that had hired Richard to sell soda at the Macon City Auditorium. This time, he encouraged him to form a band, and if he did it fast enough Brantley could use him as a local opener for the national touring acts he booked.

Little Richard and the Tempo Toppers, a rag-tag bunch of good-time players, became his first real band. They traveled around the South, including a lengthy stint in New Orleans where their residency at a club called Tijuana was enthusiastically received.

Early in 1953, the band moved to Houston to explore that city's scene. They played a residency at Club Matinee, where a famous talent scout named Johnny Otis caught their act: "I see this outrageous person, good-looking and very effeminate, with a big pompadour. He started singing and he was *so* good. . . . I remember it as being just beautiful, bizarre, and exotic, and when he got through he remarked, 'This is little Richard, King of the Blues,' and then he added, 'And the Queen, too!' I knew I liked him then" (White, p. 36).

In Houston, Richard's band gained the attention of Don Robey, head of the Peacock label. Robey, one of only a few black record company owners, was a brash disciplinarian who demanded compliance and respect from his artists. But that's not what he got when he signed Richard and the band. Robey quickly lost his temper with the sassy Penniman, and they'd occasionally end up in a physical fight. Recording sessions turned up little in the way of usable material. Even a session with Otis himself produced nothing worthwhile. Disillusionment set in on all sides and soon Richard's band broke up.

Back in Macon, Richard assembled a new band, the Upsetters, this one with more of an up-tempo R&B feel rather than the Tempo Toppers, which featured more gospel and blues. They got up to speed quickly, and soon became the premier R&B outfit and biggest draw in all of a Macon. All of the acts that came to Macon made it a point to check out Little Richard and the Upsetters. This list included Chuck Berry, then a blues singer, and Fats Domino. Both would be changed by what they saw at Penniman's show.

Another star that came to see the band was Lloyd Price, a hugely popular recording artist at the time. After the show, Price recommended that Richard send a demo tape to Art Rupe at the Specialty label, Price's own record company. Almost a year went by until Richard heard from Rupe.

In the meantime, he'd gotten himself into trouble with the Macon law for something officially termed "lewd conduct." The sentence banned him from Macon clubs just as he had reached the peak of his popularity. Because of the restriction, he and the Upsetters spent most of their time on the road, out of town.

Art Rupe's Specialty had been in business for a decade before signing Richard and had enjoyed modest success with gospel, blues, and R&B acts. Rupe had hired Robert "Bumps" Blackwell in the early 1950, a man credited with shaping the talent of artists out in Seattle, including Ray Charles and Quincy Jones. Blackwell, a classically trained musician, heard Richard's demo in 1955 and wanted him and the band down in New Orleans for a recording session.

Robert "Bumps" Blackwell, Little Richard, and Sam Cooke

One of the more underappreciated names in the pantheon of rock and roll belongs to a man named Robert "Bumps" Blackwell. Blackwell was hired by Specialty Records president Art Rupe as a kind of producer/A&R man. And he certainly proved he had an eye for talent.

Beginning in the fall of 1955, Blackwell exerted a tremendous impact on the future of rock and roll. He produced sides by Little Richard at Cosimo Matassa's J&M Studio in New Orleans with the city's best band: drummer Earl Palmer, sax player Alvin "Red" Tyler, pianist Huey Smith, and bassist Frank Fields. The same band was used by Fats Domino on that pianist's epic sides a few years earlier. After Little Richard settled on a sound, that rollicking, propulsive, piano-based explosion, Blackwell was there with him nearly every step of the way, helping to shape one of rock's most memorable careers.

Blackwell was also there when Sam Cooke, formerly lead singer of the Specialty act the Soul Stirrers, decided to opt for a secular career in pop music. In fact, many feel that it was Blackwell who convinced Cooke to leave his gospel background behind, that there was money and fame in pop music, and all Cooke had to do was say the word. Blackwell wanted Cooke's music to go straight to pop music stations, instead of the usual route a black artist's record took, firsts going to black stations, selling well in that market, then crossing over to pop. Rupe disagreed with Blackwell, that Cooke should go the traditional route. The conflict led to arguments between him and Blackwell; Cooke threatening to leave Specialty. To resolve matters, the two compromised. Blackwell gave up all his future royalties on Little Richard's records for a mere $1,500 and took Cooke and the rights to his music with him.

At the time, Blackwell had been looking for energetic, rhythmic, and "feel" musicians. He found that combination in Lloyd Price, who had a massive hit with "Lawdy Miss Clawdy." He found it in Eddie Jones, aka "Guitar Slim," and he heard it in Richard's demo. At the time, they had never actually seen him in person, let alone hear him perform. But Blackwell heard a star quality in his voice and extended the invitation. Richard went to New Orleans without the Upsetters.

"TUTTI FRUTTI"

When Blackwell and Penniman met in New Orleans to record, they were each pleased for different reasons. Blackwell got a kick out of Penniman's appearance and contrived outrageousness, and Penniman was thrilled to see that the musicians Blackwell had arranged for him to be in the studio for the recordings were among the city's best. In fact, Richard noted that most were from Fats Domino's backing band: Earl Palmer on drums, James Booker and Huey "Piano" Smith on piano, Lee Allen on tenor sax, Red Tyler on baritone sax, Frank Fields on bass, and Edgar Blachard and Justin Adams on guitars.

The first few hours of the recording session went poorly. Blackwell noticed a disconnect between Richard's singing style and his appearance. His vocals were bland, overly spiritual, without the pizzazz he looked like he could deliver. They broke for lunch over at the Dew Drop Inn. While they were there, Richard sat down at the bar's piano and started banging out some chords, perhaps in frustration.

"A wop-bop-aloo-mop a good god damn! Tutti frutti, good booty!" He sang the opening lines of a tune he'd used in his performances, mainly around Macon. He had been singing the song for years, actually, and just never figured it was the kind of tune that deserved recording.

Blackwell perked up. That was the kind of sass he'd envisioned Richard laying down in the studio. Save for some unseemly language, the song was perfect. He rang Dorothy La Bostrie, a lyricist, and had her rewrite the lyrics to make them more palatable for radio. In the 15 minutes remaining in their session, he sat Penniman down at the piano—there was no time to arrange the song for the other pianists—and told him to pound the chords and sing it like he did at the Dew Drop Inn.

The song first hit radio thanks to Nashville's powerful WLAC station and spread like a brushfire across the country. Specialty requested that Richard come out to Los Angeles and make some West Coast appearances. Demand was on the rise.

Rupe and Blackwell hastily assembled a recording contract for Richard, an unfavorable one of course, that involved Rupe buying Richard's publishing rights (for $50) and then selling them back to the company with his own name on them. Black artists, uneducated in business matters, were often hoodwinked by record company owners and Little Richard was no exception. Still, in order to be a recording artist, musicians had to play the game. Black musicians eager to capitalize on their own success were often shunned; their records were marginalized until a less savvy artist came along to take their place.

To make money—and there was definitely money to be made in this time at the dawn of rock and roll—a black artist had to hit the road. Richard's studio band did not include members of the Upsetters, all of whom were left behind. Clint Brantley, angry that the young star he discovered was so quick to abandon his people, recruited another local artist. James Brown, a superbly talented and energetic young singer, had just gotten out of jail for general misconduct. He began to front Little Richard's old band, while Richard tended to matters with Blackwell, Rupe, and his new label. The Upsetters also hooked up with another Macon talent, Otis Redding, a Little Richard fanatic, who occasionally opened the show for Brown and the Upsetters.

The white radio stations in America wouldn't touch Little Richard's version of "Tutti Frutti," despite its lyrical revisions. It still sold well, though, with white and black audiences, and reached the Top 20 on the pop singles chart. But in an indication of unfairness to come, white artists began to cover his songs, basically because they knew radio wouldn't play Little Richard's original version. Both Pat Boone and Elvis Presley rush-released renditions of "Tutti Frutti." Boone's hit number 12 in January 1956.

"LONG TALL SALLY"

A DJ in Tennessee named Honey Chile telephoned Blackwell and asked him to visit her immediately. She had something he should see. Not being one to turn a request from an all-important disc jockey down, he met with her at a cheap hotel. There was a quiet, teenaged girl, named Enortis Johnson, by Chile's side. Enortis had a doily in her hand, and on the back, some lyrics. She had walked for days from her home in Mississippi to meet with the two music executives. Her aunt was sick, and she needed to sell a song to make some money for her medical care. Blackwell saw just three lines written on the doily, starting with "Saw Uncle John with Long Tall Sally."

Blackwell, understanding the situation, took the lyrics back to his client. That afternoon, they took those few lines, fleshed them out—"Have some fun tonight" from Richard became the vocal hook—and turned them into a song. Blackwell pushed the tempo beyond the breaking point, accelerating the song's rhythm to a point in which a white singer like Pat Boone couldn't possibly get his mouth around the rapid-fire lyrics.

Released in February 1956, the song jetted up the R&B charts to the top spot and by April that year hit the pop Top 10. The song reached across the country and overseas, where young musicians like John Lennon and Paul McCartney were profoundly influenced by its sound. (Incidentally, Pat Boone *did* record "Long Tall Sally" that year and sold a million copies of it.)

When the money started rolling in, if not to Richard, at least to Rupe and Specialty, he decided to move his family to Hollywood. Rupe advanced him $10,000 against royalties for a $25,000 home. He moved his mother out of her three-room Macon home. Seeing her in that brand-new home, Richard said, was one of the happiest moments in his life.

Had he not recorded again, Little Richard's place of honor in the pantheon of popular music, just based on "Tutti Frutti" and "Long Tall Sally," would have been secure. But in the summer of 1956 he pushed the envelope even further with two Blackwell tunes: "Rip It Up" and "Ready Teddy." Both songs reached number 1 on the R&B list, while the former climbed to the Top 20 in pop. Of course, both songs were covered by Elvis Presley, Bill Haley, and Buddy Holly. The Little Richard tunes in 1956 would form the nexus of R&B and rock and roll.

At this point, management began to deal with the question of Little Richard's image. With America still a very uncertain place racially, prejudice and bias were prevalent, especially around the South. If a black performer was perceived to be sexually attractive or attracting to white women, à la Jackie Wilson, the consequences from local law enforcement and the Ku Klux Klan could be severe. So Blackwell and Penniman decided they should make Little Richard, the character, so outrageous as to be almost unbelievable, surreal.

To a degree, this worked. But Richard still cast a spell on his audiences. At a show in Baltimore, police had to intervene and remove dozens of hysterical girls from the audience, all of whom had tried to climb onto the stage and touch Richard. At the same show, one particularly wild-eyed girl removed her underwear and threw it on stage, inciting a flurry of women to do the same. Rock and roll and sex were now connected at the hip, right there, at a Little Richard gig.

With that hysteria growing, the shows became bigger, and soon Little Richard was playing to 10,000 screaming fans. Many would come to the stage and throw nude pictures of themselves at him with their phone numbers on the back.

He almost married a young girl named Lee Angel, a nude model and stripper. They spent lots of time together. He used to joke to his friends and even his audiences that he was engaged to Angel; he often introduced her as his fiancée. But they never tied the knot.

EGO TRIP

At this point, fame and fortune had gone to Little Richard's head. He was the biggest thing in popular music at the time, and people everywhere were clamoring to get a piece of him. Ego became a big factor, and he started making demands of Rupe. His first one: to make a record with the Upsetters in Macon. Rupe had always insisted that Penniman record in New Orleans, where he'd done his first two sessions. But Penniman wanted his old band back. Rupe made the concession, and Penniman was back in business with the Upsetters. That session, recorded at a Macon studio, produced "She's Got It," "Heeby-Jeebies," "Send Me Some Lovin'," and "Lucille." These were recordings as good as any Little Richard had done.

"Lucille" spent 21 weeks on the *Billboard* charts in the spring of 1957, and "Send Me Some Lovin'" stayed on the charts for 3 months after that. A follow-up session produced "Jenny, Jenny," which eked into the Top 10 during the summer of 1957, and "Miss Ann" broke the Top 60 later the same season.

"Good Golly Miss Molly" came next. It was a pastiche of a term he borrowed from a local DJ and riff he cribbed from Jackie Brenston, the sax player of Ike Turner's Kings of Rhythm. The formula worked and the song became an early rock and roll classic.

To coincide with Little Richard's unlikely rise, though, the country's social establishment, sleepy, traditional, and conservative in the mid-1950s, began to take notice and fight the growing counterculture of rock and roll. Little Richard, with his big, processed hairdo, scary pancake makeup, and insane performance antics, became public enemy number one among those who considered themselves moralistic. This wave of conservatism aimed at advertisers on rock and roll radio and sponsors of the growing number of touring caravans. Newspapers began smearing rock concerts as places of violence and licentiousness. Alan Freed's and Bill Randle's radio shows, non-segregated dances, and rock and roll package shows were seen as obscene, immoral, and anti-American. Traditional folks, those brought up in the patriotic 1940s and post-war 1950s, despised what Little Richard was doing, even as the kids who enjoyed his music saw him, along with the stellar performers he promoted, as a savior of their dreary lives.

THE GOOD LORD

The madness surrounding Little Richard generated a lot of revenue for him and the band. They'd often walk away from a particularly big show with over $10,000, much of which Richard would throw in his truck as loose bills. He was generous with it, too, handing it out to those he thought needed it. On the other hand, he didn't watch it very closely, and spent a lot of it freely.

All of this indulgence, in sex and money—but not drugs—taxed Little Richard's psyche though. It all ran counter to his religious upbringing, which seemed to find a way to addle him at the most inopportune moments. Because of this, there were deep contradictions in his character. The music he was making and singing every night, the same rabid vibrations that were lathering teens up, was being denounced emphatically as "evil," "the devil's music."

Was it? He continued to participate in various sexual practices. The thought that these things he so enjoyed doing were evil had a way of tormenting him. One day, in the throes of an inner dialogue, he heard a knock on his door. It was a missionary named Brother Wilbur Gulley, a mild-mannered representative of the Church of God and the Ten Commandments. They spoke intimately at a time when Richard felt particularly conflicted and vulnerable. Richard confided in him that he felt misused, abused, and disrespected by executives in the music business. He felt unfulfilled and unfaithful, not mention guilty about all the money he was making. He had also grown physically exhausted of the endless touring and recording schedule he'd followed for the better part of five years, and desperately needed a break.

Brother Gulley's timing was impeccable. They read the Bible together, a book Richard had always turned to in times of trouble. Richard needed rest, spiritual refreshment, and wisdom. Incredibly, in the middle of a sold-out tour of Australia in 1958, after a gig in Melbourne in which he played to over 40,000 people, he announced his retirement from show business.

He had forfeited half a million dollars in bookings and had turned the lives of all the people who'd work for him and relied on his revenue upside down. Even his family, shocked by the announcement of his religious seclusion, worried that they'd not have enough money to make ends meet. Arenas were booked, with deposits paid, for another 50 shows. He played his farewell show at the Apollo Theater in New York City to an emotional and hysterical crowd.

Publicly he blamed Art Rupe for at least part of his abdication. Rupe had forced him to feel like he'd completely sold his soul to the business. He felt like Rupe had taken advantage of him, that he couldn't stand himself for the business practices in which he'd participated. Thanks to Brother Gulley, and another spiritual friend, Joe Lutcher, a musician who had also committed his life to Jesus, Little Richard turned to a lifetime of prayer.

Lutcher and Penniman started a mission called the Little Richard Evangelical Team, in which they traveled across the country, extending ministry to those in need. In keeping with his more traditional and religious lifestyle, he abandoned his sexual practices and married Ernestine Campbell. They married in the summer of 1959 after a two-year courtship.

Penniman studied at Oakwood, a religious college in Huntsville, Alabama, where they designed a special Bible-oriented curriculum for him. He explains his conversion to *Rolling Stone* scribe David Dalton:

> I studied the Bible, a book called *Daniel and the Revelations, Steps to Christ, Daniel and the Prophets*, about Moses, about Pharaoh, about God's great plan

for man, and about how black people have ruled before, King Solomon was black. So God gives everyone a chance, and the next ruler will be him, I believe, wholeheartedly. I studied about how you can praise God through music. . . . There are a lot of people who are devoted to music, because music can bring something to people that nothing else can. (Dalton, n.p)

At Oakwood, Penniman's teachers noted that he was a natural preacher, with a gift of eloquent and heartfelt gab. But they also observed that he showed up late for lectures and disrupted classes often. The Religion Department also discovered that he had followed a homosexual path early in his career, a revelation that stunned the clergy there and got around the campus. One day, he asked a young man on campus to expose himself to him. He was reported for it. "I was supposed to have been living a different life but I wasn't. They forgave me. Oh, definitely they forgave me, but I couldn't face it and I left the church" (White, p. 101).

In 1960, Richard was preaching across the country and he ran into the Upsetters, who at the time were backing Little Willie John. Specialty had been reissuing his outtakes, songs that were deemed inferior at the time they were recorded, and they were selling well. The Upsetters and Little Richard actually recorded some songs under their own name, but they featured Little Richard as well. Soon after that, Penniman cut some gospel sides for a label called End Records.

All of this recording activity led Penniman back to Bumps Blackwell, now the A&R man for Mercury Records. Blackwell signed Penniman and hired Quincy Jones to be his musical director. They arranged the material, mainly gospel and spiritual sides, for a lush 40-piece orchestra, and together decided to smooth the edges on Little Richard's crazy delivery.

While fans were dismayed not to hear "classic" Little Richard chaos, the singer himself felt that this was exactly the kind of record he wanted to make at this point in his life—reverent, tasteful, mature. Many, including Richard himself, saw this project as Little Richard rediscovering himself, saving himself.

It didn't take long for the glow to fade.

One night, when Penniman had gone to the bus station in Long Beach, California, to hang out, eyeball patrons, and seek out sex, a cadre of police officers walked in as part of a sting operation. He was arrested again and paid the fine.

The apprehension was the last straw in his marriage with Ernestine, who'd had to struggle with maintaining any sort of relationship with her husband. She filed for divorce.

THE COMEBACK

British promoter Don Arden wanted to package a tour featuring Richard and Sam Cooke. To coerce Richard into joining the bill, he told the artist his records were still selling very well in the United Kingdom and that if he wanted to he could sing his gospel songs. Richard begrudgingly acquiesced.

On the first night of the tour, Sam Cooke's plane had been delayed due to weather and Little Richard strode out onto the stage in a white robe. He sang a couple of his gospel numbers, including "Peace in the Valley" and "I Believe." But the audience had no idea how to react. They hadn't been informed of Richard's plans. Arden, who had promised ticket buyers a rock and roll show from Little Richard in British newspaper advertisements, was stunned.

On the second night, he implored the artist to play his rock and roll. Sam Cooke's manager, J.W. Alexander, told Arden to be patient. As soon as Little Richard heard Sam's set, Alexander said, the competitive nature of Penniman would emerge. As expected, Cooke knocked the audience dead with his set. Would Little Richard do as Alexander said? When he hit the stage, there were 30 seconds of tense silence, punctuated only by Billy Preston's mournful organ. A feeling of dread crept over Arden. Penniman appeared poised to subject his audience to another gospel set. But at the end of that interminable stretch of silence, Little Richard exploded into a sequence of his biggest, loudest, fastest rockers, starting with the hit of all rock hits, "Long Tall Sally." The set had the audience in near hysterics, and, for all intents and purposes, announced the return of the original Little Richard. The King of Rock and Roll had reclaimed his throne.

That scene repeated itself all over England, where Richard wrecked place after place. This came much to the chagrin of venue managers everywhere, who watched, agitated as Little Richard would strip down to his bare chest and drive the girls in the audience wild with sexual energy.

During that same tour, Beatles' manager Brian Epstein arranged for his band to play a couple of dates with Little Richard. The Beatles, then enjoying their first flush of success with "Please Please Me" and "Love Me Do," were thrilled at the prospect of meeting Little Richard. Without a doubt, he was their collective hero. McCartney himself admitted that the first tune he ever played in public was "Long Tall Sally."

Following those dates, Don Arden booked Little Richard for two months in Germany, mostly around Hamburg, and Richard took the Beatles with him.

Soon after returning to the States, Arden called Richard with another tour proposal that was coming together quickly. The acts included Richard headlining, Bo Diddley, the Everly Brothers, and a young band from England that had just finished their first album, the Rolling Stones.

The 30-date overseas tour was a smash. But when Little Richard returned home in 1964, he encountered a changed musical landscape. The Beatles, once his charges, had taken over the pop scene. Sam Cooke, also one of Richard's biggest fans, had become a superstar. Seemingly, there was no place for Little Richard. He toyed with the idea of returning to religion, and becoming an evangelist. But the competitor in him was intent on recapturing his kingly title.

He contacted Art Rupe about going back into the studio. Specialty, Richard's label, had been in the doldrums since Penniman left the roster, and Rupe was glad to have him back. The first session, done in the summer of 1964, produced "Bama Lama Bama Loo," a traditional Little Richard–style burner. But the record fell flat, a victim perhaps of the changing musical climate. Still, Richard hit the road and played everywhere, from cheap hotels to roadhouses. The step down demoralized him; he thought he had made the wrong decision about attempting a return to glory. He had been out of the public eye for so long, the music business had passed him by.

In response, he infused his show with thousands of dollars of his own money. He tarted up his image, invested in new wardrobe and new talent. Along the way, he hired a new guitar player, James Hendrix. He now featured dancers as well as comedians, and he called it the Little Richard Show.

The emergence of Hendrix under Little Richard's tutelage wasn't surprising. Hendrix was allowed to indulge his unorthodox showmanship, and he learned quite a bit from Little Richard in the way of charisma and style. His tenure with the show didn't last long though. The rigors of the road caught up with him and he began flouting band rules, showing up late for shows and not rehearsing. Penniman's brother Robert had to let him go.

Throughout this tour, the Little Richard Show had verged perilously close to self-parody. Without any new hits, he was leaning a lot on the older chestnuts, and Little Richard began pushing too hard. The homosexual overtones became too apparent; he often crossed the line into tastelessness, turning audiences off rather than the opposite. He'd lost his intuitive feel for great performances.

In the studio, the hits stopped coming. He recorded unsuccessfully for Vee-Jay as well as for Okeh. They tried to get him to record trendy material, like the kind coming out of the red-hot Motown label. Richard resisted.

In 1968, a surprise booking came through, two weeks in Las Vegas at the Aladdin Hotel. The high-profile gig drew a glittering clientele. The Vegas types loved the act, and soon Richard was receiving invitations to appear on television from the likes of Pat Boone and Joey Bishop. It seemed he had found a new, more comfortable niche for himself, smaller than the 40,000-seat shows he played in the late 1950s, but bigger and more profitable than the snake pits he toured just a year or so earlier. He'd found a new audience who loved him for who he was, or at least the glamorous, over-the-top, rather bizarre artist he had become.

Following the Aladdin stint, Little Richard's bookings increased significantly, not just in terms of quantity and quality but also in prestige. He played the Fillmore East, Atlantic City, Harrah's in Reno, and a big gig in Central Park in New York City. The night after Central Park, he played to 32,000 fans at the city's Madison Square Garden, a gig that led to additional television appearances with Della Reese and the *Tonight Show* with Johnny Carson.

As the decade turned and Little Richard headed into the 1970s, he played another important engagement, this one at the Cocoanut Grove in Los Angeles.

As the home of many important entertainers, including Rat Packers like Frank Sinatra and Sammy Davis Jr., the Grove was more accustomed to middle-of-the-road interpreters than out-and-out rockers. His manager insisted that he take the date because his casino gigs had been drying up and a prestigious gig like the Grove was a good one. His engagement sold out in a flash; he floored audiences for two straight weeks.

The triumph led to even more television appearances, this time on the afternoon talk show circuit, with hosts Merv Griffin, Mike Douglas, and Dick Cavett. On the heels of these successes—the talk shows, the Grove gigs—a third magical occurrence happened: his first hit single in 13 years, "Freedom Blues." It charted for over two months on the *Billboard* charts and spawned a hit album as well called *The Rill Thing*. The commercial coup led to further touring and the 1970s were beginning to look quite good indeed for Little Richard.

His new contract with the Warner Bros. label Reprise was a good move as well; he produced some of the best non-peak period work of his career.

At least what he saw of it. By this time, Little Richard had begun doing drugs and drinking excessively for the first time in his life. The illicit consumption led to further activities, including outrageous sexual acts. On the road, cocaine eased the stress of travel. In the studio it gave Richard and the band energy enough for one more take. Addiction took hold.

In keeping with his ever more bizarre image, he began appearing in public with velvet, almost royal robes and ever more elaborate hairdos. When he walked into a restaurant, crowds watched as he and his entourage entered and were given a table of prominence. Quickly, he became a caricature of himself, an egotistical exaggeration that succeeded in at least earning him a huge amount of morbid curiosity.

Ego and, he said, a need for a change, convinced him to let his manager Blackwell go. In place of him he hired his family members: brothers Peyton, Marquette, and Robert. Together, they handled accounting, publishing, and management tasks.

But as the 1970s moved forward, the music scene morphed from R&B to soul, from soul to funk, and from funk to disco. Little Richard had little room to maneuver. People expected him to be a rock and roller, so when he attempted to make contemporary music, the public, and radio, had trouble branding it, accepting it, and buying it. Little Richard was a rock and roll star, and he had no place in the world of modern soul.

He took out his frustrations on unwitting promoters, a group he always distrusted. He began to miss gigs after long nights of partying. He lost weight and strength. He surrounded himself with bodyguards 24 hours a day, and those who knew him said his personality began to change. He seemed more irritable, nasty, with a scarier look in his eyes. He withdrew from his circle, pulled away from his friends and family.

He was also surrounded by violence and heartbreak. With the drugs, Richard began attracting a dark element, hangers on eager to help him partake, knowing there would always be a full supply of narcotics around. In an unrelated event, his brother Tony died of a heart attack at his home. He was a young father, and close to Richard. His death wracked him with guilt. At that point he knew he couldn't stay in show business. He knew that he had to give his life back to God. It was a familiar story, but, in Richard's mind, it felt as genuine as the first time, when Brother Gulley swayed him to lead a life in Jesus.

"It was as if something came over my whole being. I didn't care about money. I didn't care about popularity. . . . All I wanted was God in my life" (White, p. 193).

And so, in 1976, he withdrew from the excess and indulgence of rock and roll a second and final time. Gaunt, unhealthy, and addicted to drugs, Little Richard retreated to his home to clean up and devote his life to God's ministry. He sold Bibles and preached God's word.

In 1979, he made a gospel album, *God's Beautiful City*, and set out on a national evangelical campaign. His preaching techniques were taken directly from his rock and roll showmanship. His style was mesmerizing, whether he's singing "Long Tall Sally" or "You've Got a Friend in Jesus." His energy tapped into that mystical place, whether singing hard R&B or praising Jesus.

He performed God's work through the mid-1980s, when he eased back into show business with movie roles (*Down and Out in Beverly Hills*) and other appearances. His return to the spotlight helped him regain his iconic status as one of the progenitors of rock and roll. In keeping with that status, he was inducted into the Rock and Roll Hall of Fame at its very first induction ceremony in 1986, alongside Elvis, Chuck Berry, James Brown, Buddy Holly, and a handful of others that were present at the genre's birth. He received a star on the Hollywood Walk of Fame, and had a boulevard in Macon, Georgia, named after him. The spirited manifestation of rock and roll, the very persona of rebellion, the embodiment of sexual energy, is now a smoothed-over icon with only a modicum of the original abrasiveness and unease that defined him. Nevertheless, he is an icon loved today by many.

LEGACY

There's no question that some rock icons learned how to do what they do by watching and hearing Little Richard, from the cascading "whooo's!" on the Beatles' early records to the androgynous abandon of Prince in concert. But let us consider for a moment what music was like before Little Richard.

> Richard screamed so hard. His dynamic range was so terrific. Richard would be singing like this [whispers] and then all of a sudden Bow!! The needles would just go off the dial. I never overdubbed Richard's voice. Richard was full on, all the way. Richard's style of playing really brought the piano to the forefront in this music. He was such a powerful player, he'd beat the piano out of

tune and break the strings. He was the only guy I knew who would beat the piano so hard he'd break an eighty-gauge piano string. He did it several times. (White, p. 75)

Little Richard sang songs in which the words were vague and often nonsensical. He made them classics with the intensity and power of his unique voice, which was so frantic and exhilarating that the listener was compelled to follow its incredible pace to the end. His extraordinary range embraced both the wildest rock and the precision and control of an opera singer. Elvis had sexuality, Chuck Berry had fine stories to tell, and Fats Domino had New Orleans boogie to fall back on. But it was Little Richard who had them all trumped in terms of sheer exuberance and power. His music changed life, and the way of life, for entire generations.

Penniman also jump-started the careers of people like Otis Redding, who idolized him back in Macon. Likewise he inspired James Brown, another Macon man who stepped in to front Penniman's band the Upsetters when Penniman was out of town singing in New Orleans. He also hired James (aka Jimi) Hendrix as a guitar player. It would be the first time that Hendrix felt so comfortable on stage, this being the early 1960s, that he could play his guitar behind his head and with his teeth. After all, this was Little Richard's show and virtually anything was possible.

The Beatles and the Rolling Stones idolized Little Richard, even took some of his vocal mannerisms with them as they established rock and roll in its own right. Perhaps more than any other performer, Little Richard touched the hearts and styles of the people who heard him. He merged the fire of gospel music with the rollicking rhythms of New Orleans R&B to come up with the ecstatic abandon of primitive rock and roll. Though he was only a hitmaker in the literal sense for a few years, his songs sent repercussions through the musical universe and have endured to this day as fresh as those glorious days in the 1950s when they were born.

"Rock music may be a bunch of noise to some people, but to me it was the music of love. My music brought togetherness, happiness. My music broke barriers that had seemed unbreakable. It drove tunnels through walls that no one had been able to get through. My music did that. It was called 'race music' till I came on the scene. I'm grateful for that" (Dalton).

And so are millions of rock and roll fans.

SELECTED DISCOGRAPHY

Here's Little Richard (Specialty, 1957)
Little Richard (Specialty, 1958)
Little Richard Is Back (Vee-Jay, 1965)

The Specialty Sessions (Specialty, 1990)

The Georgia Peach (Specialty, 1991)

Shag on Down by the Union Hall (Specialty, 1996)

The King of Rock and Roll: The Complete Reprise Recordings (Rhino Handmade, 2005)

FURTHER READING

Dalton, David. "Little Richard, Child of God." *Rolling Stone*, May 28, 1970.

Hackford, Taylor (dir.) *Hail! Hail! Rock 'N' Roll*. Image Entertainment/Universal, 1987.

White, Charles. *The Life and Times of Little Richard: The Quasar of Rock*. New York: Harmony Books, 1984.

Courtesy of Warner Bros./Photofest.

Fats Domino

THE REAL KING OF ROCK AND ROLL

They call him "the Fat Man." With his boogie-woogie, triplets-saturated piano style and affable vocals, Antoine "Fats" Domino put New Orleans–style R&B, a genre that came to be known as rock and roll, on the map. A pianist, singer, and songwriter born in 1928 on the Mississippi River outside the Crescent City, Domino would go on to sell more records, a whopping 65 million of them, than any rocker not named Elvis Presley.

    Fats was by far the most popular R&B singer in the history of the genre. Between 1955 and 1964, *Billboard* lists no fewer than 65 Fats singles on the pop charts, making him the most popular pop presence on the charts save Elvis. Had the charts been less segregated before 1955, Domino would have given the Pelvis a run for his money, as his own sales began in earnest in R&B back in 1950.

In fact, between 1950 and 1963, Fats landed on the pop Top 40 37 times and the R&B singles chart 59! He did so with style and elegance with songs like "Blue Monday," "Ain't That a Shame," "Blueberry Hill," "I'm Walkin'," and "Walking to New Orleans." Fats produced a bounty of classic rock and roll hits—often referred to as R&B—many of which still sound fresh today.

Domino was born into a musical family. His father was in a Dixieland jazz band and taught him musical appreciation, as did many of his nearby relatives, including his brother-in-law Harrison Verrett, a mentor who taught Fats not only how to perform, but to have confidence in his abilities.

Like piano greats as Albert Ammons and Amos Milburn before him, Fats began performing for small change in local honky-tonks while working odd jobs to make ends meet. As an iceman in New Orleans he knew his clients with pianos in their homes and he'd often deliver ice and pound out a few tunes at the same time. By 1949, Domino had a steady gig at the Hideaway Club, where he met Dave Bartholomew, a man who'd go on to become Fats's musical right-hand man, handling production, arranging, and songwriting responsibilities. Bartholomew introduced record label owner Lew Chudd to Domino one night after a Hideaway gig and together the three of them would reinvent popular music.

Domino possessed a quiet, reserved personality, not exactly the happy-go-lucky one behind the smile depicted in his publicity shots. He was a family-oriented man who loved kids, his friends, and his native hometown of New Orleans. He also proved to be quite human, with a handful of vices that consumed him, but never actually brought him down. That he fought through those weaknesses to exhibit incredible staying power is a testament to the solid musicality of his recordings and the inexorable exhilaration of his live performances. Fats dominated the 1950s.

He was also the culmination of 100 years of Creole piano playing tradition, which is one big reason why he was able to turn such hoary standards into great popular numbers like the 1911 tune "Put Your Arms Around Me Honey" and "Blueberry Hill." He played everything with a broad smile, which made him an unthreatening alternative to the sexier, more lascivious performers like Etta James and Jackie Wilson. This is not to say that Fats was an innocent bystander. In his book *The Heart of Rock and Soul: The 1001 Greatest Singles of All Time*, Dave Marsh says that Fats was "the smiling personification of bottomless horniness . . . rock's ultimate one-track mind. Never has anybody made sexual frustration more pleasant and attractive—almost like fun" (Marsh, p. 314).

EARLY YEARS

The Domino family made its homestead outside of New Orleans along the Mississippi River, on the back end of the famed Laura Plantation, a sugarcane farm and the setting for all the Brer Rabbit tales featured in *Song of the South*. His father Antoine "Calice" Domino and Donatile "Zoot" Gros, a woman of Haitian/Creole descent, had eight children.

The older boys worked with their father plowing rows of cane, back-breaking work for which they earned no more than $1 a day. The women occasionally worked in the field, but more often they stayed at home, sewing quilts for sale and tending to household chores.

While they worked hard, the Dominos played hard as well. They had parties every Saturday night, where the family and friends on the plantation would work off the stress of a full week's work with strong drink, sweet cakes, and lots of music. Antoine's father Calice played banjo and fiddle.

But a flood over the banks of the Mississippi altered the landscape at Laura, and the damage prevented Calice from making as much money as he had previously. So he and his family joined his brother Gustave on land Gustave had purchased in a rural section of the city called the Ninth Ward. Calice built a shotgun shack for his family next to his brother's home on Jourdan Avenue, and his oldest son John built a house along the same road. The homes had large porches and small rooms, and made for a communal atmosphere, similar to life on the plantation. It was here that Antoine was born, the youngest of eight, in February 1928.

By the early 1930s, Calice and his sons were working miles away from home at the New Orleans Fairgrounds Race Course, a place that would later host the New Orleans Jazz and Heritage Festival that baby Antoine would headline as a rock and roll star.

When he was old enough, Antoine, a quiet but genial and cooperative kid, would chop wood for the kitchen fire and help around the house. He played some baseball and enjoyed boxing as well. His childhood hero was Joe Louis, a man he'd later befriend. There was an old Victrola in the house, and Antoine loved music. Even when the turntable broke, Antoine would spin the 78 RPM vinyl recordings with his finger to hear it. A radio brought the sounds of Ella Fitzgerald and Glenn Miller into the home. The family continued their Saturday night party tradition in New Orleans, with blues and jazz music.

Antoine learned to play piano as a child. The family had obtained an old upright piano with worn ivories, and his brother in-law, Harrison Verrett, a sort of father figure and mentor to Antoine, taught him how to play. He wrote the notes on the keys to facilitate the boy's learning. His enthusiasm grew quickly, and soon his interest in music eclipsed his desire to study in school.

And who could blame him? The Macarty School in the Ninth Ward, populated by poor urban children, was a dilapidated school with atrocious facilities.

Antoine's timid temperament held him back and soon the only thing he looked forward to every day was playing his piano. In the fourth grade, Antoine quit school and went to work.

Jobs as an iceman and a stable boy followed, helping him bide the time between stints on the piano. He discovered Clarence "Pine Top" Smith's "Pine Top's Boogie Woogie," a song that launched a genre. Antoine loved Smith's upbeat pounding, the way a pianist could be a rousing, one-man band with the ability to entertain at parties. In fact, at the family parties Antoine began entertaining the guests with his own brand of boogie-woogie. He also sat in with Verrett's jazz band, and began making tips, off of white patrons, in the courtyard patios of French Quarter restaurants.

At the time, jukeboxes began blaring the sounds of a new cadre of talented musicians, including Amos Milburn, Louis Jordan, and Charles Brown. Antoine especially loved Milburn, and not just for his playing. "Amos Milburn was the only blues singer I tried to sing like" (Rick Coleman, *Blue Monday: Fats Domino and the Lost Dawn of Rock 'N' Roll*, p. 22; New York: Da Capo, 2007).

In fact, aside from a few lessons he had courtesy of a teacher Verrett assigned him to, Domino learned most of his material by ear, listening to songs by these artists and others and committing them to memory. He especially enjoyed playing Albert Ammons's "Swanee River Boogie," and began making that the climax to his many Ninth Ward appearances.

TURNING POINT

The summer of 1947, with Antoine just 19 years old, proved to be a watershed one for the young piano player. He met a bandleader Billy Diamond, at one of Antoine's backyard shows, and was impressed enough with his boogie skills to invite him to play with his band. Domino hesitated at first, intimidated by the opportunity. But once Verrett offered to join him on the gig, Antoine consented. That July performance, at the Rockford Pavilion, the largest venue on the Ninth Ward, would be Antoine's first professional gig.

Soon after, Antoine married 17-year old Rosemary Hall, a pretty girl from Ninth Ward even softer-spoken than Antoine. They had met through business—Rosemary's father was a hunter that sold his game to customers. When Antoine went in to buy some meat, he saw the family had an upright piano. He sat down and started playing, noticing all the while the pretty girl in the background. She went to his gig at the Rockford Pavilion; saw him from the front row. Oddly enough, it would be the last time she'd ever seem him play live.

Antoine's gigs with Diamond continued. One night at the Robin Hood, a Ninth Ward nightclub, Diamond talked to the crowd after an exciting banging from Antoine. Diamond stepped up to the microphone to explain he had nicknamed him "Fats," because he'd be famous someday like "Fats" Waller, another well-known pianist. Domino blushed at the reference. Indeed, his five-foot-five-inch frame had bulked out, thanks to his mother's Creole cooking. He bristled at the reference, but never ran from it.

Domino's neighborhood band achieved local notoriety, but because they didn't make much money, they had a hard time impressing people with their presentation. Domino often showed up at gigs not in a tux but in denim. He hadn't made enough to invest in sharp threads, so he and Verrett were perceived as a rag-tag band. One night, in early 1948, after slightly upstaging early rock and roll icon Roy Brown with Diamond's band—Domino sang a few tunes, when they were only supposed to be playing instrumentals—Brown angrily dumped the band, leaving them on a dusty sidewalk with nowhere to go.

The rejection steeled Domino, who was more resolute than ever to make music his life.

In the spring of 1948, Diamond's band, including Fats, would become the house band of Charley Armstead's nightclub, Club Desire on Desire Street, a much publicized and fancy new spot that featured New Orleans talent as heralded as Dave Bartholomew, the so-called architect of the New Orleans sound.

About the same time, Fats secured some time at a nearby saloon called the Hideaway, an earthy spot where folks didn't bother with "fancy" and Fats's raw boogie was more welcomed. And better still, he could wear his working-class wardrobe without embarrassment. The Hideaway, where he played three nights a week, was just what Fats needed. He developed confidence there, in this small combination, which featured a drummer and two sax players. He'd pound out "Swanee River Boogie" to a delirious reception. The raucous, dancing crowd jumped up on tabletops to the piston-like work of Fats's incredible piano-playing hands.

The elation was understandable, at least for Fats. He and Rosemary just had their first child, Antoinette, in January 1949.

Word on the street of Domino's Hideaway gigs spread quickly and soon luminaries from around the city and beyond were popping in to see what all the fuss was about. Bartholomew, who had once turned his nose up at Domino in his dusty jeans and inelegant style, caught a few shows, as did area talent like Memphis Slim (né Peter Chatman) and an acerbic Hollywood talent scout named Lew Chudd.

Chudd, born a Russian Jew, fled the czar in the mid-1880s, first to England then Harlem, where he eventually set up an independent music label. Like other indie label owners and various musical entrepreneurs, Chudd was open-minded, more so than the major corporate labels, who were often restricting in terms of race and color. Many of the indie labels of the day were owned by ethnic and minority businessmen, including Atlantic, Modern, Peacock, King, Specialty, Aladdin, and Chess. Even the famed recording venue in New Orleans, J&M Studio, was owned by an Italian American, Cosimo Matassa. "The rise of black music during segregation would have been impossible without their colorblindness" (Coleman, p. 37).

Cosimo Matassa, J&M Studios, and the Birth of Rock and Roll

Despite its utter prominence as a critical epicenter of popular music, New Orleans never had a record industry to speak of. The loci of the record business were still on the coasts, in New York and Los Angeles, as well as in Chicago, Memphis, and Nashville. But New Orleans did manage to record a great deal of music thanks to Cosimo Matassa, the son of an Italian food store proprietor. As an enthusiastic jazz fan, Matassa, then 18, played an important role in New Orleans music, providing the room in which virtually all of its most prominent musical talents recorded. It started out in 1945 as a music store, selling record players, LPs, and 45s, J&M Music Shop on North Rampart Street in the city's French Quarter. Then when Matassa hit on the idea of creating a place for local musicians to lay down their grooves, he opened up one of the shop's back rooms.

At first, he brought in musicians to record live to acetate tape, where a recording was inscribed directly onto a shellac platter, truly primitive and an inconvenience. But it was a cheap place for musicians to commit their music to wax, only $15 per hour. As the demand from outside record labels like Specialty and Imperial grew, he invested in his first tape machine in 1949. Tape machines had been invented in Germany during the war and were not widely available when J&M first opened.

Depending on the recording session, Cosimo either engineered them right in that tiny back room, essentially a closet with a window and a microphone, or he'd schlep his equipment down to Booker T. Washington High School, where there was more room. He'd set up on the stage and pull the curtain across to dampen the sound.

Day after day, Matassa presided over recording sessions, many of which would become milestones in the history of popular music, from Fats Domino to Lloyd Price, from Dave Bartholomew to Little Richard. Ray Charles, Lee Dorsey, and Dr. John also recorded with Cosimo, as did Smiley Lewis, Guitar Slim, and Lowell Fulson.

Like many boutique recording studios at the time, Cosimo had a house band at J&M. Musicians included drummer Earl Palmer, now in the Rock and Roll Hall of Fame, saxman Alvin "Red" Tyler, bassist Frank Fields, guitarist Ernest McLean, and others. Together, they made classic R&B, with a thumping beat: strong drums, heavy guitar and bass, rolling piano and light horns. Most importantly was a strong vocal lead. This sound served as the bridge to rock and roll.

Given the impact they were unknowingly making, the house band members were paid small hourly wages, but given the opportunity to work regularly. Little did they know that in the process, they'd be making some of the most enduring recordings in the rock and roll generation.

In 1955, based on his success and enlarged prominence as a recording outlet, Matassa moved to a bigger space near the French market on Governor Nicholls Street. He expanded again in 1960 to a building next door to that one, and opened up the Cosimo Recording Studio. He'd eventually start his own label, sign artists, and make his own records. But he'd never have more success, and more of an impact on the national scene in that first little studio on North Rampart, where he hosted and presided over the very birth of rock and roll.

In the summer of 1947, Chudd and Dave Bartholomew met in a Houston club called the Bronze Peacock, where Bartholomew was playing a two-month residency gig at Don Robey's club. Robey would later go on to form the influential indie label Peacock Records. Their meeting would have wide ramifications for the evolution of popular music in America.

POLITICS AS UNUSUAL

In 1948, desegregation began. First, President Truman, who took a strong stand on black civil rights during his election campaign, announced its application in the armed forces. It would be the first of many applications as the country inched towards the 1954 decision of *Brown v. Board of Education*.

In New Orleans, popular black performers like Dizzy Gillespie, Louis Jordan, and Nat "King" Cole began insisting on desegregated audiences or they'd cancel their New Orleans tour stops. Other musical events happened in the city. Vernon Winslow was named as the first black disc jockey. Roy Brown hit the airwaves with his revolutionary "Good Rockin' Tonight," years before Elvis's oft-referenced version in the mid-1950s. Dave Bartholomew began selling records nationwide, drawing attention to New Orleans–style R&B. Professor Longhair did the same.

New Orleans would be at the forefront of desegregation in America, thanks to the active music scene in the city and the staunch support of the concept from many of its most famous citizens. The dream of desegregation was now within reach of the people of the Crescent City.

Chudd and Bartholomew, on the lookout for new talent, went to see Domino in 1949 at Hideaway. Chudd was blown away. "How would you like to make records?" (Coleman, p. 50). Domino, reticent as ever and dressed in mismatched attire, hesitated, as he would at virtually every important crossroads in his career.

Later in 1949, Domino entered J&M Studio under the auspices of Chudd and with Bartholomew as bandleader. They had decided to remake one of Fats's best-loved live tunes, a version of Champion Jack Dupree's "Junker's Blues," a song about a dope addict. They'd call it "The Fat Man," in honor of Domino's new nickname.

In the studio Fats ripped through the track, with the help of a studio band that included drummer Earl Palmer, bassist Frank Fields, and guitarist Ernest McLean, along with a horn section. The session, led by the domineering hand of Bartholomew, lasted six hours.

"The Fat Man" sent ripples through the popular music scene. Domino's powerhouse performance, led by a dynamic left hand on the keys, introduced a potent rhythm into the boogie-woogie style, and turned that fluid genre into a more thumping rock and roll beat. Domino's driving piano propels the rhythm section, not the typical drums and bass. The B-side was Fats's "Detroit City Blues."

While the success of "The Fat Man" put Domino on jukeboxes all over the city and sold 10,000 copies in its first few weeks, Fats was still a struggling musician working traditional day jobs. He, Rosemary, and the baby were living in her parents' house, waiting for the day that they'd be able to make a home for themselves. With his first check from Imperial, he bought himself a 66-key Spinet piano. The new home would have to wait.

Bartholomew booked Fats on a Western tour, his first jaunt away from home. He fretted the change. He didn't want to leave his family or his city, especially without his companion Verrett, who was away. Verrett gently nudged him to go, and Domino agreed. Little did he know that he'd be on the road steadily for the next 50 years!

GOING SOLO

With a couple of hits under his belt, including "Little Bee," which was said to be too risqué for radio, Domino gained confidence. One night, playing with Diamond's band, Fats, under the influence of alcohol, boldly asserted that *he'd* be the band's leader from now on. Of course, Diamond took offense to his audacious assertion, and he sent Fats packing. He'd lead a band, yes, but not *Diamond's* band.

He went on the road again with Bartholomew's band, saxophonist Lee Allen, and Professor Longhair (né Ron Byrd). The tour was difficult though, with the band enduring bad contracts and poor weather. They came home broke and spent. When Bartholomew went into Chudd's office to get an advance on his pay, Chudd sent him away. Bartholomew quit Imperial, leaving Domino without his right-hand man.

Still, Domino sallied forth. He hired a manager, Creole businessman and club owner Melvin Cade, who in turn introduced Fats to legal counsel named Charles Levy Jr. Domino signed a tall packet of papers, giving Levy his power of attorney, a power Levy enjoyed, some say at Domino's expense, for the next 30 years.

Fats put a new band together, featuring his longtime friend sax player Buddy Hagans, bassist and former bandleader Billy Diamond, young guitarist Walter Nelson, saxman Wendell Ducong, and drummer Cornelius Coleman. It was a scruffy group; a couple had drug problems and they were young and feisty. Ducong, Nelson, and Coleman all had a taste for marijuana, and Nelson preferred heroin, too. He often spent his money on drugs and gambling, and was arrested several times. Jimmy Gilchrist, an opening act on many Domino dates and a replacement for Roy Brown, died of an overdose in his sleep.

Despite all the trouble, Fats often remarked how his first band, this lineup, would never be rivaled by any of his future groups, so together was their sound. This would also be the band that would create the sound that many feel formed the foundation of rock and roll.

By the end of 1951, "Rockin' Chair," Fats's first national hit, was blaring all across the South's greasy spoons and juke joints. The easy, loping rocker provided another style in his growing repertoire. Lloyd Price borrowed the song's melody and style for his hit, "Ooh Ooh Ooh," and both Professor Longhair and Little Richard would cover the tune.

In March 1953, Domino happened to be in the studio when a 19-year old named Lloyd Price stepped anxiously into the studio for Art Rupe of Specialty Records. Domino wasn't supposed to do work for anyone outside of Chudd's Imperial label, but he couldn't help himself. His rolling piano sound, on Price's groundbreaking wailer, "Lawdy Miss Clawdy," was a milestone in popular music.

The record also heralded the arrival of the "New Orleans sound," a signature of Domino and Bartholomew, and the harbinger of rock and roll's first few baby steps.

In 1952, Fats, now back together with Bartholomew, having re-signed with Chudd and Imperial, struck again with "Goin' Home." The song, a bluesy, chiming story, was inspired by his band members who were always eager to get home to New Orleans from the road. The song was covered by a slew of R&B artists like Little Richard and James Brown. The hit, Fats's first R&B number 1 (number 30 pop), prompted promoters to bombard Domino with requests for tours.

As the 1950s progressed, so did R&B. Younger and younger audiences began catching on to it, and bills featuring so-called R&B artists were gaining in popularity as well as in attendance. Once the younger generation got hold of it, trouble began to brew and the idea of rock and roll became a political topic. A March 1952 R&B revue in Cleveland ended in a riot when a large contingent of black youth couldn't gain admission to the already sold-out show.

The strife led to skepticism and even deeper segregation in many parts of the South, which made touring difficult. The more popular Fats became, the more often he hit the road, and, in turn, the more trouble he encountered touring with his band. Jim Crow affected everything, from restaurants and rest rooms to hotels and highways. (Speaking of highways, while speeding toward a Louisiana gig, his car rolled over, killing his manager, Melvin Cade.)

Even in the North, musicians often had to stay in rooming houses or private homes. Nightclub owners often set up tables in the kitchen for the main attraction, because they weren't allowed in the audience. Fats often cooked Creole dishes for his band when the situation allowed.

In 1954, the Supreme Court outlawed segregation via *Brown v. Board of Education*, but this didn't alleviate the problems Domino contended with on the road. Still, R&B smoothed the way for the beginnings of integration. White audiences looked on as black music fans danced in the aisles, wondering why they couldn't shake free of their own strict moral stances and enjoy themselves. Younger white audiences had less trouble loosening up than their more mature counterparts.

The Ku Klux Klan stood and watched, ensuring the race mixing was kept to a minimum. In Atlanta, a white DJ was kicked off the air for advocating R&B. But in the end, their presence didn't deter to the masses from absorbing all the jubilant music. The Supreme Court decision had indirectly opened R&B up to the world, and all of a sudden every black R&B artist had wider access to vastly wider audiences. It would take a while for these changes to kick in. But the seeds had been sown. Especially in the South, and certainly musically, if not politically, integration was key in introducing teenagers to rock and roll.

DOMINO AND BARTHOLOMEW

They made an unlikely team. Domino was humble from birth, and with only a rudimentary insight into music's more formal side. Bartholomew had been royalty in New Orleans for years, and had been accustomed to wearing tuxedos and smelling the money. Still, they made a formidable team, the first in popular music, predating by a few years the work of Jerry Leiber and Mike Stoller.

Fats wrote many of the tunes, the lyrics, and the melodies, while Bartholomew arranged it. Bartholomew admits that Fats would normally jot down the basic ideas for a track, but it was the arranger who fleshed them all out. "Fats, like many great songwriters, did not read or write music, but he nonetheless came up with the strong tunes and direct, emotion-packed lyrics" (Coleman, p. 83). When Bartholomew wrote, on the other hand, he came up with more complex material.

It's said that Bartholomew envied Domino's incredible rise to stardom. He had been a successful recording star himself, but never rose to the same heights as his partner. Domino appreciated the work Bartholomew did, while not giving him as much credit for the final products as Bartholomew was looking for.

However it worked, the Domino/Bartholomew collaboration *was* working. In March 1954, shortly after Rosemary gave birth to their fifth child in four years, Domino was named the top-selling R&B artist in a *Billboard* poll. That same year, the demand for rollicking music from American teenagers began to crescendo.

In Memphis, Elvis released his own version of Roy Brown's "Good Rockin' Tonight," a song that Brown had cut seven years earlier and had been heard, thanks to Vernon Winslow's *Poppa Stoppa* radio show all throughout the city at the time. In New York City, disc jockey Alan Freed at WINS began his nightly parade of rhythm and blues songs, in an attempt to convert audiences on the East Coast. Bill Randle, a popular disc jockey back in Cleveland, did the same thing there.

Presley's version of "Good Rockin' Tonight" didn't make any impact at the time. It didn't include one of the key ingredients that had made Brown's such a hit on the R&B scene, specifically drums, an instrument not accepted at the time in the state of Tennessee, where the instrument was considered too "jungle." Rockabilly the way Elvis played it, however, did not catch on, and Presley went with the more bottom-heavy mix he heard from his favorite R&B artists: Fats and Little Richard in particular.

Bill Haley knew how to get that rhythm, which he did that same year, 1954, with "Shake, Rattle, and Roll." The song was originally recorded by Big Joe Turner in New Orleans with Dave Bartholomew's assistance. But Turner's version didn't boast the same drive as Haley's, with the latter's booming sax and propulsive beat capturing the true spirit of the young rock genre.

Also in 1954, the first R&B package tour came together courtesy of the Gale Agency, featuring the Spaniels, Roy Hamilton, the Drifters, and Faye Adams. Jazz and pop package tours began losing money at the time, as entertainment dollars were channeled toward big beat music. Alan Freed changed the name of his New York City radio show from *Moondog Party* to *Rock 'n' Roll Party* after losing a lawsuit to the eccentric street musician whose name Freed repurposed.

Wholesale change was under way and Fats Domino found himself at the epicenter of it. From here on, as R&B morphed into rock and roll—at least semantically if not musically—Fats would be swept away as one of the emerging genre's very first stars.

ROCK 'N' ROLL PARTY

In January 1955, Freed put together a rock show, called the "Rock 'n' Roll Jubilee Ball" at an old boxing venue in New York City. All the acts on the bill, including Fats, the Clovers, the Drifters, and Clyde McPhatter, were black. The place was sold out, and half the audience was white. But the rhythm, the tempos, the beats, and the dancing united everyone.

Up until this time, Fats Domino had never truly appealed to a pop music audience. His hits between 1949 and 1955 had been big sellers in R&B, but never crossed over. This all changed as well in 1955 when, inspired by the crossover work of Nat King Cole, he and the band, now including formally trained sax wildman Herbert Hardesty, went into the studio. This time, they hit a Hollywood studio called Master Recorders to record two tracks: the simple "Ain't That a Shame" and its B-side, "All By Myself." Two weeks later at the same studio, Chudd suggested they record "Blue Monday." All three would reach number one on the R&B chart. Pop success awaited.

In the spring of 1955, "Shame" had hit number one in R&B just as Domino encountered some publicity tangles. In New Haven, one of his gigs had been canceled due to a riot and the venue announced he'd be banned from ever performing there. At the same time, Bill Randle, the Cleveland radio host, got a copy of the song from Chudd. Randle hustled the acetate over to Dot Records, who passed it along to their white recording artist Pat Boone. A student at Columbia University at the time, Boone cut the song immediately, and his version trumped Domino's own.

Even though Boone's sanitized renditions—he also covered Little Richard's "Tutti Frutti"—hit number one on the pop chart, his tactics would soon catch up with him. Savvy audiences began seeking out original versions of Boone's tunes. Domino's original "Ain't That a Shame" followed Boone's bowdlerizing copy up the pop chart, reaching number 10. Fats's crossover to the growing white audience was under way. By now, a large portion of Domino's audience, well over half, was white. Music was accomplishing what the Supreme Court and the politicians could not: integration.

"Fats made integration," said his bassist Billy Diamond. "Fats was the Martin Luther King of music. He brought whites and blacks together, Indians, everybody" (Coleman, p. 114).

In 1955, Fats received his second consecutive Top R&B Artist award from *Billboard*, with "Ain't That a Shame" named as the top R&B recording. He dominated the R&B charts with other songs that year, including "I'm in Love Again," "Bo Weevil," and "Poor Me." His only competition at the time was Bill Haley and the Comets, though Haley's flame would die off the next year, his profile dwarfed in the shadow cast soon after by Elvis Presley. Haley reached the Top 10 for the last time in 1956 with the aptly titled "See You Later Alligator," a song Fats turned down. Fats, on the other hand, would not be denied. He remained a viable chart presence for another 10 years. In fact, between 1955 and 1963, he racked up an astonishing 35 Top 40 singles.

PERSONALLY SPEAKING

Much is made of Fats's wide grin. Though he was notoriously reserved—even his closest friends admits he is an intensely private person—his genial, smiling publicity shots project him in a flattering light. (Because Fats didn't like photos, though, Chudd had to reuse a few of those shots over and over.) Fats came across as a foil to the evil incarnate persona of Little Richard, a character the white population, and even most blacks, had a hard time accepting. Roy Brown opened the door for Little Richard's shouting, and Little Richard may have opened the door, in turn, with his epic "Tutti Frutti," for other black performers, but Fats Domino served as the palatable alternative for mature white pop fans who didn't care to spend time pondering Little Richard's sexual appetites.

But Fats himself wasn't always the scrubbed clean man he came across as to his audiences. Despite having a growing brood of children and a wife waiting for him at home, Fats enjoyed fooling around with women. He frequently had "dates" wherever he went, a vice fostered by the many months of the year he spent on the road throughout the latter half of the 1950s.

He enjoyed spending time with friends as well, and did so often as a respite from the pressures of life on the road. Fats also had a taste for drinking and gambling. He'd spend hours after shows in the casinos or in back rooms, throwing back whiskey and spending the money he made at the night's show. Fats also had a problem with punctuality. Perhaps as a cultural affectation—Fats's Big Easy personality resulted in him moving very slowly—he was habitually late for shows, rehearsals, and recording sessions. Occasionally, he'd miss them altogether. And the more success he enjoyed, the more exaggerated his flaws would become.

In January 1956, his bassist Billy Diamond couldn't stand it anymore. Fats was always late, always trying to make up time. As a former bandleader himself, Diamond had originally hired Fats on piano before Fats declared himself the leader of Diamond's own band, Diamond understood the importance of planning and punctuality.

One night, with snowy conditions and a long drive ahead, Fats appeared to be dragging his feet, putting the band behind schedule once again. Exasperated, Diamond left the band.

Domino soldiered on, replacing Diamond with Lawrence Guyton. He never admitted the critical role Diamond played in the band; there was too much happening at the time, in early 1956, to fuss over lineup changes. Elvis had decided to render his own covers of the great R&B hits like "Lawdy Miss Clawdy, "Tutti Frutti," and "Shake, Rattle and Roll." Because he was white, however, he got to do his thing on the *Ed Sullivan Show*, if only from the waist up. Black performers wouldn't be accepted on national television for many years, not even from the waist up.

Fortunately, radio continued to make changes in its own policy, occasionally filtering black or "race" music onto its playlists. If commercial stations didn't, at least curious music fans could find genuine R&B on stations with smaller signals. Domino's "Bo Weevil" came next, but it too was whitewashed by a singer named Teresa Brewer, whose version hit the Top 10. Domino's broke the Top 40 in pop.

In April 1956, Fats released his first album, *Rock and Rollin' with Fats Domino*. It sold 20,000 copies the first week of release and broke into the *Billboard* album chart, unheard of for a black artist, reaching the Top 20. He was 28 years old, and now had seven of his eventual eight children at home waiting for him when he quit the road.

In June, Fats entered Master Recorders in Hollywood again, this time with Harrison Verrett, to cut a song he'd wanted to record since hearing Louis Armstrong do it when Fats was a boy. "Blueberry Hill" had already been a hit in the hands of Glenn Miller in 1940, the same year Gene Autry sang it in *The Singing Hill*. He needed another hit to compete with the surging Elvis Presley, who cut "Hound Dog" at the time, and was staying step for step with Domino in terms of popularity.

On September 2, 1956, Domino made his national television debut on the *Steve Allen Show*. He sang two songs, "When My Dreamboat Comes Home" and "I'm in Love Again," while the droll Allen proclaimed that R&B was "here to stay." Domino, of course, would see to it almost single-handedly with his next recording.

Bartholomew hated Fats's "Blueberry Hill," as he did most of Fats's conceptually simple tunes. To exacerbate matters, Domino never captured the feel of the song that day in the studio, so engineer Bunny Robyn did a patchwork job to get the final take.

Given the circumstances, Chudd placed "Blueberry Hill" on the B-side of "Honey Chile," a track Imperial felt had a better chance of making chart impact. It didn't take long, though, for DJs to flip the record over to play the B-side and listeners called in to hear the song repeatedly. It topped the R&B charts for nearly three months and stayed at number two on the pop charts for 3 weeks straight, 27 weeks total. It even climbed the country charts, and ended up as one of country's biggest selling records of the year.

The song would eventually be covered a number of times by music's biggest stars, but Domino's would remain the definitive rendition. Its impact shifted the pianist's reputation as a major artist into high gear. Months later, "Blue Monday" also reached the pop Top Five just a few months later, in January 1957. A few months after that, Bartholomew and Domino hit huge once again with "I'm Walkin'."

Riots across the country continued at rock and roll shows, including some in the presence of Domino. Little Richard upped the ante with songs like "Jenny, Jenny" and "Good Golly Miss Molly." Rock and roll became an outrage to politicians and an embarrassment to the older generation of Americans, who did not understand it. Through it all, though, Domino remained relatively impervious to the outrage. Surrounded by violence and unrest, segregationists, liberal youths, and conflicted politicians, Domino simply wanted to make the music he'd been making all along. Still, his association with R&B made him a threat in traditional white America.

Which is why his appearance on the *Ed Sullivan Show* in 1957 made Domino nervous. Sullivan was nervous, too. He demanded that Domino's band play behind a curtain, so only the smiling pianist could be seen. His performance of "Blueberry Hill" "alone" on stage made Fats appear as a solo artist, similar to the likable man who had made the song famous years ago, Louis Armstrong. His appearance on the show pushed the song over the million in sales mark. That year Fats won a handful of awards, including Top R&B awards in *Billboard*, *Cash Box*, and *Down Beat*.

To date, he broke attendance records in almost two dozen cities, and had 12 gold records so far. It all translated to money in the bank for Domino, who, in 1956, grossed half a million dollars.

THE BIGGEST SHOW OF STARS

In 1957, the second installment of the so-called Biggest Show of Stars featured what is often referred to as the greatest package tour in the history of rock. When it was assembled, the artists on the roster had a cumulative total of 22 number one hits and most would end up in the Rock and Roll Hall of Fame. Domino headlined the show, supported by the LaVern Baker, Frankie Lymon, Chuck Berry, Clyde McPhatter, the Crickets, Eddie Cochran, the Everly Brothers, and the Drifters.

Despite its cachet, though, conditions were less than luxurious. While Fats rode in his Cadillac, most of the rest of the caravan traveled in the bus, shooting dice and drinking. Most didn't even stay in hotels, sleeping en route and then showering at the venues.

Fats didn't interact much with the other performers on the tour. He drank heavily, played cards, and hit the road following his set. He began to withdraw, and, according to the promoter, he hated to perform. Anxiety set in. The tour proved grueling even for a seasoned artist like Domino.

Thankfully, Domino's popularity was at its peak, and it didn't matter what he did or how felt: his records would sell regardless. In the spring of 1957 he placed four songs in the *Billboard* Top 100. During that same stretch, Domino's songs dominated the top slot on the R&B chart with hits for 22 straight weeks. Only Chuck Berry's masterful "School Days" had what it took to knock Fats off the pedestal.

More national television appearances followed, including a milestone for black performers on the *Perry Como Show* in May 1957. *American Bandstand* with host Dick Clark went from a local and regional spectacle to a national one in August of that year. Domino happened to have a weeklong stay in Philadelphia, where the show was taped, and he stopped by the set twice to record performances with Clark. Interestingly, the first time Domino showed up that week, Clark's set didn't have a piano, so Domino lip-synched his way through "When I See You" standing alone. The second time Domino was more comfortable, seated on a piano bench. Clark later explained that Domino was one of the few artists to play live on his program.

The exposure on *American Bandstand* and on the incredible Stars dates bumped Domino's sales figures into the stratosphere. In October, he and Chudd at Imperial celebrated sales of 25 million total records. Along with sales of a hot new artist, Ricky Nelson, Imperial was cranking, selling a million records a month. In December 1957, *Down Beat* readers chose Fats as the R&B Personality of the Year, ahead of Ray Charles and Elvis Presley.

1958 AND BEYOND

With Fats's incredible success came pressure to stay on top. Chudd especially, with so much at stake at Imperial, worried about Domino's slight slide down the charts. A couple years ago Domino's hits climbed high on their lists, but these days his songs would attain only moderate success.

Chudd, Bartholomew, and others fed him material that softened his sound. They wanted a wider audience, and Fats's people thought that meant more palatable songs. Chudd specifically requested that Bartholomew "sweeten" Domino's sound. Chudd was obsessed with white pop music at the expense of the many New Orleans R&B artists that helped him build Imperial's early success. In early 1958, *Fortune* magazine ran a story on Chudd's spectacular financial success, adding that he ran the country's largest independent music company of the day.

In the studio, Bartholomew thought Fats should simply stay with the rollicking sound that made him famous. Trouble was, Fats didn't want to go either way; he didn't care to work at all.

"Domino was a 'pain in the ass to record,' recalls Cosimo Matassa. Fats often made a kingly entrance into the studio with his valet and chauffeur carrying a case of Teacher's Scotch and two gallons of pigs feet. His personality likewise took on a rough edge when he was drinking" Coleman, p. 192). Like many of the stars in his day, Fats would show up late for recording sessions, occasionally not at all. At this point in his career, this happened frequently; he'd leave Bartholomew and the band waiting in the studio and never show. So rarefied was his star, though, this behavior never had consequences.

Chudd's strategy to go more pop backfired and Fats's singles stalled. Ricky Nelson's "Poor Little Fool" hit number 1, while Fats's "Young School Girl" barely cracked the Top 100 at number 92, and disappeared after a single week in September 1958. His sales dropped to number 2 at his own label, behind Nelson, whose star was clearly rising. Imitators began to pop up and score bigger and, frankly, better songs with their own work. Fats felt himself drifting into mediocrity. While the country was undergoing massive change, Fats knew he needed to do something.

Energized by the challenge of recapturing his elite status as a hitmaker, he resorted to undergoing a media campaign, unusual for Fats, who generally shied away from the press at every opportunity. He made several national TV appearances, including two with Dick Clark. The push paid off. In November 1958 Fats revisited the Top 10 with "Whole Lotta Loving," a tune he recorded at Cosimo Matassa's studio in September of that year. As was customary by this time, Bartholomew expressed reservations about the simplistic track. He always did when Fats took control of a recording session. But Domino's instincts proved correct and the song reached number six, selling a million copies in the process.

He did it again a year later with "I Want to Walk You Home," another tune that found the Top 10 and remained on the charts for a full 13 weeks. It was Domino's 30th song to hit the charts. The B-side, "I'm Gonna Be a Wheel Some Day," even broke the Top 20. Both did so in the summer of 1959.

At the same time, there were setbacks for rock and roll. The Day the Music Died struck when the plane carrying Buddy Holly, the Big Bopper, and Ritchie Valens went down in February 1959, killing all three. The blow to rock was palpable, stunning. Politicians everywhere began calling for the music's ban, even as it was helping to pave the way for true integration. Sam Phillips opened two radio stations for easy listening music, stating the kids were tiring of rock and roll. Payola scandals brought down DJs nationally. Elvis left the building, enlisting in the army.

The first Grammys were announced that year, and were without a Rock and Roll category. R&B had become the less controversial option, and the nominees for that category were Harry Belafonte, Nat King Cole, Perez Prado, Earl Grant, and the Champs. Missing rather conspicuously were Fats, Ray, Elvis, Little Richard, and Chuck Berry. The Grammy organization had made its feeling about rock and roll clear.

THE RISE OF SOUL

Concurrent with all this rock and roll resentment was the rise of soul music. Gospel, doo-wop, and R&B had all been evolving through the 1950s. Sam Cooke and the Soul Stirrers had enjoyed widespread popularity as had Billy Ward and the Dominoes with Clyde McPhatter and, later, Jackie Wilson, both of whom would go on to incredible solo careers.

Ahmet Ertegun, a Turkish immigrant, along with Jerry Wexler, started up Atlantic Records in the late 1950s and had already broke talent like Ruth Brown, Ray Charles, the Clovers, and LaVern Baker. All of these acts took the spirit of doo-wop and the passion of gospel in creating a stunning fusion of rhythmic dance music. Radio didn't care for it much, but it had been making its presence felt with audiences.

In 1959, Ray Charles offered up the revolutionary "What'd I Say" while the Isley Brothers did the same with "Shout." Both were blissful, gospel-injected call and response anthems that radio could not deny.

Domino finished out the decade of the 1950s—one in which he ended up recording a total of 50 hits, including 9 Top 10 pop hits all by the time he turned 32—with a couple of rockers: "Be My Guest" and "I've Been Around."

But with civil rights now on the front burner as an issue critical to integration, Fats Domino was at risk of seeming irrelevant to blacks. Young blacks especially, motivated to fight for their own civil rights, saw Domino as an object of white affection, not someone who'd help them achieve their goals of black power and equal rights. After all, Domino had the full support of a white audience. They were buying tickets, enjoying his television performances, and picking up his records. Fats himself said he didn't worry much about segregation. Asked whether he'd play to a segregated audience, he said, "Of course." In his rather apolitical mind, he simply wanted to have fun playing his songs for people, regardless of color.

But his timing was off. At a time when issues were becoming more and more important, Domino's response, his first single in 1960, was the innocuous "Country Boy." On stage, his band, middle-aged men in dapper suits, with brass, didn't reflect the musical climate of the time and almost seemed like a throwback. His career had finally begun to ebb.

Fats spent much of 1960 off the road, which had been his second home throughout the previous decade. By now he had seven children and he wanted to stay home with his family, close to his friends. He still ducked into the studio occasionally, and played a few local gigs. But Fats was more into rejuvenation. He did take some time to fly out to Los Angeles where he was given a star on the Hollywood Walk of Fame.

Ironically, Rosemary filed for separation in August of that year. As expected, Fats's old habits of philandering, drinking, and disrespect were destructive to his marriage and Rosemary had finally had enough. She accused him, through her attorney, of cruelty, infidelity, and public humiliation, among other slights. She asked to return to the family's original home. (They had moved into a larger house in the Ninth Ward several years previous.)

But then she took it all back. Rosemary withdrew her petition to separate and divorce. As the story goes, Rosemary's mother, Rita Hall, brought the Dominos back together. A deeply religious woman, Rita convinced the family to stay together, to turn more seriously to God, which Fats and the family actually did. Of course, Fats's behavior, while changed temporarily, would return to its original habits of wine and women to accompany his song, not to mention the fact that he had developed an insatiable gambling reputation. But he did manage to salvage his relationship.

In the summer of 1960, a Los Angeles woman filed a paternity suit against Domino, claiming he fathered her child. Sam Cooke had settled a similar predicament with $5,000. Domino simply avoided the city, telling a magazine he had never been more than friends with the woman.

To rekindle his popularity, Fats went over to Europe for the first time in 1962 in search of enthusiasm. He hated flying, which was why he'd put off the trip even this long. The reception overseas surprised Fats and the tour was an overwhelming success both in terms of cash and publicity. He didn't hit England this time, but would revisit the United Kingdom in 1966, to passels of enraptured fans.

At the end of 1962, he recorded a new song called "Won't You Come on Back." It would be the first single he released not to hit the charts.

LAST CALL

Fats left Imperial after Ricky Nelson signed with Decca. Rumor had it that Chudd planned on closing Imperial after Nelson's departure. When Chudd couldn't guarantee that he was keeping Imperial's doors open, Domino followed Ray Charles to ABC-Paramount. In 1963, he made his first recordings for the new label, including "Song for Rosemary" and "Red Sails at Sunset," both concert staples. "Red Sails" hit the Top 40.

But it wouldn't be enough. Fats saw his box office attendance falter considerably, as young music fans were now interested in a variety of other movements happening at the time, from Motown to the British Invasion. The Beatles and the Stones both grabbed a significant portion of America's entertainment dollar, and Fats was soon playing half-full venues. After the Beatles played on Ed Sullivan's program in February 1964, few could dispute who the real kings of rock and roll were.

In September 1965, Hurricane Betsy hit New Orleans hard. The Ninth Ward flooded as the levies didn't hold up and Rosemary had to retreat to the second floor of her home with all eight of her children. Then on the road, Fats flew to New Orleans and needed a boat escort to get to his home. He lost many personal possessions, including cars and recording equipment.

More tragedy occurred when his mentor and best friend, Harrison Verrett, died that October, and his brother Lawrence, the closest member of his own family, also died. He'd been shot by a white woman who thought he was trying to break into her home.

In the late 1960s, thanks to enthusiastic demand for classic rock and roll, there was a 1950s revival of sorts. Jerry Lee Lewis, Little Richard, and Fats Domino all enjoying a spike of popularity, perhaps more as a gesture of appreciation of the impact they had on the ever-expanding world of rock and roll than anything of commercial value.

Fats parlayed that enthusiasm into regular Vegas gigs, a place he considered a home away from home, given his obsession with gambling. Between sets he'd hit the tables, have a few scotches, and throw money around. In the mid-1970s Fats hit the Hilton with his friend Elvis Presley in a rock and roll revival double bill.

It was on one of these trips to Vegas that a car full of Fats's bandmates collided with a tractor trailer on the highway outside the city. The new station wagon, driven by a drowsy Jimmy Davis, was crushed. Clarence Ford and Buddy Hagans suffered serious injuries. Temporary guitarist Ramon Estrada made it out unscathed. But Jimmy Davis died in the accident. All but Estrada had been with Fats since 1956.

THE 1970s AND BEYOND

The 1970s found Domino cashing in on the same nostalgia trip many early rock veterans enjoyed to see out the end of their careers. They exploited that appreciation over in mainland Europe, where fans hadn't been able to enjoy firsthand the experience of original rock and roll.

But Fats didn't exactly share that enjoyment. Domino's bandleader Roy Montrell was a wicked man with a nose for heroin. He'd often pawn instruments for cash, buy drugs with the proceeds, and ask Fats for money to replace the instrument.

Domino, a man who appreciated creature comforts, had lost many of his longtime band members and friends. He became increasing isolated, offering food and drink to his younger musicians as a bribe so they'd sit down and play cards with him. Behavior deteriorated. On the road, one car traveled with the druggies, while the other carried the drinkers. Fats began locking up his jewels, a box of which he preferred to carry with him on the road. And he also began carrying a gun.

"The younger band members sometimes joked that Fats was 'The F.B.I.'—Fat, Black, and Ignorant—behind his back, though they depended on his largesse" (Coleman, p. 266).

Montrell's drug appetite became ravenous. One day Domino, fed up with the depravity, denied his bandleader drug money, chasing him away with his gun. Rock and roll had developed a reputation for hard drugs and its users. In 1970 both Janis Joplin and Jimi Hendrix died, bringing attention to the gravity of drugs in music. Ironically, Fats Domino's band members had been using hard drugs, and dying from them, since the mid-1950s. In 1979, Montrell died of an overdose of his own.

Throughout the 1980s, Domino toured, fighting to prevent his act from lapsing too deeply into "Blueberry Hill" nostalgia. He toured with Ricky Nelson in 1985 in a sort of Imperial Records Reunion jaunt. Later that year, on the same plane many of Domino's musicians flew in, Nelson and six others were in a fatal crash.

In 1986, Fats was inducted in the inaugural class of the new Rock and Roll Hall of Fame in a ceremony at the Waldorf-Astoria Hotel in New York City alongside the biggest names in the history of the genre: Little Richard, James Brown, Elvis Presley, Buddy Holly, Ray Charles, Sam Cooke, Chuck Berry, the Everly Brothers, and Jerry Lee Lewis. Billy Joel gave Fats's induction speech, essentially thanking him for turning the piano into a rock and roll instrument.

The next year, Domino earned a Grammy Lifetime Achievement Award with Ray Charles and B.B. King. It would, ironically, be the first acknowledgment Domino ever received from the Grammy committee. In 1995, the Rhythm and Blues Foundation recognized Domino with a Ray Charles Lifetime Achievement Award.

In 1997, Fats and Rosemary marked their 50th wedding anniversary. That same year the couple had been struck by tragedy when their son Andre died suddenly of a heart attack.

Fats played intermittently for the next few years, accepting accolades. They commemorated J&M Studios and the contributions of Cosimo Matassa in 1999. In September 2005, he weathered Hurricane Katrina, barely. Refusing to leave the comforts of his own home even in the face of the worst hurricane in the history of the city, Fats had to be publicly rescued from his Ninth Ward home. A few days had passed in which his whereabouts were uncertain and reports circulated that he had died in the storm.

But a few days later, it became clear that he had survived, just as he had survived the many turbulent decades as a progenitor of rock and roll. He made a record in 2006 stating his endurance, titled *Alive and Kicking*. Proceeds of the album benefited the musicians of New Orleans who had been put out of work after the hurricane.

LEGACY

New Orleans has, famously, been known as a city familiar with having a good time. At the center of that ability lies its music. Rich, rollicking rhythms are everywhere in the Big Easy. Music is more than a pastime in the city; it's a way of life. At the center of that music, are its pianists: Allen Toussaint, Dr. John, Professor Longhair, and James Booker. Fats Domino, the subject of this chapter, is a party-happy musical city's most prized pianist.

Many felt that Fats perfectly embodied the laid-back music of his native New Orleans with the upbeat release of rhythm and blues. Domino's musical signature came from a cross-section of disparate elements inherent in New Orleans. He borrowed generously from the rich musical backdrop of the city—from Cajun blues and zydeco to the French Creole influence—still a dominant force in the music culture of the region. Fats Domino became the most conspicuous and talented proponent of that blend, beginning in the early 1950s and enduring vitally through much of the 1960s.

With the help of two critically important people—writer/arranger/ accompanist Dave Bartholomew and Imperial Records founder Lew Chudd—Domino was able to bridge the divide separating so many areas: white and black, old and young, R&B and rock, North and South.

Of course, Fats isn't just a pianist, he's a legend, the most important musical figure after Louis Armstrong to come out of New Orleans and on the short list of founding fathers of rock and roll. During the course of his career, Fats achieved an amazing appeal that had transcended his music. "Though he was an R&B icon, his audience was more white than black. He was respected for his jazz and blues roots, and yet adored by teenagers who loved the simple fun of his beat. He had headlined the greatest shows in the short history of the music, whatever it was called, but it was a fleeting moment. Rock and roll's frenzy had reached its peak," and Domino was there to make it happen (Coleman, p. 178).

That he earned inaugural induction into the Rock and Roll Hall of Fame as part of the institution's flagship class is an indication of the impact he had on popular music. Elvis Presley, another of the inductees in that inaugural class, quipped that Fats, not he, was the king of rock and roll. Few would dispute that claim.

SELECTED DISCOGRAPHY

Out of New Orleans (Bear Family, 1993)

Walking to New Orleans: The Legendary Imperial Records 1949–1962 (Capitol, 2002)

Fats Domino Jukebox: 20 Greatest Hits the Way You Originally Heard Them (Capitol, 2002)

FURTHER READING

Coleman, Rick. *Blue Monday: Fats Domino and the Lost Dawn of Rock 'N' Roll.* New York: Da Capo, 2007.
Friedlander, Paul. *Rock and Roll: A Social History.* New York: Westview Press, 2006.
George-Warren, Holly. *Shake, Rattle and Roll: The Founders of Rock and Roll.* New York: Houghton-Mifflin, 2004.
Werner, Craig. *A Change Is Gonna Come: Music, Race and the Soul of America.* New York: Plume, 1998.

Courtesy of Photofest.

Ruth Brown

MISS RHYTHM

In contrast to icons of rhythm and blues like Ray Charles and James Brown, Ruth "Miss Rhythm" Brown does not have a sizable canon to stand behind. Her body of recorded work doesn't at all do justice to the immense impact she had on popular music. Hard work, hard luck, a magical voice, and a lifetime of determination characterized her career more than any stack of highly regarded LPs. Brown had real audacity, a gutsy style, and her commanding voice mingled moxie with little girl sweetness.

Many say that in her heyday—generally from 1949 through the mid-1950s—Brown became the original diva, a force of musical nature, a fusion of extraordinary ability and down-to-earth toughness that had stardom emblazoned across it. Blessed with jubilance, sass, high spirits, and wonderfully expressive features that simply broadened over time, she influenced such greats as Etta James, Stevie Wonder, Bette Midler, and Aretha Franklin. Little Richard himself credited Brown's squeals, records, and style with being a major influence.

At the outset of the 1950s, when R&B was a spark waiting to ignite, Brown's single recordings did incredible business, selling millions. Those sales and the revenue they generated were critical to the financial well-being of her record company, Atlantic, so much so that many referred to it as "the House Ruth Built," in a sly reference to Babe Ruth and Yankee Stadium. These early 1950s sides not only helped Atlantic stay in business, they inspired hordes of both fans and artists. Between 1949 and 1955, Brown's songs were on the R&B charts for a total of 129 weeks, including five number one hits. She'd become the seminal label's very first superstar.

Brown's success also allowed the record company to either sign or retain many other important acts like Ray Charles, the Clovers, Chuck Willis, and Joe Turner. Ray Charles himself used Brown's touring band as his own first band. These artists would serve as the cornerstones of R&B and help to establish the genre as viable commercially, not just as "race music," as it was referred to in the early 1950s. Brown's dominance was so thorough, many in the industry quipped that it was no coincidence her initials were R.B., standing as they did for "rhythm and blues."

In fact, an equation emerges regarding Brown's importance to popular music. Given the influence R&B had on the first strains of rock and roll—many insist rock and roll wouldn't have existed at all if it weren't for the early R&B acts—and given the importance of Brown to R&B, you could draw the conclusion that Ruth Brown, with the help of a very few others, single-handedly changed the topography of popular music. Elvis, Little Richard, Ike Turner, Chuck Berry, and Bill Haley were among the first artists to take Brown's music, add blues and country flavors, and come up with the magic formula for rock and roll.

Such was the powder keg of popular music; all the elements were in place, and the electrifying Brown simply lit the match. She was belatedly recognized for her accomplishments, and for her link to rock and roll in 1993 when she was officially inducted into the Rock and Roll Hall of Fame. She was the third black woman to be admitted, behind Aretha Franklin (1987) and LaVern Baker (1991), and alongside Etta James that same year.

Brown began her singing career as a precocious and talented teenager, "the girl with a tear in her voice." But as she matured as an interpreter, she grew more confident and began injecting her act with muscle and nuance. She also gained enough sway early on, and received enough financial assistance from Atlantic, to recruit the most talented R&B sidemen, producers, and arrangers in the industry.

Brown swaggered, for example, on "Teardrops from My Eyes" and turned haughty on "(Mama) He Treats Your Daughter Mean," her voice rising in an irresistible squeal. There was a universe of pain in her songs, an insistence on justice, a self-assuredness in her voice—"Miss Rhythm" as "Miss Righteous."

Brown's concentration on R&B did not keep her from associations with the jazz world. In fact, she was a surprisingly versatile talent. She brought a distinctive, soulful flair to her jazz vocals, too, and understood intuitively how to make her jazz standards swing.

"What I loved about her," said Bonnie Raitt, in an interview with the Associated Press done after Brown's death in November 2006, "was her combination of vulnerability and resilience and fighting spirit. It was not arrogance, but she was just really not going to lay down and roll over for anyone."

Brown's no-nonsense persona was never more evident than one night backstage at the Apollo in Harlem in the early 1950s. Brown was a young singer, appearing on a bill made up of many stars, new and old, including irascible R&B/blues icon Little Willie John. Unimpressed with Brown's act, John insulted Ruth after her set, telling her she was nothing special, that he didn't know what all the fuss was about. The quip didn't set well with Brown and she hauled off and smacked him, knocking out his two front teeth. "I was kinda brazen," she said. "Didn't step back off of nothing or nobody."

Like most first wave R&B icons, Brown drifted from the limelight in the 1960s, a victim of a rapidly changing music business and evolving tastes. During that time, her faith was tested mightily. As gigs dried up, she held a variety of menial jobs, from driving a school bus to scrubbing floors, to support her two young sons and keep her life together. She hit bottom not once, but several times, only to emerge again, each time with more purpose.

Thanks to that characteristic perseverance and tireless work ethic, Brown slowly rekindled her career in the 1970s and remained busy until her death. The surprising aspect of this revitalization was that she didn't reemerge as a singer and recording artist, but as an actor. She starred on Broadway, at the movies, and on television, winning a Tony and a Grammy in the process. She also became a popular host on two National Public Radio shows (*Harlem Hit Parade* and *BluesStage*). Brown also became a steadfast advocate for artist rights. She spoke out constantly, on stage and in interviews, about the exploitive contracts musicians of her generation had signed. Many of the early superstars of popular music, especially black music, never recouped their so-called debts to their record companies, according to official accountings, and so were not receiving any royalties at all, sometimes for decades.

Shortly before Atlantic Records held a 40th birthday concert at Madison Square Garden in 1988, the label came to an unprecedented agreement with a handful of their pioneer R&B artists: to waive unrecouped debts and to pay 20 years of retroactive royalties.

So in addition to several million-selling hits, induction into the Rock and Roll Hall of Fame, and a bevy of awards—one was the Ralph Gleason Award for Music Journalism she received for her 1996 autobiography, *Miss Rhythm*, often quoted in this chapter—Brown had in her last two decades become something of a hero for her efforts, for what she represented to the many under-appreciated and underpaid talents of her generation, and for her undying belief in the power of great R&B.

GOSPEL ROOTS

Ms. Brown was born Ruth Weston on January 12, 1928, in Portsmouth, Virginia, the oldest of seven children. Her father, Leonard Weston, was a dock worker and church singer with a penchant for drinking and her mom, Martha Jane Alston, was her spiritual leader and tough-nosed role model. In summers as a child she and her siblings picked tobacco at her grandmother's farm in Macon, North Carolina. "That helped make me the strong woman I am," she said in an AP interview in 1995.

Because her father sang in the choir and other glee clubs, Ruth was always around music. She made her vocal debut in the church, the Emmanuel African Methodist Episcopal Church in Olde Town, Virginia, when she was four. By the time she was six she was singing at weddings, standing up on the piano, belting out "Ave Maria" and "I Love You Truly" in her little soprano voice. At 10, Ruth was touring a circuit of local churches, belting out hymns and other spirituals. She managed to develop a significant vocal repertoire relatively early on, but she never learned to read music. "In school, we had music classes, but I ducked them," she said in 1995 in an AP interview. "They were just a little too slow. I didn't want to learn to read no notes. I knew I could sing it. I woke up one morning and I could sing."

Working in the fields all those years as a child also exposed her to the rural music of the black South, that spontaneous singing and humming that helped to make a heavy work load a little lighter. The music was accompanied by either a comb and paper or a Jew's harp. "The blues don't have to come from any place but the heart and soul of man, they don't require fancy orchestration, and they sure didn't get any from us as the sounds traveled from field to field" (Ruth Brown with Andrew Yule, *Miss Rhythm: The Autobiography of Ruth Brown*, New York: Da Capo Press, 1996, p. 30).

Ruth came of age listening to this music and the music of the church, but she also enjoyed blues and jazz, including the voices of Billie Holiday, Ella Fitzgerald, and Dinah Washington. When not singing spirituals, she worked on patterning her own singing techniques after them. Radio at the time, the mid-1940s, mainly focused on the white music of Bing Crosby, Vaughn Monroe, and Hank Williams, rather than the "race" records by black artists. Still, there was a local radio program called the *Mailbag* Ruth listened to as soon as her father went off to work. At the same time, Ruth began to take note of the black artists making the club scene around town: Oran "Hot Lips" Page,

Betty Roche, Doc Wheeler. These acts were important to Ruth's budding aspirations as a singer. "I dearly wanted to discuss my developing interest in singing for a living, but I knew Dad would hit the roof if I did" (Brown/Yule, p. 37).

Brown attended a local high school, where she was a cheerleader. She also helped her grandmother as a nurse's aide in convalescent homes, which she felt to be important work. But her heart remained devoted to singing. As a teenager, she would tell her family she was going to choir practice and she performed instead at USO clubs in nearby naval stations. In the many cases where she didn't tell her parents anything, but still had a singing engagement, Brown would sneak out through a window in her bedroom.

By the onset of World War II, Brown had learned enough Bing Crosby songs to serenade crowds at stations like Langley Field, Fort Eustis, Camp Lee, and Little Creek. But her parents, strict with their oldest child, would never had let Ruth go had they known it wasn't "choir practice." She was after all, underage and here she was visiting neighboring naval towns like Newport News, Norfolk, and Virginia Beach. "I lied a lot to get to where the music was," she told the *Virginian-Pilot* in one of several articles about her life. "I was supposed to be going to choir."

Once she recalled getting caught. A few songs after being introduced, she saw her father coming toward her. "He stood up on that stage, and I stopped singing immediately. I think he probably whipped me for about ten blocks" (Venable andStone, the *Virginian-Pilot*, November 18, 2006). In fact, Brown's father whipped her in the center aisle, in front of an audience and her 12-piece band. "It makes no sense to wait," she remembers him telling her. "You did it here. I'm gonna whip you here" (Brown and Yule, p. 39).

But Ruth, undeterred by her father's treatment and sporting a sizable rebellious streak, couldn't stay out of the clubs. Eventually she secured a job at one of the bases serving soda, a position that enabled her to leave the house with no risk and much less suspicion. After many appreciative performances, some soldiers at one of the bases drummed up enough cash to send Brown up to New York City to sing at the Apollo Theater's amateur night.

Tiny Bradshaw led the band the night Ruth appeared, and she sang "It Could Have Been You," a song she'd heard Bing Crosby croon many times on the radio. She got such a reception after that number, the night's MC asked her to reprise the song later on, a first for the weekly contest. It wouldn't be the last time Brown received that kind of reception for the song. It would become one of her signatures and a song she'd sing for most of her career.

Her Apollo performance led to a first place prize, $15, and a return weeklong engagement at the theater. The money she took. But she declined the booking, figuring she'd already pushed her luck. Still, the victory left a big impression on Ruth and all those who heard her sing. Her dreams were now too big to ignore. In 1945, at the age of 17, Ruth Weston left home to pursue her dreams as a singer, despite her father's threats that she'd never be welcomed back.

AT 17

Her first move wasn't far, only a five-minute ferry ride across the Elizabeth River from her hometown. Initially she busied herself touring regional bases in North Carolina, Georgia, and Kentucky. An encounter with bandleader Raleigh Randolph resulted in Ruth standing in as his lead singer, after Randolph's previous vocalist inexplicably disappeared.

One night in Norfolk while singing at a base with Rudolph, she met a man named Jimmy Earle Brown, an 18-year old midshipman who dabbled on trumpet. Brown skipped out of his duty to see Ruth whenever he could and he occasionally sat in with the band. After a brief courtship, the two became engaged; he was discharged from the service and began playing with the Randolph band along with his fiancée.

Billed as "Brown and Brown," the two began dueting with Randolph, singing together on songs like "Trust in Me" and "If I Didn't Care." Audience response was tremendous and soon they were featured attractions at Randolph gigs. For Ruth "Brown," the excitement was intoxicating. Jimmy met pro trumpeter "Hot Lips" Page, and began an informal tutelage with him. Their stock, individually and collectively, were on the rise. Ruth, madly in love with her new young partner, envisioned their name together up in lights all over the country. They got married on the fly, without notifying her family.

Unfortunately, it didn't take long for the marriage to turn sour. Ruth was shocked to find out, after coming across an old news clip in Jimmy's wallet, that her new husband was in fact already married. Devastated, she ran home, risking serious reprimand from her father, and confessed her story to the family. They forgave her misdeed and supported her.

Oddly enough, Ruth forgave Brown. After some agonizing, she had the marriage annulled, but not before her "husband" convinced her that *she*, not his first wife, was the one he truly loved. Satisfied with the explanation, she kept his last name, and together they continued to make music. They called themselves "Jimmy Brown and the Band of Atomic Swing, featuring Ruth Brown." For a period in the first half of 1947, business was good. They toured bases with a six-piece band and began developing a repertoire.

But as quickly as their act became a hit, the Brown/Brown gigs began to dry up. Learning the business, getting paid, and dealing with the shark-infested waters of promoters and booking agents, became difficult and a source of education for the young artists. The turmoil took a toll and in the summer of 1947 Brown and Brown disbanded.

After Jimmy got accustomed to being a bandleader, he also seemed to increase his womanizing. Rather than fight it, and try to wean him off his bad habit, Ruth thought it best to simply go her separate way. Moe Barney, owner of Barney's, a black neighborhood club in Petersburg, Virginia, petitioned Ruth to sing at his place as a solo act, and she seized the opportunity. Moe, a well-connected music biz personality, dug Ruth's act and told her he'd heard there was an opening for a girl singer at a place called the Frolic Bar in Detroit, Michigan. She sought out the opportunity and was hired on the spot, based largely on the vibrant recommendation she received from Moe.

While at the Frolic Bar she was spotted by Lucky Millinder, a cranky, forthright but tremendously successful bandleader, with an ear for young talent. After the performance, and a private audition in which Brown cranked out a handful of her strongest ballads, Millinder liked her enough to sign her on as his second vocalist. She was ecstatic. "I could hardly believe my luck! I was joining a group with a bunch of hit records to its name. I really felt the big time was beckoning" (Brown and Yule, p. 51).

She was right. But not before she confronted more adversity.

Things had been going reasonably well for Brown on Millinder's tour, though she wasn't called on to sing much. One night in Washington, D.C., after doing credible renditions of two songs Lucky had arranged expressly for her, he found her carrying a tray of Cokes to Millinder's band. He was infuriated. How could she, one of his star singers, stoop to the level of waitress? The petulant boss fired her on the spot, took her luggage off the bus, and left her alone, hundreds of miles from home. Fame would have to wait.

While stranded in D.C., a childhood friend she met at a bar introduced Ruth to a woman named Blanche Calloway. Blanche was the sister of international big band superstar Cab Calloway and a real pioneer in African American music. Like her brother, she had been a bandleader, the first woman of color to do so. But when Cab's career took off, she chose to leave her own behind and support him. In D.C., she ran a club called the Crystal Caverns.

It was here that Ruth began to regain the confidence Millinder had stripped from her. She started with some light work, a few numbers nightly and some at the piano, where Blanche would set up a kitty for her tips. The venue was busy, populated by locals as well as touring musicians and music industry types. One of those personalities was Willis Conover, a DJ billed as "the Voice of America." Conover loved Ruth's act and referred her to two men he knew—Ahmet Ertegun and Herb Abramson—at a fledgling company called Atlantic Records. They had opened their doors in 1947 and were looking to sign new artists.

Ertegun was the son of the Turkish ambassador to the United States, and Abramson, a dentist, had a little music business experience with a label called National. Before she knew it, Atlantic's A&R rep, Blacky Sales, was at the Crystal Caverns listening to Ruth. Blanche, now serving as Ruth's manager, as well as mentor and friend, advised her to sign on with Atlantic. And that's exactly what she did. They packed up for an important date at the Apollo; her driver, Blanche, Brown, and her "husband" Jimmy Brown, who magically reappeared in her life to patch things up.

Unfortunately, they wouldn't make it to the Apollo that night.

In the wee hours of the morning in late October 1948, the car they were in suffered a terrible crash. No one was killed, but Ruth was severely injured, breaking both legs. She was put in traction for 11 months in a Chester, Pennsylvania, hospital at perhaps the most important point of her budding career.

Then there was the matter of the letter from her husband. He had decided to leave her, seeing how she would likely never walk again. While his prognostication was wrong, Brown's legs would bother her for the rest of her life. Thankfully, the accident didn't sway Atlantic from keeping their newly signed artist on the company roster. The little label was struggling but ambitious and they maintained high hopes for Brown. They even picked up a portion of Brown's hospital bill.

A HISTORY OF HITS

Still recovering from her injury, Ruth hobbled into Apex Studios on crutches in the spring of 1949 for her first Atlantic recording session. Her inaugural A-side was "So Long," a bluesy ballad made famous by Little Miss Cornshuck, and it would become her first hit. The song remained on the R&B charts for two months, and reached the Top 10. Atlantic was thrilled. But the success was only momentary.

Ruth's four follow-up singles went nowhere and the label pow-wowed, reconsidering their approach. During her time with Ertegun and Abramson, Brown had experimented with a considerable amount of material, from Yiddish tunes to spirituals. But they decided, along with Ruth's input, that her strength was in ballads: bluesy, belted, storytelling ballads backed by lush arrangements.

Brown broke her dry spell in the fall of 1950 with a song written for her by Rudy Toombs called "Teardrops from My Eyes." The tune landed on the top of the R&B list, staying for nearly 3 months, and enjoyed a total chart run of 26 weeks. The record also made history because it was Atlantic's first 7-inch 45-rpm, an advancement over the customary 10-inch, 78-rpm.

It was about this time that Frankie "Mr. Rhythm" Laine, a headliner at one of Ruth's gigs, saw the hysteria surrounding her "Teardrops" hit, and deemed her "Miss Rhythm." Brown liked it enough to use it as her nickname, and it began showing up on handbills and other advertising material. Two other Toombs/Brown collaborations, "Daddy, Daddy" and "5-10-15 Hours (Of Your Love)," kept Brown's spotlight bright and she began the 1950s as one of the hottest R&B acts on the national scene. She toured the theater circuit hard, in particular the five black theaters in the country: the Apollo, of course, in New York City, the Regal in Chicago, the Howard in D.C., the Hippodrome in Richmond, and the Regal in Baltimore.

It was also about this time that Atlantic became referred to as "the House that Ruth Built," because of the money she was making for the label. Here's what Miss Rhythm had to say about that. "Even if this is an exaggeration, few would deny that I contributed a solid portion of the foundation as well as quite a few of the actual bricks. No doubt the cement was the matchless team at the company. . . . together with the incredible mix of outstanding musical talent they employed and nurtured" (Brown and Yule, p. 68).

Despite her chart success and despite the money she was earning for her label, Brown was beginning to realize how difficult it was to make money for herself. Her recording sessions, staffed by some of the best R&B musicians available and most skilled technical talent around, were put on Ruth's account and served as expenses against her royalties. In addition, when she toured, she was responsible for keeping 12 people on the road. On tour, she also absorbed the expense of wages, transportation, lodging, food, and anything else that came up. To make matters more complicated, Brown and her crew discovered that concert promoters were an unscrupulous bunch and often made off with the ticket money before she could hit them up.

Once entrenched in the industry, Brown began to see not only the doors that were open to her, but the doors that were closed as well. To most American radio stations and music retailers, R&B stood for "race and black" music as well as "rhythm and blues" and they turned their backs on even the most prominent artists in the genre. In their place, they focused on white performers, many of whom were doing the exact same songs, only tamer versions, as the black artists. White singers like Patti Page and Georgia Gibbs scored hits of songs that black artists like LaVern Baker and Brown had cut originally.

"It was tough enough coming up with hit sounds, therefore doubly galling to see them stolen from under our noses. Few seemed to stop and question the morality of this, least of all the publishers, to whom it was a case of the more the merrier" (Brown and Yule, p. 77).

Brown was also denied royalties from overseas sales, none of which were tracked anyway. Domestic labels and their accounting departments had no system in place to monitor those funds, so executives took advantage of the situation and pocketed whatever royalties their acts generated overseas. This unprincipled practice would come home to roost, though much later in the story.

Her first crossover hit came in 1953, when she released "Mama He Treats Your Daughter Mean." It topped the R&B charts, but also hit number 23 on the pop list. The success of the song surprised Brown, who didn't care much for the tune when she first heard a demo of it. She couldn't relate to the subject matter and didn't appreciate the up-tempo feel Herb Abramson superimposed on it. He had to coerce his singer to tackle it.

The way Abramson tells it, the songwriters, Herb Lance and Johnny Wallace, heard a blind blues singer on an Atlanta street corner sing the title line, and they were sold. Back in 1949, Abramson recalled that Atlantic had made a recording of Blind Willie McTell singing "Last Dime Blues," a track that included the line, "Mama, don't treat your daughter mean," a song, and a line, that dates back to the 1920s and seminal blues singer Blind Lemon Jefferson.

Despite Brown's reluctance to perform it, the song struck a proverbial chord. Audiences went wild over it. Brown tells the story of how one night in Charleston, South Carolina, she had to sing the song eight times before the crowd let her leave the stage. In Kansas City, Nashville, and virtually any city she played, the song became a showstopper and a riot queller. In Nashville, the mics were shut off after Ruth's set, but the crowd was still restless, eager to hear more music. Brown sang her signature tune one more time without the benefit of electricity, just to appease her fans. The song was voted the number one R&B record of 1953 by *Downbeat* magazine. That same year she won the Bessie Smith Award for Best Blues Singer handed out by a Pittsburgh newspaper.

The hits kept coming, though not as epic. "Wild Wild Young Men," whose byline reads "Nugetre" (Ertegun spelled backward) joined the hit list in the summer of 1953. The next year Brown hit number one on the R&B charts with two songs, "Oh What a Dream" and "Mambo Baby." The former was arranged by Jesse Stone and written solely for Ruth by Chuck "Gator" Willis, a beau of Brown's who met the singer while playing tenor sax for her band. The record was barely on the streets when a duplicate version of the song was rush-released by none other than Patti Page. Page's version siphoned off most of Brown's sales, though Page's success also had a way of keeping the name of Ruth Brown on everybody's lips.

At this time, Ruth had become the biggest female voice in all of R&B. "At that point, she was bigger than Dinah [Washington] or anybody. She was *the* thing. Ruth Brown appealed to anybody that heard her—she didn't just appeal to black listeners. Many of the records they called 'rhythm and blues'—which is a euphemism for 'race and black'—were not played on some general stations. It would mean she would be big in a city like Detroit where there's a mass black population and therefore two or three radio stations that played black records. In a city where there's not much of a black population and no black station, she wouldn't be as well known" (Nipsey Russell, liner notes, *Miss Rhythm*).

In late 1955 she hit number three with "I Wanna Do More" and the next year she teamed with Clyde McPhatter for the Top 10 Atlantic single "Love Has Joined Us Together." Her work with McPhatter, a former Drifter with a splendid and unique voice, spilled over into Ruth's personal life, and they had a torrid affair. But McPhatter's personal life also included bisexuality, and rumors of it, along with his excessive drinking, began to detract from his career.

"Lucky Lips," recorded in New York in September 1956, was the biggest song ever for Ruth in terms of pop achievements. This tune, along with "Mama" and "5-10-15 Hours," comprised Ruth's trio of million-selling singles. She continued to make records, and a few of them actually charted, but her late-period success was infrequent compared to her first half-dozen years. Songs like "Why Me?" garnered attention in 1958 and "Don't Deceive Me" hit the charts in 1959. It would be the last time her material would chart. She only recorded one stand-alone, full-length recording—the other LPs were collections of singles. That title was *Late Date with Ruth Brown*, and was recorded with arranger Richard Wess, from Bobby Darin's team.

Brown's sales numbers for the decade are staggering. In the 1950s, she had a total of 13 Top 10 R&B hits, including five number ones. In 1955, Ertegun and Abramson presented Brown with a plaque commemorating the sales of 5 million records. Brown's impact on R&B and the subsequent rock and roll revolution is undeniable. In 1948, when she joined Atlantic, the label ranked 25th in sales in the field of R&B. By the time 1951 rolled around, after Brown, and a few other acts, had handfuls of hits put the label on the map, the Atlantic label would rank number one in R&B.

The onset of the rock era marginalized black acts for a few years, as the music consuming public digested the euphoria of the new beats. But by that time, Ruth Brown had made a lasting impression on popular music.

SEGREGATION AND OTHER HEARTBREAKS

As she played to more and bigger audiences in the South, Brown and her band began seeing the results of segregation. While they tried to play as many "all-black" venues as they could, many cities and towns didn't have that sort of theatrical accommodation. And even if they did, Brown's crossover success prompted her bookings to open up to larger, and whiter, audiences. Still, she often encountered racial tensions and prejudice.

On tour with prominent acts like George Shearing, Count Basie, and Billy Eckstine and His Orchestra, all of whom employed biracial bands, Brown found the racial atmosphere, largely in the South, intolerant. She was nearly arrested for simply dancing with a white musician on her tour, and witnessed Shearing get booed simply because the blind bandleader had a mixed-race ensemble playing behind him.

Once, while in a ladies room in Alabama, police broke the lock and carried her out half-dressed. Apparently, it was a whites-only rest room, and Brown failed to obey local rules. She was jailed and paid a stiff fine. Another occasion found Brown on the receiving end of a gun barrel, when she barged in on what she thought was the venue's dressing room. Afraid for her life, the cop had called her a "black bitch" and pressed his gun into her midriff, Brown was rescued by her tourmates: Ray Brown, Charles Brown, and Amos Milburn.

Not long after that, Brown's Cadillac, emblazoned with *Miss Rhythm*, on the side and sporting New York license plates (an attention-getter down South), was pulled over by police on a bogus speeding charge. When the officer noticed the musical equipment in the car, he assumed it to be contraband. When Brown and her band insisted they were a band, and the goods were legitimately their own, the officer forced them out of the car to play a song, to prove they were indeed a band.

"Add separate black and white water fountains, curtains in railroad dining cars to separate the races, signs everywhere with crudely painted hands pointing the way For Coloreds, and a thousand more of the so-called civilized indignities, insults and affronts we had to suffer" (Brown and Yule, p. 121).

Fortunately for Brown, the music revived her. And the audiences, white and black, also there for the music, had a similar attitude.

> The local people just waited for the music to come, and for those of us who brought it to their neighborhood—the Charles Browns, the Clovers, the Drifters, the Sam Cookes, the Clyde McPhatters, the Coasters, the Jackie Wilsons, and the Little Richards. All these people, all these groups, with their great backing musicians, they're the ones who suffered every sling and arrow the South had to offer in those days. It was for the sake of the music that we did it. And maybe we helped the progress along a little. (Brown and Yule, p. 121)

In August 1953, Brown lost her father, at the age of 42. Close growing up, the two had a falling out when Ruth left home as a teen. At the time, the hard-drinking choir director swore she'd never be able return home or look to him for help should she need it. But it didn't take long for him to renege on his vow. Together, they had patched things up, especially when he found out that Ruth's first fiancé, Jimmy Earle Brown, was already married. He flew to her side, his oldest daughter, and the two remained close until his early death.

After her father died, and news of his infidelity surfaced at his funeral, Brown grew closer to her mother, Martha, going so far as to build her a new home in an upstart development on the outskirts of Portsmouth. She saw to it that her mother was comfortable before heading back out on the road.

BOY TROUBLE

It didn't take long for the next bombshell to hit. By fortuitous circumstance she discovered that the man she'd been spending the last year or so with, Chuck "Gator" Willis, was, like Jimmy Brown, married and with children of his own. The tenor sax player had been residing with Ruth for much of the time they'd been together, and Ruth felt the relationship was on solid ground. Of course, when she found out, in a conversation with Willis's friend, she was devastated. Her second relationship in so many tries had failed by the same deceitful premise. The event crushed Brown, until she met Drew Brown, her next beau, and, unbeknownst to Willis, the father of her first child.

When Brown found out about her pregnancy, she informed Willis, who at the time had drifted from her and she from him, even though they shared an apartment. She never told Willis about Brown, preferring to keep the pressure on him to come through as her baby's father. Ironically, word had gotten out that the real father's legal spouse was also pregnant.

When Brown went into labor, a miffed Willis refused to pay for a cab to the hospital. And shortly after Brown came home with the baby, in January 1954, Willis left. He removed his furniture from the apartment and left Brown alone with her infant, Ronald David Jackson.

"I could pick a good song, but I sure couldn't pick a man worth a damn" (Brown and Yule, p. 141).

Brown constantly had a man on her arm, and often times those men were there for the wrong reasons. Jimmy Brown and Willis, both horn players, had women "back home," before shacking up with Ruth.

Then there was McPhatter, the former Drifter. After recording "Love Has Joined Us Together" as a duet, Brown and McPhatter had a brief but passionate affair. But when his bisexuality leaked to the press, he began drinking to drown the shame, which only set him reeling further. He'd appear for his sets completely soused, and his bookings dried up quickly. Word has it that he literally drowned himself in drink, dying at age 39. (Decades later, Brown told her son he was actually McPhatter's, not Willis's. He now sings with a latter-day lineup of the Drifters.)

Drew Brown, another beau, also known as "the Great Bundini," was an entertainment charlatan, acting like a prince even as he was a drunken pauper.

In 1955, on tour with the Griffin Brothers Orchestra, Brown met another tenor sax player, Earl Swanson. Swanson was another womanizer, as well as a drug user and wife beater. Not only did he beat Brown, he beat anybody who came between him and his victim. Once, Ruth's personal assistant, Thelma Manley, got in the way of a Swanson punch and paid the price.

At the time, Ruth felt her career flagging, and Swanson convinced her that he was the man to revive it. He promoted her shows as "Earl Swanson Presents: Ruth Brown" or "The Earl Swanson Band featuring Ruth Brown." But these billings were just another way he duped her into thinking he was indispensable. When Brown felt confident, he'd smack her around and bring her back to earth. Long sleeves and makeup covered the bruises. But Brown's heart was what truly hurt.

"As a woman I was ashamed that I had become so obsessed and weak that I would allow a many to treat me that way. I had seen the other edges of it with my dad, and had always sworn it wouldn't happen to me" (Brown and Yule, p. 140).

As luck would have it, Brown was pregnant for the second time, this time with Earl's child. The pregnancy and delivery were difficult, and Earl Jr. came into the world reluctantly. Delivered by caesarean, he required a full blood transfusion at birth, and would go on to suffer other problems as well.

Brown continued to cower under Swanson's abuse. She began touring five weeks after the birth of the baby, but the toll it took on her was obvious. She took to drinking to get her through, Seagram's Golden Gin.

"I never had drunk before and I did not handle it well. The warm-up swinger was no problem, the trouble started with the ballad. With my confidence leaking all over the place, there was one song I was really scared to sing, believer in lyrics that I am. It was 'He's Funny That Way' " (Brown and Yule, p. 141).

Brown weaned herself off drink following her separation and subsequent divorce from Swanson. Earl Jr. was eight when he finally got to meet and know his father. He surprised Ruth with his paternal instinct.

In the late 1950s, Brown coupled with a young trumpet player named Danny Moore, and stayed with him for nearly four years. While the relationship progressed rather uneventfully, Brown broke up with Moore when she realized she was mothering him as well as her two sons.

ROCK AND ROLL HITS

In the latter part of 1955 through 1957, rock and roll fever struck and suddenly, "race music," or black R&B, began to catch on with white teen audiences. DJs at heretofore white radio stations began to spin race discs, and sponsor tours, where many of the acts they were sending out over the airwaves would play their hit song live on stage, in a sort of cavalcade of performers. They were called "supershows."

The benefits were obvious. It was mass commercial exposure for the black artists, especially the ones on the Atlantic imprint, who'd until now had hit serious snags earning it. But logistics for this exposure were nearly impossible, as acts were doing 35 dates in 35 cities, appearing for one song only, then packing up and barreling down the highway to the next destination.

Sales picked up, of course, but the routine took its toll, especially on Ruth's voice. Often she'd have to sing a song, one song, her *hit* song, five or six times in a day. She had a tonsillectomy and her voice changed ever so slightly, deepening a fraction. The change of voice didn't affect Ruth's career at the time, but the oncoming stampede of rock and roll acts sure would. A few more attempts at hits—three brief chart appearances in the early 1960s—and Brown's career as a recording star, at least the very bright initial phase of it, was over.

In 1962, Ruth found a lump in her breast. And though it was diagnosed as benign, the radiation treatment forced her hair to fall out. At first, losing her hair devastated her. She had always worn her hair tightly back in a pony tail with spit curls, and the style did nothing to hide her thinning tresses. In the beginning, Brown resorted to hair patches, covering the bald spots. Then she moved on to wearing a wig. Fortunately for Ruth, wigs would soon become fashionably popular.

SUBURBAN BROWN

Ruth Brown met Bill Blunt through a mutual friend. Blunt, a gentleman from Long Island, was a police officer for over two decades when he met Brown.

Blunt, eight years Ruth's senior, led a secure, sedate suburban life and the prospect of sharing the same became appealing to Ruth. She dearly wanted a stable environment in which to bring up her two boys, and now that her career had sagged and the musical climate had grown less accommodating to her, she decided this would be the time to settle down.

In the months leading up to their marriage in 1963, Ruth was still gigging in the clubs, often opening for comedians, like Pat Morita, Redd Foxx, and Nipsey Russell. Admittedly, the slots weren't great—she rarely received billing—but the work was steady and Ruth managed to keep at least one foot in the music industry.

Blunt, a dedicated father, enjoyed the kids, enrolling them on sports teams and in the Boy Scouts, and gave them the opportunity to at last lead normal lives. But in exchange for all that stability, Blunt requested one thing: that Ruth leave her performing career behind and become a stay-at-home mother.

The deal went against everything Brown had worked toward her entire life, and was a bitter pill. She tried her best to acquiesce with the terms, singing infrequently for a few years. She'd occasionally sing, without compensation, at Police Department events, when her husband could oversee the details. Once she even performed for the officers with none other than Duke Ellington. Duke led the band and Brown sang. The gig, said Ruth later, was like "teasing an alcoholic" with a drink.

Little by little, she defied her husband and took other gigs. This helped start the fissure that would destroy the relationship. For Brown felt she needed show business to sustain herself and her life. Blunt demanded she devote herself to her family. As much as she wanted to respect his wishes, though, and as good as he was with her boys, she couldn't stay away from her music.

She and Blunt separated in 1966. She took her boys and moved to a neighboring Long Island town, Deerpark, and rented a home. But in their newly independent existence—Brown made no claims on Blunt—debts piled up quickly. Despite gigs, mostly poor-paying ones, she often had to live off of the generosity of her mother and siblings. Some months she had trouble paying the rent. In the winter, when the electric bills rose, she lit her home with candles. In the spring, the boys would study outside until the sun went down.

She joined the Pentecostal Church and began singing at funerals and cooking and cleaning for the clergy. The church staff told her she needed to provide these services to atone for the all sins she'd committed while in show business. The clergy even tried to secure her vocal talents for their Funeral Package, a no-fee deal, but Brown drew the line.

Brown also took a job as a teacher's aide, and then a proper teacher, at a local Head Start program, while sneaking out at night to sing at local clubs. The salary she obtained from the program at least enabled her to apply for financial aid to get her kids through school. She also qualified for food stamp assistance and rent subsidies. She sought work wherever she could, cleaning homes, babysitting, elderly care, doing hair and makeup, teaching school. The work was humbling and often desperate. She couldn't even afford the expense of a telephone; the business next door, a garage, would take messages for her. Brown could not help but think how far she'd fallen from the glory days of her career.

One of the pursuits that helped her maintain a modicum of self-respect was at the International Art of Jazz, an organization founded on grants by the National Endowment for the Arts. Brown, along with jazz greats like Thad Jones and Clark Terry would give day-long jazz workshops to students, sometimes two or three a week.

This mingling with musicians led to a few recordings, including *Black Is Brown and Brown Is Beautiful* on Skye Records, a 1968 album that yielded a Grammy nomination for Best Rhythm and Blues Performance for a version of Paul McCartney's "Yesterday." That same year she recorded, *Fine Brown Frame* with the Thad Jones–Mel Lewis Big Band. A final album, *Brown Sugar*, made with producer Swamp Dogg, aka Jerry Williams, down at the Muscle Shoals studio, proved a scam. Her $600 advance check for the disc bounced and Williams made off with the tapes. A year or so later a primitive recording of the session was released, with no frills and no production value, just the bare-bones rhythm tracks she'd laid down. Brown, embarrassed with the result, was at the end of her rope. When she and her brother Leonard tracked Williams down to demand payment, he screamed at them and slammed the door in their faces. "I had been through a lot, but in some ways this was the worst of all. . . . I was mortified to have been humiliated like that" (Brown and Yule, p. 141).

ACTING IN THE 1970s

Many an artist's story could well have ended there, but not Ruth Brown's. In the early 1970s, she had made arrangements, thanks to some government assistance, to send both of her boys off to college. Ronnie attended Howard University in Washington, D.C., where he studied engineering and played football. Earl began his college years at the New York Institute of Technology, close to home.

One night in 1976 a friend asked her to attend something called the Westbury Music Fair. There she'd run into old friends Billy Eckstine and Redd Foxx. Foxx, in particular, would play a vital role in the rest of Ruth Brown's career.

As the story goes, and as Foxx tells it, in the early 1950s, when Brown was reaching her apex, Foxx was a struggling young comedian. At the time, Ruth had just finished a headlining gig at the Fillmore West in San Francisco, and was paid handsomely for the night. Foxx, who had first met Brown back in her Virginia days, was broke and desperate. He knocked on Brown's hotel room door and basically pleaded with her for assistance. She showed him her night's take and told him to take whatever he needed. Foxx grabbed $450, enough for a plane ticket back East for a fresh start.

That good came back around a quarter century later. Brown spilled her story to Foxx and the comedian, empathetic to her current situation, vowed to help. He invited her to California, telling her there were many things she could do there, and he'd take care of all her expenses.

In Los Angeles, thanks in large part to Foxx, Brown began acting. She did a handful of cameo appearances on Foxx's *Sanford and Son* and played the part of Mahalia Jackson on Foxx's production of *Selma*, a musical about the civil rights movement. While in L.A., she met Herb Jeffries, once a singer for Duke Ellington, also known as "the Bronze Buckaroo" from the black westerns of the 1930s.

When Brown ran into Jeffries, he was ditching a singing arrangement he'd made at an off-strip Vegas theater called the Tender Trap. She insisted she could sing in his place and soon she was on a plane to Sin City to fill his billing. That run led to a more legitimate headlining slot at a place called the Gilded Cage on the Strip. The show, billed as "the Real Ruth Brown," was a hit, as her black audience came out in numbers to support their former idol.

Back in Los Angeles, she nabbed a part in *Guys and Dolls* and *Livin' Fat*, a hit comedy, which in turn led to a Normal Lear–produced sitcom called *Hello Larry*, with McLean Stevenson. That show, and a second, *Checking In*, a spin-off from *The Jeffersons*, were ill-fated and short-lived, not to mention the end of television for Brown.

Still, the experience under her belt, along with a jolt of confidence and a little financial security, proved vital, and Brown decided to head back East where she had designs of taking back the singing career she had lost over a decade ago.

She returned to New York City in 1982, and ironically, moved back in with her former husband, Earl Swanson, who had an apartment in Riverside. Once in the city, she embarked on a staggering 18-week headlining stint at a club called the Cookery, managed by Barney Josephsen. Helen Humes had been booked but fell ill, and luckily, Josephsen had heard Brown was back in town. That successful run helped jump-start Brown's career on the East Coast. One night she had a visit from none other than Stevie Wonder, who said to the crowd, "I didn't come here to sing. I want to tell you something. . . . I came here because they told me Ruth Brown was singing here tonight, and this is the lady, take my word for it, who started it at all. Wasn't for Ruth there wouldn't be no Aretha, wouldn't be nobody! I'm here to tell you this lady is a true legend" (Brown and Yule, p. 184).

Unfortunately, her reunion with Swanson didn't last long. Earl began checking in with her between shows, badgering her to be accountable and subservient. The beatings, at first infrequent, became violent, and Brown again began losing her dignity and self-respect. To make matters even more difficult, Brown had to contend with the death of her mother.

That same year, 1982, she recorded *The Soul Survives*, with Norman Schwartz, the man behind her *Black Is Brown* set in 1968. That work led to Brown being cast in a musical adaptation of James Baldwin's *Amen Corner*.

Ever resilient, Ruth also picked up some theater work. She appeared in off-Broadway productions including *Stagger Lee*, and in 1985 she went to Paris to perform in the revue *Black and Blue*, a musical memoir of the Cotton Club days. The run was so successful that she rejoined that production later for its Broadway run.

About the same time, Brown began recording radio shows for National Public Radio producer Felix Hernandez and his Ceiba Productions. She hosted over 100 episodes of programs called *Harlem Hit Parade* and *BluesStage*, signing each one off the same way: "Remember, R&B stands for Ruth Brown."

Ruth also had a memorable role as the disc jockey Motormouth Maybelle in outrageous director John Water's play *Hairspray*—and on Broadway, where she won a Tony Award for her role in *Black and Blue*. And while that may have seemed like a peak to her comeback, Ruth continued to gain ever wider exposure.

A heart attack in 1989 slowed her down, but not for long. In 1992, her body slowed her again, this time her legs, which required surgery. She had had problems with her legs since the car accident in 1948 and the operation managed to get her back on her feet with much less pain.

She began recording again for more specialized blues and jazz labels. In fact, her album *Blues on Broadway* (Fantasy, 1989) won a Grammy for Best Jazz Vocal Performance, which looked just fine lined up next to her Tony. In 1990 she played a show with Koko Taylor and Irma Thomas called "Three Legendary Ladies." Along the same lines, she joined LaVern Baker and Etta James at the 15,000-seat Wolf Trap venue in Virginia in a show billed as "Three Divas." She opened for B.B. King in front of 60,000 fans. She played the Montreaux and Newport Jazz Festivals, Carnegie Hall, and the Hollywood Bowl.

Back home in Portsmouth, Virginia, the city held a Ruth Brown Weekend and dedicated the street where she grew up Ruth Brown Avenue. She had met and entertained U.S. presidents. The circuit was complete. Ruth Brown had after five full decades in entertainment, recaptured her original success and with some semblance of the electrifying energy that lit a fire under the world of R&B back in 1950.

FINAL CHAPTER

On January 12, 1993, Ruth Brown was invited into the Rock and Roll Hall of Fame on her 65th birthday. Her name had been on the ballot for five years, even dropped for two years. Brown and many in her circle held little hope for induction, considering the fact that Ertegun was a large backer of the institution and Brown had, after making hits for his label, been a thorn in his side thanks to her dogged pursuit of just artist royalties.

When they finally did induct her, they sent her notification to an old address and the news languished for a month. She read about her own induction in the papers, like everyone else. On the night, Brown duetted with Bonnie Raitt on "Mama, He Treats Your Daughter Mean," earned enough votes for induction. Raitt inducted her with a short speech and Ruth followed with some words of her own, a few of which were directed at Ertegun, who was in attendance. The parry was good-humored though, and Brown enjoyed the moment.

Brown, Begle, and the Quest for Royalty Reform

Midway through the 1960s, Ruth Brown was destitute. Recently divorced from a man who forbade her to perform, she had trouble meeting her bills and supporting her two young boys. She held jobs cleaning houses, driving buses, bathing the elderly. This was an inexplicable predicament for Brown, who nearly single-handedly built the empire known as Atlantic Records with her R&B hitmaking in the early 1950s, the same artist who, on paper, sold a million copies of her biggest hit, "Lucky Lips," in 1957. Incredibly, when pressed, her label insisted that Brown, when all expenses were added up, actually *owed* them money. When touring, recording, promotion, musicians' fees, and other expenses were tallied against Brown's advances, Brown was in the red. Attorney Howell Begle, a fan of Ruth's, thought the situation was preposterous, and together with Brown, they sought to right what they perceived as a severe injustice.

Begle, a communications and entertainment lawyer and ardent R&B fan, made Brown's cause a personal crusade in the early 1980s, working pro bono on her behalf and signing up several other former Atlantic artists, including the Coasters, the Drifters, and Big Joe Turner. None of these acts had received royalty statements in 25 years. When Begle and Brown pressed Atlantic for a royalty statement at the time, it showed she had made $785 in domestic and foreign revenues combined, in 20 years of working.

Begle considered the cause a travesty of justice. In his research, he determined that Brown, the Clovers, and Big Joe Turner landed Atlantic 36 Top 10 R&B hits, including eight number ones. The numbers, including those number ones, didn't add up. The Clovers, it was determined, had made $2,500 in 25 years, a total of $100 a year or $20 a person.

Begle and Brown's first visit to Atlantic's offices in April 1984 was not well received. But through some sniffing around and some record checking, it was determined that Atlantic had not kept any sales figures for foreign accounts throughout the 1960s. Their accounting systems were primitive and manual entries were non-existent.

Now panicked, Atlantic back-pedaled. These acts had not sold as many units as were originally publicized. For example, Brown's "Lucky Lips," a hit Atlantic had proudly touted as a million seller, actually only sold 200,000. Still, they insisted, Brown and the Clovers owed the label somewhere between $10,000 and $30,000.

Soon, the press got wind of the predicament, and the royalty scandal blew wide open. A program called *West 57th* called attention to the plight, and brought in performers from other labels, like Hank Ballard and Bo Diddley.

Moving forward, Brown brought her case to Congress, where she testified in front of the House Judiciary Criminal Justice Subcommittee. Her appearance earned her sympathy, understanding, and muscle. Atlantic began softening. A class action lawsuit threat under RICO (Racketeer Influenced and Corrupt Organizations Act), got the music industry's attention. Faulty bookkeeping, improper accounting of session costs, underreporting of domestic sales, and underpayment on foreign sales all factored into the suit.

Begle eventually partnered with attorney Chuck Rubin, a man on a similar crusade who represented artists like the Coasters, Sam and Dave, Carla Thomas, Brook Benton, and the estate of Clyde McPhatter. The newly enlarged roster came with more muscle, and more hits. In a surprising coup, they also added Gerry Bursey to their payroll. Bursey was the head of Atlantic's royalty accounting division, but had been recently terminated. Further, Jesse Jackson, a fan of the cause, recruited Bud Wolff at AFTRA (American Federation of Theatrical and Radio Artists) to examine the company's handling of their federally insured pension contributions. If there was a problem, it could potentially be a federal offense.

The movement was gaining strength and Ahmet Ertegun, president of Atlantic, began showing up at meetings.

At the tail end of 1987, Atlantic had hammered out a timetable for royalty repayment. They would be announced in 1988, at its much-ballyhooed 40th anniversary celebration.

The details were a compromise: all of the artists' debts would be erased, but the backdating of royalties would only revert back to 1970, an 18-year period. This conveniently excluded these artists' most productive period—the 1960s—but it was a settlement nevertheless. $250,000 had been set aside for payment to the suit's first 7 artists and their estates, and the label agreed to conduct audits on behalf of the 28 additional pioneers who'd recorded for Atlantic in the 1950s and 1960s. Brown's $30,000 check was her first from Atlantic in more than 20 years.

The agreement also included funding and grants for the Rhythm and Blues Foundation, which Brown helped to establish. Atlantic set aside $1.5 million for the foundation, while Warner Communications committed $450,000. This money would be used for tax-free grants for pioneers and artists in need.

Her work with the Rhythm and Blues Foundation, an organization set up with the assistance of attorney Howell Begle, Atlantic Records, and Warner Communications, who pledged nearly half a million dollars, as well as celebrities like Dan Ayckroyd, was a landmark in popular music and royalty reform, in particular. In part it was set up to provide tax-free grants in recognition of artists' contributions to the music and determined by need to pay for medical or funeral expenses and the like. There was also an effort to reform royalties among all record labels, not just Atlantic.

Her campaigning was tireless and found her involved in artist rights for five decades of her life. This crusade would, along with her profound musical legacy, be one of the true and lasting achievements of her life. Ruth Brown died in Las Vegas, in November 2006, at the age of 78. The cause was complications following a heart attack and stroke she suffered after surgery and had been on life support.

SELECTED DISCOGRAPHY

Miss Rhythm: Greatest Hits and More (Atlantic, 1989)
Rockin' in Rhythm: The Best of Ruth Brown (Rhino, 1996)
A Good Day for the Blues (Rounder, 1999)

FURTHER READING

Brown, Ruth with Yule, Andrew. *Miss Rhythm: The Autobiography of Ruth Brown, Rhythm and Blues Legend.* New York: Da Capo Press, 1999.

Courtesy of Photofest.

LaVern Baker

EMPRESS OF ROCK AND ROLL

A versatile vocalist, LaVern Baker melded blues, jazz, and R&B styles in a way that opened the door to a new idiom: rock and roll. She was one of the sexiest divas gracing the mid-1950s nascent rock and roll circuit, boasting a brashly seductive vocal delivery tailor-made for belting the catchy novelties "Tweedle Dee," "Bop-Ting-a-Ling," and "Tra La La" for Atlantic Records during rock's emergent first wave, beginning in 1953. On songs like "Soul on Fire," "Tweedle Dee," often thought to be the first rock and roll pop hit, and "Jim Dandy," LaVern's voice, a fascinating mixture of sophistication and down-to-earth power that evoked Bessie Smith, resonated at a time when jazz, swing, and big band were mutating quickly into rockin' blues and rhythm. Baker was at the fulcrum of that critical transition.

Baker recorded for the Atlantic label until the sizable racial barriers came down, and she enjoyed considerable success, particularly on the R&B charts, all the way through her zesty 1962 recording of the public domain tune "See See Rider." Her statuesque figure and charismatic persona made her a natural for TV and movies. She co-starred on the historic R&B revue segment on Ed Sullivan's TV program in November 1955 and did memorable numbers in Alan Freed's rock movies *Rock, Rock, Rock* and *Mr. Rock & Roll*. Her Atlantic records remained popular throughout the decade, especially with her 1958 torch song "I Cried a Tear," the rousing Leiber and Stoller–penned gospel rave "Saved" in 1960, and her lovely Bessie Smith tribute album, *LaVern Baker Sings Bessie Smith* (1958) before leaving Atlantic in 1965.

Baker was a charter member of the first rock and roll tours that criss-crossed the country, playing to screaming teenagers everywhere. On one particular caravan in 1957, since billed as the greatest compendium of rock and roll talent ever assembled, her travel companions included Buddy Holly, Chuck Berry, Fats Domino, Bo Diddley, and Little Richard, which gives some indication of the company she kept during her peak early years.

Though she cut half a dozen singles that rose to high positions on both the pop and R&B charts, Baker's frequency on the pop charts doesn't tell her whole story. As a pioneer in the R&B vernacular, Baker, like Ray Charles, Jackie Wilson, Ruth Brown, and Etta James, suffered from the segregationist impulses of the larger culture by having her songs re-recorded almost immediately by white singers like Georgia Gibbs and Patti Page. Their sanitized versions, bolstered by racist sentiment and the support of record stores and commercial radio, greatly outsold the original so-called race records; they robbed the original creators of their full rewards, not just in monetary compensation but in terms of social recognition as well. Eventually, the youth of America saw through the ploy and prejudice and, despite their lack of commercial airplay, sought out the originals. Today, history recalls those originals and only the originals; LaVern's enduring impact in R&B and early rock and roll sounds will never be forgotten.

THE EARLY YEARS

LaVern Baker, née Delores Baker, was born in Chicago on November 11, 1929, amid intense poverty, though little else is known about her childhood. Most historical research on Baker picks up where she begins singing in clubs, as her original stage persona, "Little Miss Sharecropper." Details on her adolescence are sparse.

It's certain, though, that music played a significant role in her life from a very early age. Her extended family included members with deep musical backgrounds. Merline Johnson, for example, was LaVern's aunt on her father's side. Johnson, known as "the Ya Yas Girl" for her lovely stature and feminine figure, sang with Big Bill Broonzy and Blind John Davis in the late 1930s and 1940s Chicago. She was born in Mississippi, but moved to Chicago with the great Northern migration in 1936 and she became famous for singing brash tunes like "Jackass for Sale" and "Running Down My Man." The Bakers boasted another famous family member in Memphis Minnie, an aunt on her mother's side. Memphis Minnie was the most famous black, country blueswoman of her time. Known as Minnie McCoy, she came from Louisiana via Mississippi and Memphis, and she moved to Chicago in 1930 on her way to becoming the blues' premier female performer. LaVern Baker came directly from this bold and trailblazing bloodline, so it's no surprise that she developed an equally unique and impressive vocal style.

She developed her style, as many did, through singing in the Baptist church in her Chicago neighborhood. Blessed with a powerful voice, she began impressing churchgoers immediately, and by the time she'd hit 12, she'd regularly take leads in the choir. As soon as she turned legal, at 17, she performed cabaret at the nightclubs on Chicago's South Side. Still known then as Delores Baker, she adopted the stage name of "Little Miss Sharecropper"; the persona involved wearing a tattered cotton sack dress and looking like a young slave. Of course, this persona wasn't far from the truth. Her grandparents were former slaves.

The name's origins are uncertain, although a performer at this time, Mildred Cummings, aka "Little Miss Cornshucks," was also performing through the 1940s and Baker was said to have enjoyed her rustic comedienne act. It was said that she adopted the Little Miss Sharecropper alias to appeal to the hordes of Southerners new to the Chicago. At night, after hours, she often went by the name Bea Baker, perhaps after Memphis Minnie's real name, Merline Baker. The concept of having dual aliases indicates that Baker understood how to appeal to not one but two audiences.

One of Little Miss Sharecropper's first high-profile gigs was at a popular Chicago joint called Club DeLisa. There she found a devoted following, a mixture of the city's urban sophisticates and the newly migrated country folk from "down home." Both got a kick out of the singer, who belted in the tradition of great shouters like Big Joe Williams.

Encouraged by her rapid progress, she moved from Chicago to Detroit, and out of the blues. In the Motor City in the late 1940s, things were bustling. John Lee Hooker had just arrived in town, Johnnie Ray had not yet begun to wow 'em at the Flame Show Bar, and the young future record mogul Berry Gordy was still splitting his time between the assembly line, the boxing ring, and early attempts at songwriting.

Industry in Detroit buzzed, especially the automotive industry, resulting in a huge influx of Southerners looking for good-paying assembly line work. The flush of money enhanced the optimism of the city and music was everywhere, especially after hours, where autoworkers would adjourn to the bars for a drink and some music after a hard day of work.

Gospel, blues, jump blues, and doo-wop saturated the city and it was under these circumstances that LaVern got a gig singing at the Flame Show Bar. The manager of the bar, Al Green, who'd also go on to manage Jackie Wilson, was so impressed with Baker's act that he became her personal manager.

With talent scouts abounding in Detroit, it didn't take long for Baker and Green to attract the attention of renowned big band leader Fletcher Henderson, who heard her sing one night at the club. She cut a test recording with Henderson called "Little Miss Sharecropper," but the session didn't go well and the effort was never released. It has since vanished without a trace. Still, based on this early association with Henderson, Baker's reputation in Midwestern clubs continued to rise.

Her first official appearance on record came when LaVern was hired by the Eddie "Sugarman" Penigar Band to front his act as Little Miss Sharecropper. They commuted between Detroit and Chicago, striking it big in both cities and soon Baker's character was a major attraction on the club circuit. LaVern made her first legitimate recording with Penigar for RCA Victor in 1949, including "I Wonder Baby" and "Easy Baby." In 1950 she cut "Sharecropper's Boogie" with Hot Lips Page and Red Saunders for Columbia, but the track was never released.

In 1951, she was hired to front Maurice King and His Wolverines. Together, they cut a couple of sides for the Columbia/Okeh imprint. Baker is credited on these sessions not as Little Miss Sharecropper but as Bea Baker.

But with big band jazz on its last legs, musicians that had cut their teeth on swing and jazz were now making their living playing the harder, faster, and more vibrant new format that hip folks around the country were calling "rhythm and blues." Even though Detroit's major R&B revolution was still a few years off in 1947, the times were undergoing massive musical change. The Todd Rhodes Orchestra was at the vanguard of change, its music pointing the way forward to the rock and roll era while still maintaining its links with the fast-dying swing years.

As well as being a bandleader and musician of stature, Todd Rhodes was a seasoned talent spotter. Many of the musicians who later found fame as part of Motown's celebrated Funk Brothers got their start in the Rhodes band, among them drummer Benny Benjamin, who powered nearly every important Motown recording from the 1960s.

It was under this circumstance that Rhodes spotted LaVern Baker. Rhodes had just lost his singer, Kitty Stevenson, and had seen Baker singing at the Flame Show Bar. In 1952, at 23, LaVern was recruited to sing with the popular ensemble. Under Rhodes, she adopted the name LaVern and her recording career shifted into high gear.

She debuted with Rhodes's orchestra on the impassioned ballad "Trying" for Cincinnati's King Records, along with a couple of other sides, also on

King, and together they toured constantly. The exposure proved invaluable for Baker, as would her association with the hot bandleader Rhodes, and she made the decision, with the help of Green, to tour without Rhodes's support.

But instead of going across America again, they decided to head to Europe, Italy mainly, for several months, spanning the end of 1952 and the beginning of 1953. The adulation and the enthusiasm of the Europeans floored Baker, and upon her return to the States she felt it best to parlay her growing confidence into a solo career. She craved more of the spotlight than simply as a vocalist for a big band. Two music men, Jerry Wexler and Ahmet Ertegun, hungry to sign up and coming talent, would be happy to oblige her.

THE ATLANTIC YEARS

LaVern signed with Atlantic as a solo artist in 1953. At the time, Atlantic had been a functioning label for five years, and its principals were beginning to get a handle on the massive transformation popular music was about to undergo. Ertegun and Wexler may have seen traces of the great blues singer Bessie Smith in Baker, with her growl and forceful delivery. Both Wexler and Ertegun were fond of the early blues belters, and they were eager to give Baker a shot at that same glory.

Atlantic had already signed one R&B singing sensation, Ruth Brown, back in 1949, and her career was well under way. They envisioned Baker to be a solid, bluesy complement to Brown, rather than competition. Baker's first session with Atlantic was in June 1953. She and her two bosses composed a couple of songs and they cut them with a New York City band featuring Freddie Mitchell and Pinky Williams on saxes, Jimmy Lewis on guitar, Lloyd Trotman on bass, Sylvester Payne on drums, Hank Jones on piano, and arranger Gene Redd. This essentially was the Atlantic label's house band.

Baker debuted with the incendiary "Soul on Fire," her first single and a generous hint of what was to come. Her muscular delivery, with splashes of smoldering sexiness, came across beautifully on the record. It pushed the boundaries of pop at the time with its gospel urgency and it foreshadowed the impassioned vocalizing for which she'd become very well known. Stylistically, it suggested her work with Rhodes though, and wasn't one of LaVern's tracks that eventually prefigured rock and roll. The record didn't chart, but has since become an early R&B classic.

" 'Soul on Fire' is as tough and bopping as anything any of the guys on the circuit could claim. Baker's melismatic growls at the end of the tune illuminate the gospel origins of her style, but her smooth confidence with the worldly lyric, her patience in allowing the song to develop, and her empathy with the small combo backing her all suggest her nightclub experience" (Dave Marsh, *The Heart of Rock and Soul: The 1001 Greatest Singles Ever Made*, New York: Da Capo Press, 1999, p. 357).

Less than a year later, LaVern recorded a pair of similarly sexy ballads: "I Can't Hold Out Any Longer" and "I'm Living My Life for You." But neither of these sold commercially and didn't provide the breakthrough that Ertegun and Wexler were expecting. These tracks are considered among Baker's lesser work.

In October 1954, Baker returned to the studio, this time with Sam "The Man" Taylor on sax, the Atlantic House band, and the label's background singers, the Cues, listed on the release as "the Gliders." For her first effort she and the band re-cut Lonnie Johnson's hit from 1948 "Tomorrow Night," injecting it with her characteristic spiritual passion. At the same session she laid down "Tweedle Dee," a Winfield Scott track with the simple flair of a children's rhyme. At the time, the sound came out of the radio like a blast of fresh air, thanks to Baker's playful but brawny singing and Taylor's roaring sax solo.

The result was smashing and the biggest record of Baker's career thus far. It reached the Top Five on the R&B charts, where it remained for almost four months. More important, and with great significance, it hit the pop charts in January 1955 and stayed there until the spring, reaching number 14. In placing that song on the charts, she'd become the first of Atlantic's R&B artists to cross over to pop.

Baker, along with two other Atlantic artists, Ruth Brown and Clyde McPhatter, and New Orleans pianist Fats Domino, became the principal figures to represent the gradual acceptance of black musicians by white audiences. That attention precipitated great scrutiny, but also great notoriety, not only for herself but for other R&B artists. Because she crossed over, music fans nationwide began to step up their support of a wide array of R&B artists, which meant that Baker's style opened the door to virtually all other pop, R&B, and early rock and roll artists to follow. White audiences were attracted to Baker, who was beautiful, unthreatening, and talented, proving to record labels across the country that R&B artists were viable commercially. And as soon as R&B caught on, and it was catching on faster than a fire in a hayfield, rock and roll was not long to follow.

The coy, Latin-tempo "Tweedle Dee" was a smash throughout 1955 and it set Baker's career on a skyward trajectory. Unfortunately, given the fact that black artists still weren't accepted by commercial radio for most of the 1950s, Baker's great material was pillaged by white artists who *were* accepted on the radio. This song theft—often referred to as "whitewashing"—happened regularly in the 1950s. One of the main perpetrators was a singer named Georgia Gibbs, whose management regularly pilfered black hits, cleaned them up, and presented them to white audiences. Gibbs's version of "Tweedle Dee" was on the street a matter of weeks after the original, and it stole a substantial amount of the sales Baker's own version would have enjoyed without the competition. Gibbs's copy hit number two on the pop charts and remained on the list for a full 19 weeks, selling over a million copies.

White Artists and Black Songs

When Georgia Gibbs died, historians were torn between writing a respectful In Memoriam, and an acerbic diatribe about her dubious role in the annals of music. Gibbs, along with other white artists like Patti Page and Pat Boone, had a number of enormous hits and an equal amount of success. In fact, in the 1950s Gibbs and Boone were among pop music's biggest stars. Trouble was, they had hits doing cover versions of black artists' material.

Back then, radio wouldn't touch the music of black artists, and neither would many record stores. The Jim Crow policies at media outlets and the marketing power of major record labels limited the careers of black performers unable to sell as many records as their white counterparts. The theft angered many black artists and their white executives, but they were powerless in the face of it all.

White covers of black hits were fairly common then, and black artists suffered because their originals, usually on small independent labels, got the short end of the deal. The diluted covers were usually much milder, giving consumers the black songs without the black singers.

After Gibbs had covered "Tweedle Dee," "Tra La La," and "Jim Dandy" by LaVern Baker (she also had a hit with Etta James's "Roll with Me Henry"), Baker sent Gibbs a life insurance policy naming her as the beneficiary in case something should end Baker's career. After all, "if anything happens to me," she was heard to have said, "you're out of business." On a more serious note, Baker was so infuriated after Gibbs sold a million copies of her "Tweedle Dee," she considered legal action and consulted with her congressman, who called a federal hearing. Unfortunately, even after that, no action was taken. Despite that, Baker's approach exhibited her fiery rock and roll spirit; that same spunk and wit infused her hits with greatness.

While the sanitized versions of inimitable black hits greatly outsold the originals, and the segregationist impulses of the white-led music and media industries infuriated the artists and songwriters responsible for so much of the great tunes of the 1950s, eventually, teenagers discovered the difference and became increasingly determined to hear, and to buy, the right thing.

An infuriated Baker filed suit over the whitewashing, but lost. By that time, though, her star had ascended nonetheless. Another big hit, "Bop-Ting-A-Ling" followed "Tweedle Dee," and "Play It Fair," a subsequent smash, followed that. On the latter, Sam Taylor's inspired sax break sends the tune to the next level, and serves as the perfect complement to Baker's full-throated vocal. "Bop-Ting-A-Ling" hit number three on the R&B charts, and "Play It Fair" reached number two (both in 1955). It would take a while longer, but LaVern would eventually place a song at number one.

"Bop-Ting-A-Ling" and "Tweedle Dee" were two of Baker's so-called nursery rhyme numbers, simplistic, humorous, sing-songy tracks. Other attempts at nursery rhyme tunes included "Tra-La-La" and "Fee-Fee-Fi-Fo-Fum." As a serious artist, Baker resented having to sing so many of these silly tracks. Still, their success helped ease that frustration.

"Tra-La-La" was featured in the low-budget, 1956 Alan Freed film *Rock, Rock, Rock* along with performances by the Flamingos, the Moonglows, the Teenagers, and Teddy Randazzo. Just prior to that film, Baker embarked on one of Freed's legendary rock and roll revues, this time at the Brooklyn Paramount Theater where she shared the stage with the Penguins, the Moonglows, the Clovers, B.B. King, and Danny Overbea.

ROCKIN' AND ROLLIN'

By this time, roughly the summer of 1955, music industry and fans were calling the music they heard in these shows and on their radios "rock and roll." And with Baker at the very top of the heap, she became known as one of the first queens of the original rock and roll era.

On November 20, 1955, New York DJ Dr. Jive was invited onto "The *Ed Sullivan Show* to bring 15 minutes of R&B into the nation's collective living room. He brought with him the 5 Keys, Willis "Gator Tail" Jackson's Orchestra, Bo Diddley, and LaVern Baker (singing "Tweedle Dee"). This was the kind of rarefied publicity every R&B artist yearned for and it was Baker's first taste of national exposure. This appearance with Sullivan would jump-start the most successful phase of her career: the second half of the 1950s.

During this time, Baker cemented her prestigious position as one of rock's first women. She enjoyed her second clutch of rugged hits, including "Jim Dandy" and "Jim Dandy Got Married," both of which combined the soulfulness of the blues with a hint of rock and roll backbeat, to establish her as a permanent figure in the rocky creation of pop music. They all made it into the R&B Top 10 over the next couple of years.

"Jim Dandy" hit the charts in December 1956 and didn't leave for five months. The tune, a silly Lincoln Chase composition about a man always helping girls out of trouble, featured such an infectious vocal that it went on to become Baker's first number one song. Audiences and disc jockeys loved it, and spun the record faithfully through June 1957. On the flip side of that single, "Tra-La-La" didn't chart on the R&B list at all, but did manage to hit the pop charts. The irony was not lost on Baker and her career; she relished the opportunity to cross over and did so with jazzy and gospel-fired elegance. *Cash Box Magazine* bestowed Baker with its prestigious "Best Female R&B Vocalist" award for 1956. With a lengthening string of hits, Baker, just 29, prepared to take the next step.

"Jim Dandy" was such a huge hit that songwriter Chase was commissioned to write a follow-up. LaVern's next release was "Jim Dandy Got Married," which posits that it's easier to rescue women than to be married to them. This made it to the R&B Top 10, but only climbed to number 76 on the Pop charts. Enough "Jim Dandy" was apparently enough.

Baker embarked on a tour of Australia in 1957, along with the Platters, Joe Turner, and Bill Haley and Comets. At the airport, before her flight, she half-jokingly took out an insurance policy, with none other than Georgia Gibbs named as the sole beneficiary. Gibbs, of course, had made a name for herself, and lots of money, by copying a few of Baker's tunes without permission. LaVern sent the insurance policy to Gibbs with a note saying that if anything happened to her, she wanted to make sure that Gibbs didn't lose any money from not being able to cover her records. The stunt was widely publicized and gave Baker's profile in pop a boost.

On May 11, 1957, LaVern was one of the guests on Alan Freed's second half-hour TV show. Also on the show were Ivory Joe Hunter, Charlie Gracie, and Jimmy Bowen. Later in 1957, Atlantic released "Humpty Dumpty Heart," which was featured in the Freed film *Mr. Rock and Roll*, a movie released in October 1957. Other stars in that flick included Little Richard, Frankie Lymon and Teenagers, Chuck Berry, Clyde McPhatter, the Moonglows, and Brook Benton. "Humpty Dumpty Heart" would be another Baker tune to hit the pop charts but not R&B.

In September 1958, LaVern went into a New York studio with Jerry Wexler to cut what would become her biggest hit. "I Cried a Tear," a torch song by Fred Jacobsen and Al Julia, featured Reggie Obrecht as arranger and conductor. Alongside the big band ensemble and the choir backing is saxophonist King Curtis, who plays a devastating solo. The record was rushed into stores and radio stations, where DJs and proprietors were anxiously awaiting it. It broke on the charts in December 1958, hit number six on the pop side and stayed there for five months. It finally faded in April 1959.

"I Cried a Tear" was also the first serious single that Baker had released in a few years, and her relief in singing it was palpable. She "complained long and bitterly about being saddled with such rock and roll novelty numbers as 'Tweedlee Dee' and 'Jim Dandy.' Those remain the records by which she's best remembered, which is fairly awful evidence of the puerile tastes of most of those who've written rock and roll history so far, especially since 'I Cried a Tear,' one of the great R&B torch tunes, was her biggest hit, and the only one to make the pop Top Ten" (Marsh, p. 386).

For the next few years, Baker recorded a handful of memorable songs. In 1959, there was the Neil Sedaka tune "I Waited Too Long," the gospel-based "So High, So Low," which echoed the Brenda Lee melody of "So Deep," and "Tiny Tim," a tune that made it to number 63 on the pop chart. At the end of the year, Baker resuscitated two of Kay Starr's Top Five tracks: 1954's "If You Love Me" and the 1952 chestnut "Wheel of Fortune," neither of which did nearly as well as the originals. In 1960, Baker reprised Faye Adams's 1953 hit "Shake a Hand," and charted with the quirky "Bumble Bee." The work subsequent to "I Cried a Tear" didn't fare well commercially, but it demonstrated Baker's expanded versatility. In retrospect, many of these tracks exhibit the same steamy romance and sultry summer melancholy that they did back in the late 1950s when pop fans were first hearing them.

As rock and roll gained traction in the late 1950s and the start of the 1960s, so too did Baker ramp up her approach to her singles. She teamed up with the Drifters' lead singer Ben E. King for her own track "How Often," a pairing that made perfect sense at the time, coupling two of pop's biggest stars. Why it was never released as a single, with its King Curtis sax solo, remains a mystery. "You Said" is classic early rock and roll/late vintage R&B with a searing vocal performance and a Mickey Baker guitar solo. She did another duet, this time with Jimmy Ricks, called "You're the Boss." Ricks had previously sung lead for seminal R&B vocal group the Ravens.

In December 1960, LaVern went into a New York Studio with Jerry Leiber and Mike Stoller, the songwriter/producers responsible for many late 1950s hits for the Drifters ("On Broadway"), Ben E. King ("Stand by Me"), and the Coasters ("Charlie Brown"). Leiber and Stoller collaborated with Baker on the revival-meeting rocker "Saved," a Bible-thumping, slightly humorous uptempo tune that featured an all-star cast of New York session players, including Rudy Powell and Al Sears on saxes, Bert Keyes on piano, Phil Spector on guitar, and Abie Baker on bass.

"Saved" cracked the Top 40 in the spring of 1961, reaching number 37. Not exactly the commercial result Baker's team longed for, but it signaled the singer's dedication to her gospel roots, and her effectiveness performing within that idiom. Unfortunately, "Saved" also signaled the beginning of the end of Baker's hit-making period. Throughout the 1950s she had remained one of Atlantic's most consistent producers of charting tunes. "Different times, different grooves," Baker told Armenta. "I got to Atlantic at the right time, that's all" (D. Armenta, "My Brush with Greatness: The Amazing and True Story of '50s Diva LaVern Baker,", p. 1).

But the pop music scene's overhaul began in 1961, when Motown, the Beatles, and the British Invasion took popular music by storm. A few R&B artists like Sam Cooke and Ray Charles managed to escape the ambush. But virtually every other R&B/rock act had great difficulty maintaining any kind of commercial footing. Soon, the airwaves would be saturated with the Supremes, the Miracles, the Temptations, the Beatles, and other English pop rockers.

Still, Baker notched one of her final hits in 1962. "See See Rider," a traditional song with American folk roots going back to the early 1920s. Baker certainly heard the versions of it done by blues greats like Ma Rainey and Bessie Smith, both of whom covered it famously. Also, Big Bill Broonzy and Mississippi John Hurt did as well. "See See Rider," or "Easy Rider" as it had

LaVern Baker

evolved semantically, is a blues metaphor for "sexual partner." Originally it referred to the guitar hung on the back of a traveling bluesman.

Baker turned the classic song, with its hard-spun lyrics and gritty storytelling, into a masterpiece. Produced by Atlantic's Ahmet Ertegun, it remains one of the long-running public domain tune's best interpretations. In December 1962, the song crept into the charts, climbed for eight weeks and nestled into the Top 10 on the R&B side. On the pop list it reached number 34.

There was one further hit in Baker's future, "Fly Me to the Moon," which made just a minor impression on the chart in the early part of 1965. Indeed, there was no room on the upper segments of the charts now that soul, R&B, hard rock, blues, and singer-songwriter folk were all competing for prominence. LaVern left Atlantic that year, after more than a decade with the label. She had released 33 singles, 15 of which hit the R&B charts and 19 had reached the pop charts. As music had changed, so had the needs of the label. Unfortunately, the mutual separation left both of the parties with only one leg on which to stand.

BRUNSWICK AND BEYOND

After parting ways with Atlantic, LaVern signed with Brunswick, now one of the fast-rising soul labels climbing in the long shadows cast by Motown. Brunswick had been a part of the music industry since the 1920s, originally releasing its back catalog of recordings through the U.S. arm of Decca. By the 1950s the label had started working with new repertoire and in 1957 had wised up to the fast-rising R&B scene. Jackie Wilson had become Brunswick's first popular music signing and his hit-making presence helped the label change with the times.

Baker's time on Brunswick would be short, though. Her voice, best suited to jazz and gospel-tinged rock and roll and R&B, didn't feel comfortable in the pocket of a pop song. She achieved moderate success on a few poppy soul numbers, including the notable duet with Jackie Wilson called "Think Twice" that earned a brief berth on the pop list in January 1966. A few months later, Nat Tarnopol, the Brunswick head honcho, and some other ill-advised executive at the label convinced Baker to do a spin-off of her "Jim Dandy" hit, only this time it would be a tribute to a popular television show of the day, called "Batman to the Rescue." "Wrapped, Tied and Tangled" in 1967 was a little more like it, though still not one of Baker's classiest performances. Her duet with Wilson was her only Brunswick work to ripple the waters.

Still, Baker was content with her life and career. She had managed to weather the storm of pop soul without drowning completely, even find a place for herself as a live attraction. Audiences still showed interest in watching her perform, even if it was to hear her "oldies." Her youthful, statuesque beauty and powerful voice were garnering a lot of interest from movie producers as well.

At home, she had a loving relationship with her husband, comedian Slappy White, whom she married in 1961.

ASIAN FLEW

Shortly after her single with Jackie Wilson was released in 1966, LaVern embarked on a USO tour to Vietnam to entertain the troops. While performing through rainy season storms and flooding, LaVern fell ill with pneumonia. Like the professional she was, she performed right up until her lung collapsed. She was airlifted to a decent hospital in a remote part of Thailand, where she recuperated for three months. In the meantime, the USO tour had continued without her and then returned to the States. Baker returned to the Philippines. In 1987, she regaled Armento, a navy air traffic controller and part-time DJ for Air America Radio stationed in Subic Bay, with her version of her very strange penultimate chapter.

> I didn't know what to do, who to go to. The tour was gone and I was in a strange country where telephone service was practically nonexistent. I hitched with farmers on wagons to Bangkok, where I thought I could at least find some Americans. I found some U.S. Marines there on "R and R," and they took me to the Air Force base. I'd had to slog through rice paddies in water up to my shoulders in some places to get to Bangkok, so by the time the Marines got me to the base I'd had a relapse. (Armento)

LaVern was airlifted out of Thailand back to a naval hospital in the Philippines, where she spent another four months recovering from her second case of pneumonia, along with dysentery picked up from the local water. When she was well enough to be released, LaVern was in a quandary as to what she should do next.

> I had a husband back home who had no idea where I was or even if I was alive; some of my friends from the USO troupe had told him I was deathly ill and airlifted out, but no one knew what happened after that. I tried to get a military flight back, but that was wartime, you know. As a civilian I had the lowest priority for a flight Stateside. Most of the room was taken up by poor boys who were badly injured, or had died on the field and were being shipped back to their families. I knew I had to raise some money to get a commercial flight back out of Manila, so I asked the commanding officer of Subic Bay if I could get a job. (Armento)

Baker began singing in the Subic Bay's NCO Club, earning money to eventually make her way back home. She tried desperately to contact her husband, to no avail. Communications were primitive and frustrating. "I tried and tried to call my husband, but never got through. I don't know to this day if it was the radio system or he just wasn't answering or what. It was hard to tell if you got a connection with all the background static. For all I know, he heard my voice and hung up. Probably did, the no-good &%@$#!!" (Armento).

Reportedly, White, her husband, had assumed the worst. He got a divorce and took steps to have her death made official. In her absence, and presumed death, he also managed to assume rights to all her recordings and revenue from other sources. Not only that, her agent had dropped her as a client as well. The U.S. Embassy in Manila finally found out from the States that she had officially been declared dead. She issued appeals through the embassy, but the situation felt futile each time she tried to make contact. She gave up hope.

Baker found a cheap place to live off the base in Olongapo City, where she began making friends and a modest life for herself. She grew accustomed to her little home and began enjoying her life for what it was. "I decided to quit tearing myself up and accept the fact that I wasn't going home anytime soon. I wasn't even sure I wanted to go, seeing as my own husband just up and declared I was dead so he could make some money off of my records. He never even tried to find out about where I was or if I was alive. Who wants to go back to that?" (Armento).

LaVern ended up spending over 21 years in the Philippines, from 1967 to 1988. On the day she decided it was time to go back home, she called up an agent to announce her return.

BACK IN THE USA: THE 1988 COMEBACK

Upon her arrival home, her return was announced at a mega-gala, which also happened to be Atlantic Recordings' 40th anniversary commemoration in New York City, where she performed at a celebration in Madison Square Garden. Wexler and Ertegun trumpeted her homecoming.

LaVern's career then took off in new directions. Her Rip Van Winkle–like absence saw her "sleep" through an incredible number of changes in the U.S. music scene, one that she was unable to comprehend and, in fact, contend with as a recording star. Instead she turned to Broadway, to act, a format toward which she'd been headed before taking off to go overseas.

In 1990, she slipped effortlessly into the starring role of *Black and Blue*, a character previously played by her colleague, seminal Atlantic recording artist and R&B icon Ruth Brown, in her comeback. From there, it was further success and renown, including a comeback recording, *Woke Up This Mornin'* (1992) and a song on the *Dick Tracy* soundtrack called "Slow Rollin' Mama." Her comeback effort earned credible reviews from critics, most of whom hailed her surprisingly strong singing and lithe backing music. A cadre of New York session aces, including guitarist Cornell Dupree, drummer Bernard Purdie, keyboardist Paul Griffin, and bassist Chuck Rainey, added all the right touches. The repertoire was standard and slightly predictable, but LaVern's singing was not.

Her performance and her story led her to reviving her career. In 1990, the Rhythm and Blues Foundation granted her a Career Achievement Award and in 1991 the Rock and Roll Hall of Fame inducted her as well. She put on tremendous performances at prestigious outlets like the Newport R&B Festival and the Chicago Blues Festival that put her emphatically back on the map. At the former she commented to the audience, "I was there before Buddy Holly got on the bus!"

Sadly, just as her career showed signs of renewal, she was slowed by various health problems. Baker suffered two strokes and eventually had to have both legs amputated due to complications related to diabetes. Once again LaVern was dealt a difficult hand, but she pulled through and continued to show the spunk and gutsiness she displayed years ago. Despite her illnesses she continued to perform. She worked constantly, right up until the end. On March 10, 1997, LaVern Baker's heart gave out and she passed away in a New York hospital.

> LaVern Baker believed in luck. "I've had the best and the worst of luck. I'm hoping that it's on the upswing this time." But you can't survive all that she has survived, then come back again successfully after 22 years without creating some of your own good luck. She was not the type of woman to buckle under harsh circumstances or to walk around with a chip on her shoulder about the unfairness of life. She was a realist and a pragmatist who dealt with life as it came. "I just did what I had to do. Don't we all?" (Armento)

LEGACY

Entering the scene as she did at this time, during the convergence of jazz, gospel, R&B, blues, and rockabilly, LaVern Baker was one of the first divas in modern music, and many credit her with being the first female rock and roller. A true trailblazer, she broke open the doors of the music industry for other women as well as African Americans, before America and the world had accepted the idea of "popular music." This came with great difficulty and struggle. LaVern and other musicians faced many prejudices slogging their way through the music industry.

By the mid-1950s, men were garnering most of the headlines with a new music first called R&B and then, once the white boys took hold of it, rock and roll. Black women like Etta James and LaVern Baker, schooled in gospel and the blues, were turning out ripping R&B sides. Ruth Brown's fusillade of hits, from "5-10-15 Hours" to "Wild, Wild Young Men," made the nascent Atlantic Records the House that Ruth Built. But in the 1950s, vocal expression by women was about as segregated as the nation was during those Eisenhower years. Ruth Brown never made it past the 20s on the white-dominated pop charts; Etta James's classic "Tell Mama" got to number 23. LaVern Baker, with her stately beauty and deceptively powerful voice, climbed past these accomplished singers with revolutionary work and passionate resolve.

The building success of rock and R&B was challenged every step of the way—for men, yes, but African American women especially—largely by political and religious leaders that opposed this new style of musical expression. These leaders felt that because rock and roll's roots were in the black community it deserved condemnation. The presence of suggestive lyrics, the emotional frenzy the music generated in live performance, and the fact that blacks and whites were able to freely mix at such performances confirmed that rock was nothing but immoral behavior with a strong backbeat.

LaVern Baker's determination and the considerable support of Atlantic Records—of course, they also had a lot to lose should the music be outlawed—helped her overcome many of the establishment's early hurdles. Listening to her music today, it's easy to hear the sense of courage, a tenor of defiance, in the beauty of her voice. She is unquestionably the Bessie Smith of her day, a true force of nature, who today is often overlooked in terms of her influence and impact on R&B, rock and roll, and women in popular music. To honor that critical role, the Rhythm and Blues Foundation in 1990 chose LaVern as one of the first eight recipients of a Career Achievement Award. That same year, Baker earned induction into the Rock and Roll Hall of Fame.

The success she achieved is highlighted by her long catalog of R&B and pop hits spanning the years 1955 to 1965. During that time, she exerted a massive impact on the scene. Even to this day you can hear the echoes of her singing style in the explosive 1960s work of Elvis Presley.

LaVern's sound also embraces the qualities of legends like Billie Holiday and Louis Armstrong. But her talent didn't begin and end with her a beautiful voice. Her exquisite figure and exuberant personality provided her with the perfect traits for a Hollywood starlet. Her appearances on Ed Sullivan's TV program in 1955 and in Alan Freed's rock and roll movies furthered her successful career.

Her hits—there were over 30 of them in both pop and R&B—featured Baker brashly belting out lyrics over a driving horn section, and often made as great a splash on the pop charts as they did on the R&B charts. Yet while she's best known for these novelty tunes, which were lightweight, Baker's genuine fans prefer her more serious, albeit less successful releases as being her defining work. Her 1959 cover of Leiber and Stoller's "Saved" is a vintage chestnut centered around the singer's hell-raising delivery that deserves a much higher place in the pantheon of pop than it now occupies. But because it died commercially, it hasn't endured in the idiom's annals. Even so, her body of work stands side by side the giants of popular music. In her prime, she possessed the complete package: poise, personality, presentation, and passion, along with beauty, talent, and some of the greatest music made in the early rock and roll era.

SELECTED DISCOGRAPHY

LaVern Sings Bessie Smith by Bessie Smith (Atlantic/WEA, 1990)
LaVern Baker Live in Hollywood '91 (Rhino/WEA, 1991)
Soul on Fire: The Best of LaVern Baker (Atlantic/WEA, 1991)
Woke Up This Morning (DRG, 1992)

FURTHER READING

Armenta, D. "My Brush with Greatness: The Amazing and True Story of '50s Diva LaVern Baker." Available online at www.associatedcontent.com/article/156936/a_true_story_in_honor_of_black_american.html.
Brackett, David. *The Pop, Rock, and Soul Reader: Histories and Debates*. New York: Oxford University Press, 2004.
Gaar, Gillian. *She's a Rebel: The History of Women in Rock and Roll*. New York: Seal Press, 2002.
Marsh, Dave. *The Heart of Rock and Soul: The 1001 Greatest Singles Ever Made*. New York: Da Capo Press: 1999.
Rolling Stone Editors. *The Rolling Stone Illustrated History of Rock and Roll: The Definitive History of the Most Important Artists and Their Music*. New York: Random House, 1992.

Courtesy of Photofest.

Sam Cooke

THE MAN WHO INVENTED SOUL

Of all the voices to come out of the soul era, Sam Cooke's was the most miraculous. Many call his the most important voice in the history of the soul genre. No one has ever sung with his verve and panache, with his tonal control and natural modulations. Along with Nat King Cole and Frank Sinatra, Sam Cooke possessed the most memorable, if not the *best* voice in all of popular music.

Jerry Wexler, the head of Atlantic Records, a pioneer in R&B, and an authority on the subject, called him "the best singer who ever lived, no contest." In 1964, Muhammad Ali said, "Sam Cooke is the world's greatest rock and roll singer—the greatest singer in the world" (ABC-TV Interview, February 25, 1964).

A subject of adulation from both the black and white music communities, Sam's appeal was many-faceted. Early on, as a gospel singer with the Soul Stirrers, he was nothing less than a saint, a young, striking figure with the voice of an angel and the physical presentation of a god. People called him "that pretty child." He was the first teen idol the gospel field had produced. On stage with his gospel group, he must have made quite a few of the women, and perhaps some men, have impure thoughts amid all the hymns. Certainly, after he crossed over to the secular side of music, this became a dominant part of his appeal.

"He wore me down," Aretha Franklin once said of Cooke. Rumors circulated at the time that she and Cooke had a thing going on. "Ooooh, I just loved him. That man could mess up a whole room full of women!" (Franklin and Ritz, 1999). Besides blazing a trail from the gospel to the secular, Cooke also became an important role model as a businessman in the industry. He was among the first black musicians to start his own record label and a publishing company as an extension of his career as a singer and composer. His example, followed by performers such as Ray Charles and Curtis Mayfield, would lead many away from the pitfalls of financial ruin, pitfalls that plagued so many of the more naive black artists in the 1950s and 1960s.

In the annals of modern music, Cooke's journey from gospel to pop is also among the most controversial. As an iconic gospel performer, Cooke was unequaled at the time, and had he never recorded a note of music as a solo artist his place in the gospel pantheon, high and mighty, would have been secure. With the Soul Stirrers he had become the biggest star gospel music had ever seen, and he had become an important member of the black community, with a fiercely loyal following thanks to performances like "Jesus Wash Away My Troubles" and "Pilgrim of Sorrow." Had he stayed on with the gospel idiom, he could have taken the musical style to new heights.

But his goal changed, the bar raised, as he became more and more popular with the Soul Stirrers. He wanted to reach beyond the gospel community to the general public. He wanted to sing not only to the black population but to the general population. This meant leaving his gospel roots, which, in turn, meant sacrificing everything he had accomplished to that point. Leaving gospel to go to pop was tantamount to making a deal with the devil.

This is the road Sam Cooke chose. It alienated and angered his gospel fans that considered singing for God, especially the way Cooke did it, to be a blessing. Still, lured by the idea of reaching a wider audience—and the money, girls, and notoriety that came along with it—singing pop became too powerful to resist. He began dabbling in pop soon after Elvis debuted, when he, along with the rest of the nation, began witnessing the appeal of rock and roll among American youths. But he did so delicately at first, recording under a different name so as to not disturb what he had already accomplished in gospel. But even this small toe in the water got Cooke dismissed from the Soul Stirrers and abandoned by his record label.

But Cooke turned gospel's loss into his advantage, and he began using his real name as a performer. One of his first sessions on the pop side, "You Send Me," produced by famed producer/A&R man Robert "Bumps" Blackwell and issued on the tiny Keen Records label, became one of the most famous and popular singles of the 1950s, hitting the top of the pop and R&B charts. The song has lived on as vintage Cooke, fusing elements of gospel, pop, and soul in such a way that had never been heard before. It fast became Cooke's signature sound, and a pioneering sound in pop music for the next 10 years.

Cooke also served his black community in the struggle over civil rights, a movement that paralleled his own rise as a star. When he died in 1964, black America plunged into despair. He had been a ray of light, a symbol of hope, an emblem of equality and racial balance. In fact, so outraged were his fans that his death provoked accusations of a conspiracy. To this day, because his murder has never been solved with certainty, the gospel community believes its prodigal son was killed by the Mafia. Even though it had never been proven that Cooke had Mafia ties, he did lapse into his share of vices as a rich pop star and celebrity. His taste for women, one of whom was accused of his murder, was not surprising or a secret. He had also grown quick-tempered and egotistical, so it would be no surprise either that his disposition, formerly so genial, upset many people.

Having died early in his life and with so much career left ahead of him, the real tragedy of his passing is that he never truly got to make the music he should have. Having spent his first five years in gospel, he was just beginning to find his footing in the R&B and soul music of the 1960s when he died. Before that, as a mainstream pop artist, he was constantly obliged to customize his music to a white pop audience, the one with all the money. But in 1963, a glimpse at what might have been came in the form of a recorded live date at the Harlem Square Club. Cooke proves that underneath the saccharine pop he tailored to radio, he could sing real, gritty soul as well as anyone.

Experts and fans alike imagine that he would have arrived at that point had he stayed his current course. Unfortunately, like so many others in pop who were snuffed out too soon, the world is only left with a guess.

> The story of Sam Cooke is about music, religion, romance, race, politics, and history. But most of all it is a story about longing—Sam's longing for the most stirring sound, the perfect song, the most impassioned response, as well as his longing for wealth, fame, and a better life. It is a story about one half of a divided nation longing for freedom, equality, opportunity and respect, and how Sam used his celebrity to help ensure that a change was indeed gonna come. (Michael Hill, liner notes, *Sam Cooke: The Man Who Invented Soul*, RCA/BMG, 2000, p. 3).

THE EARLY YEARS

Sam Cook was born on January 22, 1931, in the blues hot bed of Clarksdale, Mississippi, one of eight children of a Baptist minister, Charles Cook, and his wife, Annie May. His father worked as a servant in a Victorian mansion owned by a wealthy white family. On the weekends, when he wasn't working at this job, Cook was a Baptist preacher working for the Lord.

Early on, Sam showed considerable musical promise. In the backyard of his family home in Clarksdale, Sam would put sticks into the ground from a pecan tree and sing to them, as if they were his fans. Practicing, he'd tell those who'd snicker at him, practicing for his future fans.

Eventually, the Great Depression wiped out his employers and the Cooks were forced to move north to Chicago as part of the parade of black men seeking work in the city's stockyards. The family settled in Bronzeville on the city's South Side. Charles Cook found a church nearby and quickly became a major spiritual figure in the area. At the same time, four of his enthusiastic kids formed a gospel group to sing at local churches. In the group, called the Singing Children, Sam deferred to his older siblings, Charles and Mary, relegated to harmonizing.

At the time in Chicago, the gospel scene had exploded. Mahalia Jackson and Thomas Dorsey among many others had made an impact on the national scene and the Cook kids were hooked on the style. When the Singing Children decided not to continue on, Sam latched onto a gospel quartet that had formed on a neighborhood street corner, called the Teenage Highway QCs. Like many young gospel groups, they sang beautifully, dressed nattily, and had their eye on popular appeal, especially with the ladies.

Even young gospel singers like Sam were aware of what was happening in the pop scene. He favored singing groups like the Ink Spots, an influence that would crop up in his later work as a pop artist. The QCs were ambitious; they performed in churches and at religious gatherings and soon became a popular outfit in Chicago's spiritual community. They asked a member of the Soul Stirrers at the time, R.B. Robinson, to be their musical trainer, which he did. Sam learned the technique quickly and his tutelage from Robinson also put him on the Soul Stirrers' radar—a shrewd move.

In 1948, the group hired a manager and began reaching outside of Chicago. They made some ripples in Detroit, where they met the Reverend C.L. Franklin, Aretha's father, and turned a few heads in Memphis as well. But despite young Sam Cook's dazzling affect on the ladies he sang to as lead singer of his group, they returned home without a record deal. About this time, Sam started writing his own music, which added another facet to his understanding of music.

THE SOUL STIRRERS

It didn't take long for the Soul Stirrers' karma to come back to Sam. In 1950, after the QCs had problems making ends meet, the group extended an invitation to Sam to replace Rebert Harris. Harris, it should be noted, exited the group because he had trouble abiding by the moral aspects of singing gospel. Sam, now 20, jumped at the chance to join.

The Soul Stirrers had formed in Texas back in the 1920s and had developed an unparalleled heritage as a gospel group. During that time they had developed and polished a sublime formula, marked by glittering harmonies, heartfelt, spiritual singing, and a powerful performance ethic.

It was in this tightly knit group that Sam Cook began to make a name for himself. But it wouldn't be easy. It began with spending countless weeks and months on the road. Ten months of every year were spent traveling, the quintet wedged into a single car and subsisting on bologna sandwiches.

Cook began discovering his natural vocal technique. He avoided the stereotypical image of the pained, deep-feeling man often found singing lead in many gospel groups. Rather he chose to sing with smoother, more accessible edges. He'd still channel the sounds of Jesus, but he also drew fans in with his elegance and composure. Even early on, he's credited with breaking the established mode of gospel lead men, and he quickly began building a reputation of his own.

It took a while for Soul Stirrer fans to accept Cook as Harris's successor. Harris was legend in gospel and so any new lead presence would be an acquired taste. But Sam's presence also changed the complexion of the audience at Soul Stirrers shows. Where in the past young girls often spent the time giggling near the back of the halls, they were now pushing their way up front to get a better look at Sam. He sure looked striking in that crisp white suit.

"He went out there and started singing, and [people] would not believe his voice," said Bobby Womack, a singer who had cut some sides with Sam in the 1960s.

> And in the midst of the show, he would comb his hair and look in the mirror at himself, which was in very bad taste in a church. But that's the kind of guy he was. Matter of fact, when he came to sing pop, he became a little more conservative than when he sang gospel. But I could not believe it. Here's a guy who had a song called "Wonderful'—how his God is wonderful. And he was combing his hair and singing, and chicks were screaming and trying to show their legs and stuff. It was like a rock and roll show. (Hill, p. 7)

Art Rupe, the head of the Soul Stirrers label, Specialty, didn't care much for Sam. He preferred Harris because Harris had made Rupe money. He sold records. One year after the Stirrers cut the hit "By and By," they showed up in his studio not with lead singer Harris, but with a pretty-boy upstart. Rupe didn't care much for taking chances, but he entered the studio and put young Sam to the test. Rupe was intent on protecting his investment, the Soul Stirrers recordings, and he wanted to make sure this wouldn't be a gamble he'd regret.

Art Rupe and Specialty Records

In 1945, Art Rupe wanted to start a record business. So he took $200 and went down to Central Avenue in the ghetto of Los Angeles to buy what were then called "race records." When he took them home, he analyzed each one to determine why some were hits and others weren't. Out of this he established a set of rules or principles that he was to use in making records of own. (For example, he noticed many successful records had the word "boogie" in the title.) He also discovered that jukebox operators were the biggest customers for these race records and they acted as wholesalers for small independent companies.

Next, Rupe sought out artists that fit his profile, searching the club scene for prospects. A band called the Sepia Tones released "Boogie #1," the debut release on his Juke Box label. It sold 70,000 copies and enabled him to record others, including Marion Abernathy aka "the Blues Woman," Roosevelt Sykes aka "the Blues Man," and Roy Milton and His Solid Senders.

Encouraged by Jules Bihari of R.P.M. Records, later of Modern, Rupe started a new label, Specialty, after enduring a bad partnership. Rupe persuaded Milton to come with him to Specialty and right away he became a huge success. Rupe's recollection of the black churches of his youth and the gospel music he loved helped him negotiate contracts with gospel greats such as the Soul Stirrers, the Swan Silvertones, and the Chosen Gospel Singers. He also brought in secular artists like Guitar Slim, Don and Dewey, and his biggest star, Little Richard. While on a talent hunt in New Orleans he discovered 17-year-old Lloyd Price. In Specialty's first recording session in New Orleans Rupe produced Price singing "Lawdy Miss Clawdy" using Dave Bartholomew's band featuring Fats Domino.

From his modest beginnings, Rupe would go on to record some of popular music's most seminal sounds, from Little Richard's "Tutti Frutti" and "Good Golly Miss Molly" to Sam Cooke's "I'll Come Running Back to You." Cooke left the label soon after his crossover pop success.

Over time, Specialty's fortunes rose and fell. The loss of Little Richard, the breakup of Rupe's marriage, and frustration of losing Cooke rankled Rupe and he lost interest in the record business. He shuttered Specialty and pursued his oil and land interests. That is, until he received a call from Little Richard in 1964. Richard, who had only recorded gospel music since leaving Specialty, was considering recording secular music again. As a side note, Richard had been touring Europe with four British musicians who excited him and wondered if

Sam Cooke

Rupe was interested in the group. Rupe said no to the Brits, but he was definitely interested in recording Richard if he was ready to come back. That group her overlooked ended up making history: they were called the Beatles.

Usually a session consisted of four songs, eight at the most. This one stretched to 11, with Rupe emphasizing traditional material. At first, Cook, who'd never made a record before, didn't even know where to stand in relation to the microphone. Despite the fact that Sam hit all the right notes, Rupe doubted his ability to sing with passion, a critical element, of course, in gospel. When the Stirrers left those sessions, Rupe withheld his judgment of Cook, preferring him to get seasoned on the road, which he did, for another 10 months in 1951.

A year later, the Stirrers returned to Rupe's studio, and this time Rupe had insisted on a few changes. He added drums to the group's songs, anathema at the time, because he had spent some time in New Orleans and Memphis and had had his ear to the ground. Over the next couple of sessions, the Stirrers' gospel sound becomes gradually more pop-friendly. This played directly into Cook's strength, so he wound up singing much more lead as early as two years into his tenure with the group. This also relegated the other four Stirrers to background vocal roles. Still, Rupe began to understand how well the point/counterpoint of Cook and the rest of the singers meshed together.

In 1953, Rupe added electric guitar to the drums, bass, piano, and organ mix. The growth at first sounded rocky, but the sound was without a doubt in transition. Cook, up front in the mix, was developing a singing technique that would stay with him for the rest of his career: the famous "woah-ooh-oh-oh" yodel, a vocal modulation that breaks into pieces and then reassembles beautifully. This falsetto embellishment, often called "curlicues," became the young Cook's trademark. When the group recognized this quirky development, and the effect it had on their audiences, they began to feature opportunities to have him soar. Cook was beginning to understand the power he possessed as a singer and performer.

Over the next couple of years with the Soul Stirrers, Sam grew exponentially as a singer. Each gig built on the last, and he gained precious experience experimenting with his vocal technique, loosening up and allowing the natural flourish of his voice take over. Reflecting this transformation, Cook's lead earned greater emphasis and more confidence.

In July 1955, Rupe sent Bumps Blackwell to a gospel show in Los Angeles to record the program, which included the Soul Stirrers. Blackwell witnessed firsthand Cook's sex appeal and marveled at how such a gifted performer exuding such sensuality could do so in such a spiritual environment. He also wondered how Cook could still be so accepted within that environment despite the rumors that he had, by the age of 23, already fathered two children out of wedlock.

In 1956, Sam saved his best performances as a Soul Stirrer for last. On the sessions recorded for Specialty early that year, Sam let it fly on masterpieces such as "Jesus Wash Away My Troubles," "Touch the Hem of His Garment," the poppy love song "Wonderful," and the chilling "Pilgrim of Sorrow." He tackled this work with precision and elegance, and laid down some of the best lead vocals gospel had ever heard. "Were You There," one of his last gospel performances in the studio, sounded as if he knew he'd be crossing the great divide to pop, and he wanted to give it one final, memorable send-off. His desperation and passion are palpable, his performance unparalleled.

In fact, Sam Cook must have known he was about to cross over. Egging him on was none other than Blackwell, who had identified Cook's appeal, and pushed him to do it. Blackwell at the time was also working with another gospel/secular performer, Little Richard.

"Bumps said I had the voice," said Cook at the time, "the confidence and the equipment to work as a single [sic] and that I ought to give it a try. Making a living was good enough, but what's wrong with doing better than that?"

Bumps also noted that there was a void in the pop music landscape, a gaping hole aching to be filled by an artist who could sing with the passion of gospel and the precision of pop, a style of music that was evolving with alacrity. He knew the landscape of pop and rock music intimately. One month after the show in Los Angeles, Bumps traveled to New Orleans to record a gospel shouter named Little Richard and his song "Tutti Frutti." At the same time, a white boy out of Memphis named Elvis Presley was beginning to make waves at Sun Studio with Sam Phillips. Clearly, the music scene, the entire topography of popular music, was changing, and Blackwell knew that Cook would be a part of that change. There was just something extraordinary about him. With his stunning looks and angelic voice, Blackwell knew he had lots to offer. He just had to lure him from the sacred to the secular. It just took a little cajoling.

Since seeing him in the summer of 1955, Blackwell had been nudging Cook to try his hand at secular material, quietly, though, when no one else was listening.

EX-COMMUNICATION

Finally, in the winter of 1955, there was a breakthrough. Sam sent Bumps six songs on tape featuring just him playing his guitar. Among the tracks were "I'll Come Running Back to You," and the earliest version of "You Send Me." Encouraged, Bumps decided to press Cook to do a recording session with him in New Orleans the next year. But first, Sam wrote to Art Rupe for permission: "'A friend I've been knowing for quite a while asked me if I would consider recording some popular ballads ... ' Sam has 'one of the major recording companies' interested and material ready," (Daniel Wolff, liner notes, *Sam Cooke with the Soul Stirrers*, Specialty Records, 2002, p. 28).

Cook recorded in New Orleans in December 1956 under the name Dale Cook, so as to protect his gospel identity. "That was so the religious people didn't frown on him, but come on—they knew the sound," said Lou Rawls. "How were you going to get around that?" (Hill, p. 9).

"Lovable," one of the songs they cut, is a reworking of the gospel tune "Wonderful" with a pronoun switch from the sacred "He" to the much more secular "she." On the tunes, Cook is obviously searching for a pop style. But his hesitation is not surprising, for he's essentially betraying not only the Soul Stirrers, but his entire spiritual foundation. The conflict disturbs his performance, and he sounds tentative, unsure, doubting.

After his New Orleans studio date, he hurried to the Apollo Theater for a Stirrers Christmas performance. The group skipped their annual February studio session in 1957, instead opting to hit one in April, a studio date that would be their last. Ironically, after he recorded it in New Orleans, no one gave "You Send Me" a second thought—despite its stripped-down elegance. It was passed off as merely fluff. But Blackwell knew when something was worthwhile.

Blackwell invited Sam into the studio again in June 1957, in order to improve on their first material, he and Sam hit a studio in Los Angeles with guitarist Cliff White, drummer Earl Palmer, and arranger Rene Hall, to cut not the songs Cook had sent him but, oddly, a pop arrangement of George Gershwin's "Summertime" he felt certain would be a hit. As an incentive, they recorded a couple of Cook's tunes as well, including "You Send Me" and "I'll Come Running Back to You." Through the grapevine, Art Rupe heard what Bumps and Sam were doing, covering Gershwin, and he lost his temper. "Why on earth would the kids dig opera and all that stuff?" he inquired of Blackwell. Specialty had been recording early rock and roll avatars and R&B icons. Why would Bumps serve up a warmed-over cover of an old chestnut? Miffed, he fired Blackwell.

Amazingly, the session continued, perhaps because no one was altogether sure if Rupe was serious" (Barney Hoskyns, "The Soul Stirrer," *Mojo*, January 1995).

Blackwell bought his contract out from Specialty to focus on Cook. He waived all future royalties from his previous Specialty productions, asked for $1,500, and took Sam with him, along with two songs: "Summertime" and "You Send Me." Blackwell's next stop was an upstart label called Keen Records. They promptly hired him as their A&R man, and they liked the sound of "You Send Me." The secular journey of Sam Cook had begun.

"Crossing over in the arena of gospel meant leaving the world of spirit for the world of the flesh, rejecting the joys of the sacred for the allure of the secular sound, the potential profits of pop" (Hill, p. 7).

Of course, there are many similarities between gospel and R&B. Their rhythms are intertwined, the roots of each, especially qualities like emotion and passion, are shared. In many cases, R&B hits were gospel hymns with a few syllables changed. Ray Charles's "This Little Girl of Mine," is a good example. The gospel version had the word "light" in place of "girl." Despite those similarities though, few gospel performers dared cross the line over to pop. Jesus was watching over them, and to turn one's back on gospel meant to do so not only to the audience, but to Him as well.

The Soul Stirrers were the most popular gospel group in the country, and so all eyes were on Sam, their lead singer. Everyone who knew gospel, knew Sam Cooke. Despite that, despite the risk of losing everything he had worked toward, something was compelling Sam to convert. His gospel days were numbered. Bumps Blackwell would see to that.

Sam spent the summer of 1957 living in Blackwell's apartment, while the Keen label spent their time pushing the "Summertime"/"You Send Me" single. By September it was clear that the B-side was the side everyone wanted to hear. The record, essentially the debut release by Sam Cooke—he and Blackwell chose to tack an "e" onto his surname—wound up selling 80,000 copies in Los Angeles alone, on its way to selling over one and a half million nationwide. It hit number one on the pop chart, despite being covered by a white female singer, Teresa Brewer. Its simplicity and Sam's purposeful, drilled-in repetition stuck to the lips and imaginations of millions.

Overnight, with a single song, Sam Cooke became a secular superstar, with audiences consisting of black and white, men and women, young and old. American radio ate it up and he soon received invites to all the prominent TV programs, including *American Bandstand.*

The assault on Sam's business had also begun. A white agent at William Morris convinced Sam that he'd be a natural talent for white audiences, and that, he said, he could move Cooke into a non-black market. Meanwhile, Art Rupe, kicking himself for letting Sam go so cheaply to Blackwell, rushed out "I'll Come Running Back to You" in an attempt to cash in.

Encouraged by this early success, Blackwell and Cooke rushed into the studio and cut more sides, including the prototype slow dance "You Were Made for Me," "Lonely Island," and "Love You Most of All." These were tuneful songs, pure and simple. They weren't intricately arranged pieces with verse-bridge-chorus structuring. Rather they hinged on pure, transcendent melody. For his part, Sam knew how to construct these songs, and not just from a vocal perspective. He understood what made a great song, a solid groove, and even though he didn't play an instrument beyond rudimentary guitar, he knew how a song flowed and he heard the arrangements and instrumentation in his head.

Sam also seemed to savor each word he sang, and his idiosyncratic vocal mannerisms—some co-opted from his Soul Stirrers stylings and some, like the way he sang "ooh" right before launching into a lyric, created off the cuff—became the very quirks that made his voice so irresistible. And what made him so impressive in the studio was his preparation. He'd go in completely prepared, having worked out his parts beforehand so as not to waste any time. He reveled in his studio freedom, and enjoyed the success that came because of it.

Another aspect that made this time so enjoyable was that he discovered his gospel colleagues had not, as he expected, turned their backs on Sam. He reconnected with his Soul Stirrer bandmates and would be loyal to them however and whenever he could. Senior member Roy Crain would eventually become Sam's road manager, and he'd often supply the group with tour slots, song material, and resources. Eventually, when Sam opened his own recording label, he offered them a contract.

Nor did his fans turn their backs on him. Perhaps this was because Sam chose not to perform risqué and material otherwise at odds with his gospel experience. Rather, songs like "You Send Me" were polite, sweet, and smooth, and not all that different in sentiment than what he was doing with the Soul Stirrers. This allowed him to bring most, if not all, of the enthusiasm he'd generated with his previous group into his new pop project.

Sam's effective crossover proved unexpected and welcome. But not just for Sam. Many other gospel performers had been watching Sam's progress, wondering if they too should attempt the same leap. Aretha Franklin, Lou Rawls, Patti LaBelle, and Gladys Knight, for example, were all gospel singers eyeing the same crossover. And after Sam Cooke proved it could be done, and justified the result, they too all made the same successful transition.

BREAK ON THROUGH

Sam toured both the Chitlin' Circuit, where he knocked audiences dead nightly with his combination of smooth material and soulful singing, and the more sophisticated supper club touring stops, where he had trouble connecting with his audiences. In fact, you couldn't choose two more disparate crowds. The former yearned for soul and passion, while the latter preferred not to be disturbed while eating, especially by a young person intent on lifting them up and getting them dancing.

The Chitlin' Circuit shows, largely segregated, were a smash. Robert Palmer, a white critic and author, wrote about a Cooke show he sneaked into down in Little Rock in 1960.

> Halfway through the opening number he shed his tuxedo jacket. Next came the tie. Loosening his collar, singing like God's favorite angel, Cooke slowly, teasingly, peeled off his formal white gloves. . . . One landed on my table, and half a dozen women, each the size of a football linebacker, landed on top of me. Down I went, followed by the table, the chairs, and the women, who fought for the glove tooth and nail while I squirmed on the bottom of the pileup. . . . Cooke had somehow remained dapper through it all, made a graceful exit, leaving the hall in pandemonium. (Robert Palmer, *Rock & Roll: An Unruly History*, New York: Crown, 1995)

Singing to segregated audiences bothered Cooke. The Jim Crow laws that permeated Southern culture made it difficult for African Americans to find hotels, restaurants, and even bathroom facilities as they made their way across the region. The restrictions humiliated Sam as well as the many other quality artists that were marching around the South on the package tours that crisscrossed the country.

Though chafed, Sam took the high road more often than not. Despite the threats made by groups like the Ku Klux Klan and the restrictions inherent with the Jim Crow laws, Cooke often refrained, at least in public, from showing much anger. He sang about it, often in veiled terms, except for the obvious references like his hit "Chain Gang."

In some cities, depending on the artist, a venue would be split into two halves with the stage in the middle. On one side there would be whites, on the other blacks, and the performer would have to choose whom to sing to. Sam led the movement, as a black artist, to sing to his black audiences. Many other R&B and soul artists followed his lead.

Because Sam appealed to both black and white audiences, he often found himself in difficult circumstances. White girls were frenzied at his gigs as well, and this prompted insecurity with police and other military presences, to make sure Sam didn't make any untoward moves on a girl not of his color.

"I have always detested people of any color, religion, or nationality, who have lacked courage to stand up and be counted. As a Negro I have—even in the days before I began to achieve some sort of recognition as a performer—refused jobs which I consider debasing or degrading" he said (Peter Guralnick, *Dream Boogie*, New York: Little, Brown, 2005, p. 336).

LIFE AND LOVES

Sam's first girlfriend, Barbara Campbell, knew what she was dealing with when she got acquainted with Sam. She knew of Sam's magnetic attraction to women around the time he began singing lead for the Soul Stirrers, but that didn't prevent her from hanging around. Sam made promises to Barbara, just enough of them to keep her within arm's reach. In the summer of 1952, after they had been seeing each other casually for a few years, Barbara got pregnant. Sam still lived at home with his parents, and Barbara lived at hers, and so her condition became problematic.

At the same time, Barbara wasn't the only entanglement Sam had to worry about. A girl he met in Cleveland, Marine Somerville, also became pregnant with his child, and, as the story goes, another girl, this one in Chicago, informed him of *her* pregnancy, also with his baby. He was all of 21.

Sam began to understand that the allure he held on stage, his ability to captivate audiences, could also transfer to his personal life. Girls fell in love with him rather easily, he realized. It made him feel powerful, potent. It also completely tangled up his personal affairs.

On tour in Fresno, Sam met Dolores "Dee Dee" Mohawk through a friend, Lloyd Price. She was a Texas girl who grew up, as Sam did, in the Holiness Church, and they spent two weeks together. During that time, Sam, 22 at the time, fell in love. Meanwhile, Marine was having Sam's first baby, Denise, and two days later Barbara was having a girl, Linda Marie Campbell.

Sam's relationship with Dee Dee deepened quickly, and the development surprised everyone, including Sam's own family. His group knew well that Sam enjoyed his share of the pleasures of the flesh, sometimes more than one "flesh" at a time. He and his friends at the time could choose from a group of girls. So when Sam and Dee Dee announced their intentions to get married, few could have admitted that they expected such news. Sam's family felt that Dee Dee, who already had a son of her own, had simply reeled in a big catch; she wasn't good enough for their son and they didn't bother attending the wedding. Barbara Campbell was crushed. She loved Sam, and had fond memories of their time together.

But the relationship teetered recklessly, a casualty of Sam's own "sinful world" and Dee Dee's jealousy. In 1958, the turbulence came to a head and the two admitted they'd married too early. They divorced that same year. Months later, Dee Dee, while driving around her hometown of Fresno, on anti-depressants and drinking, crashed her car and died.

Even prior to his divorce from Dee Dee, Sam had rekindled his relationship with Barbara. She had been living with Fred "Diddy" Dennis, a childhood friend of the Cooks and something of an enterprising street-smart businessman. Barbara never really loved Dennis, but married him in part to make Sam jealous. The ploy worked. Sam began looking into Barbara's situation. She already had Linda, his child, though neither told the young girl who the father was.

At the time Sam's interest in her began peaking, she became pregnant with Diddy's child. One day, Sam ran into a friend of Barbara's, who inquired, now that he was free again, if he was still interested in giving a relationship a second try. He told her he'd take Barbara back with his little girl, Linda. But not if that package came with Diddy's child as well. Linda had an abortion and went to visit him again.

They were married in October 1959. Sam dearly wanted to be with his daughter, and Barbara was a lovely, down-to-earth girl. Still, in the back of Barbara's mind all the time rested the fact that Sam married her because he wanted to be closer to his daughter. She could tell because the marriage lacked intimacy. Who knew what was happening with Sam while he toured? Not Barbara, but she knew his presence remained detached at home. He spent lots of time reading to Linda, drawing pictures for her, and playing her music. But Barbara felt Sam arranged this domestic tableau to be near Linda, and she was right. She coped with this conflict by smoking marijuana.

In December 1961, she gave birth to Sam's son, Vincent Lance Cooke. Sam shared the good news with everyone, but he spent little time with the baby and Barbara to enjoy the occasion. He had been in the studio immediately before the birth and returned immediately after.

But Sam was a different person at home than he was in his world of music. He liked lounging in his silk pajamas, having a cigarette, and sipping on a scotch. He retreated into his mind at home, often working out songs on his acoustic guitar, sketching out lyric ideas, or flipping through books. Barbara may as well have not been there. In fact, Sam only truly bonded with Linda. He failed to cultivate much of a relationship with Vincent as he grew older, or with Tracey, born less than a year after Vincent. Throughout this period of his life, when fatherhood should have played a significant role, Sam would spend lots of time out with his friends, something he prohibited Barbara from doing. In fact, he despised it when she invited her friends to the house.

Sam never remained faithful to any of his wives or girlfriends. Like others in his situation, he had trouble resisting temptation. He didn't discriminate between assignations either. White, black, twins, married, it didn't matter. One night, he even took the wife of one of his tourmates in a hotel bathroom for a quick interlude, while he was in the room. When it came to women on the road, Sam was surrounded, and he had no scruples.

He had a meaningful affair with Zelda Sands, an executive at Sam's SAR label. Sands handled most of SAR's administrative odds and ends, the nuts and bolts of running the label, and it was widely believed they were sexually involved.

One day, she received a call from Sam and Barbara to come to Chicago from her office in Los Angeles; they just wanted to get together with her and talk about things. Confused, Zelda hopped a plane and met with them in a hotel room. Barbara confronted Zelda directly about her interest in Sam, who sat by quietly.

But the feud didn't end there. Barbara traveled back to Los Angeles and marched Zelda out of the SAR office at gunpoint. She returned only to gather her things. Sam didn't care to acknowledge what Barbara had done, and so Zelda left SAR. But she also took Mel Carter, the label's only promising star, with her as her management client.

BUSINESS AS USUAL

Sam's first foray into the business side of music came when he and Pilgrim Traveler J.W. Alexander set up a publishing company called KAGS Music. Alexander, a gospel singer and longtime friend of Sam's, had initiated the idea. But for some time Sam had demonstrated a serious interest in controlling his own career and money. In 1959, he and Alexander followed their instincts as

Sam Cooke

music men and formed a label, SAR Records, using the initials of himself, Alexander, and his new road manager, former Soul Stirrer S.R. Crain. His first single? The Soul Stirrers' "Stand by Me Father."

Over the first few years of SAR, Sam released albums by Johnnie Taylor (a former Soul Stirrer), Bobby Womack, and others. In 1963, he set up another label, called Derby, to showcase some harder-edged soul music, including an up-and-coming piano player named Billy Preston.

Ironically, as he was putting his own roster of artists together, Sam's label, Keen, was coming apart at the seams. It certainly wasn't built for the kind of mega-artist Sam had become. "You Send Me" happened to be its inaugural release, so while it enjoyed the success, an infrastructure wasn't in place to handle all of its new Cooke-related responsibilities. Cooke's squabbles with Keen owners increased as they debated issues like recording budgets and tour support.

Seeing this turmoil, the music industry responded. Many labels made appeals for Sam's business. Atlantic Records was one of the first to make an offer. Ahmet Ertegun and Jerry Wexler, the two executives behind the label's early success, wanted to sign Cooke badly. Had they (and not RCA) signed him, Sam Cooke's career would arguably have been entirely different. Wexler's hard-core R&B roots would have steered him more in the direction of real R&B. Instead, Sam chose RCA, mainly because they had helped boost Elvis Presley's career, the man who invented rock and roll. When RCA got their hands on Sam, they, in turn, billed him as "the man who invented soul."

RCA'S HUGO AND LUIGI

> If only he'd signed with Ahmet Ertegun and Jerry Wexler and spared the world the saccharine, string-saturated atrocities he was to record with RCA's hotshot duo Hugo Peretti and Luigi Creatore. All Sam should really have needed to know about these Italian cousins was that they were the perpetrators of "Dance with Me Henry," the white Georgia Gibbs' soulless bowdlerizing of Etta James's lubricious classic "Wallflower." They may have been magnificent scammers . . . but they had even less taste than all the other scammers on the pop scene at the turn of the decade. (Hoskyns)

Hindsight is always 20/20. Many of today's critics feel that when looking back at the entire life's work of Sam Cooke, he made his best music outside "the bowdlerization" of Italian arrangers Hugo Peretti and Luigi Creatore. But that's only because we can now hear Cooke classics like *Live at the Harlem Square Club*, a recording from a 1963 date that wasn't released until the mid-1980s. We can distinguish now between Cooke's sedate soul and his passionate R&B, and compare one to the other and make a firm judgment about which is "better" or which is more enduring.

Still, it's not fair to rewrite history. Who's to say what would have happened to Cooke's career had he not encountered the Italian team? Perhaps he would have been unable to string hits together and, like many of his contemporaries, he would have fallen off the map.

Sam Cooke first met Hugo and Luigi (that was the way they were billed professionally) when he signed to RCA. The first cousins had started out doing children's music and then progressed to become chief figures in the pop music department at Mercury Records in 1954. They made a name for themselves creating rather bland pop hits marked by melodic simplicity, and over five or so years they notched a consistent track record of success, with hits by Sarah Vaughan and Georgia Gibbs. They often sanitized R&B songs and recruited white artists to perform them, mainly because commercial radio wouldn't touch black R&B acts.

In the late 1950s they began work for RCA, with hefty salaries and big offices. Together, they selected a handful of songs, including songwriter Jeff Barry's early composition "Teenage Sonata." But the arrangement and performance of the song failed in nearly every way, so they let it drop. But the session wasn't a total wash. Hugo and Luigi had encouraged Sam to bring some of his own material into the studio. One of those songs was "Chain Gang."

The tune, inspired by a specific scene Sam had encountered on one of his drives through the South, was nothing like the experience of the scene itself. It felt placid, serene, the way Sam and his arrangers prepped it, quite contrary to the blood and sweat often coming from prisoners on a chain gang. But his vocal track came out so beautifully, his enunciation so precise, charm suffused the entire arrangement. Unfortunately, they abandoned the session before finishing the production. "Chain Gang" would have to wait.

During this initial period with RCA, Sam kept a busy schedule. There were tours and recording sessions, of course, but also numerous responsibilities for his SAR imprint. The commitments kept him moving. His work with Hugo and Luigi progressed into theme-oriented albums like *Cooke's Tour*, a sort of international-themed platter consisting of rather dated material. "Teenage Sonata" failed to make impact on the charts, but another Cooke artifact did. Over at Keen, Sam's former label, owner John Siamas discovered a demo Sam had made with Herb Alpert of "Wonderful World." That song shot up the charts, soaring right past "Teenage Sonata." Hugo and Luigi began feeling the heat.

It took a while for Sam to assert himself at RCA. Due partly to his bland work with the Italians and some bad luck, he had trouble proving his consistency. But in the second half of 1961 through the summer of 1962, Sam had begun to hit his stride as one of RCA's principal artists and revenue generators. In that time he had three Top 20 pop hits ("Cupid," "Twistin' the Night Away," and "Bring It on Home to Me"/"Havin' a Party.") He also charted an album during that time, also called *Twistin' the Night Away*. Also about this time, Sam cut some blues sides with big band accompaniment and called it *My Kind of Blues*. He enjoyed the experience so much that he delved even deeper into the blues on his next album, *Night Beat*, an album billed as his "after hours masterpiece."

In contrast to *Blues*, *Night Beat* spotlighted Sam fronting a small combo with Billy Preston on organ, Ray Johnson on piano, and Hal Blaine on drums. The record, a sort of after hours, late-night, moody concept album, features Sam in impressive voice on an array of gospel-tinged blues covers, from "Mean Old World" and "Little Red Rooster," later covered also by the Stones, to "Fool's Paradise." It is one of Cooke's most enduring overall works.

About the same time, Sam recorded *Live at the Harlem Square Club*, a brilliant work of soul and one of Sam's best recordings. But it wasn't released for over 20 years. RCA simply didn't know what to do it with it. The rawness of the tapes didn't jibe with Sam's prevailing polish, and neither did it appeal to the ears of anyone at the label. It was shelved until the mid-1980s and has since become known as one of the truest measures of Cooke's ability and a glimpse into the kind of electrifying power he possessed as a performer.

1963

During a run at the State Theater in Philadelphia in the spring of 1963, Sam met 31-year-old Allen Klein, a feisty New York City accountant. Klein had made a reputation for himself, and entered music history, by famously auditing Atlantic Records on behalf of many of their biggest performers who'd felt they had not been compensated adequately by their label. He'd also go on to work with the Stones and the Beatles as well.

Sam knew of Klein's reputation in the music business and got the idea that he could make use of his assistance. During his State Theater run, Klein was so mesmerized by Cooke's performance he attended the show every night for a week. Cooke got wind of Klein's enthusiasm and took the opportunity to introduce himself after one of his shows. He approached Klein and proceeded to go off on a gentle diatribe about how badly his label had been treating him.

"Allen Klein was a right kind of guy, a sort of Robin Hood figure with a slide rule who simply by virtue of his disconcerting ability to shut out everything but the problem at hand could make powerful record industry figures knuckle under" (Guralnick, p. 464).

Klein took a look at Cooke's situation and discovered he was heavily in debt. On Sam's behalf this time, he audited RCA's books, found $110,000 in unpaid royalties, and ended up renegotiating Sam's RCA contract to the tune of $450,000 spread over four years. He had also helped Sam set up Tracey Records, which gave him control of his material. It was the freedom and autonomy he wanted as an artist, and Klein helped him achieve it.

In the fall of 1963, Klein approached Cooke with a check from RCA, which included all his unpaid royalties. Cooke in turn, wrote Klein a check for 25 percent of it as a result of his services. Cooke trusted Klein and didn't require a contract or a receipt. And then he asked Klein to manage him.

Klein said, " 'Look, I never managed anyone before.' I wasn't being clever. I just felt awkward about it. But he looked at me and said, 'Well, before I wrote my first song, I'd never written a song before' " (Guralnick, p. 524).

When he accepted Cooke's offer to manage, Sam didn't require a contract for that either.

People say that Sam Cooke changed during the course of 1963, not least because of the tragic drowning of his 18-month-old son Vincent in the pool of a new home purchased in the Los Feliz Hills, east of Hollywood. Vincent's death rocked Sam's religious faith to its foundations and it put his marriage to Barbara—the one he blamed for his son's death—to the ultimate test. He started to drink more, and he stepped up his already active philandering. He began getting on his friends and colleagues, and he lost some of his youthful vigor. Up until this time, Sam never showed his darker side. When he felt down, he'd keep to himself and not share his anger or irritation. At his best, which was most of the time, Sam enjoyed a life, a drink, a talk. He had lots of energy, and told good stories, he made people feel important when they were around him.

But that all began to change in 1963. The music business, his life, and the tragedy of losing his son all made him question his purpose, his spiritual foundation.

Another development at this time came with the growing civil rights movement. Sam had always been attuned to the plight of the African American; his frequent travels through the South made it impossible to ignore. But now, with the help of activists like Dr. Martin Luther King Jr., the situation began to boil, and Sam became more emotionally invested in it.

The New Orleans AFO (All For One) band was led by Harold Battiste, a man as committed to the civil rights struggle as any black musician in Los Angeles. With Sam's help, Battiste conceived the idea of a network of so-called Soul Stations that would serve as gathering points for young blacks in the community. He voiced his feelings to Battiste about segregation and the movement, and how he wanted to capture it all in a song.

In response to that desire he wrote the stunning "A Change Is Gonna Come," his reaction to Bob Dylan's protest classic "Blowin' in the Wind." "The stirring prophetic song suggested a new direction in Sam's career; perhaps he planned to speak out more aggressively about the state of his people. He had befriended such key figures in the African American struggle as Malcolm X and Muhammad Ali, so, as an observer at least, he was on the front lines of race politics" (Hill, p. 18).

It possessed a rather overwrought orchestral arrangement, but it remains Sam's most impressive achievement as a songwriter. It reached out across the airwaves as a barely coded call to action for black America. It had all the power of King's "Free at Last" speech with traces of classic soul. Sam's despairing vocals recalled his best on Soul Stirrers work.

The song embodied the deep melancholy Sam was feeling at the time. Many who heard it, and knew him, had no idea from which part of Sam the song came. The loss of his son changed Sam until his own death. It cut him to the core and left a lasting scar. He carried on, writing songs and making records, but he never truly managed to rediscover his former self.

Sam opened at the Apollo on November 22, 1963, the day that President Kennedy was assassinated. After the first show, owner Frank Schiffman came out to make the announcement, and the hysteria in the theater—several women in the audience became hysterical, sobbing uncontrollably—was reflected in the country at large. There was widespread sorrow throughout the black community.

Sam himself began to revel more in sorrow. The assassination blew a hole into the civil rights movement and Sam himself felt deflated. But he had no real home to return to. Barbara's life had grown far removed from her husband's. He saw the rest of his children less and less. He grew more disillusioned with the music business every day and he had trouble keeping up appearances. He took up drinking more actively.

It was obvious that he wanted to be more than a pop singer. He wanted to make a difference, but didn't know how to go about it.

In mid-1964, Sam had released not the *Live at the Harlem Square Club* because of label concerns, but *Sam Cooke at the Copa*, a more sedate live gig. The audience was ready for that one and the platter spent 55 weeks on the charts, both before and after his death.

THE MURDER, THE MYSTERY

Sam was by all accounts a troubled man. His marriage was essentially over. For the first time, around the middle of 1964, Sam had actually spoken about the possibility of a divorce. She'd been unfaithful to him, which set in motion a double standard of Sam's logic. He could, but she couldn't.

People who were close to Cooke also claim he was beginning to feel unhappy about his business affairs. On the music circuit, two close friends, Ray Charles and Little Willie John, were in trouble with the law. Charles had just been busted for heroin and John had killed a man in Seattle. The night Sam disappeared, he had had a spat with Barbara. He had met some friends at a tony place called Martoni's, a hang-out for elite celebrities. He had several martinis, and left his friends after a few hours, saying he'd meet them at another club called PJ's on Santa Monica. A woman named Elise Boyer, a local party girl, was on his arm. It wasn't until the early morning that Sam and Elise finally appeared at PJ's, but Sam got annoyed when a flock of people approached him, and the couple drove off. Sam knew where he was going, a place where no one would recognize him: the Hacienda Motel. It was 2:30 A.M. when they checked in.

Inside the room, Sam was being rough with Elise. She didn't like the look in his eyes. He had already torn off her sweater and dress, and had begun groping her. He retreated briefly to the bathroom and when he came out, she was gone and so were his clothes.

It is impossible to know exactly what happened next. Sam put on what was left in the way of clothing—his sports jacket and shoes. He covered himself as best he could, then put the shoes on his feet and marched out the door, irate. He jumped in the car and drove to the hotel's check-in window. He pounded on the window until the motel manager shuffled over to see what the commotion was all about. Sam accused her of taking Elise. Where was she, he asked? Was she hiding there in the office? She shrugged and insisted she had no idea, but he persisted with his tirade.

The hotel manager, Bertha Lee Franklin, didn't like the looks of this unstable, half-naked man, whoever he was. He went back to the room to look for Elise, who never showed up. He turned and got his hands on Franklin and began to shake her, not easy to do to a woman of 190 pounds. She fought back, and they both fell to the floor. She bit and scratched, and he held her tightly. When she finally wrested herself free of his clutch, she lunged for a gun. There was a struggle and two shots went off without hitting anyone. The third, though, pierced both of Sam's lungs and his heart, and lodged next to his right shoulder blade.

"Lady, you shot me," he said. (Guralnick, 2005)

Between 5,000 and 6,000 people walked through the People's Funeral Home to view Sam's body on December 12. Three thousand people jammed into the Tabernacle Baptist Church in Chicago the following week, with 7,000 more packed outside in the freezing Windy City streets. Sam's body was laid out in a glass-lidded coffin, with guards stationed at either end. The body was returned to L.A. on Friday the 18th, and a similar throng turned out at the Mount Sinai Baptist Church. Frenzied scenes outside the church delayed the family's arrival for almost 45 minutes. When Barbara arrived, it was in a Rolls Royce with the 20-year-old Bobby Womack in tow, wearing one of Sam's suits. Billy Preston played organ and Lou Rawls wailed "Just a Closer Walk with Thee." A weeping Ray Charles was led up the aisle to sing "Angels Watching over Me."

Some people simply couldn't believe the idea of Sam Cooke with a prostitute in a $3-a-night motel in south central L.A. Others knew it was hardly out of character. Sam always carried large sums of money, but he was not inherently violent. He had none of that in his history. There were many questions, and not nearly enough answers. Allen Klein and J. W. Alexander hired private detectives to find out the truth.

At the hotel, a crowd of curious onlookers had gathered. They initially began singing Sam's songs, but as the mob grew so did their anger, and they began calling out stridently for Franklin to explain herself.

In March 1965, just months after Sam's murder, Barbara Campbell married Bobby Womack, a good friend of Sam's, triggering outrage in the black community. Did they have something to do with the murder? Barbara later filed papers to dissolve Sam's SAR label. In April 1966 she sold her half of Sam's publishing to Hugo and Luigi for $103,000; Hugo and Luigi in turn sold them to Allen Klein. J W. Alexander also sold out to Klein, who has won a succession of lawsuits over the catalog.

"If he hadn't have left God, left the church, it would never have happened," said a Baptist minister, voicing sentiments silently shared by many.

LEGACY

As a black American, Sam wanted to be all things to all his fans, and he often was. He recorded some of the most beautiful gospel ever made. He laid down orchestral MOR (middle of the road) for his white adult fans, he proved to be a guru and advisor to his roster of young R&B artists, while at the same time he wanted to be a gruff, tough soul singer. He wanted to sing at the upscale Copacabana, but also at the Harlem Square Club, both of which demanded completely different repertoires and approaches. He nailed both, speaking to each audience as if he'd known them his whole career.

It is in part because of this incredible versatility that he is the most underrated of all the great 1950s R&B singers. As good as his gospel sides are, and they're tremendous, and as classic as his smooth soul sides are, in some ways he was even better when he performed tough R&B.

Cooke aced the dynamic ballads, and had a great touch with more rock and roll material as well. In other words, he knew his material and he knew how to present it.

> His recordings come across with such force precisely in contrast to the mediocrities of his time, even in contrast to the banal arrangements that Hugo and Luigi gave him. The fact that Cooke could use the kind of cornball arrangements he frequently did is yet another testimony to the sheer power his voice possessed. You can ignore the near-vapidity of tunes like "Cupid" simply because his voice has all those internal catches and twists that drag you out and into the music. (Dave Marsh, "This Is Sam Cooke," *Creem*, March 1971)

In addition to being a performer, Cooke established himself as a groundbreaking black entrepreneur in mainstream music. He produced records for others, set up his own publishing company (Kags Music) and launched a record label (SAR/Derby). He also assisted artists like Bobby Womack, Johnnie Taylor, Billy Preston, and Lou Rawls in making the risky transition from gospel to pop.

In the end, despite his suspicious death over four decades ago, it's the voice on the records that endures, that uncommonly beautiful instrument that Cooke was blessed with at birth back in 1931. His sonorous vocals speak as loudly as the legacy of his influence. Atlantic's Jerry Wexler, who would conceivably have steered Sam Cooke toward the deep soul he innovated had he been able to sign him instead of RCA, said, "When I listen to his gospel work everything else goes away."

After he died, RCA posthumously issued "Shake" backed with "A Change Is Gonna Come." Regarded as one of the greatest singles of the modern era, it matched a hard-hitting R&B number (later cut by Otis Redding) with a haunting song about faith and reckoning that returned Cooke's voice to its familiar gospel home. The circle was complete.

SELECTED DISCOGRAPHY

Live at the Harlem Square Club 1963 (RCA, 1963)

The 2 Sides of Sam Cooke (Specialty, 1970)

Sam Cooke: The Man Who Invented Soul (RCA/BMG, 2000)

FURTHER READING

Guralnick, Peter. *Dream Boogie.* New York: Little, Brown, 2005.
Hill, Michael, liner notes, *Sam Cooke: The Man Who Invented Soul.* RCA/BMG, 2000.
Hirshey, Gerri. *Nowhere to Run: The Story of Soul Music.* New York: Da Capo, 1994.
Hoskyns, Barney. "The Soul Stirrer." *Mojo,* January 1995.
Palmer, Robert. *Rock & Roll: An Unruly History.* New York: Crown, 1995.
Wolff, Daniel, liner notes, *Sam Cooke with the Soul Stirrers.* Specialty Records, 2002.

Courtesy of Photofest.

Jackie Wilson

"MR. EXCITEMENT!"

In 25 years of recording and performing, between the years of 1950 and 1975, Jackie Wilson was a pioneer showman. With an acrobatic voice and an athleticism that made his performances sexy and exhilarating, Wilson embodied a lethal fusion of style and substance.

From humble origins in the street gangs and boxing rings of Detroit, Jackie Wilson would grow up to become an international star with inclusion on the roll call of the most significant black artists of the past 30 years. With contemporaries Clyde McPhatter and Sam Cooke he completed a triumvirate of the most essential stand-up singers to emerge from group apprenticeship to solo stardom in the mid-to-late 1950s. These were the first major voices of the new generation whose gospel-inflected singing styles, urban orchestrations, suave personalities, and crossover success fronted the broadly accessible side—the polished leading edge—of black music's general transition from 1950s rhythm and blues to 1960s soul.

Of his many impressive singing colleagues, Jackie was the strongest, most outrageous, and most instinctively talented of the breed, with a dynamic range that could soar from passionate whispers of love or grief to full-blown, glass-breaking catharsis. At his peak, like "Doggin' Around" from 1960, the hoary chestnut "Danny Boy," or the breathless "(Your Love Keeps Lifting Me) Higher and Higher" from 1967—he could blow the minds of an audience. Wilson laced his operatic tenor with polish, panache, and melismatic decoration—that is, the ability to bend or stretch a phrase or syllable—on a heart-stopping scale.

As a performer, too, he was the most spectacular showman of his generation. He employed the athletic training of his boxing past to execute spins, splits, thrills, and spills. Only James Brown would muster the nightly energy to surpass what Jackie Wilson brought to the stage. And when Jackie began doing it in the early 1950s, audiences, especially young women receiving their first doses of sexual energy, could barely contain themselves. They'd scream and froth in the aisles.

While awesome to hear and witness, his virtuoso singing never quite amassed the international audience he'd been built to reach. In the United States, he sent nearly 50 songs and 30 albums onto the charts during his career. But internationally, due to mismanagement, he barely got off the ground. In fact, though many of his early recordings notched chart appearances in the United Kingdom, for example, Wilson didn't visit London to nurture that audience until the late 1960s. In contrast, Motown recognized the importance of audiences internationally, and though they started later, they were in Europe by 1964.

A variety of other factors contributed to the obfuscation of Jackie Wilson's legend during his lifetime. Both management and Wilson lacked vision and often made inscrutable song choices. Unlike Gordy at Motown and Wexler at Atlantic, Wilson's label, Brunswick, couldn't anticipate the changing landscape of soul music and so they made dubious decisions based on poor instincts.

Worse, Wilson became mired in a handful of moral dilemmas that had him reeling, and, in one case, nearly dead when he was shot by a paramour. In any event, he always seemed to emerge from those prickly situations undaunted, a blazer tossed over his shoulder, and another amazing performance on the tip of his tongue.

In Van Morrison's tribute to Jackie, called "Jackie Wilson Said (I'm in Heaven When You Smile)" from his well-known *Saint Dominic's Preview* album from 1972, Morrison captures the surreal effervescence of hearing Wilson sing: "Baby, let it all hang out!"

EARLY YEARS

Born Jack Leroy Wilson in Detroit, Michigan, on June 9, 1934, Jackie Wilson was the only child of Jack and Eliza Mae Wilson from Columbus, Mississippi. The Wilsons, a well-meaning and religious working-class couple, loved their son, but were strict and disciplined. Wilson had some trouble with his father, an alcoholic, but got along well with his mom. She lost two children prior to Jackie, and so doted on him dearly.

They lived in the Highland Park enclave in northern Detroit, a rough neighborhood where Jackie hung out with friends, which included the future Four Tops leader Levi Stubbs and Little Willie John. Encouraged by his parents, he began singing in his local church at six years old. Jackie wasn't particularly religious. He just loved to sing and the cash came in handy for the cheap wine he liked drinking on the sly, beginning around the age of nine. By the time he was 10 he could be seen singing on the streets of Detroit. Passers by marveled at his ability to sing in tune, pitch-perfect, in both gospel and blues idioms. By the time he was 12 he joined the Ever Ready Gospel Singers, which spent their weekends touring other black churches in the Detroit metropolitan area. The young gospel belters enjoyed great notoriety—Jackie sang some lead with the group—and they were all the rage around the city.

But Jackie's heart wasn't entirely in his singing. He also liked boxing, so much so that he began to train at a local gym. He had a strong build and was a graceful, natural athlete, so his first inclination was not to be a singer, not least a gospel singer, but rather a sportsman of some kind.

In the 1940s, boxing enjoyed tremendous popularity. Detroit native Joe Louis and Billy Conn had a fierce rivalry, as did Rocky Graziano and Tony Zale. Sugar Ray Robinson and Jake "Raging Bull" LaMotta, all captured the imagination of a nation looking for a diversion from the war. Boxing provided that, especially for young teenagers like Jackie Wilson.

Wilson attended Highland Park High School, but not frequently enough to appease administrators. Involvement with a gang called the Shakers meant constant trouble for Wilson as a young teen. Truancy landed him in the Lansing Correctional Institute not once, but twice. It was at Lansing that Jackie took up boxing to pass his days. In his mind, he'd be following in the footsteps of his boxing idol Joe Louis, then a celebrated hometown hero. To that end, he left school in the ninth grade.

Despite intense disapproval from his mother, who wanted him to be singing rather than punching, he began enlisting in tournaments. In 1950, at 16, Jackie fudged his birthday and adopted the name "Sonny" to enter a Golden Gloves amateur welterweight tournament in Detroit. Surprisingly, he won the tournament. He stepped up his training, and boxing, for the moment, became central to his persona. He aspired to become a professional boxer. He worked on his footwork, something that would later come in handy as an entertainer and dancer.

Ultimately, his professional boxing aspirations never panned out. He failed to repeat as the Detroit Golden Gloves tournament champ, and fought only a handful of fights, losing the majority of them. His mother exhorted him to return to singing, which he did. Sonny Wilson's short-lived boxing career ended almost as quickly as it began.

Like many teenagers, he took a job on an automotive assembly line, where he could be heard whiling away the hours mimicking Al Jolson and Clyde McPhatter, lead singer with Billy Ward's Dominoes, the first R&B group to place a record on *Billboard*'s Top 30. He loved pop music. He also loved a young girl named Freda Hood.

THE SONG AND DANCE MAN

Jackie was good-looking, self-confident to the point of superciliousness, and a favorite with the girls. It helped that he was both an artist and an athlete, a sensitive guy and a muscular brute. He certainly loved women.

In February 1951 Wilson, at 16, hastily married Freda Hood, 17, whom he had known since he was 10, after she had become pregnant. It would be the first of her 15 pregnancies. His child, a daughter, was born in March. At this time he was singing in a group that consisted of his friends Levi Stubbs, Sonny Woods, and Lawson Smith. They only knew a few songs, but were welcome additions at house parties where they split the $5 they earned for their performance.

Jackie was discovered at a talent show run by R&B talent scout and bandleader Johnny Otis in 1951 at Detroit's Paradise Theater. Otis, a scout with King Records, had been scouring the country looking for young talent, and had already discovered artists like Etta James and Esther Phillips. Wilson didn't win the show that night, but Otis was encouraged by his talent and he hooked Wilson up with the Thrillers for an audition. But that R&B quartet eventually signed lead singer Hank Ballard and became the Royals. Otis ended up sending the Royals to King, and they left Wilson out of the deal. Eventually, the Royals would enlist the services of Ballard and change their name to the Midnighters. Otis also signed future legend Little Willie John to King.

In late 1951, Jackie hooked up with Dizzy Gillespie's short-lived Dee Gee label based in Detroit. Gillespie had seen the R&B scene sprout up nationally and he was looking to take advantage. Wilson, still going by the name Sonny, released two singles from Jackie's session in early 1952, the standard "Danny Boy" backed with "Bulldozer Rock," and "Rainy Day Blues" backed with "Rockaway Rock." His cover of "Danny Boy" became a top requested number among his club audiences.

In 1953, a friend of Jackie informed him that Clyde McPhatter, lead singer of Billy Ward and the Dominoes, was leaving Ward's band to begin a solo career, and they were holding auditions to find his replacement. Jackie tracked down the details and showed up, aged 19, with a girl on each arm. When they asked him his name, he called himself "Shit" Wilson.

Despite the arrogance, Ward was impressed by Wilson's voice and presentation. He took his telephone number. Within a few months, Ward rang him up and invited him into the band, but not initially to replace McPhatter. Rather he viewed Wilson's role as something of an apprenticeship in which he joined the Dominoes for tours rather than recording sessions.

Originally, the Dominoes formed as a gospel act, and as such appeared on the *Arthur Godfrey Talent Show* television program. With Clyde McPhatter on lead and Ward on piano, the Dominoes opted early on to sing more blues and R&B material when those styles gained wider acceptance.

In the early 1950s, the McPhatter-led group hit the R&B charts with a couple of numbers, including "Do Something for Me" and "Sixty Minute Man," the latter with its searing vocal considered to be a rock and roll prototype. Wilson listened and learned while with the Dominoes. Before joining, he worshipped McPhatter's voice and he began picking up elements of McPhatter's vocal techniques in his own performance. At the time, other voices made an impact on him as well, including the seminal gospel voices of the Soul Stirrers prior to Sam Cooke joining and Ira Tucker, leader of the Dixie Hummingbirds. In pop, the Ink Spots and Mills Brothers caught his attention, as did the operatic Mario Lanza and Vaughn Monroe. Yet perhaps the most critical influence in Wilson's young life was Al Jolson. Jolson's act, full of wild writhing and excessive theatrics, shaped Wilson's ideas about what an exciting performer should do on stage and what a thrilling performance should include. In Wilson's mind, Jolson, along with Louis Jordan, another idol of his, should be considered the stylistic forefathers of rock and roll.

Wilson also benefited from Ward's vocal coaching. "I learned just about everything I know from him. Breath control and how to dance during one number and then come back and sing a ballad. That's hard" (Bill Millar, liner notes, *Reet Petite*, Ace Records, 1986, p. 2).

McPhatter left the Dominoes in 1953, first to enter the U.S. Army and then, upon his return, to form a group of his own, the Drifters. Wilson replaced McPhatter as lead singer, and would go on to record dozens of tracks. Only one of those cuts reached the R&B charts; "Rags to Riches" hit number three in late 1953. Wilson first reached the national Top 30 on the group's recording of "St. Therese of the Roses" in 1956. During Wilson's stint as lead singer of the group, the Dominoes solidified its legacy by becoming one of the 1950s' truly seminal R&B vocal group pioneers.

Educated and now tested, Wilson was ready to go out on his own. The four years of touring and recording gave him the experience he needed to build confidence. He had developed a gorgeous vocal sound—a combination of gritty Southern R&B and Al Jolson–esque theatrics—and a stunning performance style—flamboyant, agile, sexy, acrobatic, and crowd-pleasing. Many noticed early on that Wilson had the unprecedented ability of melding both black and white singing styles. This gift came in handy, especially in Vegas, where the Dominoes played to predominantly white audiences.

His sweaty, lean physique, which he often exposed by unbuttoning his shirt in performance, drove women to hysteria. His star quality was undeniable. Wilson was ready to go it alone.

When he left the Dominoes to pursue a solo career, Jackie contracted the services of local talent agent Al Greene. Almost immediately, Greene put a call out around Detroit for fresh material Wilson could tackle. At the time, a young entrepreneur named Berry Gordy, a Detroit scenester and music fan, responded. Gordy also dabbled in songwriting and had compiled a decent collection of songs that he could show Greene and Wilson. In fact, he'd auditioned some of his material for a few of Greene's previous clients. Greene liked what he heard and based on the material, secured a record deal with the Chicago-based Brunswick.

Brunswick had been a part of the music industry since the 1920s originally releasing its back catalog of recordings through the U.S. arm of Decca. By the 1950s the label had started working with new repertoire and in 1957 had wised up to the fast-rising R&B scene. Wilson would be Brunswick's first popular music signing and his presence there would change the course and identity of the label.

Gordy, a former featherweight boxer himself, knew Wilson from the fight circuit in the late 1940s. The two bonded and Gordy set about writing for Wilson. The first composition Gordy tackled was with co-writer Billy Davis (aka Tyran Carlo), a struggling songwriter Gordy met through his sister Gwendolyn. "Reet Petite," recorded at the Pythian Temple recording studio in New York City, is a brassy, rockin' R&B track about the "finest girl you'd ever want to meet." and with one brisk track Wilson's solo career was set into motion.

"Novelty Rock 'n' Roll, it was not a coherent statement so much as a storm-tossed word salad about a girl who filled her clothes from head to toe. High pitched and ecstatic, Wilson ripped it up with considerable brio. 'Reet Petite' was a funny one,' said Wilson. 'Berry wrote it the way I sang it so if I hadn't come along, God knows who could have recorded it'" (Millar, p. 3).

The tune showcased Wilson's versatile vocal technique, complete with yodeling chorus, and it's easy to pick up a couple of Gordy's early signatures: with the answering horns in the chorus, and a rock and roll stop-start technique later heard in the Miracles' early track "Mickey's Monkey," which would show up on Motown just a few years later. The song almost hit the Top 10 in R&B, and its success affirmed Wilson's potential as a solo artist. In the United Kingdom it hit the Top 10 on the pop charts in 1957.

In subsequent Gordy/Wilson collaborations, other Motown elements would appear. The bold sound of the baritone sax in "I'll Be Satisfied" and the ubiquitous tambourine used to bolster the rhythm track of "That Is Why (I Love

You So)" would both show up in Gordy's early songwriting for Tamla/Motown artists.

"To Be Loved" and "I'm Wanderin'," released in 1958, cleared the way for a deluge of weepy ballads that would become another one of Wilson's trademarks. This lush style of arrangement complemented Wilson's eccentric vocal qualities and it appealed to a middle-class black audience. A song like "(You Were Made For) All My Love" demonstrate the Wilson's fondness for the operatic singer of his childhood Mario Lanza, who had a serious impact on his artistic sensibility.

While Wilson wasn't creating material close in spirit to the blues like Etta James and other early R&B trailblazers, he filled a critical need in the black music market somewhere between the big band sounds of Louis Jordan and the more palatable sounds of white, easy-listening artists like Perry Como and Bing Crosby. Jackie's own track, "Come Back to Me," with its prototypical Chuck Berry/Bill Haley guitar licks, also reflect a real rock and roll influence.

These early Wilson hits brought the team of Gordy, Davis, Greene, Greene's assistant Nat Tarnopol, producer Dick Jacobs, and orchestra leader Milton DeLugg. Gordy would continue writing for Wilson until 1959. He and Davis wrote his first 6 hits and 10 of the songs on his first two albums. Berry's sister Gwen would go on to contribute to this partnership as well on tunes like "Lonely Teardrops," "I'll Be Satisfied," and "That's Why (I Love You So)." These tunes all charted, and Wilson became a regular visitor to the upper reaches of the R&B and pop charts.

By the late 1950s and early 1960s, Wilson had "become" the Brunswick label, accounting for almost all the label's album releases. After all his songwriting success, though, Gordy began to wonder where all the money was going. He'd written a handful of hits, some of which crossed over to the pop charts, and he still had no money to show for it. Monies generated from songwriting successes would often go to the artist, producers, the record company, or the music publisher—often all four—before reaching the writer. And in the event the writer has a royalty arrangement, proceeds from a hit song take time, often months, to pay dividends. The lack of a return frustrated Gordy, and his wheels began to turn. Within months he'd rectify that situation by setting up his own recording venture, first called Tammie, then Tamla, then Motown.

" 'You can go broke with hits if someone else is producing them,' Gordy complained" (Millar, p. 3). Within months, Gordy would quickly consolidate the lessons he learned from his crash-course working with Wilson at the Brunswick label, and he applied them to his own start-up venture.

Wilson brought his hurricane performance style to the silver screen for his seventh hit, "You Better Know It," when he performed live on stage in the film *Go Johnny Go*, a sort of late 1950s rock and roll time capsule roughly outlining the rags-to-riches career of Jimmy Clanton.

In his performance, indicative on this film, Wilson was a force of nature, doing back flips and exhibiting the kind of dazzling, boxing-derived footwork Muhammad Ali would have appreciated. It also made conventional 1950s moms and dads, not yet accustomed to the gyrating and innuendo-saturated nature of taboo-busting rock and roll, squirm with discomfort. Jackie often removed articles of clothing, first his jacket, then his tie, and then his shirt, which he at least untucked and unbuttoned.

Criticism came from all sides. Wilson's act was immoral! Wilson was too overtly sexual. He used his microphone in rather suggestive ways. He often pantomimed unzipping his fly. What right-minded mother would allow her children, especially her girls, to witness the super-sexual Wilson in concert?

His unabashed sexuality rattled the foundation of traditional performance. To the older generation, Jackie Wilson was unacceptable. To younger folks, though, he was the black version of Elvis Presley, talented, dashing, and sexy enough to make girls swoon.

"If people were supposed to act like that man does in public, then we wouldn't wear clothes and have our own houses," wrote one woman to a magazine called *Soul*. "Everyone would just run around nude and party in the streets. I suggest you quit running stories and pictures on that man until he either cleans up his act or quits singing altogether. To think white people got upset over Elvis Presley" (Millar, p. 4).

Wilson explained away all the controversy by saying he was doing what came naturally. That, and he simply took what Elvis was doing at the time and adapted it to his largely black audiences. Elvis, of course, said that he took much of his act from Wilson. But like Elvis, and other possessed performers like Jerry Lee Lewis, Wilson simply communicated most explicitly the physical nature of soulful, rhythmic rock and roll.

THE NEXT PHASE

In 1958, Wilson's manager Al Greene died shortly after Jackie inked the Brunswick/Decca deal, leaving Wilson's affairs to Nat Tarnopol, Greene's 23-year old assistant. Once in charge of Wilson, the enterprising businessman didn't delay. He began remodeling Wilson's presentation in a striking new direction. Early on in the Wilson/Tarnopol relationship, when the latter was simply apprenticing with Greene, Tarnopol heard Wilson singing some Mario Lanza songs, only half-kidding. Wilson's versatility impressed Tarnopol so much that he thought, why not adapt some of his classically themed performances for an R&B audience?

The adaptations proved to be a brilliant ploy. Not only did it engender enormous sales for Wilson, crossing him over to an ever-larger white audience, but it also cast Wilson in a totally different light than the lascivious one many had already witnessed.

A succession of adaptations from classical themes brought enormous sales. "Night" was lifted from Camille Saint-Saëns's *Samson et Dalila* aria "My Heart at Thy Sweet Voice." "Alone at Last," another smash, introduced a Tchaikovsky piano concerto (B-flat minor) to the Top 10. "My Empty Arms," a pop version of Leoncavallo's "On with the Motley" from *Pagliacci*, also hit the Top 10. In fact, these classically influenced tunes would comprise three of his five Top 10 hits.

Some thought Wilson was ill-served by a manager who wanted to turn him into an opera singer, but the singer trusted his boss's decision. Now they knew he wasn't simply a screamer. He'd be accepted by the white world without losing his black audience.

The decision not to limit Wilson to rock and R&B meant that Tarnopol had to bring in a veteran bandleader. Enter Decca arranger Dick Jacobs. Jacobs went on to produce most of Jackie's recordings from 1957 through 1966. Jacobs knew Jackie's vocal abilities, how he reveled in all styles, so he teamed him with huge orchestral accompaniments.

The new material came off in stark contrast to his lubricious reputation and soon Jackie had prestigious and sold-out performing engagements at major Los Angeles, Las Vegas, and New York nightclubs. His success allowed Jackie to gain trust in Tarnopol's instincts and he soon assigned him his power-of-attorney.

Wilson's dual appeal to both black and white audiences was carefully calculated. On the A-side, Tarnopol would place his rollicking, rock and roll–flavored dance nuggets, and on the B-sides, something a more mature white audience could find: the tear-soaked blues ballads, songs like "A Woman, a Lover, a Friend" and "Tear of the Year." His masterpiece "Doggin' Around," a classic combination of blues, soul, easy-listening, and country-politan overtones, feels today like a Ray Charles classic and is still one of Wilson's most appreciated and best-known tunes. It became one of his biggest hits. In November 1958, the tune reached number seven on *Billboard*'s pop chart.

Later in 1961 Wilson had major pop and R&B hits with "Please Tell Me Why" and "I'm Comin' Back to You," followed by moderate success with "Years from Now" and "The Greatest Hurt." He subsequently formed a songwriting partnership with his lifelong friend Alonzo Tucker that produced a top R&B and huge pop hit with "Baby Workout" in 1961. Later R&B and pop hits included "Shake a Hand" and "Shake! Shake! Shake!"

All this hitmaking made Jackie Wilson quite the star. He set Apollo Theater box office records and earned the *Cashbox* Entertainer of the Year Award in 1960. In fact, at the tail end of that year he was among the most highly regarded black artists in America, alongside Ray Charles and Sam Cooke. With that stardom—and given his sex appeal—came women, lots of them, many of whom would throw themselves at Wilson. Married to Freda since 1952 and now with four children, Jackie didn't allow his domestic situation to interfere with his love life, and he played the field while on tour, philandering on many opportunities.

Jackie's Close Call

Jackie Wilson's reputation of being a real lady's man served him well for most of his career. But there's was one time when it quite nearly knocked him dead. It happened with a woman named Juanita Jones.

Jackie was cheating on his wife with Jones. But Jones found out that Wilson had been cheating on her with a woman named Harlean Harris. This meant, incidentally, that Wilson was cheating on his wife with two women at once. Anyway, on February 15, 1961, all the duplicity caught up with him when Jones, a jealous lover and covetous of her time with Wilson, caught the singer returning to his Manhattan apartment with Harris on his arm and shot him twice. Despite his wounds, Wilson made it downstairs where he was taken to Roosevelt Hospital. Doctors performed life-saving surgery. He lost a kidney and was laid up for months, in the hospital for six weeks. He ended up with a limp that dogged him for years and one of the bullets in his body, too close to his spine to remove, stayed there for the rest of his life.

In the meantime, Wilson's record company, Brunswick, was desperate to protect his reputation as an upstanding family man. Had the story gotten out about his infidelities, and there were many, his career would be ruined. So Nat Tarnopol, Brunswick chief and his press agent fabricated the following story that ran in all the major papers.

In the early hours of 15th February 1961, after a business meeting and a late movie, he headed back to his New York apartment. Passing through the lobby, he noticed a fan he'd seen at many a local concert. As politely as he could, he spurned her request to talk and went upstairs to his apartment. Moments later he answered a knock: the woman stood in the hall where she explained, quite simply, that she was going to shoot herself. Wilson lunged for the .38 caliber revolver in her waistband and the couple tangled on the floor. A bullet entered his lower back and another lodged in his abdomen. Stumbling out into the street, he was rushed to Roosevelt Hospital where he fought for his life. Juanita Jones, a 28-year old ex-Army WAC, was taken away for questioning. "I'm all mixed up," she sobbed, "I hope I didn't hurt him."

Wilson emerged from the hospital some six weeks later, with his wife on one arm and his mother on the other.

MORE TROUBLE

When he returned home and set about working again, he ran into difficulties of another type, this time financial. In 1962, the IRS seized Jackie's Detroit family home, a palatial estate in the city's Highland Park section, for non-payment of taxes. The previous tax year he had declared annual earnings of $263,000, a giant salary compared to the average worker. But Tarnopol and the accounting department at Brunswick failed to report much of what he earned, thus the IRS attaching his home. Jackie made arrangements with the IRS to make restitution on the unpaid taxes and to re-purchase the family home at auction.

A more thorough review of Wilson's finances showed, stunningly, that he was broke. Despite his incredible career, he had nothing to show for the hits, the songs, the successes, the fame. Tarnopol had thoroughly mismanaged Wilson's financial future. In some cases, he scribbled his own name on some of Wilson's best material so as to earn publishing moneys from them. "Doggin' Around," for example, was originally credited to Tarnopol's aunt, Lena Agree, who didn't write music. The song was actually written by Alonzo Tucker, Wilson's friend and co-writer. Tarnopol's criminal behavior did not surface for some time. So Wilson had no reason to be suspicious.

To set matters right, he increased his recorded output. In 1962, he released his first live album *Jackie Wilson at the Copa*. Recorded live in New York in 1962, the effort is the only live album Wilson released during his lifetime, and it's less a showcase for Wilson's talent than a textbook of pre-Beatles showbiz practice, meaning Wilson presents him as a sort of all-around entertainer in the vein of Sammy Davis Jr., not the R&B titan he's best remembered as.

Backed by a big TV-style band and chorus, he tackles standards such as "Tonight," from *West Side Story*, "Body and Soul," and Cole Porter's "Love for Sale." The sprawling band accompanies Wilson on his more characteristic hits, including "Lonely Teardrops," and "That's Why (I Love You So)" as well.

The album sold well, put him back on the pop charts, and convinced Brunswick to keep Wilson as their flagship artist. Decca, Brunswick's parent corporation, even went as far as to give Tarnopol 51 percent, or majority control, of the label in order to keep Wilson signed.

The climate for artists like Wilson was changing though, based on the up and coming work of artists at Motown, Berry Gordy's rising label. Gordy's early tunes with the Miracles, the Marvelettes, and the Temptations were beginning to change the face and sound of black music. The days of easy listening and quasi-classical ballads were fading and the pop-soul sound of Motown roared to the forefront of popular music. Compounding that, the sound of the Beatles and the British Invasion with its raucous guitars and melodic rock hooks, also began sweeping the country. Wilson and Tarnopol responded with a style that corresponded with the sound coming out of Detroit.

The Wilson team re-introduced the churchy growl of his past, phased out the Lanza-esque approach, and upped the tempo to a frenetic pace. "Baby Workout," with Gil Askey's tremendous big band arrangement, landed on the desired target, back in the pop Top 10. Another track, "Shake Shake Shake," also met with success, and pushed Wilson's artistry toward more gospel-inspired soul music.

Unfortunately, the din created by Motown and the British Invasion drowned virtually everything else out, and the years of 1964 and 1965 were dismal for Wilson. Wilson's follow-ups to "Baby Workout" were diffuse, concealing a sense of bewilderment and lack of direction. Once guaranteed to reach the Top 20 with virtually any record, his songs now hovered at a distance, floundering around the lowest reaches of the Hot 100. Tarnopol's choice of material became increasingly confused. The pair threw everything at the wall to see what would stick: dance fads, Christmas carols, standards, inspirational ballads, and more of Wilson's patented pop operatics. In all, almost a dozen of Wilson's recordings failed to assert themselves over the charts.

One of the songs that came closest was "Shake a Hand," Wilson's duet with Linda Hopkins. Born in New Orleans in 1925, Hopkins was, like Wilson, an extremely versatile singer. She had a long list of stage credentials alongside her vocal skills, which included classic, traditional, and urban blues, R&B, soul, jazz, and show tunes, all with distinction and style. Hopkins long idolized the seminal blues singer Bessie Smith and won critical plaudits for her portrayal of Smith in the theatrical presentation *Jazz Train*. Despite recording for numerous labels since the 1950s, the only charting track she had was "Shake a Hand" in 1963. It narrowly missed the R&B Top 20, peaking at number 21. Good for her, not particularly successful for Wilson.

To exacerbate matters, his wife Freda's patience had finally run out. She'd had it with Jackie's dalliances with other women and filed for divorce in 1965, bringing an end to their 13-year marriage. Freda received the house, $10,000, and a modest $50 per week for each of their four children. Throughout the rest of his life, Jackie treated Freda and the kids as though they were still a family.

But the trouble didn't stop. In March 1967 Jackie and his friend and drummer, Jimmy Smith, were arrested in South Carolina on morals charges. Both were arrested in a motel with two 24-year old white women. Lurid details of the case appeared in the newspapers. Tarnopol, in another slick spin effort, decided that to restore Jackie's public image, Wilson had to marry longtime girlfriend Harlean Harris. The civil ceremony was held the next month. Jackie had been going with Harlean from at least 1960 and they'd had a son in 1963. Wilson and Smith were only fined a few hundred dollars and the "morals charges" were soon forgotten.

THE SOUL YEARS

Wilson finally dug out of his creative slump in 1967. Now 30 and with 28 hits already under his belt, Wilson moved his recording base to the CBS studios in Chicago and began working with producer Carl Davis. This partnership commenced what is referred to as Wilson's Soul Years.

In his Chicago base Davis had rekindled the defunct but seminal blues label Okeh for CBS/Epic, and he also collaborated successfully with the former

Impression Curtis Mayfield on artists like Major Lance, Walter Jackson, and Billy Butler. Davis recalls speaking with Tarnopol at a black DJ convention at the Waldorf-Astoria in New York City.

"Jackie had been doing pop-oriented things with plush string arrangements," he recalled in a 1977 interview. "He had gotten 'cold' as a chart artist and my job was to bring him back into what was happening" (David Nathan, liner notes, *Jackie Wilson: The Soul Years, 1966–1975*, Brunswick, 1999, p. 2).

A secretary at the studio named Barbara Acklin, an aspiring songwriter who would go on to chart success herself, gave Davis and Wilson a cut called "Whispers (Gettin' Louder)." When she wasn't answering the phone, Acklin wrote songs in her spare time. She expressed an interest in recording, but Davis wasn't in the market for a female artist on his roster. She did however manage to slip the song to Davis, and Wilson heard it. They liked it and decided to take a crack at recording it. The Acklin song became Wilson's biggest hit since "Baby Workout" in 1963, grazing the Top 10 and lodging at number 11.

As it turned out, "Whispers" gave Acklin her first taste of success. Thanks to the recommendation of Wilson and a couple of other Brunswick recording artists, including Gene Chandler, Davis signed her as an artist on the Brunswick label. It didn't take long for her to score a couple of hits: "Love Makes a Woman," which hit number 15 in the summer of 1968, and "Am I the Same Girl."

With "Whispers," the new working relationship between Davis and Wilson began auspiciously. So auspicious in fact, Tarnopol brought Davis into the Brunswick fold full-time to collaborate with all of the Brunswick artists. At the time, Davis began working with arranger Sonny Sanders, fresh from a stint at Motown. Davis had also wanted to recruit the Funk Brothers—that is, the rhythm section at Motown—for his sessions with Sanders, but studio/label owner Gordy had severe restrictions in place for his staff musicians. So the musicians had to slip away at night and come to Chicago, where they backed Wilson on the sly. The accompaniment gave Wilson's sound a needed boost, a lively punch that felt right for the singer.

Coming through with a follow-up to "Whispers" wasn't as easy, though. Wilson misfired on his next three singles—"Just Be Sincere," "I Don't Want to Lose You," and "I've Lost You"—before knocking another one out of the park. "(Your Love Keeps Lifting Me) Higher and Higher" sent Wilson back into the Top 10 almost a year later.

Originally, songwriters Gary Jackson, Carl Smith, and Raynard Miner had given the song to Billy Davis at Chess, and Davis, the same guy who worked with Berry Gordy on songs like "Reet Petite" and "Lonely Teardrops" for Wilson, planned to give the song to his act, the Dells. At the time, Davis and the Dells were on a roll, and the song was tailor-made for the act. But unbeknownst to Davis, the writers of the song also took it to Carl Davis at Brunswick, and before the Dells had a chance to cut and release it, Wilson beat them to it. Brunswick had rush-released it and the song hit radio immediately.

"Higher and Higher" is considered by many to be the best recording of Wilson's career. Once again, the Funk Brothers came to Chicago to moonlight in the studio. "My luck really changed because Carl came up with some good stuff. I always wanted to try things like that and to me 'Higher' was more gospel than R&B, nearer to what I'd sung as a kid. I felt more at home" (Nathan, p. 3).

The comfort level remained for another single, "Since You Showed Me How to Be Happy," which nearly broke the Top 30 on the pop charts. But then, another rather bizarre choice arose from the Brunswick camp. They decided to have Jackie record an entire album with Count Basie. This is not in itself a terrible idea. Basie had been searching for an artist to serve as a conduit to attract a young audience and Jackie was the perfect man for the job. But for Wilson, the situation proved a little pricklier. He'd just come off a couple of solid, up-to-date soul singles, and appeared to be on a roll. He had worked with the Motown band, the hottest label and sound in the country on "Higher and Higher" and "Whispers" and the partnership gelled perfectly.

The Basie liaison resulted in an album, *Manufacturers of Soul*, and two singles, a cover of Sam Cooke's "Chain Gang" and a cover of the Impressions' "For Your Precious Love." Neither made an impression though and the confounding Brunswick plan resulted in tripping up Wilson's momentum, and he never truly recovered. He managed to team up successfully with renowned New York City urban music producer Van McCoy, who'd later record "The Hustle," for the Burt Bacharach pop-meets–Philly soul of "I Get the Sweetest Feeling." That song glanced the Top 30, peaking at number 34 in the summer of 1968—the last time Jackie would hit the Top 40 in pop music. It rose high on the R&B charts, and in the United Kingdom as well. But it was the sound of Wilson going out not with a bang but a whimper.

His American fortunes began waning again. In a revealing interview with Bob Fisher, he admitted that politicized black consciousness had brought its problems: "I found it difficult to adjust, very much so. All of a sudden black was black and white was white and each wanted to perform his own music. For someone like me who had been used to both audiences it was an insult to record one thing and not the other. It left me quite shattered" (Bob Fisher, *NME*, February 1975).

Conflict between his record company and management contributed to the slide. There were R&B hits, "You Got Me Walking" for example, was a song co-written for him by Chi-lite lead singer Eugene Record. But Wilson's career was swallowed up by the extremes of black music. No longer was it feasible for a soul artist not on Motown to appeal to a white audience. In the early 1970s, too, black was black. The funk of Sly and the Family Stone, and the slinky bass lines of blaxploitation soundtracks filled the air in urban locations. At the same time, white was white. The sound of white America became obsessed with the loud rock bands like Led Zeppelin and Deep Purple, the Southern rock of the Allman Brothers, and the garage rock of the Kingsmen.

Jackie Wilson

Neither black nor white audiences had any purpose for Wilson, and he spiraled downward. Rumors of alcoholism, drug addiction, and complex financial difficulties surfaced, sullying his reputation further. His visits to the recording studio decreased significantly in the 1970s, an indication that he had lost enthusiasm for the art of making music. In 1975, he made one of his last recordings, "Nobody But You."

The song itself was a dramatic soul ballad written by the famed songwriting team of Barry Mann and Cynthia Weil, veterans of New York City's Brill Building songwriting factory. In Wilson's hands, it became a soaring, majestic gospel blues song along the lines of Bill Withers's "Lean on Me" and Carol King's "You've Got a Friend," both of which are purposely paraphrased in "Nobody But You." "It became more like a personal testimony to some of the trials and tribulations Jackie Wilson endured during his lengthy career as a recording artist and performer" (Nathan, p. 4).

Regardless of the power in Wilson's performance, his acceptance continued to diminish. He had made ill-fated attempts to keep up with the times when he covered songs like the Beatles' "Eleanor Rigby" and the Doors' "Light My Fire," both of which were more laughable than laudable. On the other hand, he did prove he could cover standards, with incredible versions of "Over the Rainbow" and "Georgia on My Mind," neither of which charted, but both attest to his incredible versatility and interpretive skills.

Still, the pop hits dried up in the 1970s and Wilson saw the writing on the wall. In an effort to recoup his dignity and make a little money at the same time, Wilson threw in the towel. He quit trying to keep up with pop music's Joneses, and joined the oldies circuit.

DEATH AND DYING

The '70s were tragic for the Wilson family. In September 1970 Wilson's oldest son, 16-year-old Jackie Jr., was shot and killed during a confrontation on the porch of a Detroit neighbors' home. Also Jackie Wilson's daughter Sandra Wilson Abrams died from a heart attack in 1977, and another daughter, Jacqueline Wilson, was an innocent bystander when she was shot and killed during a drug-related drive-by shooting.

Jackie's own life was not immune to tragedy either. On the night of September 29, 1975, while performing at the Latin Casino near Cherry Hill, New Jersey, Wilson was stricken with a massive heart attack during his performance as part of the *Dick Clark Revue*, an oldies road show. When he fell, he hit his head. Clark, in the wings on the side of the stage, thought it was part of his act and implored Wilson to get up.

One of the first to reach Jackie was Cornell Gunter of the Coasters who immediately noticed he wasn't breathing. Gunter applied resuscitation and got him breathing again. An ambulance quickly got him to the nearby hospital.

He had suffered severe brain damage ascribed to oxygen deprivation. He lapsed into a coma that lasted three months.

Although Wilson regained consciousness, he had total impairment of his faculties. He couldn't walk, talk, or feed himself and he communicated with blinks and sounds. In the years that followed, Wilson was transferred from facility to facility, and his estate went completely bankrupt. In 1977 Jackie Wilson was then institutionalized in the Medford Leas Retirement Community. Artists like the Spinners and Barry White contributed significant sums of money to his ongoing medical care. There were benefit concerts that raised goodly sums. But apparently much of the money was spent on litigation as family members fought over his estate. The IRS submitted a six-figure tax bill to Jackie's estate, and all of those fighting over rights to his recordings backed off, unable to assume that tax liability.

In 1984 after eight years and four months in a vegetative state, the great Jackie Wilson finally passed on at the age of 49. Due to the significant debt and legal wrangling, Jackie died virtually alone. After a well-publicized funeral attended by around 1,500 relatives, friends, and fans, he was buried in an unmarked grave in his home city of Detroit. In life, he had dazzled vast audiences, and in death, he had become a pariah and a pauper.

This sad state of affairs was later corrected in 1987 when a fundraising campaign collected enough cash to install a proper gravestone on his burial site.

LEGACY

Jackie Wilson's honey-rich falsetto-tenor voice thrilled millions throughout the world. Few could outdo him in terms of sheer vocal prowess. Combine that voice with his electrifying performances on stage and a legendary combination results. He wasn't just one of the pioneer singers of the rockin' soul era. He revolutionized singing. He was at the fulcrum of R&B's important transition to soul music, and more than any other artist of his time, he embraced first R&B then soul with equal aplomb.

Like only a handful of other icons—Sam Cooke and Ray Charles come to mind, both of whom also crossed over—Wilson appealed to massive, international audiences, men and women, black and white.

And like both Cooke and Charles, the latter especially, Wilson tackled a wide array of material, from gospel-tinged blues to opera-derived pop songs à la Mario Lanza. No one in the history of pop had that kind of versatility or the kind of audacity it took to feed his audience such a wide spectrum of material. And he did so with incredible chart success. His work from 1958 to 1975 generated a total of 47 charting singles, including six number one hits.

It could also be said that if it wasn't for Jackie Wilson there might not now exist a legendary record corporation called Motown. For it was Jackie's dynamic and broadly successful versions of Berry Gordy's early compositions that gave the unknown Detroit hustler credibility as a songwriter and spurred him on to more ambitious goals. Perhaps Gordy was destined to establish an empire come what may. Nevertheless, Jackie's first few hit recordings of his songs, "Reet Petite," "To Be Loved," "Lonely Teardrops," "That's Why" and others from 1957–59 were enough to motivate Gordy to look for a fortune on his own.

The only reason he is not mentioned in the same breath as Cooke and Charles is that Wilson often suffered from poor choices of songs. He was "something of an underachiever in the studio" (Richie Unterberger, *AMG.com*). While much of popular music's black talent had informed labels and visionary music people helping to call the shots—Aretha had Jerry Wexler, Otis Redding had the Stax band, Motown artists had Berry Gordy and others—Wilson didn't have that luxury. *His* right-hand man, Nat Tarnopol, was more or less strictly business and didn't possess the same visionary instincts. Thus we have Wilson's career missteps, miscalculations, and studio failures.

Of course, this can also be looked at as a positive. With such an inspired voice, he did not feel the need to neatly conform to any commonly recognized category of entertainment. In particular, it was the brash orchestration of so many of his records that set him apart from whatever was hitting the charts at the time. That he happily and frequently veered from intense soul-blues to adapted classical themes by way of supper-club standards only confused the issue the more. But perhaps Jackie Wilson preferred it that way, to keep his listeners off balance with his choices. While it prevented him from attaining stratospheric, unprecedented heights on the written pages of history books, at least he did things his way.

Wilson left an indelible imprint upon a generation of superstars. Some say Elvis Presley took his act in total after watching Wilson perform and Van Morrison placed his firm approbation on record with the song "Jackie Wilson Said." More recently, his material has been revived by high-minded stylists like Lionel Richie, Michael Jackson, Luther Vandross, and Peabo Bryson. To many who grew up with them, and even some who learned of him much later, Wilson's memory outshines the brightest of contemporary soul singers to remain one of soul's true stars.

SELECTED DISCOGRAPHY

Jackie Wilson at the Copa (Brunswick, 1962/2000)
Whispers (Brunswick, 1966/2002)
Higher and Higher (Brunswick, 1967/2000)
The Very Best of Jackie Wilson (Ace, 1993)

FURTHER READING

Carter, Doug. *Jackie Wilson: The Black Elvis*. New York: Heyday, 1998.
Douglas, Tony. *Lonely Teardrops*. New York: Routledge, 2005.

Michael Ochs Archives/Getty Images.

Etta James

THE MATRIARCH OF R&B

Few artists have experienced the horrifying travails that Etta James has and lived to tell about it. After leaving school in the ninth grade, she broke big into show business in 1954 at the premature age of 14 when West Coast R&B icon Johnny Otis heard about her and called her to his hotel room for an audition. At the time, she'd been singing with an all-girl, street-corner trio called the Creolettes. She describes herself then as a 15-year-old "juvenile delinquent, ditching school, hanging out, drinking wine."

The trio's first record for the Modern label was called "Roll with Me Henry," a so-called answer song to Hank Ballard's lascivious R&B jumper "Work with Me, Annie." It hit radio in 1955 and exploded instantly. Otis, a man on the spot (who also took a writing credit on Etta's tune even though he hadn't touched it himself) changed the Creolettes name to the Peaches and took them on the road with his revue.

But by the time the 1960s rolled around, she succumbed to a fierce drug habit that lasted through much of the decade and beyond, stunting her career, and preventing her from reaching the heights for which she'd been destined. When she finally checked into the hospital in 1973, she "went down in the record books as the sickest person ever to have detoxed off of anything in the history of Los Angeles County."

A rhythm and blues star since her first record in 1954, she was introduced to white music 20 years later by patients at the psychiatric hospital where she successfully underwent rehabilitation. Oddly enough, she didn't even know that Rod Stewart had covered her hit "I'd Rather Go Blind," until one of the young women in the rehab ward played it for her.

Still, her addiction didn't seem to affect her singing voice. Throughout a career that has spanned six decades now, Etta has made an incalculable impact on popular music. She is known in wide circles as one of the towering voices of R&B, and near the top of a short list of female singers in the pop music era.

In the 1960s, Etta James was to the Chess label what Aretha Franklin was to Atlantic. Both at the time were competing for the crown, then still up for grabs, as the Queen of Soul. James had given the Chess label, also the home to blues greats like Chuck Berry, Howlin' Wolf, and Muddy Waters, a string of hits in the early 1960s, before biding her time a few years during the onset of rock and roll. For her part, Aretha was gathering steam through her developmental Columbia years with John Hammond, getting ready to soar.

Like Aretha, Etta went down to Muscle Shoals to cut some important sides, making four trips to the famous Alabama studio in 1967 and 1968. Jimmy Ray Johnson, one of the guitarists at those sessions, remembers the recording experience with Etta fondly. "She and Aretha both possessed the ability to sing a song immediately. . . . Every note you hear was done with the band live. The band would freeze to death with chill bumps while we were doing it" (Lee Hildebrand, liner notes, *Tell Mama: The Complete Muscle Shoals Sessions*, Chess/MCA, 2001).

They intersected briefly in the mid- to late 1960s, while Etta, floundering personally, attempted to come to grips with her addiction. We know who won that unspoken contest today. Aretha has reigned since those heady days of classic R&B as the undisputed Queen of Soul. But one could only have imagined what would have happened had James held heroin at bay long enough to truly attain her real potential.

Etta remained in the here and now long enough to cut a dazzling array of solo R&B hits throughout the 1960s, including "Stop the Wedding," "Pushover," and "Tell Mama." Her best-known track, "At Last," was recorded way back in 1961, and is heard constantly today on both the big and small screens, at weddings, and on oldies radio stations. It is *the* quintessential soul ballad, and it is all Etta.

Nat King Cole was a fan of Etta before he even knew her name. When his road manager put a coin in a jukebox in restaurant where he and Cole were having a cup of coffee, the song that played, sung by Etta, stopped him in his tracks. "Dick," said Cole, addressing his companion, "I don't know who that girl is, but she's one of the finest singers I've ever heard" (Morry Roth, liner notes, *Tell Mama*, Chess, 1968).

EARLY YEARS

Jamesetta Hawkins was born in 1938 and raised in Los Angeles by a variety of caregivers. Her natural mother, Dorothy Hawkins, was only 14 when she gave birth to Jamesetta. Mother Hawkins, a light-skinned beauty with a flair for the glamorous, flitted in and out of her daughter's life for decades. She dressed in black, wore fishnet stockings, spent hours applying makeup, and kept bizarre hours, especially for a mother. She loved jazz, adored Billie Holiday, and attracted men like flies to a flame. But she certainly wasn't ready for motherhood and because she had no natural maternal tendencies, she ended up spending much more time out of their Watts apartment than in it. She was gone so much that Etta herself refers to her mother as "the Mystery Lady."

Another early mystery concerned Etta's father, as in, who exactly was he? Even her mother didn't know with any certainty. To this day, Etta does not know the true identity of her father. One theory she holds is that it was none other than Minnesota Fats, the white pool shark, born Rudy Wonderone. A friend of Dorothy's named Willie Best, an actor, also had a close friendship with Fats, and in 1937, he had been in Los Angeles frequently on business. Dorothy, when pressed, actually admitted Etta's father was white. She just didn't admit (or know) which white man it was.

In place of Dorothy, Etta's early parenting came from Lula and Jesse Rogers, the couple that owned the boarding house in which Etta and her mom lived. Mama Lu served as an attentive guardian, and the person who kept the closest watch on Etta, an adventurous child. The Rogers had decent money and were able to provide comfortably for their adoptive offspring.

At the age of five, Etta became a singing sensation. It happened, like many of the back stories of early R&B stars, in the church. St. Paul the Baptist Church in Los Angeles had one of the hottest choirs in the city, the Echoes of Eden Choir, led by Professor James Earle Hines, and one of the city's most flamboyant preachers, Reverend Branham. Because of the strength of the services, the church would be filled to capacity every Sunday. Guest stars like Sister Rosetta Tharp would show up and perform, and the service was broadcast live on local radio.

Choral leader Hines was a classic gospel belter, a manly singer with a bellowing voice that invoked the gods. Etta loved hearing him, and she began humming along to the choir's booming tunes. Mama Lu, who brought Etta to the services, noticed her interest in song and encouraged her to take voice lessons. This she did, with Hines, and she also took piano lessons with his wife.

While she didn't remain patient with learning very long, she did discover a love for singing. Her voice, a raw instrument, would remain raw, and Hines, recognizing it as such, nurtured it. He didn't push Etta, but he didn't let her off easy either. He prepared her to sing in front of the congregation, which she did, at age five.

She remembers standing on top of a stool to sing, an overweight little girl with curly ringlets hanging down to her waist. The congregation encouraged her mightily those first few times, and Etta felt her confidence growing. After the service, Branham and Hines stood by their new prodigy while the congregation filed out. They were proud. They had a new attraction to boast of at the church; Etta had become a drawing card.

Dorothy, her mom, never bothered to come see her sing at the church, though Etta doesn't know why. Neither did her adoptive father, Jesse, who even before he came to know Etta swore he'd never set foot in a church. But the more popular his daughter became, the more he felt compelled to check what all the fuss was about.

As the story goes, Jesse (aka "Sarge"), saw profit potential in his new young talent. And rather than showing up at church to merely witness her ability, he attended, and intended, to serve as her manager. Seeing firsthand how big an attraction Etta had become, Sarge began asking the church for money. He came between his daughter and her choir, and his actions turned Hines and Branham against the family. When Sarge threatened to bring Etta to another church if they didn't meet his wishes, they called his bluff and bid them all adieu: Mama Lu, Sarge, and Etta, a victim of greed. St. Paul's had been her second home, one in which she was no longer welcome.

When Sarge found his family a new church, with an even bigger congregation, he was excited to introduce everyone to his daughter's talents. But Etta didn't want to sing. She didn't feel inspired. In fact, she'd never sing in a church again.

To this day, Etta can't sing on request. She never liked encores, rarely granted them throughout her career. "For me, singing's linked to real-life emotions. If I don't feel it, I can't sing it" (Etta James with David Ritz, *Rage to Survive*, New York: Villard Books, 1995, p. 21).

Dorothy made periodic stops at Mama Lu and Sarge's place to visit Etta. Occasionally, she'd take Etta for a few days, and even bring her around town at night. Dorothy loved the nightlife, and so, it turns out, did Etta. In 1940s Los Angeles, joints were jumping. Etta would peek into clubs and see through all the smoke and booze the high glamour of the day, the excitement, mystery, and mayhem of the scene.

During that same period, Etta soaked up as much music as she could. Johnny Moore and the Three Blazers with Charles Brown, T-Bone Walker, and Amos Milburn were all blaring from jukeboxes. Dorothy would take her to see jazz outfits like the Stan Kenton Orchestra with June Christy and the slinky, gorgeous Josephine Baker, after whom Etta imagined Dorothy patterned herself. She got the scoop on Art Tatum and Duke Ellington.

As a young teen, she was surrounded by doo-wop on the street corners; the feel-good vocal vibe became another building block in her foundation. Clearly, her musical education had quickly segued out of the church and onto the streets.

When Etta turned 12, Mama Lu, 68, suffered a damaging stroke. She held on for a while, but ultimately died, leaving Etta without a mother figure and primary caregiver. Swooping in came Dorothy, in her gauzy black clothing and glamour-girl cosmetology; she lifted her daughter out of Los Angeles and delivered her to San Francisco for a new beginning.

Of course, Etta's life with Dorothy ended as quickly as it began. In fact, Dorothy didn't even have enough money to get the two of them to San Francisco; the bus driver kicked them off at Fresno for lack of the proper fare.

Always resourceful, Dorothy called her brother Frank and his wife Mary, a childless couple who'd grown accustomed to being alone. They paid the rest of the way, and actually took custody of Etta. The transition was rocky, interrupted by infrequent and unannounced visitations by Dorothy. Etta was happy to live with her real mom, if only for a brief while. The change of scenery did her good, and deep down, despite Dorothy's super whimsical nature, she actually enjoyed the mystery and excitement that time with the woman brought.

In the early years of the 1950s, Etta transformed into a tough, resentful street girl, a handful at home. She skipped school most days, and when she did attend, she refused to sing in Glee Club, a mandatory class. She joined a gang called the Lucky 20s, no surprise considering she had no real family of her own at the time.

At 14, hormones began acting up. She went with boys, beat up other girls, smoked pot, shoplifted jewelry to pay for musical recordings, and eventually ended up in Continuation School, a limbo stop before Juvenile Detention Center. She loved and listened to jazz, but it was the street corner sounds of doo-wop and the gutbucket feeling of down-home blues, all sexy and sultry, that really got her going.

About this time, she formed a singing group with a couple of her girlfriends. The Mitchells, Jean, 14, and Abye, 23, were, like Etta, toughies hanging around San Francisco's Fillmore district. For her part, Abye was more interested in the men and boys on the music scene than actually participating in it as a performer. Etta and Jean, too young to play that game, did their best to keep up.

They called themselves the Creolettes, essentially "project girls" singing R&B covers. Their tight, three-way harmonies were patterned after groups like the Moonglows, the Orioles, and the Chords, all of the hippest vocal acts. Their first few performances, at amateur shows, record hops, and other revues, helped them gain confidence and work out a few dance moves. Thanks largely to Etta's strong lead vocal, they were well received, and it didn't take long for the Creolettes to make a name for themselves around the city.

One afternoon, when the Creolettes were singing at a hop, Hank Ballard stopped by with his band the Midnighters. At the time, Ballard was the hottest R&B act in the country, and their song, "Work with Me, Annie," dominated the airwaves. The bobbysoxers were thrilled to be in the presence of greatness, especially when, after the show, Ballard gave them a vote of confidence.

The episode emboldened James. She went home and penned an answer song to Ballard's hit. At the time, answer songs—that is, songs written as responses to existing hits—were popular, and a surefire way to get a little attention, if not score a companion hit. James's composition, "Roll with Me, Henry," got immediate attention, largely because the song it replied to was such a huge hit. The year was 1954 and Etta's life, if not the other Creolettes, was about to change.

The tune caught the attention of West Coast R&B guru Johnny Otis, a debonair Greek with olive skin and an encyclopedic knowledge of R&B. Abye made sure of that when she slipped backstage after an Otis gig and caught the bandleader's eye. That night, in the early morning hours, Abye called Etta and Jean and insisted they come down to the gig. Johnny Otis wanted to hear them sing.

In the hotel room that night, Etta, still half-asleep, agreed to sing, but only in the bathroom, with her back to everyone. Singing on demand still didn't feel right to her. Despite the uncomfortable situation, Otis enjoyed the girls enough to invite them on the road with them as an act in his touring revue. After, of course, Etta and Jean lied about their age and forged a note from their "parents" saying as much. They'd be paid $10 a night and they were no longer the Creolettes. They were the Peaches.

While touring was difficult for all of the Peaches, they were able to get into the studio to record a proper version of "Roll with Me Henry." Etta's friend Richard Berry came in to sing the part of Etta's sexy counterpart.

The girls didn't have to pay for the session, though Etta noted later that Otis had sneakily appended his name to the writing credits. During the session, Otis took Etta's name, then still Jamesetta Hawkins, and changed it to Etta James. At 15, her professional recording career had begun.

The record, issued by the L.A.-based Modern imprint, came out not as being sung by the Peaches, but by Etta James, with the other two Peaches on backing vocals. And while it shot up the R&B charts, it was also promptly banned from American radio for being too sexually frank.

To circumvent that problem, Modern renamed the song "The Wallflower," but they couldn't do anything about the suggestiveness of the lyrics. The record sold well in stores, but suffered from a lack of airplay. Yet what truly galled Etta came a few weeks later: Georgia Gibbs, a white singer, coyly adapted the song using more polite lyrics and less suggestive posturing. The song, renamed "Dance with Me Henry," reputedly sold over 4 million copies. Changing the word *roll* to *dance* smoothed over any sexual connotations and the song became a massive hit. "I was happy to have any success, but I was enraged to see Georgia singing the song on *The Ed Sullivan Show* while I was singing it in some funky dive in Watts" (James and Ritz, p. 47).

The lesson proved to be a painful one. Etta, embittered at the irony of the "Henry" episode, learned just how rebellious she needed to be. She'd vowed to stay true to herself, and to help her along, learn about the music industry. This would be the last time she'd get stabbed in the back. Too many black artists throughout the history of pop had drawn the short straw. Not Etta. She began her unofficial music business schooling when Gibbs released "Dance with Me Henry."

For four or five more years Etta continued to record for Modern Records, cutting some of the best female rock and R&B of the era with tunes like "Good Rockin' Daddy" and "Tough Lover." Along the way, she met Ruth Brown, one of the women in R&B that had blazed the trail Etta now traveled. At the time, Ruth had a big hit with "Mama, He Treats Your Daughter Mean," and she was headlining all over the country. She and Etta met on the circuit frequently, and James admired the example she set, not just for her but for other women on the R&B scene: the way she looked and acted, the way she sang, and especially the way she conducted herself, not taking any funny business from anyone. Etta pocketed the lessons she learned from Ruth during the late 1950s and made good use of them when necessary.

Etta toured with the hottest groups in the country at the height of her Modern years. In addition to Brown, she toured with another Atlantic act the Clovers, influential R&B act Little Willie John, and even played some dates with Elvis Presley, whom she recalls at the time being a perfect gentleman. Her run-in with an arrogant Bo Diddley, though not exactly amiable, resulted in an answer hit to his "I'm a Man," with Etta's "W-O-M-A-N."

At 20, Etta struck up her first relationship with a man. Though she had seen some things on the road that would make a sailor blush, she'd refrained from any real commitment. Harvey Fuqua, a member of the popular singing group called the Moonglows, served as her initiation into the world of full-time companionship. Older by 10 years, Fuqua was a player. He knew the ropes of the music business; Etta soaked up his knowledge and learned from his experiences.

About the same time, Etta met a man named John Lewis, a tall, distinguished-looking man who learned the ropes of the music business from his father, Howard Lewis, a famous promoter. A charmer, John was a pimp in his earlier days, and a womanizer, having courted many well-known women in Los Angeles. Lewis recognized Etta's talent and the two enjoyed a business relationship, with Lewis serving as her manager, from 1957 to 1964.

Lewis, and many others, including the often mild-mannered Sam Cooke, tried to keep a lid on Etta's emotional outbursts. As a young teen, she hadn't been disciplined all that much, and her propensity for free expression and speaking her mind often got her into trouble. On the road throughout the South, where busy, traveling R&B acts were often pulled over by state police cars, she rarely bit her tongue. The fact that they were pulled over because of the color of the passengers' skin peeved her, and she let the officers know.

Often, too, in the cutthroat world of booking and promoting concerts, agents would occasionally tell the acts they'd booked that there was no money to pay them, that ticket sales were slow. Etta would have none of it, going so far one night as to pull a gun (loaded with blanks) at a hapless promoter. He ended up chucking a suitcase full of green to her across the floor.

Her temper and wild nature were well known across the entire country. Singers like Dinah Washington and Sarah Vaughan, queens of soulful blues and jazz, knew how talented Etta was, but they had also seen the downward spiral of Billie Holiday firsthand. Etta demonstrated some of the same characteristics and tendencies, with her impetuous actions, her penchant for partying, and her rebellious temperament. And to this point she hadn't even been exposed to the hard stuff.

With the help of Fuqua and young fan-turned-manager named Greg Harris, Etta hooked up with Leonard Chess of the infamous Chess Records label. Fuqua's group the Moonglows, featuring a young Marvin Gaye, were already on the label. Harris secured Etta's release from Modern, and struck a deal with Chess. The year was 1960 and Etta was just 21.

Leonard Chess, a former juke joint owner in Chicago, started out by selling records out of his trunk. His close affiliation with electric blues artists in the city gave him a leg up on his competitors during the 1960s blues boom. But as his business grew, he desperately needed women artists to fill out his roster. He already had Waters, Berry, Little Walter, and many others. Etta became Chess's first female star.

Chess put Etta on staff as a singer and songwriter, and he paid her room and board. She wrote and did session work on her own, and as a backing singer. (She sang behind Chuck Berry's "Back in the U.S.A." and "Almost Grown.")

It was at this time that Etta began her transformation from a rocking rhythm and blues singer to a skilled interpreter of pop, soul, and jazz standards. Early on, Leonard Chess had planted the seed with Etta that he intended for her to cross over into pop, like Sam Cooke and Ray Charles had, or were in the process of doing. Berry did the same in rock and roll, writing songs aimed directly at white teenagers. Like Berry, Etta was ready. Chess saw the opportunity, and the dollar signs, and champed at the bit.

"AT LAST"

Harvey Fuqua wrote for Etta, and the songs, with simple chord changes, were the perfect beds for the singer's interpretive abilities. "At Last" became the first song to hit it big. The song fulfilled Chess's desire and crossed over to pop. James's canny phrasing, slightly jazzy and full of heart, combined with lush string arrangements, resulted in her best performance and the song vaulted her to superstar status. It also proved to be a departure for Chess, who had made most of its money thanks to the tried and true I-IV-V blues chord progressions and Chuck Berry's vintage rock and roll.

"At Last" opened the floodgates for Etta, and suddenly every record she cut became important. "Something's Got a Hold on Me," "Pushover," and "Stop the Wedding" were young rock and roll kind of tunes with a gospel spirit, while other tracks were quieter and more poignant. "Pushover," recorded in 1963, actually outdid "At Last" on the charts at the time, but is not as well known today.

Whatever Etta sang, Etta owned. She felt her performances deeply, and made her audiences empathize, if not outright relate, to what she was singing. Songs charted by the bunches, and everything Etta touched turned to gold, if not literally, certainly figuratively. For three years she reigned as the queen of what would become soul music, though no one was calling it that at the time.

But while this goodness was all happening, while the world began to appear at her feet, a seamy underside began to surface. Hard drugs like heroin and cocaine cast a spell.

> More than booze or weed or cocaine, heroin hit me hard. I loved it. Heroin became my drug of choice. It took me where I wanted to go—far away, out of it—and in a hurry. All pain, though, and confusion melted under its lazy, hazy spell. I grooved on the zapped-out sensation. . . . I was living in that place where junkies love to live, the never-never land of unreality, the place of spaced-out cool. I got hooked real quick. (James and Ritz, p. 108)

It didn't take long for Etta's reputation as a junkie to precede her. Business people and friends worried about her, how she assumed an addiction at such a young age. Outsiders tsked-tsked. They were morbidly curious. Etta became a pathetic character, from hitmaker to junkie, in the span of a few months. But she couldn't have cared less. The rush those drugs provided her became her sole focus.

The Billie Holiday comparisons were frequent and obvious. "I'd get in the same habit [as Billie] of going for the double dose. I liked seeing the needle stuck in the vein between hits. Thought it was cool. In a world where cool meant so much, junk pushed me into the perilous territory of the extra cool. The danger was thrilling" (James and Ritz, p. 108).

As a bonus, Etta discovered that the heroin helped her lose weight. She'd been portly all her life, and for the first time she felt more attractive. The idea of being a slim and peroxide blonde, with all these hit records out, fulfilled her entire self-image. Only the hit records stopped coming. As she wrestled with drugs, the quality of her work suffered, and between 1964 and 1967, only one song, her duet with Sugar Pie DeSanto, "In the Basement," made both the pop and R&B charts.

She lived among the junkies, pimps, and gangsters in Chicago. She got high before gigs, and went out into the early morning hours afterward. On tour, she had no business to attend to; that's why she had a record label and manager. It occurred to her that she might actually be living the life Dorothy, her mother, would have admired, dressing to the nines, prowling the streets. "I wanted to be nasty" (James and Ritz, p. 111).

Her junkie phase was punctuated with periods when she'd stay clean. During one such period, Dorothy would take her to Muslim temple in Los Angeles. In Atlanta, where she also spent some time, she returned to another Muslim temple, this one presided over by a man named Louis Farrakhan. She related perfectly to the religious rebel vibe emitted by the temple and Farrakhan. She felt the undercurrent of violence in her involvement with her Muslim brothers, and was attracted to it. When she moved to the Theresa Hotel in New York City, she came to know the work of Malcolm X as well. All along she studied the Koran, and, over a period of 10 years or so, called herself, off and on at least, Muslim.

She never changed her stage name—though she did add an X to her name for personal purposes—and didn't bother abiding by some of the strict rules the religion posed.

In the mid-1960s, Etta did all she could to keep her career together during her addiction. John Lewis, her manager, kept her professional life afloat, while at the same time keeping her and his own wife, incidentally, stocked with drugs. He booked the Midnighters, Hank Ballard's band, to back Etta on one tour, an arrangement that thrilled the singer. Most important, though, Lewis took care of scoring for Etta.

For a while, this worked out fine. But Etta's attitude became desperate and ungrateful. Lewis, frustrated with his client after a few senseless arguments, threatened to fire her. But backed into a corner, Etta fired him without thinking. He was her lifeline, her connection to her career, to her drugs, to her reality. Lewis, though, had grown tired of the struggle and he left.

Not content to leave her be, Lewis had the police bust in on Etta and find her hidden stash of heroin. While the charges were dropped, the relationship deteriorated.

Tragic episodes continued. Butch Navarro, a member of Etta's traveling crew, died of an overdose while shooting up with Etta. Leonard Chess approached Etta one day and told her she'd die if she didn't get help. Only a few nights previously she'd been walking the streets of Chicago, throwing up in garbage cans, desperate for a fix. She found drugs in the possession of Fred, a sordid, 80-year-old dealer. He demanded oral sex in exchange for the right to buy smack. The notion of that debasement, the utter humiliation of it, drove her away and she somehow made it through that night and the next day without scoring. She had hit proverbial rock bottom.

DETOX

The Stern's Convalescent Home was just outside Chicago in Harvey, Illinois. Upon her arrival, John Lewis fixed her a batch of heroin so as to make her withdrawal gradual. But the process became complicated. After a few days, tetanus set in, and fluid built up on her brain. She was in danger of swallowing her tongue, so they tied it to a wooden stick. She had a massive seizure and was rushed to the nearest hospital. Doctors slapped her to keep her from crashing. They yelled constantly to keep her conscious and from becoming comatose. The ordeal saw Etta come within seconds of death. When she came to, she felt like she'd been beaten in a brawl.

Her doctor told her she deserved congratulations. She was only the second person in the history of Illinois medicine to survive tetanus. Over the next few weeks, Etta had successfully returned to a sleeker and more alert version of her former self. She had lost weight and gained inspiration to return to show business.

But her new attitude didn't last long.

On her way back to New York from Chicago, Etta ran into John Lewis, now a junkie himself. She rode with him in a cab and watched as he pulled a bag of smack out of his pocket, dipped his finger in, and snorted it. The temptation was too great for Etta to resist. She succumbed to Lewis's offer and relapsed.

Her drug narcosis lasted for a few more years, through a few more abusive relationships. One that was so abusive in fact that she had to hire a bodyguard after she broke it off. She avoided total uselessness though, and hit the touring circuit again. In Detroit, she sang at the Greystone Ballroom, and connected with the Motown crowd, which was growing and beginning to make a real impact on popular music. After one Greystone gig, she partied with Marvin Gaye, whom she had known through Harvey Fuqua and the Moonglows. They snorted coke and wrote music.

She made interesting choices in songs at this time. "Fool That I Am," "Fools Rush In," "These Foolish Things," Seven Day Fool," all gave some indication of her down-sliding self-image. She began to feel the hypocrisy of her life: how she slayed audiences at her gigs, but couldn't hold her own life together at all.

She scored with Jimi Hendrix, Miles Davis, and anyone else who could serve as her supplier. Lewis, her manager, had been in jail so that pipeline had shut down. Living in Harlem, playing the Apollo Theater whenever she cared to, proved to be a good arrangement for Etta, and she survived doing it.

Back in Chicago after her stint in New York, things went from bad to worse. Still using, she and a friend were busted at a friend's house on the city's South Side. She'd been arrested for possession as well as for writing bad checks, which had been a bad habit for Etta. For four months she called Cook County Jail home. Leonard Chess was there to pick her up at the time of her release.

Jail didn't clean Etta up for good, though. She returned to Los Angeles and started back in on drugs. Every once in a while, Etta traveled to New York or Chicago to do another recording session. One notable moment involved her unstoppable yearning for heroin. She was awakened, at 2 P.M., by the smell of smoke and sirens. The house was on fire. People yelled and screamed for her to get out, but Etta had other things on her mind. As was her usual routine, she got up, went into the bathroom, and fixed. It took precious minutes that she could have used to escape the fire, but Etta paid no attention. She needed to use. She got out of the house at her leisure, much to the relief of the firefighters pounding at her bathroom door.

She met and started a relationship with Billy Foster, a tough-minded, egotistical forming boxing champ with a love for drink. He and Etta's love/hate existence resulted in many beatings for Etta. "When Billy came home screaming like a lunatic and throwing me out of bed, beating me upside the head with his fists while I screamed, 'Oh, God, why are you doing this?' and he replied, 'Bitch, I'm God and never forget it!'" (James and Ritz, p. 161). Etta discovered later that Foster was a wannabe pimp who spent his late nights chasing waitresses to work for him. Still, she had trouble extricating herself from abusive relationships. She and Foster moved to Anchorage, Alaska, in 1967, where Etta had taken a lounge singer job. At a time when Motown and the Motown Sound were cresting in popularity, and lesser singers were at the top of the charts, Etta was confined to underachievement. She recognized the irony, but felt powerless to do anything about it.

In 1967, Aretha Franklin went down to Muscle Shoals, Alabama, at the behest of Atlantic's label producer Jerry Wexler to record some Southern soul. The idea made sense, and the music that came out of Aretha's session, including the single "I Never Loved a Man (The Way I Love You)," rationalized the time and expense. Otis Redding, Joe Tex, Sam and Dave, and others were all recording R&B hits in the South and Leonard Chess picked up on the trend. He decided to send Etta South, several months pregnant, to do the same.

Rick Hall, a former country fiddler, owned Fame, the Muscle Shoals studio. "I was happy with those sessions," says Etta. "It went real cool. Rick Hall didn't tell me what to do, he told you what not to do. He let me do my own thing" (Peter Grendysa, liner notes, *Etta James: Her Best*, Chess/MCA, 1997, p. 9).

Rick Hall and Fame, the Muscle Shoals Studio

Rick Hall, a former country fiddler, opened his recording studio in Muscle Shoals in the early 1960s. He called it Fame, and the name would be a harbinger of things to come. Hall recruited a skilled, rag-tag bunch of musicians, both white and black, to serve as the house band at Fame. You might not recognize the names: "Bowlegs" Miller (trumpet); Charles Chalmers, Aaron Varnell, Floyd Newman (saxes); Carl Banks (organ); Jimmy Ray Johnson,

Albert Lowe Jr. (guitars); Barry Beckett, Dewey Oldham (piano); David Hood (bass); and Roger Hawkins (drums). They weren't as recognizable, and still aren't, as the Stax studio band in Memphis—Steve Cropper, Booker T, James Washington, and Duck Dunn—but they were every bit as soulful and talented.

It wasn't long after opening that the Muscle Shoals hits started coming. Beginning as early as 1962, Hall and the studio had success with artists Arthur Alexander and Jimmy Hughes.

But the floodgates of Fame opened in 1966 when Jerry Wexler of Atlantic Records brought Wilson Pickett to the studio first to cut "Land of 1,000 Dances," and then to record "Mustang Sally." All of a sudden, Muscle Shoals was on the map. With Pickett's hit in the pocket, Wexler and Hall teamed up for some Aretha Franklin sessions in 1967. While friction between Aretha's manager Ted White and some of the musicians disrupted those sessions, and they were finished in New York City, they still yielded Aretha's breakthrough hit, "I Never Loved a Man (The Way I Love You)."

"It was a time of rapid fire changes and breathtaking productivity, a period of almost uninterrupted success—for Rick, for the studio, for the studio musicians, and for the artists themselves, all of whom were coming to believe that there was something magical about Fame and Muscle Shoals, that Muscle Shoals had what the world was looking for" (Peter Guralnick, *Sweet Soul Music*, New York: Little Brown, 1986, p. 219).

When Leonard Chess saw his New York City counterpart Wexler cashing in on Aretha and Pickett, he decided he wanted in. He sent his artist, Etta James, down there, even though she was pregnant with her first child. The first single from those sessions was a version of Clarence Carter's "Tell Daddy," called "Tell Mama." That song hit the Top 10 on the R&B charts and broke a dry spell for Etta. The B-side of that single, "I'd Rather Go Blind," is the song that today people remember, perhaps right behind "At Last" as one of the singer's most memorable performances.

While Hall, the studio's sole arranger, enjoyed other hits during this period, there was dissatisfaction fomenting among his ranks. During their biggest year, 1968, his musicians made $17,000 apiece. But soon after that, Hall struck a production and distribution deal with Capitol Records. The agreement, made because he felt like Atlantic wasn't compensating him fairly, stung Jerry Wexler. Wexler's artists had made Muscle Shoals a recording destination, and without them Fame would have foundered. Still, Hall signed onto Capitol for $1 million. But despite the windfall, he gave each band member a bonus of only $10,000.

The parsimonious Hall, not willing to acknowledge his band's role in the studio's success, turned his musicians against him, and his entire studio outfit, minus the recording equipment, split off and formed Muscle Shoals Sound in an old casket factory. (The name took advantage of the destination's notoriety.) Their first big client? Jerry Wexler. "We just built the business from the clients Rick threw out the door," says Jimmy Johnson (Guralnick, p. 378).

> In the 1970s, Muscle Shoals Sound became a hit-making entity unto itself, cutting records by Simon and Garfunkel, Willie Nelson, Sonny and Cher, Bob Seger, and the Rolling Stones whose epic singles "Brown Sugar" and "Wild Horses" were cut at the studio in 1969. Meanwhile Hall soldiered on at Fame, cutting hits by the Osmonds, Paul Anka, Mac Davis, and Bobbie Gentry.

Letting Etta "do her thing" resulted in the glorious *Tell Mama*, the album and song of the same name. Many say that the record is one of the crowning achievements of 1960s soul. It certainly is among the top dozen or so recordings of the era, and is Etta's own defining moment record-wise.

"Tell Mama," the song, was a spin-off of Clarence Carter's "Tell Daddy," which Carter recorded with Hall a year previous, but which had only moderate success. Etta's version succeeded, though, and it hit the Top 10 on the R&B charts in 1967 and it crossed over to pop as well. That session yielded another classic on the B-side as well in the wrenching "I'd Rather Go Blind." The latter was a song she'd been inspired to write after getting to know Ellington Jordan, a convict.

While an inmate at Chino Prison, Jordan had given Etta the tune's first verse; she ran with the rest, though, in a cruel twist of fate, the byline reads "Ellington Jordan/Bill Foster." Regardless, 30 years later, the song remains relevant. Rod Stewart covered it on his classic album *Never a Dull Moment* from 1972.

Etta returned to Muscle Shoals another handful of times, a testament to how much she enjoyed the experience. The second time she ventured to Alabama, in 1968, she cut a rendition of Otis Redding's "Security" as well as a spin-off of Redding's "Mr. Pitiful," calling it "Miss Pitiful." At the same session, Etta covered Aretha's "Do Right Woman, Do Right Man." While she was there, she spoke with Redding via telephone, and the two made plans to record some duets. But the idea never came to be; Otis died tragically in a plane crash soon after that conversation.

Also in 1968, almost 30, Etta gave birth to her first child, Donto. The elation of birth, however, gave way to a sad reality. Etta, still delving into drugs and the wild life, had no business being a mother. Their apartment resembled a hippie hangout, and Etta was still coming to blows with her partner Foster. When Donto was just six days old, Dorothy, Etta's mother, saw the debauchery surrounding the baby and kidnapped him. She told Etta's friend she was taking him for a ride—and didn't return him for three days.

One time, Etta, Billy, and the baby were traveling across country so Etta could perform. But the baby had trouble breathing and they rushed him to the hospital. The ward wouldn't admit him, however, without a deposit. Etta attempted to pay, but soon realized she had no money left in the bank; Billy had gambled it all away. Desperate to get help, she pawned a ring and the spare tire off her mobile home. Things had gone from bad to worse and were about to get even lower.

There was an arrest warrant outstanding from a time she had jumped bail in Alaska, and bounty hunters working on commission were hot on her trail. While she was on the road she returned to find the door to her apartment off its hinges. Knowing they were in pursuit, Etta moved around during the night, often crawling through backyards to escape detection. She couldn't see her baby, who was now in the hospital with a respiratory illness, and she had no home to speak of. She still had to perform. One night, when she pulled up to a gig, she saw several cars angling toward her. She wheeled around and escaped, forfeiting a paycheck. The next day, she turned herself in. The day after that, in January 1969, she came before the judge in Anchorage. They put her back in jail.

Etta's time in prison wasn't long, 10 days, but it was tortuous. While there, Donto had to have risky emergency surgery. But without a way to communicate with those with her baby, she had no way of finding out for days what had happened. Eventually, a friend of hers, Fred Johnson, the husband of a woman who owned a nightclub Etta performed at, came to tell her the operation had been successful and that he had the money to bail her out.

She met, dated, and fell in love with a man named Artis Mills, a hulking but down-to-earth country boy from Texas. He served as a calming influence on Etta, whose only narcotic vice now was marijuana. They married in the spring of 1969. Things were looking up. She had a husband who loved her, a healthy baby, and a new outlook on life. She had every opportunity to make a fresh start as the 1960s turned into the 1970s. But it didn't happen.

THE 1970S

Mills despised hard drugs, so that forced Etta to score and shoot up on the sly. She'd buy her drugs from a dealer—often saying she was going out to buy "chicken"—hide them at home, and shoot up when her husband was out of the house. She hid her stash in her wig holders, of which she had many. Eventually, Artis found her stash; it was difficult for Etta to keep her habit under wraps.

But what Artis told her surprised her. "If you're going to keep on doing this, I'm gonna do it with you" (James and Ritz, p. 190). And that was the day her husband also became a junkie.

Etta's sound at the turn of the 1970s followed the trend of most black music. That is, it became funkier. Acts like Sly and the Family Stone, Curtis Mayfield, and the Temptations were emerging as major acts and their sound reflected the grit of urban existence much more than the polish of Motown or the down-home sounds of Stax.

With the death of Leonard Chess from a heart attack in 1969, Etta had more control over what she recorded. Funk, as well as the white rock of Hendrix,

Janis Joplin, Rod Stewart, and the Rolling Stones had surged, and Etta picked up on that both in her vocal approach and on her records. In Janis she saw a protégée, a rebellious upstart carved directly from her mold, especially in her hallucinogenic indulgences. Like every good junkie Etta was into experimentation. She began dipping into acid and taking trips.

She befriended Sly Stone and indulged in hallucinogens plenty with him. The bohemian appetites of hippies from the late 1960s to the early 1970s dovetailed nicely with Etta's own ravenous narcotic appetite. And now with Artis imbibing right alongside her, she had everything she needed. One night, Sly Stone, who ran an informal stolen car ring, offered the couple a Cadillac, free. Things couldn't get any better, at least for a while.

But the good times quickly turned bad. When money became a problem, Artis and Etta resorted to holding people up. They'd pull a gun on a dealer or a friend, and demand money, drugs, or both. Word got around that the couple had become untethered. They ran scams, and turned friends into enemies.

Eventually, the illicit activity caught up with the couple. They were seized in Texas and thrown once again into jail. Artis, being a gentleman, didn't want Etta hanging out in a Texas prison, so he took the fall, assuming responsibility for all the charges: the holding, the using, the bad checks. He'd spend a decade in jail. Etta was freed on bail and she returned to New York City with Dorothy and Donto, where the prospect of cheap heroin lay ahead.

Etta's rock and roll journey began with producer Gabriel Mekler, a pop and rock-oriented producer who had enjoyed some success with Three Dog Night. They chose material from rock and pop songwriters like Tracy Nelson of the band Mother Earth and Randy Newman, whose rebellious spirit Etta identified with. The record 1974's *Etta James*, fell on deaf ears, though, and its failure brought on great disappointment.

With no management or career to speak of, Etta headed to a methadone clinic, courtesy of the folks at the Chess label, which was now located in New York. Following rehab, the label hired her for a desk job, with a weekly salary and an additional stipend for her methadone treatment.

Not surprisingly, Etta became addicted to methadone, and began supplementing her legal doses with illegal heroin. A few months later she was apprehended again by the police, this time on a warrant for drug possession and writing bad checks in Texas and California. The judge sent Etta to Riker's Prison this time, for a total of three weeks. Upon her release, she promised to resolve her criminal charges in both Texas and California. A judge in California, recognizing her drug addiction, sentenced her to Tarzana Psychiatric Hospital outside of Los Angeles. She'd spend the next 17 months there.

The experience at Tarzana was life-changing. She was demeaned, verbally abused, mentally and physically tortured by counselors and other inmates. She had to wear a diaper and a baby bonnet, and a sign around her neck that read "I'm Etta James and I'm a spoiled baby."

Group sessions would last up to 48 hours. Patients would get completely broken down and reassembled. Doctors penetrated Etta's steely exterior to get to the hurt beneath. She would exercise excessively, attempting desperately to get free once and for all of the addiction that gripped her.

Eventually, Etta made progress. And the more progress she made, the higher she was elevated in the ranks at Tarzana. As a senior coordinator, she began leading groups of her own. Etta bought completely into the program and for the first time she began to understand herself, her own life, a little better. She had the power to change, and she made it happen.

During her time at Tarzana, she received permission to record an album. Released in 1974, *Come a Little Closer* is miraculous in that it was made at all. It finds Etta in the painful throes of withdrawal, but also in incredibly strong voice, especially on a song called "Feeling Uneasy," a wordless moan of a song that is one of the unrecognized highlights of Etta's career and a breathtaking musical depiction of a junkie trying to clean up.

After two years at Tarzana, she left, rather unceremoniously after boozing it up one night with some other staff members. Still, she left with a man named Sam Dennis, one of the therapists Etta had been working with. Also an ex-junkie, Dennis would keep Etta in line. After leaving Tarzana, she became pregnant with Dennis's baby and gave birth to another boy, her second, in the spring of 1976.

As Etta's luck would have it though, Sam became nasty, and it didn't take long for her to feel endangered in his presence. He'd tour with her, but the relationship became unsteady fast.

At the same time, her tenure with the Chess label, a time that had lasted 16 years, was also coming to a close, making Etta feel uneasy and uncertain about her future. Along came Jerry Wexler, who had left Atlantic and now worked as a freelance producer. He contracted Etta to a one-album deal with Warner Bros.

Deep in the Night is one of Etta's most memorable recordings. While it featured songs of the period like Alice Cooper's "Only Women Bleed" and the Eagles' "Take It to the Limit," it also featured a lot of Etta's outstanding vocals and a session band up to the task. Names in the studio included Bonnie Raitt, drummer Jeff Porcaro, and guitarists Larry Carlton and Cornell Dupree.

To Etta's credit, she and Wexler fought back the temptation to go disco, which at the time had been mesmerizing the country. The album didn't sell well enough for Warner Bros. to contract another project, but the fact that Etta was back on track, without compromising, had been encouraging enough. Next up: an album with R&B producer extraordinaire Allen Toussaint.

While Etta got her footing as a recording artist again, Artis Mills, her husband, emerged from 10 years in jail. The year was 1981.

After rehab, Etta had taken up cocaine, in small amounts at first. But as her appetite grew, so did her desperation to use; little by little her priorities changed from her career to her habit. In 1980, Etta hired Lupe de Leon to be her manager. For a while, he tried booking her, and experienced a bit of success. But the struggle became too great for de Leon, and soon, Etta was without effective representation and a booking agent once again.

Fed up with finding a new manager, she started booking her own gigs, as bleak an activity as any artist could ever undertake. In fact, this was still another dark period for James. She even posed over the telephone as her own agent.

Etta met an old friend and former junkie Esther Phillips who turned her onto an intimate L.A. club called Vine Street. There she reacquainted herself with her classic material, and a more nuanced vocal approach. Through the 1970s she had become a shouter, a visceral singer with more power than poignancy. But at Vine Street she had cleaned up her act, and, with discipline and a renewed commitment to Artis and her sons, freed herself from cocaine.

For some reason, Etta's 1980s work resulted in her becoming known as a blues singer. This is a misnomer; she never made a conscious decision to alter her material in that direction. Perhaps it's because R&B phased out in the 1980s at the hands of dance music and blues. Stevie Ray Vaughan helped reintroduce audiences to electric blues, and promoters, eager to fill that new need, began searching for possible performers. Etta happened to be in the right place at the right time. The coincidence boosted her profile at the time and carried her through the next several years.

In the late 1980s, another addiction, this time to codeine, knocked her off track. And another rehabilitation stint, this time a month at the Betty Ford Clinic, was the next stop for Etta.

Cleaned up again, Etta got back on track recording in 1988. *Seven Year Itch* reminded fans why she had such a great reputation for her 1960s work in Southern soul, and 1990's *Sticking to My Guns* said it loud and proud. In 1992, Jerry Wexler returned with *The Right Time*, and several other albums saw her exploring jazzier directions.

Etta also began enjoying some recognition for her entire body of work. Most important, in 1993 she was invited into the Rock and Roll Hall of Fame, at a ceremony in which Wexler served as her presenter.

In 1994, she did something she'd been wanting to do for many years, but never got the chance. She dedicated a recording, *Mystery Lady*, to her mother, Dorothy. It won a Grammy, her first, for Best Jazz Vocal album.

She was inducted into the Blues Hall of Fame in 2001 and the Grammy organization bestowed her with a Lifetime Achievement Award in 2003.

LEGACY

Jerry Wexler, the legendary producer at Atlantic and the man who worked with so many of the great R&B performers, described Etta James as "the greatest of all modern blues singers . . . the undisputed Earth Mother" (www.rockhall.com/inductee/etta-james). Her raw and moving vocals and red-blooded passion has influenced many important singers of the commercial pop era, including Janis Joplin and Bonnie Raitt, both of whom have served as touchstones for many younger artists. Her early hits, like "Roll with Me Henry" and "Good Rockin' Daddy," essentially vintage rock and roll songs of the 1950s, assure her place in the early history of rock right alongside seminal artists like Little Richard and Chuck Berry. In the same way, her R&B/soul work in the 1960s deserves its place alongside Aretha and Otis.

Unfortunately, being a junkie was as significant to Etta as being a singer and for 17 years her career suffered from terrific swings of elation and depression. But to her credit, her tremendous personal problems never completely got the best of her. So great was her urge to sing, it didn't matter how deep her addiction or desperate her plight. She always managed to come out of it, survive somehow, and live to sing about it.

Etta's odyssey is the stuff of rock and roll lore, a harrowing tale of soaring highs and unimaginable lows. Through it all, her legacy remains, as one of pop music's most enduring singers, as a true artist who despite her struggles, managed to express herself in ways no other artist has before or since.

SELECTED DISCOGRAPHY

At Last! (MCA/Chess, 1961)
Tell Mama: The Complete Muscle Shoals Sessions (Chess/MCA, 1968/2001)
Come a Little Closer (MCA/Chess, 1974/1996)
Deep in the Night (Bullseye Blues, 1978/1996)
Her Best: The Chess 50th Anniversary Collection (MCA/Chess, 1997)
Love Songs (MCA/Chess, 2001)
The Chess Box (MCA/Chess 2000)
Best of the Modern Years (Blue Note, 2005)

FURTHER READING

Gaar, Gillian. *She's a Rebel: The History of Women in Rock and Roll*. New York: Seal Press, 2002.
Hildebrand, Lee. *Etta James: The Chess Box*. Liner notes. MCA/Chess 2000.
James, Etta and David Ritz. *Etta James: Rage to Survive*. New York: Villard, 1995.

Courtesy of Photofest.

Ike and Tina Turner

THE KING AND QUEEN OF RHYTHM

Before all the horrific details of their relationship came to light, before the biopic and Tina's book *I, Tina* engulfed them, Ike and Tina Turner made a massive musical impact on the world of R&B. Ike was an architect of the early rock and roll sound and a precursor to Elvis Presley himself. He helped nurture the music and careers of many who'd go on to legendary fame, including B.B. King, Little Richard, and Ray Charles.

One of his most famous clients happened to be Tina herself. A true project when she met Ike, Tina would go on to become one of R&B's most dynamic performers. With Ike behind her as a svengali-like bandleader, Tina foisted herself on audiences with rabid, otherworldly energy and mesmerizing stage presence.

One reviewer in 1968 described the vision of Ike, Tina, and their backing singers the Ikettes, like this:

> It was obvious, from her first number, that Tina Turner is the most exciting female performer in the Rhythm and Blues idiom today. Superlatives like "wild" or "primitive" cannot do her justice. With the Ikettes remaining on stage, Tina, in a figure-hugging red mini, opened with "Sweet Soul Music." It's almost uninteresting now that everyone features it but Tina, but the Ikettes made it unmistakably theirs. How she manages to dance like she does one will never know. On "A Love Like Yours" the Ikettes wailed in authentic gospel style while the band ceased playing and Tina preached with an intensity which was embarrassing for some. (Bill Millar, "The Ike & Tina Turner Revue," *Soul Music Monthly*, April 25, 1968).

Ike and Tina Turner spent 16 years on the road together with the Ike and Tina Turner Revue, from 1960 to 1976, turning on audiences with pure, unadulterated musical exhilaration. They won fans all over the world with a tight ship of a show the likes of which only James Brown could approximate.

Ike was a throwback to the post-war blues musicians of Clarksdale, Mississippi. Tina was a throwback as well, to blues belters like Big Mama Thornton and Bessie Smith. Together, their outsized talents helped their shows become epic events. Unfortunately, the same could not be said for their recordings. Ike and Tina waxed only a handful of memorable full-length albums. A couple of their singles, including the controversial Phil Spector creation "River Deep, Mountain High," "Proud Mary," and "Fool in Love," of course, will reside high in the pantheon of pop. But their recordings often died quick commercial deaths.

This could be because Ike produced relatively few original tunes, and when he did, they were often imitations of tracks he had already written. He and Tina also didn't spend much time studying trends, which prevented them from making false stylistic moves simply to keep up. But it also gave them an air of stodginess at points during their career, when they should have been keeping it young and changing with the times. Occasionally, as on their Beatles' cover "Come Together," or on the Stones' "Honky Tonk Women," they turned in innovative renditions of popular songs. This kept their live repertoire fresh without having to belabor the act of writing too many original compositions.

Ike's pursuit of money also distorted the intentions of his Revue. He made many of his musical decisions based on cash, and, more than anything, he loved doing cash business. When he finally built his own studio, for example, he stepped up his recording activity, largely because he didn't have to pay for studio time.

Still, it all happened for the Ike and Tina Revue when the gang hit the stage. For Tina, the stage was a safe haven, a place where all the fear, sadness, and violence disappeared, at least momentarily. For Ike, too, the stage had become his resting place, where concerns about money, addiction, infidelity, and frustration all wafted away in a cloud of cool cigarette smoke, electrifying music, and the exhilarating, hip-shaking moves of his partner, Tina, one of the most exciting performers in the history of popular music.

IKE'S EARLY YEARS

Izear Luster "Ike" Turner Jr. was born in 1931 in Clarksdale, Mississippi, a segregated lowland cotton town between the Mississippi and Yazoo Rivers. It's also one of the town's most responsible for producing Delta blues artists. As the last child of a seamstress mom and an alcoholic dad, Ike didn't have the kind of upbringing that fostered entitlement or stability. At an early age he began witnessing violence, learning about the pleasures of sex, and realizing the uncomfortable realities of growing up quickly.

As a youngster, Ike earned money for the family by gathering up the excess fabric from his mother's projects and piecing them together to make rugs. He also worked for a white blind man named Mr. Brown, walking him around town. When he wasn't busy, he learned guitar from Mr. Brown's wife. At seven, thanks to tutoring by local blues legend Pinetop Perkins, he began playing the piano. Ironically, even though he is better known for his innovative guitar playing, he speaks of piano as his first instrument.

"I was always very talented musically," says Ike.

> I inspired Elvis you know. I didn't know who Elvis was. I was playing in West Memphis and there was a white guy that was driving a gravel truck. He used to come around to the back of the club because people didn't mix in those days. I would pull out the piano from the wall and he would stand behind the piano and watch me play. But I didn't know him. Years later when he was famous he walked up to me and said, "You don't remember me do you? I'm the guy who used to hide behind the piano and watch you." (Precious Williams, "Ike Turner," *Scotland on Sunday*, September 16, 2001)

The first woman Ike married was Edna Dean Stewart, at 15. They stayed together for a while, living at his mother's house. But Stewart didn't want to be in Clarksdale and Ike endured his first trying split. The second woman, Alice, came along in Helena, Arkansas, but didn't stay faithful enough for Ike. The next Mrs. Turner was Anna Mae Wilson out of Greenville. They lasted through Ike's eventual move to east St. Louis.

In time, Ike managed to make a name for himself as a local musician. By 16, Ike was broadcasting his favorites and his own tunes via WROX out of Clarksdale, and gigging on the side as a pianist with Sonny Boy Williamson and guitarist Robert Nighthawk. He also proved handy with musical instruments.

He'd fix busted pianos, mend broken guitar strings, make reeds from sugarcane; do whatever possible to keep instruments in circulation. The repairs helped him understand the inner workings of many instruments, and he soon became skilled on a number of different ones.

TINA'S EARLY YEARS

Anna Mae Bullock was born in a Brownsville, Tennessee, hospital in 1939 and raised in a four-room shotgun shack on a plantation in the segregated, back-country town of Nut Bush, a tiny burg rich with arable farmland. The child of parents Zelma and Floyd Richard Bullock, Anna Mae had a sister, Alline, who was older by three years. Zelma was a feisty woman of Native American blood, who'd been smoking and shooting guns from the time she was 10 years old. Husband Richard was a strong personality as well, the resident overseer on a sharecropping farm, owned by whites, called Poindexter Farm. Richard was also a deacon at the local church, and he needed all his spiritual reverence to deal with the constant conflict he found himself in with his wife. They fought endlessly and loudly.

The domestic strife took a toll on young Anna Mae. She didn't receive much affection from her parents, who viewed her as a product of a floundering marriage, an unwanted child. Alline, born when the couple experienced happier days, enjoyed what little tenderness her mother and father could muster. But there was little left over for Anna Mae.

Anna Mae looked very different from her sister. She had reddish skin and fair hair, with unusual facial features. Alline was very dark-skinned, with the traditional African American features of her father. Not surprisingly, given the emotional pall generally cast over the house and family, there wasn't much music present. There were no musical instruments around the house. They did enjoy lively singing every Sunday as part of their church service. But the musical dimension of growing up began and ended there.

With this, and virtually everything else related to her childhood—love, friendship, pastimes—Anna Mae had to go and find it for herself. Busy and mischievous, she was a tomboy who loved getting into scrapes, exploring, and shaking things up at home. Her sister was quieter and slower, more cautious. The two got along; Alline tried her best to watch out for her little sister. But Anna Mae always seemed to have plans of her own.

In the mid-1940s, when her parents moved across Tennessee to work for a new wartime defense facility, Anna Mae and her sister split up. Alline went to live with her mother's aunt and uncle, while Anna Mae was assigned to the strict and religious family on her father's side. Life with them was dreadful. From day one she wanted desperately to get out, to be rejoined with her own family. In a few years, when her parents were more established in their new jobs, they finally sent for their children and Anna Mae got her wish.

But even when Anna Mae and the Bullocks came back together under the same roof, this time in Knoxville, Tennessee, the emotional isolation from her parents continued. Her mother and father's marriage, still embattled, interfered with any kind of harmony the Bullock girls craved and their lives felt unsettled. To avoid the negativity, the sisters made their own way, going to school, learning the popular spots in Knoxville, and making friends around town.

During the summers she and her sister would help out on the farm, picking cotton and strawberries. When Anna Mae was 11 her mother had finally had enough of her father, and she disappeared without telling her kids. She had moved to St. Louis to live with her aunt. Not long after their mother left, her father took up with another woman. The relationship progressed quickly and together they too left the house, for Detroit. The Bullock girls were passed along to another aunt, Georgie.

Neither parent paid much attention to their kids after they left. Father Bullock sent some child support money weekly, but that stopped after a while, and Alline and Anna Mae were left to fend for themselves. Anna Mae took a job working for a white family, the Hendersons.

A teacher and a car dealer, the Henderson couple was a typical, well-adjusted family, something Anna Mae had never seen before. They taught her by example what it was like to live in a happy household. They cared for her like parents, and set Anna Mae on a somewhat straighter path.

In high school, Anna Mae came into her own. She got involved with organizing hops and she excelled on the basketball team. Interestingly, she also came out with the cheerleaders at halftime, where she'd do stunts in her game uniform. She had lots of friends and socialized every chance she got.

In spring of 1956, Aunt Georgie became seriously ill and passed away. Anna Mae's mom came for the funeral and took her back to St. Louis with her. Alline, her big sister, had already made the trip.

THE KINGS OF RHYTHM

Now 17, and Alline already 20, the two would go to clubs around St. Louis and east St. Louis. At the time, R&B was in full swing, and the rough and tumble clubs of east St. Louis had all kinds of great music blaring from their open doors. One night she and Alline went with a group of Alline's girlfriends to a place called Club D'Lisa to see a notoriously popular R&B act called Ike Turner and the Kings of Rhythm. Anna Mae remembers the music this way:

> [Ike] hit one note and I thought: "Jesus, this guy can play." And that joint started rocking. The floor was packed with people dancing and sweating to the great music, and I was just sitting there, amazed, staring at Ike Turner. I thought, "God, I wonder why so many women like him. He sure is ugly." But I kept listening and looking. I almost went into a trance just watching him. (Tina Turner with Kurt Loder, *I, Tina*, New York: Avon Books, 1986, p. 50)

The first edition of the Kings of Rhythm formed when Ike was still a teenager. He and a few of his classmates began as a cover band. They dug R&B, jump blues, and boogie-woogie, the kind they heard by the likes of Amos Milburn, Roy Brown, Charles Brown, and Ray Milton. Hungry and talented, they gigged around Clarksdale. On Saturdays they'd back up a couple of trucks, block off some streets, and have a battle of the high school bands.

The Kings of Rhythm featured saxophonists Jackie Brenston and Raymond Hill, drummer Willie Sims, guitarist Willie Kizart, and singer Johnny O'Neal. Ike played piano. They set out for Memphis in early March 1951 to wax their debut recordings. A man named Sam Phillips was managing a place called the Memphis Recording Service, where he taped the work of local musicians and peddled them to indie labels.

They had a few tunes ready to cut including Ike's own "I'm Lonesome Baby" and "Heartbroken and Worried." Ike sang both of those tunes, but not very well and Sam recommended that some other band member give it a try. So when the next tune came up, "Rocket 88," saxman Brenston took the lead vocal. The song still featured Ike's jagged guitar line and distorted rhythm. In the editing room, after the band was long gone, Phillips would later mistakenly credit this song to Jackie Brenston and the Delta Cats when he licensed the tune to Chess. But everyone present knew that it was simply another Kings of Rhythm tune, only with Brenston on vocals. Oddly enough, it is this song that has secured a lofty position in the annals of rock and roll. Many call the 1951 Phillips track the first true rock song.

"Rocket 88" became a regional hit, but it caused problems within the band almost immediately. Singer O'Neal signed with King Records; Brenston's ego swelled and he left, as well. Ike dissolved the band and moved on his own to west Memphis.

At the time, a new young Clarksdale guitarist named B.B. King had been at a Memphis recording session for Modern Records when Ike turned up on his bicycle. The session wasn't going well, and the band needed a break. Ike jumped in on the piano and label owner Joe Bihari loved what he heard. After Ike told them about his Mississippi roots—that he knew the Mississippi blues scene and all the artists in and around Clarksdale and Greenville—Bihari and his two brothers signed Ike to the label as a talent scout.

The generous salary thrilled Ike. The Biharis bought him a car and paid his travel expenses as well. Ike was in his element; he referred musical talent to the Biharis as a full-time employee at Modern. While there, Ike turned up talent like Bobby "Blue" Bland, and he had a hand in bringing people to the label like Little Walter and Muddy Waters. Ike brought Howlin' Wolf to prominence as well; he took him to Sam Phillips, who in turn signed him to Chess. Wolf also recorded for Modern.

At this time, the Modern label demand for material grew. So Ike began writing songs for the label's new artists, and he'd often accompany them on piano or guitar in the studio. This was a particularly fertile time for Ike, who came into his own as an artist and talent evaluator. He contributed dozens of songs to the Modern roster and to various Sun Sessions by the likes of Johnny O'Neal, his then-wife Bonnie Turner, Billy "the Kid" Emerson, and Raymond Hill, all of whom were members at one time or another of his Kings of Rhythm band.

Turner's Kings of Rhythm also came back together in Memphis. O'Neal's deal with the King label never worked out and Jackie Brenston returned to the fold after being unable to follow up his "own" hit "Rocket 88." When Ike picked up and moved to St. Louis in 1954, frustrated at his inability to have a hit with his busy slate of Memphis recording sessions, most of the band came with him.

It was in the shadowy clubs of east St. Louis, that part of town across the river from the much cleaner (and whiter) St. Louis, that Ike and the Kings of Rhythm began clicking. But east St. Louis was a very different place than Memphis. The Tennessee city populated its clubs with hip, generally well-dressed and sophisticated inhabitants. Not so in east St. Louis, where the streets were full of trouble-seeking rabble-rousers.

Ike was street-smart enough to cope with the edginess and degenerate nature of his new home. In fact, he referred to the Kings of Rhythm, an eight-member band, as a gang. And as a gang, they were often faced with defending their turf physically as well as musically. There were often fights at their east St. Louis gigs, and the band was forced to carry guns.

Further, Ike began gambling in the city. He considered himself lucky, and, as a steady gambler, would-be bandits knew he was often in possession of large amounts of cash. Ike's gun, the permit for which he'd received from the city's police department as an honorary deputy, came in handy on a frequent basis.

Envious musicians also threatened them after they were turned down at Kings of Rhythm auditions. One musician, this one not particularly violent, who made it into the band's lineup was a guitar wiz named Jimmy. But Ike had some problems with his freelancing sound, and his overuse of effects. It got to be so incongruous with the band's sound that he had to let him go in favor of rehiring Willie Kizart, his original guitarist. Of course, the rest of the world would come to know the canned guitar player when he changed his name to "Jimi," as in Jimi Hendrix.

Bonnie Turner, Ike's wife at the time, also gained fluency on the piano, which freed Ike up to spend more time on guitar. Like Hendrix, Ike picked up a Strat and began making unruly noise. His innovations and unfettered experimentation on the instrument—even though he didn't read music—were obvious from the start, and Ike soon became known more as a guitar player than a pianist.

At first, they began playing east St. Louis gigs on Sunday afternoons to black teenagers, innocently enough. But soon white teenagers, hearing what all the fuss was about, began turning out to see the show and trouble started brewing. Police came with paddy wagons to bring the white teens home. A friend of Ike's, witnessing the enthusiasm of white audiences, opened a white-oriented teen club and soon, the Kings of Rhythm began playing that venue as well.

Ike prided himself on the racial diversity of his audience and made it a policy to play only in venues in which both whites and blacks were allowed. The club scene in east St. Louis may have been a tough place to make a living, but it was also a wonderland of work opportunities, and Ike developed a reputation as one of the city's real showmen. He was hard-working too. After a while Turner and his boys were playing over a dozen jobs a week.

Club owner George Edick recalls that he was also one of the city's strictest bandleaders:

> Ike's band had to be dressed—they wore suits and ties. And he wouldn't let them have drinks up on the bandstand. There was no drinking at all. He used to rehearse at my place sometimes, and if one of his men was late or something, he would raise holy hell with him. That's why he changed musicians so much—he would just get rid of guys if he had trouble with them. Ike was a strict businessman. He played three or four gigs a night, and he was strictly straight. He was just a workaholic. (Turner and Loder, p. 59)

IKE AND TINA MEET

The more Anna Mae watched the Kings of Rhythm, the more she felt the urge to get up on stage with the band to sing. Ike often invited girls on stage to try their hand at singing, and Anna Mae would watch woman after woman, all apples of Ike's eye at least for the night, get up on stage and sing, mostly poorly. Of course, he invited them up in return for other favors, after hours.

Anna Mae first sang in public at the Spring Hill Baptist Church as a child in the gospel choir. She demonstrated some talent as a singer, but considering music wasn't exactly in the family, no one took special notice. Her father did have a radio and the family would gather and listen to weekly serials shows. Anna Mae remembered those rare times of family togetherness fondly.

The music Anna Mae typically heard growing up was country and western, though some of her uncles appreciated down-home blues. That gritty style didn't appeal to her much though. As a teen, she preferred to listen to the songs on popular radio, mainly R&B. She sang them at home all the time, and though she wasn't performing, she built her voice up enough to sing with power.

One night at an east St. Louis roadhouse called the Manhattan Club, Anna Mae begged her sister's boyfriend, Gene Washington, Ike's drummer, to ask Ike to give her a chance. When he did, Ike said, "Sure." But Anna Mae never heard her name called from the stage. Frustrated, she waited.

Between sets, as Ike was doodling on the organ, Gene Washington decided not to wait any longer. He grabbed a drum microphone, which was on a long cord, and pulled it all the way to Alline and Anna Mae's table. Alline, bashful, pushed the microphone away from her face. But Anna Mae lit up. She took advantage and started singing. Ike had been tapping out a song she happened to know and she sang along with it.

The pianist perked up fast. He came off the stage, curious, and asked her what other songs she could sing.

> I told him I knew some Little Willie John songs and some of the blues stuff, and a lot of the songs that he and the band were playing. So Ike started playing the things that I knew, and I started singing and the band started drifting back in with their women—who are all wondering, "Who's that girl up there?" But once they got a good look at me, they fell in love with little Ann—because I was no threat to any of them.' (Turner andLoder, p. 62)

Anna Mae finished out the night fronting Ike's Kings of Rhythm band; it was the first time he'd ever used a woman singer, and it was also the first time she'd ever been in the spotlight. She left the Manhattan Club stage that night feeling like a true star, perhaps knowing that her life was about to change. From that point on, Anna Mae became a prime attraction for the Kings of Rhythm.

"Back in those days, people weren't that crazy about women singers," said Ike. "But I let her sing at the club 'cos the people liked her. I never paid her any money, but I gave her gifts instead and I wasn't charging her for any of the tutoring or singing lessons I gave her" (Ike Turner and Nigel Cawthorne, *Takin' Back My Name: The Confessions of Ike Turner*, London: Virgin Books, 1999, p. 72).

From that point, Ike and Anna Mae (the band called her "Little Ann") became good friends. Ike taught her the finer points of voice control and performance. He tutored her on the band's large repertoire, and they spent a lot of time together. In Ike's words, they did "everything together except have sex." At the time, Ike was doing this with many other women.

Ike was living with a woman named Lorraine Taylor, with whom he had a son, Ike Jr. Anna Mae took up with Ike's sax player, Raymond Hill. In a short time, she had his baby, a son named Craig. The turn of events—a career with a disreputable rock band, a baby out of wedlock—set Anna Mae's mother off. She was too young to give birth, and not the kind of girl who should be fronting a bar band on the wrong side of town. Her mother put Anna Mae out of the house to live on her own with the baby.

The arrangement strained Anna Mae. At the time she had a job as a nurse's aide. She was rehearsing with the band, and had sole responsibility for the baby. To aggravate things, Hill had left her. Affording an apartment became difficult, but Ike wasn't about to bail her out. He paid her just a few dollars a week to help her with bus money to and from rehearsals and gigs, and no more.

For the next three years, the band featured Little Ann in its act. But neither the Kings of Rhythm nor Little Ann made much more than regional impact. One day in 1959, Ike wrote a number titled "A Fool in Love" for a singer named Art Lassiter, a guy Ike had chosen as a lead singer for the band. But Lassiter never showed for the recording session, and the band had booked expensive studio time. Little Ann had helped Lassiter learn the tune and had demoed it for Ike before the band entered in the studio.

When Lassiter didn't show, Ike and the band decided to use Little Ann to cut a "dummy" vocal, a singing track to be erased and replaced by Lassiter's when he decided to show up. Anna Mae's vocal was high-pitched and screechy, largely because Ike had written the tune to be sung by a man. Still, it was a decent performance, and a tape of the song circulated around local clubs. A local disc jockey, Dave Dixon, heard it and suggested that Ike send the song over to Juggy Murray at Sue Records. Murray liked it and bought the master.

"All of those blues singers sounded like dirt," said Murray after hearing the tune. "Tina sounded like screaming dirt. It was a funky sound" (Al Quaglieri, liner notes, *Proud Mary: The Best of Ike and Tina Turner*, EMI/Sue, 1991).

"A Fool in Love" has been called "the blackest record to creep into the white pop charts since Ray Charles' gospel-styled 'What'd I Say'" the previous summer, (Turner and Loder, p. 79).

Juggy Murray, the principal behind Sue, drew up a contract and Ike got his act in order. He received a $20,000 advance for recording and publishing rights. He named his all-girl back-up singers the Ikettes, and renamed Anna Mae "Tina," to rhyme with his favorite television character Sheena the Queen of the Jungle. Another reason he made up a name for her was to prevent Anna Mae from taking off with the name. Should Anna Mae leave, Ike could find another Tina, no problem. He called the whole production the Ike and Tina Turner Revue.

THE BIG TIME

It didn't take long for the revue to start making waves with Tina out front, screeching and screaming like a cornered bobcat. "A Fool in Love" hit the charts, as did follow-up singles like "I Idolize You," "I'm Jealous," and "Poor Fool." But the folks at Sue were dismayed by the lack of pop appeal and they sent Ike and Tina to New York City to record with some bigger names and top-notch talent.

"It's Gonna Work Out Fine" featured the songwriting team of Mickey Baker and Sylvia Vanderpool. The song, hinging on Sylvia's guitar playing and Baker's booming voice, accomplished the Sue label's wishes. It climbed the charts, peaking on the Pop list at number 14, and preventing Ike and Tina from being a one-hit wonder. Capitalizing on the temporary attention, they booked a week at the Apollo Theater. Tina electrified audiences, those notoriously difficult to please, with her high-energy stage persona. She played four shows a day for seven days that week, and in doing so the Ike and Tuna Turner Revue became a must-see traveling road show.

It was at about this time in her career that Tina began to develop her personal style, at least aesthetically. As the story goes, Tina got a bad dye job at a local hairdresser. They had put too much bleach in her hair and left the heat cap on too long. As a result, almost all of her hair fell out; her scalp was visible, with nothing left but stubble. She was mortified. Her hair was ruined! Then the solution: Tina began wearing wigs, long, flowing wild wigs, the crazier the better. They'd soon become one of her stylistic signatures.

"I got to like wearing wigs. Because I loved movement, especially onstage, and I had this image of myself and the Ikettes singing and dancing, and all of our hair constantly moving, swaying to the music. It seemed exciting, but at the same time very classy" (Turner and Loder, p. 87).

Also about this time, the nature of her relationship with Ike changed, even though Ike was still with his wife Lorraine. In fact, his wife had escaped for a while, taking Ike Jr. with her. While she was away, Ike had partied and was drunk. Tina brought him home to sober him up, and the evening ended in a compromising clutch.

"The first time I went with her I felt like I screwed my sister or somethin'," said Ike. "I mean, I hope to die—we really had been like brother and sister. It wasn't just her voice. . . . Anyway, Ann and me was tight" (Turner and Loder, p. 74).

Tina became pregnant soon after, but not from her interlude with Ike. The father was her ex-boyfriend Hill. Still, the situation embarrassed Ike and made it seem a little suspicious. Given the act's name and Tina's pregnant form, audiences everywhere figured they were married. Indeed, hanky-panky had been going on. And Taylor, returning from St. Louis to be with her husband and father of her children, was suspicious. Ike had some explaining to do.

But his explanations didn't wash. Taylor knew something was going on between Tina and Ike and she wanted to know the story.

She marched into Tina's room—they lived in the same house—and aimed a .38 caliber gun to her head. Tina, half asleep, yelled out for Ike. Lorraine sprinted from Tina's room and locked herself in the bathroom. The gun rang out. Taylor shot herself in the chest in a failed attempt to kill herself.

Fortunately for Ike—who would almost certainly have been indicted for what appeared to be a murder—Taylor survived. She and Ike stayed together with their children while the Revue continued to log miles on the road. Oddly, Ike didn't let the close call at home deter him from rekindling his relationship with Tina. He slept with her frequently while on the road and their comfort level with each other deepened.

HITS AND MRS.

As the pressure mounted for him to come up with more hits for Sue Records, Ike began acting erratically. The closer he and Tina had become, the more he demanded from her. And when he perceived that she wasn't being straight with him, that she let him down, or wasn't giving a performance her all, he often resorted to physical abuse. He'd take his shoe off and hit her with it, fatten her lip. Then, when he was finished beating her, he often insisted on having sex. The emotional vicissitudes of the relationship were dramatic.

One day in 1962, Ike and Tina, in a moment of tenderness, agreed to marry. Tina, wary of Ike's mistreatment, said she consented in part because if she didn't she'd figured she'd be beaten. To consummate the marriage, Ike and Tina, along with their band, took a ride from Los Angeles down to Tijuana. Ike had heard about the sex shows and other ribaldry south of the border and thought it would be fun. Tina figured they'd find a justice of the peace. As they drank at a Mexican cantina, Ike in his oversized sombrero, a man with a camera approached the table. Looking at the lovey-dovey Ike and Tina, and asked them if they wanted to get married, which they did. Skeptics observed that Ike married Tina due to worries over being sued by his previous wife, Lorraine Taylor, for child support and alimony. Rumors have it that Ike married 13 times, though only four of them were public ceremonies. With enough money to be comfortable, Ike, Tina, and the band decided to move west and make Los Angeles their home. Tina brought her two kids in to live with them, and Ike brought his two from his time with Lorraine. For the first time in Tina's life, the living arrangement felt like a real family.

Now settled, Ike stepped up activity for the band, booking recording sessions whenever he had a few spare hours. His productivity was so great that he felt compelled to reconnect with the Biharis at Modern Records to catch some of the overflow, while still under contract with the Sue label. In 1964, Sue's Juggy Murray, encouraged by the progress Ike and Tina were making, offered a generous contract extension to keep the band on the label.

Murray recalled Ike being a tough negotiator. "He made me put in the agreement that he could cut what he wants to cut, and not what I want him to cut. I gave him $40,000 and what does he do? He sends me the worst shit in the world" (Quaglieri).

Turner's plan, Murray figured, was to ditch Sue as soon as he could. He took the advance cash and bought the expensive home in Los Angeles even as subsequent Sue material stiffed commercially. But the truth was that Ike had real limitations in terms of his songwriting abilities. He had the roadhouse blues idiom under his belt, but he couldn't reach beyond that to a poppier sound. His limitations frustrated him, and his relationship with Murray at Sue deteriorated.

Ike had also lost most of his Revue musicians, mainly in disputes over money, so he was faced with the constant challenges of recruiting and rehearsing new band members. The stress took a significant toll on him, and he often let his steam out when Tina was around.

At this time of few hits, touring revenue was crucial. They'd gig for 90 days straight in dates around the country, and this with a skeleton crew where musicians had to lug all their own gear on a nightly basis. There was no technical crew either, so the band was responsible for setting up, not to mention be around for rehearsals. These tours were not glamorous at all and they put a real strain on Tina.

Ike didn't mind it, though. His philandering continued while on tour. He'd sleep with one of the Ikettes, or pick up a woman from the audience, at the same time sending Tina home early after a show.

"I'd known what he was like when I met him—all the women—and now I was beginning to realize that he'd never change. That I would never be enough for him. That no woman could" (Turner and Loder, p. 103).

In addition to the womanizing and the violence, Ike began to develop a fondness for drugs. Until this time, he'd been a coffee and cigarette guy, even while his band members, including the Ikettes, enjoyed smoking marijuana on occasion. Of course, if Ike felt drugs were hampering any of his musicians' performances, he'd either fire them on the spot, or dock their pay substantially. One night, though, he took a toke with the Ikettes to see what all the fuss was about. His drug use swung from casual to serious in a short time.

Ike also began having trouble with the Ikettes. In the spring of 1965, they had a hit record, and the spotlight brightened on them as a prime attraction on Ike and Tina's Revue. They were offered tours on Dick Clark's pop Caravan of Stars and started receiving commercial attention that Ike and Tina were not. Ike resented the emphasis and he began training other women to take the Ikettes' place in case the originals left the tour.

For the Ikettes, Ike's treatment was humiliating. Given the time and energy they put into Ike's tour, they thought they had earned special consideration, and a little respect, not to mention more money. Ike kept the girls on salary, but didn't give them any publishing credit or a percentage of the revenues from sales on their solo recordings. Ike owned the name, he thought, and therefore the concept. In September 1965, the Ikettes walked.

RIVER DEEP AND MOUNTAIN HIGH

For all their industriousness, all their studio time, and all their on-stage gigging—they seemed to tour 365 days a year—Ike and Tina never managed to make a quintessential recording. Ike's limited facility in the studio never truly took advantage of Tina's powerhouse vocals, and rarely did they attempt to bring in outside help. This was the case until they signed with Loma Records, run by former Warner Bros. executive Bob Krasnow.

Krasnow's first handful of Ike and Tina singles also flopped and he'd hit a crossroads with the act fairly quickly. Then, one day, the young producer Phil

Spector bailed him out. He phoned Krasnow and asked if he could make a record with them. At the time, Spector had a reputation as being the teen-pop king of the early 1960s, having produced hits by the Ronettes, the Crystals, and the Righteous Brothers. And he was still on the youthful side of 30. He forked over $25,000 for the right to record with them, with every intention of creating his biggest hit.

Spector didn't invite Ike to the session at all, a fact that didn't bother Ike. He had been in charge for so long he considered it a relief to let someone else make his record. Tina though, worked like a dog, laying down vocal track after vocal track for weeks. But somehow, things didn't go as planned.

> Tina's magnificent performance of Phil Spector's "River Deep-Mountain High" is part of the story of a record that should have been an automatic Number One but never made the charts. Backed up by what sounds like 10,000 Ikettes, challenging and conquering the difficult changes of mood Phil created for the production, Tina outsang Bill Medley (Righteous Brothers) and the Crystals and put herself on a level with Darlene Love (Ronettes). . . . The power of its emotion might be compared to Dylan's "One of Us Must Know," but the musical inventions of Spector and Tina's control over her almost anarchic vocal weapons make any comparison pointless. It stands alone. But it bombed. (Greil Marcus, *Rolling Stone*, May 17, 1969)

While the Spector album, mainly a run-through of their greatest hits ("Fool in Love" and "It's Gonna Work Out Fine"), R&B standards, and a few big-production efforts from Spector, was certainly their best full-length recording, no one in the United States really even cared. It fell between the cracks of R&B and pop; both formats thought the other should handle it, so neither did and the record died a quiet death. Indeed the entire album languished toward the bottom of the pop charts. The eccentric producer was appalled.

In the United Kingdom though, the reaction was quite different. The song shot to number one and captivated the country, staying on the charts for five months. It was such a sensation, the Rolling Stones tapped Ike and Tina to open for them on a tour in 1966.

In response to the differing acceptances of his work, Phil took out ads in trade publications stating "Benedict Arnold Was Right!" when the record scored in England. Then he quit the music business temporarily and dissolved his record company. Many who knew him say he was distraught about the record's lack of success and didn't know which way to turn.

The Rolling Stones tour lasted six days, but Ike and Tina's Revue made a massive impact on everyone involved. Tina's performance had a powerful influence over Stones' frontman Jagger, who began using some of Tina's dance moves later in his career.

They parlayed that reception into a worldwide tour through Europe and Australia, where they were adored by ecstatic crowds. "It was as if they had never seen nothing like my show. There was nothing like my show, though, and I don't think there is today. Even so, I was surprised by the reaction we got abroad. I just didn't expect to be that big. People were just overwhelmed by our Revue" (Turner and Cawthorne, p. 116).

The tour helped Ike and Tina gain momentum. They booked a month in Germany for a quarter of a million dollars, 25 dates in 30 days. Tina sang through that booking after having a tumor surgically removed from her neck. Each night the blood from her fresh incision would bleed through the gauze, but still, she soldiered on.

With all the money, Ike began buying bigger quantities of drugs. At a stint in Las Vegas, he first tried cocaine. It gave him a feeling of exhilaration, and it turned the otherwise weary Ike on. With a little white powder, he now had the energy to write, perform, have sex, and party every day. He was so impressed by the drug's effects that he turned his band onto it as well.

The antics got more outlandish. After shows, they'd retire to their hotel rooms, a bowl of cocaine on the table—pounds of it at a time—a freshly stocked whiskey bar, and all the girls they could handle.

"The drug thing just got bigger and bigger until finally it was totally uncontrollable. As long as I had money and knew where to go and get stuff, I would go" (Turner and Cawthorne, p. 145).

Meanwhile, Tina would watch the goings on, and do nothing about it. She had no choice but to keep to herself. She learned to tolerate Ike and the band's outrageous behavior, and only interrupted when she was told to bring Ike food. For Tina, the humiliation cut deeply.

THE SPLIT

Tina recalls that it was about this time she fell out of love with Turner. The philandering, in her face and in the open for all to see, became too much to endure. The drugs often turned Ike into a monster, and with that transformation came violence. Tina did her best to keep her distance; she turned out to sing every night, but couldn't possibly share his bed.

In fact, this was one stipulation she demanded directly from Ike. If he was going to sleep around, she asked him, please don't do it in her bed, the marriage bed. Of course, one day Tina came home and found him doing just that, with still another of his consorts and the relationship was essentially over. Still, despite his cheating, Ike kept Tina close at hand. She felt miserable.

"There was no life outside the house, the studio and the road. I couldn't even go to a movie on my own. . . . So by this time I was real unhappy. I didn't care about anything: on the road, I'd just go to the job, and then afterwards go back to the hotel and go to bed" (Turner and Loder, p. 127).

Tina's depression worsened in 1968 and 1969. The band was touring, and playing command performances all over Europe, but on a personal level Tina was spent. She hung around with a woman named Ann Thomas, an amiable woman Ike had also fallen in love with. Tina and Ann became close friends and helped each other emotionally. Ironically, they both found out they were pregnant at about the same time, and by the same man.

Things went from bad to worse. One night before a show in 1969, Tina got a beating that resulted in a broken jaw. Ike forced her to sing that night anyway, and she did so with the taste of blood in her mouth. She began to plot a way out. (source)

She got a prescription for Valium from her doctor, 50 pills. He felt she needed some tranquility in her life and these would afford her at least that. What he didn't expect was that Tina would attempt to punch her ticket out. One night before a show in Los Angeles, with girls and drugs and alcohol surrounding her, she entered the ladies room and took all 50 pills.

Ike's personal tour assistant, Rhonda Graam, discovered Tina and rushed her to the hospital to get her stomach pumped. She nearly died on the way, but doctors managed to revive her. When she awoke, Ike was there, demanding they return to the club to perform. Tina could hardly stand up. "It serves you right," said Ike. "You wanna die? Then die!" (Turner and Loder, p. 147).

Tina's resignation regarding her marriage with Ike turned to loathing and their relationship withered. They were now strictly business. Fortunately, business was good. The Stones tour had launched them back onto the radio, first with a cover of the Beatles' "Come Together," a song backed by a cover of the Stones' "Honky Tonk Women." They followed that with a rendition of Sly Stone's funk epic "I Wanna Take You Higher." Ike and Tina's version actually topped out on the charts higher than Sly's original version a short time earlier.

Their hits gave them leverage and they signed a lucrative five-year deal with Minit Records, a subsidiary of Liberty. Their nightly fee jumped to $5,000 from less than $1,000. They appeared on the *Ed Sullivan Show* as well as on Andy Williams's TV program. The Revue was in high gear.

At the end of 1970, they had a few days off in Florida and Ike brought the band into a local recording studio. He wanted to wax a song that the Revue had been incorporating into their live set for over a year. "Proud Mary" was written by Creedence Clearwater Revival frontman John Fogerty, and, in the hands of Tina, became one of the most joyfully chaotic records ever to come out of rock and roll at the time. It was pure mayhem, and a perfect vehicle for Tina's frenetic stage persona.

The recording managed to capture that craziness and the song zoomed up the charts. In fact, it became Ike and Tina's first Top 10 pop hit, and their first million-selling record. It also earned Tina her first Grammy Award for Best R&B Vocal Performance. In October of that year, *Rolling Stone* magazine featured Ike and Tina on their cover.

The song got the year off to an explosive start. Indeed, in many respects, the year would be the band's high-water mark. Somehow, Ike and Tina managed to put aside their differences and work together musically. Their shows and recordings at this time featured tremendous chemistry, if not personally, at least musically.

With all the cash flowing in, Ike began to indulge in just about everything: excess was the name of the game. He surrounded himself with women, drugs, and party-goers. While Tina was in the hospital with a bronchial illness following a tour, Ike had their entire house redone, in Tina's words, "like a bordello from hell," and he built Bolic, a new studio with state of the art equipment. He could now record whenever he pleased; he was freed of all temporal and financial constraints.

Ike surrounded himself with cash. Literally, he'd carry around suitcases of money, just in case. One night he threw $70,000 on the floor of a dressing room to see what kind of reaction he'd get. The Revue was paid in cash, sometimes as much as $20,000 a night, so there was plenty of green to go around.

Over the next few years, Ike and Tina rolled through well-paying gigs, even though the singles and albums didn't fare very well. Early in 1974, Tina was selected by director Ken Russell to appear in the movie version of the Who rock opera *Tommy*. She'd been chosen to play the character of the Acid Queen and sing a song of the same name in the film. Ike wasn't invited to be in the cast.

The appearance boosted Tina's profile as an artist and her confidence. She began to feel inner strength, that perhaps she could offer audiences something of her very own, unconnected with Ike Turner. The reviews of Tina's performance in *Tommy* were positive and suddenly people were talking as much about Tina as they were about Ike, the longtime star of the show. The resentment irked Ike, but bolstered Tina's damaged self-image.

That confidence manifested itself in her very first solo album, *Tina Turns the Country On*, a collection of country music cover songs. It was recorded at Ike's studio, but worked on by outside producers. The recording, a curious choice for Tina's solo debut, didn't do well on the charts. But it did give Tina a chance to set out on her own, a place that she enjoyed being, especially in light of the fact that by this time Ike and Tina's collaborations were disappearing from the charts.

The pieces were in place for Tina to go it alone. One of those considerations, the Turner kids, was getting older, approaching adulthood, which meant Tina didn't feel as obligated to be around for them. At the same time, Ike's drug habit increased. At Bolic, his studio, he'd hole up for days, freebasing cocaine and having orgies. On any given night, he'd use $2,000 or $3,000 worth of drugs. When he did cocaine, he went on a bender for seven or eight days at a stretch, never returning home. He did more partying at Bolic than actual recording, and his career backslid significantly.

"When I was doing cocaine, I would sit up and philosophize and procrastinate. I would talk about what I was going to do, but I wouldn't do shit. I'd work on one record for two months. At first the song would sound like a smash hit, then the next day I'd change all of it."

IKE'S FALL

After his United Artists contract was up (UA had purchased Liberty and all of Liberty's artists), Ike signed a contract with Cream Records that had a key person clause in it, meaning Tina had to be part of the deal or the contract was void. But Tina had every intention of disappearing as soon as possible.

In 1976, the Revue was set to play a huge show in Dallas at the Hilton. They flew in together, but Tina had fought with Ike on the flight over and tensions ran high. Ike was moody on the plane, and didn't have any drugs to quell his uneasiness. Tina had been holding on to the frayed ends of her rope for almost a year and was ready to let go at any moment.

In the limo, on the way from the airport to the hotel, Ike and Tina continued to fight; this time Tina fought back, kicking and scratching at Ike. Ike punched Tina several times in the eyes and face, bloodying her. When they got to the hotel, they went their separate ways. At show time, with the band on stage ready to play, Ike showed, but not Tina. She was gone. Ike was devastated.

"We had to cancel everything I had booked. My life ain't been right since then. Because that was all of my life, man, building the Ike and Tina Revue. . . . So I wasted my whole life building something and then it got taken away from me" (Turner and Cawthorne, pp. 182–83).

In the years that followed, Ike lost everything. His investments all went sour for one reason or another, his studio burned down, and, most important, the people who surrounded him while things were going well, all the people who constantly reminded Ike how great he was, and how much he was loved, began disappearing. At one time, his payroll numbered up to 30 people. Now, the band had broken up and all the hangers on, seeing the writing on Ike's studio wall, decided to find more promising situations.

He returned to St. Louis to be with his sister, fatally ill with cancer. While he was in the studio back in Los Angeles he had written a powerful blues number, regretting his life and missing his mother. He played that for his sister, and watched as she died in front of him.

Things had unraveled. One night, completely depressed, he put a .57 Magnum in his mouth and pulled the trigger. For some reason, though, the gun didn't go off, then the phone rang. A worried friend showed up at the same time to check on him. His life, he figured, wasn't meant to end prematurely. And yet, it ostensibly did when he lost the Revue.

From this point, he went into a 15-year tailspin of partying and darkness. His music production shrunk to nothing. He married his old flame Ann Thomas, the only person who stuck by him when the light grew dim. He found contentment temporarily in his marriage, but found more in the copious amounts of drugs he was ingesting.

The problem was he didn't have the money coming in to afford his habit. At first, he enjoyed pure cocaine straight from Peru. But as time passed and his revenue dwindled, he settled for vastly inferior grades.

He tried rehab a couple of times, for a month at a stretch. Neither time stuck. After the second effort, he started dealing drugs, not seriously, and was nabbed in a police sting operation. In fact, in his life he had been arrested several times, but never found guilty. Call it luck. Call it prudence. But he was never caught with drugs on his person.

But this time his luck had run out. He had nothing going for him. There was no career, no money, no hope, just drugs and darkness. He was quite literally nearing that proverbial place called rock bottom. He was saved by a jail term. He cleaned up, and even made some money hustling products from the prison store. He'd behaved well, and was up for parole in a few months. But when the parole board denied his release, he was sentenced again, this time to the State Penitentiary, the California Men's Colony, to a four-year term.

> "Now I been clean since 1989. I went to the jail then for two years and I've never touched any drugs since then. So if I hadn't gone to jail I'd almost certainly be dead by now. See I learnt a lot in jail, jail was good. And I was makin' $500 a day in there, selling coffee cans and cigarettes to people in the jail. I had the Crips, the Bloods and the Spanish people in there all selling for me, in modules. I managed to save up $12,000 in seven months from doin' that." Nowadays, Ike takes nothing stronger than a handful of vitamins and a shot of wheatgrass every morning. "Lots of green," he laughs. "Lots of green vegetables. I love everything green—especially money. (Williams)

He did indeed clean up upon his release after two years, but found civilian life to be difficult. He tried to get back on track with his career, but when he called favors in no one responded, not the Rolling Stones, not B.B. King, not many of the people he'd given breaks to himself.

He soon realized why. When Tina's book came out telling her life story, with its bleak depiction of Ike, word began to get around that she'd led a wretched existence while with him. To make matters worse, Tina's side of the story went from a book to a movie called *What's Love Got to Do with It?*

When the movie hit theaters and earned international viewership, Ike became public enemy number one. The film portrayed Ike to be an unlikable, reckless, callous control freak with an addiction for both sex and drugs. Ike felt the portrait was cruel and excessive.

"I ain't that kind of dude. I got a temper, and I'm dominating and all that shit about what I want as far as music is concerned, but I ain't what they had me be" (Turner and Cawthorne, p. 229).

As Ike's sun had set, Tina's star ascended.

TINA'S RISE

After Tina left Ike in Dallas, she moved from place to place, trying to stay one step ahead of Ike, of whom she had real fear. She knew what he was capable of and she was sensitive not to expose her harborers to the possibility of violence.

She had taken up Buddhist chanting, which soothed her nerves and kept things in perspective. She stayed with a friend of a friend, Anna Maria Shorter, wife of jazz star Wayne Shorter in a place called Lookout Mountain. She felt safe there, until one day, a former Ikette, Robbie Montgomery, came knocking on the Shorter door.

Tina hid, and peeked out the window. Ike had sent Robbie in to pick Tina up. He was looking dapper, standing beside a limousine. The Shorters called the police and had Ike removed. Tina filed a petition for divorce in July 1976, less than a month after the Dallas fisticuffs.

At a meeting with United Artists, Tina met and hired Mike Stewart as her new manager. Stewart began putting together a show for Tina, bringing in dancers and a backing band. Bob Mackie came aboard to design costumes, and former *Shindig!* television producer Jack Good began putting the production together.

Rumors arose that Ike had hired a hitman to kill his soon-to-be ex. Tina started carrying a weapon in case that situation came about. With the money she earned from publishing advances and from her new label deal, she hired bodyguards to protect her. Ike had sent people to harass her, firebomb her house, and threaten her friends. Fear became a way of life.

Divorce proceedings were ugly and protracted. Ike fudged the numbers used to tally his net worth and Tina, eager to be done with the process, told the court she had no use for anything that belonged to Ike. The divorce was final in the spring of 1978.

Tina released her first post-Ike solo album, titled *Rough*, later that same year. The album didn't fare well and UA, amidst a takeover by Capitol/EMI, released Tina from their roster. Also in 1978 on UA, Ike released *Airwaves*, a collection of unreleased songs featuring Tina. But it too disappeared in the drone of disco beats and a fast-evolving popular music scene. In the many decades Ike had been making music, he rarely, if ever, paid attention to trends. To his credit, he believed in the music he was making. Unfortunately, the creative world of music, especially in the 1960s and 1970s changed at a rapid rate and Ike failed to keep pace with those changes.

Tina contracted Roger Davies, a young, burly Australian who had moved recently to Los Angeles. Davies was working for Lee Kramer, a high-powered management executive. Together, they assumed Tina as a client, as well as the debt she'd accumulated in the two years she spent with United Artists. They booked her on a lucrative, five-week tour of South Africa, and then additional tours of Australia and Southeast Asia.

Davies rearranged Tina's entire show in 1980 and 1981. In a ploy to get younger and more rock and roll, he forced her band out, told her to get rid of Rhonda Graam, her longtime manager, and made her lose the Bob Mackie clothing. He booked her at better, more prestigious gigs in the States. One in particular at the Ritz in New York City proved to be especially worthwhile. Tina hadn't played New York in a decade and the gigs, three straight nights, were all sold out.

Rod Stewart, in town for his appearance on the TV show *Saturday Night Live*, attended one of the shows and invited Tina to come on the program with him to sing his three-year old hit, "Hot Legs." Based on her incendiary shows at the Ritz, she signed a contract with Capitol Records in 1983. For her first single, she recorded a version of Al Green's romantic ballad, "Let's Stay Together." The song was a smash and became Tina's first hit as a solo act. And it wasn't a hit just in America. Britain gobbled up the song as did the continent and parts of Asia. Tina stood on the precipice of something very big.

Follow-up hits "What's Love Got to Do with It?" and "Better Be Good to Me" came next. "I didn't know that 'What's Love Got to Do With It?' had been written for me . . . I didn't think it was my style. . . . I had just never thought of singing pop. So when Roger played the song for me I just said, 'Oh, no, not that one'" (Turner and Loder, p. 240).

The album, called *Private Dancer*, took two weeks to put together and about $150,000, a big gamble for Turner and Davies. Upon delivery she embarked on a four-month tour opening for Lionel Richie.

At first, "What's Love Got to Do with It?" sold slowly. But Capitol pushed their promotions department and by the end of its second week, it had hit the Top 50, and began climbing quickly. The record itself soared to number one on the album chart and suddenly Tina was everywhere. Not long after the album hit the top—where it would stay for nearly three months—people were clamoring for her attention. Her story emerged, and so did the outpouring of sympathy, support, and appreciation.

She was chosen to appear alongside Mel Gibson in a major feature film, *Mad Max: Beyond Thunderdome*. She also hit the charts with the movie's theme, "We Don't Need Another Hero."

The American Music Awards honored her in January 1984 with top prizes in the female vocalist and video performer categories. That weekend she hit a Los Angeles studio with luminaries like Michael Jackson, Bruce Springsteen, David Bowie, and Bob Dylan to record "We Are the World" for African famine relief.

Later in the spring, amid an intense and gratifying European tour, Tina flew back to Los Angeles for the Grammys in what would become perhaps the most memorable night of her life. The voters bestowed her Grammys for Best Female Pop Vocal, Best Female Rock Vocal, and, finally, Record of the Year. All the pain and suffering she'd endured over the past 20 years must have surely disappeared that night, as the music industry finally recognized the amazing accomplishments of Tina Turner.

A major film, *What's Love Got to Do with It?* starring Angela Basset as Tina and Laurence Fishburne as Ike, came out in 1993 and received an overwhelming amount of attention. The film chronicled the Revue's ascent to stardom with Ike, portrayed as an abusive husband, and Tina's subsequent courage to break free. Ike went on the record at length to defend himself. But the fact remained. Tina had weathered her own intensely personal storm, and was now ready for her time in the sun.

IKE'S RENAISSANCE

In the mid-2000s, Ike got his act in gear once again, this time to a much more sympathetic audience. The antipathy that had arisen after Fishburne's depiction of him was significant, and Ike had to lay low for a while as the ill will subsided. But he pulled an act together, amassed some material, and went on the road. He began doing interviews, and the press, the same press that had viewed him as a villain after the movie and while he was in jail, began to rewrite their reports, now giving Turner credit where credit was due. Like Chuck Berry and Little Richard, Ike was at the vanguard of America's rock and roll revolution, and he needed to be recognized for that. Subsequent albums, 2001's *Here and Now* and 2006's *Risin' with the Blues* convinced critics and audiences alike he was ready for a comeback. *Risin'* won a Grammy award in 2007 for Best Traditional Blues Album.

LEGACY

It's almost three separate stories: Ike's, Tina's, and Ike and Tina's. But they intertwine like strands within a single rope. Ike's story began with a passion for music, a passion from which he fashioned a musical empire. Tina's story also began with a passion for music, the music she heard and loved coming from her radio. She took that passion and turned it into unalloyed energy.

It might seem that the concept of Ike and Tina, at least in hindsight, was a bad idea. Their relationship never gelled; neither truly loved the other. Being together often brought out the very worst in each one. But the fact is, neither could have reached such heights without the other. Neither would have come to create such an impressive canon of work, had they not stayed together, gutted it out, sang another song. Neither would have been inducted into the Rock and Roll Hall of Fame in 1991 (Ike was actually in prison during their induction) had they not stayed together through good times and bad, and there were many bad times.

Neither Ike nor Tina did things the conventional way. Ike came up through the mean blues world of Mississippi; Tina suffered through numerous relocations, broken families, and many disaffected years. Fortunately for Tina, she didn't sing like anyone else and the uniqueness of those pipes put her over the top. "I know that I don't have a pretty voice," she admitted. "I took a lot of my training and patterns of singing from men" (Turner and Loder, p. 204).

Ike and Tina Turner

Many believe that Tina sits within the holy trinity of women singers in the history of R&B next to Aretha Franklin and Etta James.

But their uniqueness, their willingness to simply be themselves, set them apart. They were widely considered to be one of the most potent teams in all of R&B. And once they settled on a formula, they stuck with it. The Ike and Tina Turner Revue remained relatively unchanged, but for some set list additions and subtractions for over ten years. It was a genuine embodiment of the American spirit: enterprising, high-octane, and incredibly entertaining.

The Ike and Tina Turner story started deep in the heart of the Mississippi Delta, bluesland, and it ended up at separate ends of the same continuum of the human existence; one in darkness, one in light. Along the way they had soaring highs and savage lows, triumphant gigs at Carnegie Hall, and knockdown, drag-out fight in fleabag hotel rooms.

Today, with the headlines devoted to their turbulent relationship generally behind them, they are remembered best, and thankfully, for their incredible repertoire of unstoppable R&B.

The First Rock and Roll Song

There is a great deal of debate regarding which song exactly could be considered the first rock and roll song. Initially, Bill Haley's "Rock Around the Clock" from 1954 was chosen largely because it was the first rock and roll hit heard on national radio airwaves. Rock critics often look back at Elvis's "That's All Right, Mama," from the same year. But those truly in the know counter with the fact that the first blues shouter Roy Brown sang "Good Rockin' Tonight" in 1947, over six years before Elvis's enshrined "Sun Sessions." Wynonie Harris sang the same song in 1948. Down in New Orleans, also one of rock and roll's early birthplaces, Cosimo Matassa, the owner of J&M Studios in the 9th Ward was rolling tape in the presence of Fats Domino, whose "The Fat Man" came out in 1950, Lloyd Price, who sang "Lawdy Miss Clawdy" in 1952 at the age of 17, and Big Mama Thornton recorded a raucous version of "Hound Dog" in 1953, years before Elvis took a crack at it. Little Richard cut the scene's first real barnstormer, "Tutti Frutti," also cut by Elvis, in 1955, one year before Presley's legendary emergence in 1956.

Many designate Ike Turner's 1951 classic "Rocket 88," mistakenly credited to Jackie Brenston by a careless Sam Phillips at Sun Studios, as the first true rock song. The song was wild and rough enough, built around the distorted guitar—the first time a sound like that had showed up record—and it became the first true national hit for Sam Phillips. He had sold it to Chess, the only label at the time to believe the coarser the music the better. The record enabled Phillips to quit his day job as a radio deejay and focus on recording music. The rest of that music, as they say, is history.

SELECTED DISCOGRAPHY

The Best of the Blue Thumb Recordings (Hip-O, 1997)
The Great Rhythm & Blues Sessions (Tomato, 1991)
The Kent Years (Ace/Kent Soul, 2000)
Kings of Rhythm Band: Dance (Collectables, 1996)
Proud Mary: The Best of Ike and Tina Turner (EMI/Sue, 1991)
What You Hear Is What You Get: Live at Carnegie Hall (EMI, 1996)

FURTHER READING

Bego, Mark. *Tina Turner: Break Every Rule.* New York: Taylor Trade, 2005.
Collis, Mark. *Ike Turner: King of Rhythm.* New York: Do-Not Press, 2004.
Larkin, Colin, Editor. *The Virgin Encyclopedia of R&B and Soul.* London: Virgin, 1998.
Turner, Tina with Loder, Kurt. *I, Tina.* New York: Avon, 1986.
Turner, Ike and Cawthorne Nigel. *Takin' Back My Name: The Confessions of Ike Turner.* London: Virgin, 1999.

Courtesy of Photofest.

The Isley Brothers

A FAMILY AFFAIR

When the subject is an historical retrospective on the Brothers Isley, two things stand out. The first is the most obvious. Through six decades—spanning from the early 1950s right into the new millennium—the Isleys have, quite miraculously, managed to remain relevant in one form or another for a very long time. As one of the longest running acts in rock and roll history, their distinguished career has spanned not only two generations of Isley siblings, but also massive cultural shifts and several different styles of music. Further, the Isley Brothers are the only act to hit the *Billboard* charts in six straight decades and the only act to hit the *Billboard* Top 40 in five straight decades. They had two number one albums on the Pop charts: *The Heat Is On* (1975) and *Body Kiss* (2003), and three Top 10 Pop singles ("It's Your Thing" in 1969, "That Lady [Part 1]" in 1973, and "Fight the Power [Part 1]" in 1975). Their chart impact on the R&B side is too frequent to even mention here.

If that in itself is a remarkable achievement, and it is, then consider that they've accomplished this by remaining on the periphery of the music industry.

They've done it all without the muscle and cooperation of the music establishment. They were, and are, true renegades in the business.

The Isleys were in front of people and making great music long before names like Aretha and Otis had come of age as artists, but rarely do you hear the Isleys mentioned in that same company. They were every bit as important to the fabric of R&B at the time, but you never heard them spoken of with the same reverence as the other icons of the period, ones whose names have lingered longer even though their careers have faded. Indeed, the Isleys' career has never truly faded at all, which perhaps may be the reason for their being so often overlooked: their legacy has not yet been written.

The Isleys left their home of Cincinnati for New York City in 1957 and never looked back. They began as a gospel-influenced doo-wop group and expanded into R&B, soul, funk, rock, and disco, often blending two or more within the same song. This synthesis, incorporating rock and funk elements into R&B, gospel, and soul initially came as a shock and surprise. Thanks to electrifying stage performances, the Isleys were one of the pop scene's most anticipated and sought-out acts.

During their unparalleled history, they have also become one of the most enduring acts of all time on the *Billboard* charts and one of the only groups to survive both the British Invasion and disco fever, both juggernaut trends that eliminated virtually everything in their paths. The Isley Brothers also serve as a crucial link in the development of soul music, bridging gospel and R&B, and R&B, funk, and rock. In fact, with their 1966 single "Testify," many say they actually invented the funk genre. They were also integral in creating the soul ballad, also called "Quiet Storm," in the early1980s.

Guitarist Ernie Isley is considered one of pop's great lead guitarists, and lead vocalist Ronald was a major influence on the development of modern R&B and hip-hop. As icing on the soul cake, they employed two of music's most legendary stars within their ranks: Elton John joined them as a keyboardist during their 1964 U.K. tour, and Jimi Hendrix, then known as Jimmy James, had become a full-time member of the band in 1964 and 1965, right before recording his epic solo material.

As great and influential as the Isleys and their music have been during this time, they've never truly crossed over to a singularly pop audience the way so many other R&B artists did. Still, their achievements both within and outside the popular music scene are unprecedented and legendary.

THE EARLY YEARS

The first generation of Isley siblings was born and raised in Cincinnati, Ohio. O'Kelly Isley, a navy man from North Carolina, and his wife Sallye, a Georgia girl, had three sons early on: O'Kelly Jr. was born in 1937, Rudolph in 1939, and Ronald, two years later in 1941. Vernon was the youngest of the first four

Isley boys. Two more boys, Ernie (1952) and Marvin (1953), would enter the picture a little later.

They grew up in the Lincoln Heights area outside of Cincinnati, in a modest cookie cutter home built for the employees of General Electric. The young Isleys absorbed all the elements of black culture that would provide the narratives and emotional content of their songs when they began writing. They moved to Blue Ash, another satellite town of Cincinnati, during high school.

Like so many young African American artists, the four Isley Brothers all began singing in church under the tutelage of their parents. Both Isley parents had musical backgrounds. O'Kelly senior had been a professional singer, and Sallye was an organist and choir director at the family church. Before having kids, father Isley was in a traveling Vaudeville troupe called the Brown Skin Models that traversed the South with Cab Calloway, the Ink Spots, and others. Both Mom and Dad were college educated.

They worshipped at the First Baptist Church in downtown Cincinnati. The congregation at First Baptist was animated, often excessively so. The boys recall feverish, cathartic services, full of excitement, shouting, and fainting. Interestingly, the Isleys would take that fever pitch and transfer it to their galvanic live shows.

In 1954, the four eldest Isley boys formed a gospel quartet. Throughout their young lives they had been listening to the spiritual strains of the day. "At first we patterned ourselves after Billy Ward and the Dominoes," said Ronnie Isley. "Then, listening to the Dixie Hummingbirds and Mahalia Jackson, Jackie Wilson and Sam Cooke, we developed our own style. Clyde McPhatter was a huge influence, personally and professionally. We spent a lot of time talking with him about singing styles and techniques" (Leo Sacks, liner notes, *It's Your Thing: The Story of the Isley Brothers*, Epic/Legacy/T-Neck Records, 1999, p. 33).

With those examples serving as their soundtrack, the Isleys made rapid progress. They appeared on a television show, *Ted Mack's Amateur Hour*, as kids. They won hands down that day and took home a jeweled watch. In true family fashion, they took turns wearing it. Success came quickly, and soon the Isleys were touring the region as a family group, with Vernon singing lead.

At first they toured the church scene around Cincinnati, then they branched out to points east. But as they were gaining momentum, unexpected tragedy befell the family. Vernon was riding his bike around the neighborhood when he was struck and killed by a car. He was just 13. Shaken over the tragedy, the brothers disbanded the group.

It took the Isley parents two years to coax their young sons back into singing again. They were grief-stricken, and they felt no one could sing lead like Vernon. They were also conflicted about singing gospel again. The popular music scene had been changing before their eyes with the surge of rock and roll, R&B, and doo-wop. But after a grieving period, O'Kelly and Sallye convinced their children that they owed it to Vernon to continue, that going forward would fulfill a higher purpose. Then brother Ronald stepped up and volunteered to try lead. The boys, in turn, approached their parents about singing more secular music. The sound of doo-wop was everywhere, and the brothers loved it, enjoying bands like the Diablos, the Spaniels, and the Crests.

Reluctantly, the Isleys acquiesced, and the band left Ohio for New York City. They took a Greyhound bus from Cincinnati. A friend they encountered along the way promised to hook them up on arrival in the city. They stayed at a hotel in Times Square for the first two weeks. Fortunately, Rudolph paid for those weeks up front—on the second day in the city someone pick-pocketed his wallet.

Uncomfortable but anxious in such a big place, the brothers wasted no time in contacting Richard Barrett, a talent scout who had in 1955 supervised the sessions that produced Frankie Lymon and the Teenagers' epic "Why Do Fools Fall in Love." Barrett found the boys literally on the street, but was struck by their enthusiasm and natural gifts. Ronnie, he felt, sounded like a combination of Clyde McPhatter and Jackie Wilson, which made sense, considering the group covered much of McPhatter's Dominoes repertoire. He fed them and helped them make the appropriate contacts in New York City's recording industry.

One of those contacts was George Goldner, the producer of the Lymon sessions. Goldner took the Isleys into the studio and cut their first few doo-wop sides, including "Angels Cried" and "The Cow Jumped Over the Moon," for a handful of different independent labels in the city, including Cindy, Mark X, and Teenage imprints. Those recordings, released between 1957 and 1959, never sold outside of Cincinnati, but they did earn them the attention of RCA Records.

At this time, the group had been working on their neo-gospel doo-wop, a soulful blend of the secular and the spiritual. One of their set's centerpieces was a cover of Jackie Wilson's "Lonely Teardrops." During a particularly spirited reading of it one night at a Washington, D.C., gig, one of the Isleys sang out the line, "You know you make me wanna shout!" The interjection inspired a frenzy of audience feedback. When an RCA executive heard their performance, and signed them based on that performance, he instructed them to construct their first single around that line. While the call-and-response classic "Shout" failed to reach the pop Top 40 on its initial release, it eventually became one of early R&B's classic cuts.

Unfortunately, the rest of the Isleys' work at RCA didn't inspire much commercial excitement. They were paired with the Italian songwriting and production team of Hugo Peretti and Luigi Creatore, a duo that had been assigned to work with Sam Cooke. The Italians were prone to using lush arrangements, and smooth, easy-to-digest—some would say "fluffy"—material. This style, of course, had nothing to do with the Isleys' background and experience. The work didn't ring true, and the brothers were again without a direction or a future.

The Isley Brothers

In 1961, eyes peeled for a hit, the group caught wind of a Bert Berns and Phil Medley's composition called "Twist and Shout." The song was originally cut by a group called the Topnotes, a promising act already signed to Atlantic. But the Isley Brothers decided it fit them even better—with its "testifying" elements and spiritual fire—and they took a crack at it. Produced by Berns and the group, recorded in the early spring at Bell Sound studio in New York City, and released on the Wand label, the song was an instant hit, charting in mid-June 1962 and remaining there for 19 weeks. It just missed the top spot on the R&B list, peaking at number 2, and wedged securely into the pop Top 20, at number 17. The Isleys finally had the hit they'd been waiting for. Everything was about to change for the neighborhood boys from Lincoln Heights.

"Twist and Shout"

The Isley Brothers weren't the first to record the Phil Medley and Bert Berns's song "Twist and Shout." It was originally recorded by the Topnotes in 1961. Phil Spector, then a young staff producer for Atlantic, was assigned to produce the track and it bombed, due in part to Spector's lifeless production. The Isleys recorded it the next year with Berns in the studio—he had disliked Spector's production—and the reworked version hit number 17 on the Pop charts.

Over in the United Kingdom in early 1964, the Beatles were working furiously on their first album, *Please Please Me*. They had recorded 11 songs in 10 hours and planned for "Twist and Shout" to be recorded last. By that time, John Lennon's voice was shot. Lennon was suffering from a cold and was drinking milk and sucking on cough drops to soothe his throat. With only 15 minutes left on the clock, producer George Martin had Lennon give the song two tries. Two takes were recorded and Martin opted for the first one, adding that the second one was unlistenable. The Beatles' cover was released in America as a single by Vee-Jay. It reached number two on the pop charts on April 4, 1964, the week when the first five places on the chart were all Beatles singles. "Twist and Shout" was the only million-selling Beatles single that was a cover song, and the only Beatles cover to reach the Top 10 on any national record chart.

THE HIT PARADE

The Beatles were so enamored with the Isleys' first hit that they borrowed it for their debut album in 1963. The fact that only a small percentage of music fans knew the song's origins or the original performers was an indication that the Isleys weren't at all on the national radar, a problem that would dog them throughout the decade. The song became the Beatles' own, and the Isleys, though they'd use the tune to raise the roof off of venues they played, wouldn't be able to take advantage of the song's newfound fame. They even tried releasing it twice, once in 1959 and again in 1962, without any significant success.

They did begin making money though. They moved from the streets of New York to nearby Teaneck, New Jersey. They began dressing nattily, in sharp mohair suits. They earned those outfits with another semi-hit, "Who's That Lady," for United Artists in 1964. That song would come back in a much bigger way for the band almost a decade later. Unfortunately, United wasn't the right fit for the brothers either, and they left them after a very brief association.

Their unfulfilling affiliations with so many labels grew wearisome. They were tired of hassling with different record companies and maneuvering through all the politics and the wishes of various music executives. So they decided to circumvent the system altogether and form their own company. The move was unprecedented. They would be the first black group to make this move, and one of the first black artists, with the exception of Sam Cooke, Curtis Mayfield, and Ray Charles, to ever do so. They called their company T-Neck after their hometown.

The formation of T-Neck gave the Isleys creative and financial control over their own careers, something they wanted since moving to New York. Going against the grain would be a recurring theme in the ongoing career saga of the Isleys.

ROCKIN' THE BOAT

Unfortunately, creative control wasn't the answer to their commercial woes. Over the next two years, they struggled to duplicate their "Twist and Shout" success. "Testify," their first T-Neck single, was an early Isley classic but it didn't impact the charts at all. Like "Twist and Shout," it's another blast of post-gospel rock and roll jubilation that roars with the power of a massive gospel group with a funk band backing. "Testify" is a notable track in rock and roll history if not for its high chart position, for the commercial debut of its new lead guitarist.

The Isley Brothers were in desperate need of a guitar player. They met Jimmy James, his stage name at the time, in a popular Harlem hangout called Hotel Teresa. Hendrix had just been honorably discharged from the army after a parachute accident. Not only was he looking for a band, he also needed a place to stay. So the Isleys, after what Ronnie remembers as a dazzling, "60-second audition," invited Hendrix into the band and into their home.

Hendrix was so hard up he had pawned his guitar. When the Isleys went down to pick it up for him and buy it back, it was so beat up even the strings had been removed. "He was the star of the band before the first rehearsal was over," Ernie Isley recalled. How many people can recognize the goose that laid the golden egg?" (William C. Rhoden, liner notes, *It's Your Thing: The Story of the Isley Brothers*, Epic/Legacy/ T-Neck Records, 1999, p. 26).

The Isley Brothers

The presence of Hendrix gave the band an immediate instrumental lift, and a focal point outside their extraordinary vocal skills. They also gave him more leeway than they did the rest of the band, largely because they knew he could hold his own. They bought him a new white Stratocaster to better look the part, and they allowed him to dress differently than the rest of the band members because of his outstanding skill.

On the first few numbers he cut with the band, Hendrix made such an impact that he set them, at least temporarily, in an entirely different musical direction. "Testify," for example, and "Move Over and Let Me Dance," the first two singles they released on T-Neck with Hendrix, guitar plays a prominent role in the arrangement. And while it may not have created a stir when it happened, these songs certainly are, in retrospect, the direct antecedents of classic Hendrix work like "Foxey Lady" and "Purple Haze."

It's obvious too that not only did the guitar player make a clear impression on the Isleys, the Isleys' work also had a huge impact on Hendrix. He absorbed their jubilant, fever-pitched intensity straight into his own work as a songwriter. In turn, Hendrix's influence on the Isleys would remain for years: Ernie Isley, the group's lead guitar player following Hendrix's departure in 1965, was forever billed as a Hendrix successor, even though he started with the band as a drummer, and moved to guitar after Jimi left. The Hendrix link served as both a blessing and a curse to Ernie for the rest of his career.

Two years later, the Isleys began reading about the sensation known as Jimi Hendrix, how he'd gone to England (he even asked to borrow a guitar), which is one of the reasons why he left the Isleys, found a manager, and started tearing up venues. "Around 1967 we started hearing about Jimi," recalls Rudolph, "and so we bought his album. We couldn't understand a word of it! ''Scuse me while I kiss the sky.' What was he talking about? Some of the guys in the band went to see him and *they* didn't know what he was talking about! But they knew the place was coming off the hinges!" (Sacks, p. 51).

The absence of a single to follow up "Twist and Shout" exasperated the Isleys so much that when the opportunity to record for Motown came along, they put their own T-Neck operation on hiatus. At the time, 1966, Motown was the hottest label in America, with a roster full of the hottest acts around, including Smokey Robinson and the Miracles, the Supremes, the Temptations, Marvin Gaye, Tammi Terrell, and Stevie Wonder. Motown had been responsible for the so-called Sound of Young America, a polished pop soul sound that had both black and white audiences clamoring for more. The Isleys desperately needed another hit, and one way they felt assured of getting it was by signing with Berry Gordy's Motown label.

Gordy's label did with the Isleys what they'd done with great success with so many other acts: they fit them onto the conveyor belt system from which they'd emerge from the hit factory as superstars. Gordy assigned the Isleys to the hit songwriting team of Brian Holland, Lamont Dozier, and Eddie Holland and he set about molding them into stars.

Their first song for the label, "This Old Heart of Mine (Is Weak for You)," triumphed, going to number 12 on the *Billboard* Hot 100 and number 6 R&B in 1966. Yet its success provided only temporary solace. As with "Shout" and "Twist and Shout" before it, the group was unable to follow their inaugural Motown hit with a successor. Things were happening fast at Motown, and, for a while they were given ample attention. H-D-H wrote another tune that earned moderate airplay, "Take Me in Your Arms (Rock Me a Little While)," but the song didn't break into the Hot 100 in pop and was considered a failure, certainly by Motown standards.

When the Isleys didn't create the kind of excitement Motown expected from them, Gordy pulled his resources back. He had already stretched his limited creative wherewithal too thinly, and so, like any chief executive, had to make some tough decisions. The Temptations, the Miracles, and the Supremes were still super-hot, and so were a handful of other Motown acts. The Isleys hadn't broken through, and so would receive limited assistance.

As a last-ditch effort, the band relocated temporarily to England, where "This Old Heart" and the Motown album did very well, reaching number three on the Pop chart. They thought that concentrating their energy on the one place that seemed impressed would, in turn, help them back in America. This contrary thinking often worked for the Isley Brothers, but not this time. They returned to the States to deal with what they perceived as a bad arrangement with Motown.

Of course, the Isleys had been through this before in their 10 years in the business. They had felt the slight of other record companies. As good as it was to have Motown behind them, that slight was disappointing. "Leaving Motown was considered the kiss of death," Ernie Isley said (Rhoden, p. 27). Regardless, they quit the Motown hit factory in 1968—one of the first acts in the company's history to do so—and resurrected T-Neck.

IT'S THEIR THING

To help them navigate the tricky marketing and distribution channels, they contracted the services of Buddah Records back in New York City. They reworked their image, trading out their mohair suits for wilder, more personal clothing, a mélange of velvet, furs, and leather, with radical English and French designs. The look was classy and distinguished and set them apart, at a time when across the country, "different" was good. The change served them well.

Their first album after ditching Motown, *It's Our Thing*, spawned the epic single "It's Your Thing," the group's biggest achievement to date, a number one R&B hit, number two Pop. Recorded in January 1969 at New York's A&R Studios, the musicians on the session were members of Wilson Pickett's touring band: drummer George Moreland, pianist Herb Rooney, arranger George Patterson on sax, and guitarist Charles "Skip" Pitts Jr., best known for his wah-wah work on Isaac Hayes's million-selling classic "Shaft." When the bass player failed to show, the group filled the gap with 17-year-old Ernie Isley. Self-produced, the tune topped the R&B charts for four weeks in the spring of 1969. The album of the same name stayed at number 2 R&B for two weeks while going to number 22 on the Pop list.

There was only one problem: Motown thought they owned it. They claimed the Isleys were under contract with them and therefore deserved at least a portion of the proceeds. The legal battle ensued for the next five years, with the Isleys eventually winning.

Released amid Motown fever, "It's Your Thing" did the impossible: it won a Grammy Award for Best R&B Vocal Performance, something that must have irked Berry Gordy. Since dropping off the charts back in 1969, the song has lived on ad infinitum. It sold over 5 million copies, has been covered by over 60 bands, and has become an anthem of self-expression and personal freedom.

More change was afoot in the Isleys' camp. Not only did they change their image, they also expanded their lineup. They invited younger brothers Ernie and Marvin officially into the band, along with brother-in-law Chris Jasper. And, in another example of impressive self-reliance, they put Ernie, Marvin, and Jasper through music school, so when the time came—and it definitely had arrived by 1969—they were ready to contribute musically to the band's output. Ernie contributed on guitar and drums, Marvin on bass, and Jasper on keyboards. With the singers out front—Ronnie, Rudolph, and O'Kelly—and the others forming their musical backbone, the brothers now comprised a real and formidable band.

Marvin recalls the care his big brothers gave him and Ernie. Their father died when they were young, so they'd lived their lives without a proper dad. His three older brothers filled the void. "It was like having three fathers. . . . They let us enjoy their company, they steered us from trouble. They told us stories about music and they helped us with our homework. They explained why it was important to help Mom with the housework. They acted like the difference in our ages wasn't there" (Sacks, p. 39).

As the hits started rolling, the Isleys made a subtle sonic shift. They sidestepped from a funky type of hard soul sound suggesting James Brown, to a more rocking funk sound, an integration of Brown with a heavy dose of Jimi Hendrix's syncopated hard rock. Ernie's lead guitar playing surged to the front of the band's studio mixes. "That Lady," for example, features a lead guitar solo that is inarguably the first guitar solo spotlighted in an R&B single.

Their follow-up album, 1970's *Get into Something*, didn't have the same commercial impact, but it did go over with soul audiences, boasting six Top 30 hits on that chart, including the hard-edged funk of "Get into Something," starring Pitts on guitar. If the disc didn't linger with audiences, it did manage to advance the band along its creative continuum, pushing the rock sound to accompany its funk.

In 1971, the Isleys again surprised audiences and the music industry by doing the unexpected. They released *Givin' It Back*, a collection of covers.

Nothing new in that. But in a twist, the album featured songs originally written and performed, mainly, by white pop artists: James Taylor, Neil Young, Stephen Stills, and Bob Dylan.

> Those who are old enough should recall the time whence it came, an era in which hatred and disunity over the Vietnam War, civil rights, school desegregation, the environment, and a multitude of other issues were threatening what seemed, potentially, like the beginning of a new civil war, this one not between states but between factions and ethnic and racial groups in 1,000 individual neighborhoods. The opening cut of *Givin' It Back*, "Ohio/Machine Gun," is a slap-in-your-face reminder of just how angry the times and the people were. The track evokes instant memories of the campus bloodshed of 1970, not just at Kent State but also the often-forgotten killings a few days later at Jackson State University in Mississippi, where the victims of a fusillade of sheriff's deputies' bullets were black students. . . . Blacks reacting to years of oppression had little use for mostly middle-class white college students, however sympathetic many of them purported to be to their situation, while well-meaning white students and activists couldn't begin to know what privation of the kind experienced by blacks and Hispanics in most American towns and cities was. . . . In music, too, there was a lot of division; blacks usually didn't resonate to the top artists in the white world and, in particular, were oblivious to (and even resentful of) the adoration accorded Jimi Hendrix by the white community. So, when the Isley Brothers—whose appeal among black audiences was unimpeachable—opened *Givin' It Back* with a conflation of Neil Young's "Ohio" and Jimi's "Machine Gun," they were speaking to anger and bloodshed in the streets, but they were also performing an act of outreach that was about as radical as any they could have committed on record in 1971. (Bruce Eder, "Givin' It All Back," *in The All Music Guide to Rock*. Erlewine and Unterberger et al., eds., San Francisco: Miller, Freeman, 1997)

By blurring the color lines at a time when color seemed to be so important, the Isleys created a quiet, under-publicized revolution. They broke through color barriers—though no record company publicity department was there to ballyhoo it—and cast these songs in an entirely different light. Not only did they prove themselves to be dexterous interpreters, they also emphasized the power American protest music had to move audiences. On the cover, the brothers are pictured with acoustic guitars, another nod to white audiences, this time the white singer-songwriter movement that had been surging toward prominence. Not only could the group get audiences dancing and singing. They could make them think as well. There was the distinct feeling that Isleys were on the verge of something big.

THE BIG TIME

Recorded in 1973, *3 + 3* was a major turning point for the Isley Brothers. With this album, the Isleys moved their T-Neck label from Buddah to Epic/CBS (which became Epic/Sony in the early1990s), and it was at Epic that they unveiled their new lineup. The lineup enhancement, something they called 3 + 3, referring to the older brothers adding the newer Isleys, made the family unit one of the first self-contained black bands in popular music.

A slick reworking of "That Lady (Part 1)," a song originally released as a single in 1964, triggered a new stylistic era for the band and marked the start of a period in which they dominated the black music realm. Between 1969 and 1988, they'd go on to place a staggering 50 singles on the R&B chart.

In the studio, they were constantly pushing the envelope, and on "That Lady," the aggressiveness paid off. Ernie Isley, now firmly in charge of electric guitars for the band, made history with his solo in the song. It's a high-water mark for early-1970s soul and one of the band's true classics, with a bevy of qualities that transcend its time. The guitar riff was sampled later on the Beastie Boys' closing suite to *Paul's Boutique* and its presence gave the song history and depth. The hook and melody are excellent, but it's the solo that most people remember.

"When I finished the solo in 'That Lady,' " says Ernie, "Kelly looked at me for 15 minutes straight without blinking. I felt like I had one foot on the ground, the other on Mount Olympus. . . . I went from a black and white world to Technicolor" (Sacks, p. 38). This experience is in stark contrast to young Ernie's first performance with his older brothers back in 1958. At the time, Ernie was just six years old. Together, their doo-wop performance had a choreographed move, taken politely from Jackie Wilson, in which the brothers tossed their sweaters over their shoulders casually, then walked to the front of the staged and threw them into the audience. The crowd went wild! Unfortunately, young Ernie thought the crowd was laughing at him, not enjoying the act, and the feeling traumatized him. He stopped dancing and started to cry. To this day, he doesn't feel comfortable in front of a crowd and tends to perform with his back to the audience.

Fast forward to 1992, when the Isley Brothers were inducted into the Rock and Roll Hall of Fame. Ernie Isley, once the little brother who needed tending, was jamming on Hendrix's "Purple Haze" alongside none other than Carlos Santana.

The song hit number six on the pop chart in the summer of 1973, and the album sold well. It also continued the Isleys' penchant for white pop covers, this time interpreting James Taylor's "Don't Let Me Be Lonely Tonight," Seals and Crofts's "Summer Breeze," the Doobie Brothers' "Listen to the Music," and Jonathan Edwards's "Sunshine (Go Away Today)."

FIGHT THE POWER!

They'd done so many covers during the last few years—even "That Lady" was a cover, albeit of their own tune—the Isleys hungered for good, original material. It was a fertile time in music, with Marvin Gaye, Curtis Mayfield, Sly Stone, Parliament, James Brown, and Stevie Wonder all composing and performing innovative material. Ensemble funk bands like the Ohio Players, Earth, Wind and Fire, the Commodores, Graham Central Station, the Bar-Kays, and many others were also beginning to register impact of their own on the black music scene. Real bands dominated black music, and were pushing themselves and each other to creative heights.

The Isleys, with momentum and a clearly defined creative path to follow, set to writing new stuff. At the time, Chris Jasper and Marvin and Ernie Isley were attending C.W. Post College on Long Island, getting their education in music. They also dabbled as a jazz trio.

Their first collaborative effort with the elder Isleys *3+3* became the group's biggest yet, and its first as a cohesive unit. They traveled together out to Sausalito, California, to record a follow-up at the famed studio the Record Plant. *Live It Up* was the follow-up and it featured a more sculpted and refined version of the soul/funk/rock hybrid they were pursuing. The title cut single from that album, written by the ensemble, set the pace with bar-raising performances by Jasper on keys and Ernie on electric guitar. The equally fiery "Midnight Sky (Part 1 & 2)" followed that onto the singles charts. Both lodged high on the R&B side, while showing up in the middle on the pop side.

"You know," says Chris Jasper, "all I ever wanted to do with the Isleys was make music that was meaningful. What ideas could we originate? What new avenues could we explore? That was the biggest joy—collaborating with the brothers. Just being in the studio together. . . . Personalities and business aside, it was always about the music—making positive, hopeful, healing music" (Leo Sacks, liner notes, *Live It Up,* Epic/Legacy/T-Neck Records, 1999).

It took a few years for the younger Isley generation to earn the confidence of their older kin. But during the making of the next handful of albums, *The Heat Is On* (1975) and then *Harvest for the World* (1976), Ronnie, Rudolph, and O'Kelly began stepping back to let their younger kin do some of the composing and arranging. "The older brothers saw what was happening," says Jasper, "that the younger brothers had our fingers on the pulse—that we were selling records, so gradually they grew more comfortable with us as the principals songwriters" (Sacks, *Live It Up*).

With the newcomers now in full contribution mode, the Isleys started clicking. *The Heat Is On* is notable not only as a team effort but for the inclusion of "Fight the Power (Part 1 & 2)," a Top Five pop hit, and number one R&B track, that made the Isleys one of music's juggernauts in the middle of the decade. The tune, a loose, percolating jam, perfectly encapsulated both the political edge and raw funk energy the Isleys observed swirling around them.

By now, the Isleys had established a pattern of hard-nosed, individualized non-conformity. No one, not Berry Gordy at Motown, not Atlantic Records, not United Artists, was big enough to push them around. They were now bold enough to say so in song. They took greater responsibility in politicizing their music. *The Heat Is On*, based on the courageous declaration of "Fight the Power," would be their biggest financial and critical success, and the band's unequivocal peak.

In 1975, they began to take their leadership role seriously. The next year, when they made *Harvest for the World,* they voiced their most overtly political statement to date. "Harvest for the World," perhaps in response to Stevie Wonder's politically oriented social statements on albums like *Innervisions* and *Fulfillingness First Finale* became paragons of black music, gold standards for every other black artist to come. The former, especially, one of Wonder's most important works addressing drugs, spirituality, political ethics, and life in the ghetto, was a collection of songs set to some of pop's funkiest grooves. Radio loved it, and so did the Isley Brothers.

Ironically, given the achievement, the Isleys' success on pop radio dried up after "Fight the Power." By 1977, music had completed its shifted in favor of disco, and radio squeezed most acts out of the chart picture altogether in favor of shallow, dance-oriented grooves. But the Isley brothers, true survivors, were one of the few acts to find a way to stay alive. In the five years "Fight the Power," the brothers polished up their dance beats of their own, smoothed out their ballads, and managed to keep their heads above water. After the acclaimed *Harvest for the World,* the Isleys released the equally excellent *Go for Your Guns* in 1977, *Showdown* in 1978, and *Winner Takes All* in 1979. All albums sold well, were rapturously received by R&B fans, and were shunned in the pop world. No matter, the Isleys were still getting it done. The pop charts didn't want them, but the R&B chart still possessed a fond place in its heart for their output.

Disco and dance music, and the polished production techniques of music studios at the time, began showing up on Isley records beginning with *Winner Takes All* in 1979. Tunes like "It's a Disco Night" and "Life in the City" featured a glossy sheen and dance vibe that carried over into much of their 1980s work. For every "Voyage to Atlantis," an extraordinary soul rock jam and staple in their late1970s and early1980s set, there were a handful of technically elaborate, smooth soul songs aimed at the dance crowds.

SMOOTH SAILING NO MORE

At this point, around 1980, the Isleys' formula, effective for most of the1970s, became a little trite. Even when a song worked on a commercial level, and many did on the R&B side, it was criticized for being formulaic. The young faction—Ernie, Marvin, and Chris Jasper—started running out of ideas. Frustration mounted creatively and personally. Divisions arose within the band. Squabbles occurred more and more frequently; generational fractures, the kind that most families endure, became evident as the weeks and months passed.

Albums like *Grand Slam* and *Between the Sheets* reflected the band's creative indifference. After scores and scores of recording sessions, Ronald's vocals still retained that gorgeous zeal. But it was becoming obvious that the group's continuity was fading. This was as much from dissension within the group as it was from dwindling interest in the music industry among group members.

In 1984, the friction grew to be too much to bear. Egos interfered with productivity. Ernie, Marvin, and Chris decided to venture out on their own, calling themselves Isley/Jasper/Isley. It was the end of an unprecedented 10-year run for the band and the beginning of a new chapter for both remaining factions.

"There was a generational split right down the middle, sure," admits Jasper. "That was reality. The older guys versus the younger guys. But I don't think the music ever suffered." Ernie called the upstarts, "the young lions, roaring around camp." But, he added, "there was always one camp" (Sacks, p. 29).

A year after separating, the remaining original Isleys, Ronald, Rudolph, and O'Kelly, the vocal side of the group, signed another record contract, this time with Warner Bros. To compensate for losing the young instrumentalists, they hired session musicians to round out the band's sound. Interestingly, *Masterpiece*, the group's Warner Bros. debut, centers mainly on their exquisite vocals, reducing the instrumentation, long their strong suit with the group's young lions, to a backing role. They also resorted to outside writers, giving the Isleys' new material color, variety, and dimension. It was a promising start.

Isley/Jasper/Isley signed with Columbia and had good success out of the gate with their debut LP *Broadway's Closer to Sunset Boulevard*. Their 1985 release *Caravan of Love* included the title track, their one R&B chart-topping single, which enjoyed a three-week stay at number one. They scored three other Top 20 singles in 1986 and 1987: "Insatiable Woman," "8th Wonder of the World," and "Givin' You Back the Love."

Then tragedy struck once again. Not long after the release of *Masterpiece*, O'Kelly suffered an unexpected heart attack and died. He was 48 and entering into what appeared to be a satisfying phase of his career. The misfortune sent the Isley family reeling.

Death had played a major role in the life and times of the clan, first with Vernon, then with the brothers' father. Death, it seemed, struck at those times when the family had undergone decisions to make momentous change. When Vernon was killed as a young teen, the group was speeding toward a promising career as a family gospel act. When father Isley died, the band had been on the cusp of deciding whether to fly the nest and head to New York City. And when O'Kelly died, he, Ronnie, and Rudolph had reinvented the band and embarked on a new career phase. Each time death occurred in the family, the surviving members felt struck down, devastated, and each time they rose up from the ashes, reformed, and excelled.

In response to O'Kelly's passing, though, Rudolph left music to enter the ministry, something he'd wanted to do for years. "When my brother Kelly died in his sleep of a heart attack, the same way our father did, I knew I had to make a change away from show business," Rudolph said. "Now I have a new King and I'm singing about a new kind of truth, the truth about Jesus Christ" (Sacks, p. 36).

Incidentally, Marvin Isley had been suffering from the complications of diabetes, which he had been diagnosed with in 1976. But his reluctance to follow his doctor's orders led to him having a stroke and kidney failure. He had both legs amputated in 1996.

In the late 1980s, the band contracted the services of Angela Winbush, a talented performer, songwriter and producer that had some success as part of a duet, with Rene Moore, as well as solo. After Winbush produced *Smooth Sailing*, the first new album after O'Kelly's death, Ronald began to manage Winbush's career. *Smooth Sailing* served as a tribute to their fallen brother, as did the poignant song "Send a Message."

Winbush produced and wrote the bulk of Ron's solo debut, *Spend the Night*, in 1988, an album credited as "the Isley Brothers featuring Ronald Isley." Winbush and Isley married in 1993. She also went on to produce the Isleys' *Mission to Please* set in 1996. That album featured the services of brothers Ernie and Marvin. In 1989, Ronald convened in the studio with Rod Stewart on a remake of the band's Holland-Dozier-Holland classic "This Old Heart of Mine," a song the band originally released as a Motown single in 1966. This time out the record did even better than its debut outing, reaching Pop number 10, two spaces better than in the spring of 1966.

Meanwhile, Chris Jasper, who split from Ernie and Marvin to go solo, made a couple of albums on his own, in which he played all the instruments, including *Superbad* in 1988 and *Time Bomb* in 1989. Neither sold, and the talented Jasper, unable to reconnect with the family that brought him fame, drifted into commercial obscurity.

THE 1990s

Somehow, at a time when musical trends were changing faster than the seasons, Ronnie Isley found ways to stay relevant, and he often brought his brother Ernie along with him. The hard-core rap world embraced the Isleys wholeheartedly. Bands like Public Enemy, led by Chuck D, identified with the political overtones of the Isleys' mid-1970s material and sampled it generously on their material in the late 1980s, nearly 15 years after the song's original release. Public Enemy even called one of their songs "Fight the Power," in a nod of acknowledgment to their heroes. Though the Isleys' original had a smaller purview, Chuck D used it as an anti-establishment anthem and full-on battle cry.

Other contemporary acts have sampled and recorded versions of the Isleys' music, including "Footsteps in the Dark" (Ice Cube's "It Was a Nice Day"), "Between the Sheets" (Notorious B.I.G.'s "Big Poppa" and Keith Murray's "The Most Beautifullest") and "(At Your Best) You Are Love" which was included on Aaliyah's debut *Age Ain't Nuthin' But a Number* (1994).

Ronnie had also become a sought-after vocalist for hip-hop artists like Warren G, Nas, Ja Rule, and Jay-Z. He sang the hook in Swizz Beatz's "Big Business" and its remix, "Bigger Business."

Neo-R&B crooner R. Kelly contributed substantially to the resurgence of Ronald's commercial stock. He imitated the legendary vocalist on a remix of "Bump 'N' Grind" and later on the track "Down Low" on his *R. Kelly* album from 1995, which also featured Isley's actual vocals. It was in the context of the "Down Low" video that younger audiences were introduced to Ronnie Isley via his portrayal of the character of Frank Biggs, a Mafia-like type looking to beat Kelly up for having an affair with his woman. Incidentally, the latter is a reference to Biggie Smalls (the late Notorious B.I.G.) and his own alter ego, "the black Frank White," itself a reference to the Christopher Walken character in the film *The King of New York*.

Isley's Mr. Biggs would reappear in a remixed version of "Down Low," the video for the Isley Brothers' 1996 single "Floating on Your Love," and as the uncle of Kelly Price in her video, "Friend of Mine." In the process, Ronnie had become Mr. Biggs to a new generation of listeners, as much as he has maintained his own original musical identity.

Not surprisingly, Mr. Biggs returned on *Eternal*, the first release by the Isley Brothers since *Mission to Please* (1996). *Eternal* is the synthesis of the Isley and Biggs dichotomy.

> If black popular culture has been influenced by the "gangsterization" of its core audiences, then the Isley Brothers, with the help of R. Kelly, have clearly studied the trends. It is clear that "Mr. Biggs" is present throughout the project because he moves units. Thus it is Biggs who is prominently displayed on the project's lead single reminding audiences not of the formidable legacy of the Isley Brothers and their classic recordings like "It's Your Thing" (1969), "That Lady" (1973), and "Fight the Power" (1974), but their lead singer's alter-ego. (Mark Anthony Neal, for *Pop Matters*, www.popmatters.com; *Eternal: The Isley Brothers Featuring Ronald Isley aka Mr. Biggs*, Dreamworks, 2001)

This is particularly apparent on the eight-minute title track that gives Ernie Isley ample space to revisit his Hendrix-like guitar solos. With producers Jimmy Jam and Terry Lewis in the mix, and Mr. Biggs taking a momentary back seat to Ernie Isley, the track "Eternal" becomes a metaphor for the longevity of the Isley Brothers. *Eternal* sold over a million copies.

The notoriety that the music of the era brought to the Isley Brothers' material was enough to keep the catalog moving and their new projects in the public eye. Few bands or artists could get away with having a hit in 1959 and still produce relevant songs almost 50 years later as Ronnie Isley has with "Contagious" (a Top 20 smash in 2001) and the Hot 100 singles "What Would You Do" and "Busted" (released in 2003).

"Busted" was on the 2003 disc *Body Kiss* (with Snoop Dogg and Li'l Kim), a record that debuted at number one on the album chart. It was the first number one album the Isleys had since releasing *The Heat Is On* back in 1975 and it earned a Grammy nomination for Best R&B Album.

That same year, 2003, Isley released *Here I Am: Ronald Isley Meets Burt Bacharach*, an acclaimed album featuring Isley singing the compositions of Bacharach with Bacharach conducting and arranging.

Ronald Isley parlayed his Mr. Biggs persona into a fashion magnate as well. Along with a fur company called Tendler Furs, Isley unveiled the Mr. Biggs Fur Collection. He and the Isleys had always been known as rather flamboyant dressers—once they ditched the mohair suits in the mid-1960s—and Ronald had demonstrated a flair for the fashionable. This endeavor took him out of the music industry, if only temporarily, and made him something of an entrepreneur.

LEGAL TANGLES

In 1994, Michael Bolton lost a lawsuit filed on behalf of the Isley group on the grounds that he plagiarized their music in his song "Love Is a Wonderful Thing." The Isleys recording a similar song with the same title in 1966. After a protracted battle, the courts ruled on behalf of the Isleys. They awarded Ronnie and Marvin $5.4 million in damages, 66 percent of all past and future royalties from the single, and 28 percent of past and future royalties from Bolton's album *Time, Love and Tenderness*. Since that ruling (and Bolton's subsequent loss on appeal in 2000), Bolton no longer performs the song in concert, and the well-known video is neither sold nor aired on television.

In 1997, Ronnie Isley declared personal bankruptcy after the IRS accused him of failure to pay taxes. The federal government claimed he failed to report performance and royalty income to the agency. The IRS also contended that he was involved in a host of deceptive practices relating to his finances during that five-year period, among them, a royalty check scheme where Isley deposited checks for his own use that had been issued to other members of the band, including his dead brother, O'Kelly. The government also claimed Isley bought personal cars using a business account and paid band members in cash to keep the transactions off the books.

In December 1999, the courts ordered the liquidation of the Isley estate, including the rights and royalties to over 200 Isley Brothers recordings, to pay off debts, including a reported $5 million in back taxes. He was convicted and sentenced to 37 months in prison on tax evasion charges and was ordered to pay over $3 million in fines. The 65-year-old was indicted in October 2005 on five counts of tax evasion covering the years from 1997 to 2002 and one count of failing to file an income tax return. U.S. District Court Judge Dean Pregerson called Isley "a serial tax avoider."

In a unique and rather devious turn of events, Michael Bolton emerged as one of the leading bidders for the Isley estate, offering $5.3 million for it. At the time, Bolton, still owed the Isley's $5.4 million following his plagiarism verdict. Ultimately, though, the Isleys were saved by Wall Street financier David Pullman. Pullman was responsible for issuing something called Bowie Bonds. Named after the artist David Bowie, the Bowie Bonds raise capital based on the projected future royalties of artist recordings and compositions. Given the desires of advertisers to mine classic rock and soul samples to use in commercials and movies, the bonds have been helpful to artists who have a formidable body of work, but are unlikely to find strong commercial interest in their future musical endeavors. This revenue has helped various artists, including Ashford and Simpson and the Marvin Gaye estate. The initial Bowie Bonds raised $55 million and a portion of that went to Isley.

LEGACY

With the possible exception of the Beatles, no band in the history of popular music, and certainly no African American act, has left a more substantial legacy on popular music than the Isley Brothers. From their original hit "Shout" back in 1959 to their number one album *Body Kiss* in 2003, the Isley Brothers have been a presence on American music charts for nearly 50 years. It's hard to believe that Ronnie Isley had an opportunity to make an impression on Paul McCartney and John Lennon with "Twist and Shout" in 1962, then almost four decades later, collaborate with high-profile rappers like Dr. Dre and Tupac Shakur on some of the late twentieth-century's most hard-core hip-hop music. Ronald's work with neo-soul artist R. Kelly, whose own work touched his many colleagues and protégés, had a profound effect on acts like Maxwell, D'Angelo, and Babyface.

And these are acts the Isleys touched directly. What of the Isleys' indirect influence? How could that be quantified? Their inimitable work in the 1970s, music that fused the bass-heavy vibrations of funk and the passion of soul with the driving force of hard rock, sent massive repercussions through everything that came after them, from soul and disco to funk, rock and hip-hop. Ronald's indelible, slow-jam smoothness as a singer and balladeer, Ernie's groundbreaking guitar work that seemed to pick up where Jimi Hendrix left off, Marvin and Chris Jasper's integral keyboard compositions and bass grooves all had impact on the work of the young artists who grew up listening to them.

They were inducted into the Rock and Roll Hall of Fame in 1992, alongside Jimi Hendrix, Johnny Cash, and the Yardbirds, all of whom give a good indication of the Isleys' secure place in history. They were also elected into the Grammy Hall of Fame in 1999 as well as the Vocal Group Hall of Fame in 2003.

Of course, that's not to say that Ronald Isley will not somehow find a way to endure through another decade, even beyond his prison stay. In an article highlighting the various phases of the Isley Brothers' musical journey, the *Michigan Chronicle* reminded fans that "you can count on one hand the groups that go back as far as the Isley Brothers." And it added. "As long as people can be assured of hearing the voice of Ronald Isley, the continuance of the group is a certainty" (Steve Holsey, "Artists Come and Go: Some Are Here to Stay," *Michigan Chronicle*, December 10, 1996).

SELECTED DISCOGRAPHY

Givin' It Back (T-Neck/Sony, 1971/1997)
3 + 3 (T-Neck/Sony, 1973/1997)
Live It Up (Epic/Legacy, 1974/2001)
The Heat Is On (Epic/Legacy, 1975/2001)
Harvest for the World (T-Neck, 1976)
It's Your Thing: The Story of the Isley Brothers (Epic/Legacy, 1999)

FURTHER READING

The All Music Guide to Rock. Erlewine, Unterberger, et al., eds. San Francisco: Miller, Freeman, 1997.
The Faber Companion to 20th-Century Popular Music. London: Faber and Faber, 1990.
Rees, Dafydd and Luke Crampton. *Encyclopedia of Rock Stars*. New York: DK Publishing, 1996.
Rhoden, William C. *It's Your Thing: The Story of the Isley Brothers*, liner notes. Epic/Legacy/ T-Neck Records, 1999.
Sacks, Leo. *It's Your Thing: The Story of the Isley Brothers*, liner notes. Epic/Legacy/ T-Neck Records, 1999.
Sacks, Leo. *Live It Up*, liner notes. Epic/Legacy/T-Neck Records, 1999.
Stambler, Irwin. *Encyclopedia of Pop, Rock and Soul*. New York: St. Martin's, 1989.
Vincent, Rickey. *Funk: The Music, the People, and the Rhythm of the One*. New York: St. Martin's Griffin, 1996.

Courtesy of Photofest.

James Brown

Andy Schwartz

THE GODFATHER OF SOUL

On the morning of December 28, 2006, dawn in Harlem broke cold and damp under cloudy skies. But the bleak weather had not kept hundreds of people from lining up, beginning shortly after midnight, at the entrance to the historic Apollo Theater on West 125th Street.

    They were mostly black, mostly between the ages of 30 and 60. They waited patiently and good-naturedly to bid a final farewell to the man whose body would soon rest in an open casket on the Apollo stage. That stage had been the site of some of his greatest career triumphs—the same stage where he had ruled, with fiery music and matchless showmanship, on so many nights down through the decades.

Hours later, the lines from the Apollo extended both east and west, down both ends of the long block and then around the corners of Adam Clayton Powell and Frederick Douglass Boulevards. All along the route, the dead man's recordings poured forth from makeshift sound systems attached to stores and restaurants: "Try Me," "I Feel Good," "I'll Go Crazy," "Papa's Got a Brand New Bag," "Sex Machine," "Living in America." The police had closed 125th Street to traffic, and the crowds strained against the temporary metal barriers erected at the edge of the sidewalk.

At a few minutes past 1 P.M., a white carriage turned onto the thoroughfare. It was drawn by a pair of plumed white horses, driven by two men wearing formal dress and top hats, and bore a gold-painted coffin built of 16-gauge steel. It held the body of a man known by many appellations: "Soul Brother Number One," "The Hardest-Working Man in Show Business," "The Godfather of Soul." But as the carriage moved slowly and solemnly down the street toward the doors of the Apollo, a chant rose up from the throng and his real name rang out: "James Brown! James Brown! James Brown!"

Born into abject poverty in the segregated South, possessed of both immense talent and indomitable will, James Brown is one of a handful of twentieth-century artists of whom it can truthfully be said that they changed music—not just *black* music, not just *American* music, but the sound of popular music around the world.

In the 1920s another African American genius, Louis Armstrong, defined the role of the instrumental soloist and forever changed the sound of jazz. In the 1960s, James Brown transformed rhythm and blues into funk and thereby laid the sonic groundwork for virtually all subsequent rhythm-based pop music forms. The critic Robert Palmer wrote, "The chattering choke-rhythm guitars, broken bass patterns, explosive horn bursts, one-chord drones, and evangelical vocal discourses he introduced in the mid-sixties became the *lingua franca* of contemporary Black pop, the heartbeat of the discotheques and a primary ingredient in such far-flung musical syntheses as Jamaican reggae and Nigerian Afro-beat" (Robert Palmer, "James Brown," in *The Rolling Stone Illustrated History of Rock & Roll*, New York: Random House, 1992, pp. 163–64).

In Brown's best and most influential recordings, the *song* was virtually inseparable from his *sound*. That sound was raw, intense, and indisputably black in its diction and delivery, and it could not be easily emulated or copied by white performers.

Much more than a singer, James Brown conceived and commanded a complete stage show involving crucial elements of timing and sequence. It encompassed a large instrumental group, backing vocalists, and dancers, all of whose roles were endlessly rehearsed and revised. The James Brown Show functioned as a quasi-religious revival meeting, a variety show, and a communal tribute to both Brown's innate talent and his relentless striving for success. Along with his recordings, album covers, publicity photos, and television appearances, the James Brown Show served as a forum through which he introduced new dances, slogans, and hair and clothing styles. All of these changes were closely followed, especially in the 1960s and early 1970s, by an international fan base that stretched from Manhattan to Mali.

The James Brown story is a classic American saga of upward mobility from impoverished origins to the pinnacle of pop stardom. At the peak of his influence, Brown was a figure of profound social significance in black America whose actions and statements inspired admiration, controversy, and derision. He freed himself from record company interference to gain creative control over his music and established a diversified business enterprise that included record labels, publishing companies, and radio stations.

The story also reveals the limits of the singer's real power within the music industry; it is marred by personal tragedy, professional decline, and numerous acts of willful egomania. None of these things have diminished the global impact of James Brown's greatest music, or the pleasure and inspiration which generations of listeners have taken from it.

THE EARLY YEARS

Although varying dates and locales have been reported over the years, today it is generally accepted that James Joseph Brown Jr. was born on May 3, 1933, in rural Barnwell, South Carolina, the only child of Joe and Susie Brown. Four years later, James's mother abandoned the family; he would not see her again for 20 years. Joe Brown, with only a second-grade education, toiled for meager wages on farms and plantations, in turpentine camps, and later as a gas station attendant. Driving a vegetable delivery truck, he earned $4 per week.

Father and son, along with a succession of Joe's female companions, "lived about as poor as you could be," James later recalled. Their unpainted wooden shack in the woods outside of town "didn't have windows except for shutters that you could pull together; and there was no electricity or indoor plumbing. . . . We ate black-eyed peas and lima beans, fatback [dried and salt-cured pork fat] and syrup, polk salad that we picked in the woods, and cornbread" (James Brown with Bruce Tucker, *James Brown: The Godfather of Soul*, New York: Macmillan, 1986, p. 3).

Joe Brown was overwhelmed by the responsibilities of single fatherhood and at age five, James was sent to live with his aunt Handsome "Honey" Washington in the black section of Augusta, Georgia, known as "the Terry" (for "territory"). Her two-story dwelling at 944 Twiggs Street was in fact a working brothel presided over by Honey and her bootlegger brother, Jack Scott. Often as not, James was forced to fend for himself in this house full of adult strangers coming and going at all hours, which was raided regularly by the local police.

Trombonist and arranger Fred Wesley Jr., who served two lengthy stints with the James Brown Show, later explained to writer Cynthia Rose, "We're talking about a three, four-year-old child who actually didn't live anywhere. Nobody fed him, nobody bathed him. He didn't *have* a place to live. He survived on sheer guts" (Cynthia Rose, *Living in America: The Soul Saga of James Brown*, London: Serpent's Tail, 1990, p. 22). When beds were scarce in the overcrowded house, James slept on a wooden pallet on the floor. He did not own a pair of store-bought underwear until he started school at age seven; at times he was sent home from class, humiliated, for having "insufficient clothes."

Much later in life, Brown cited music as "one of the things that helped me to survive . . . [It] was just there in the community and I fell into it, the way you will" (Brown and Tucker, p. 17). He heard the country and pop tunes played on local radio stations and tried his hand at any instrument within reach, including harmonica, piano, and guitar. (James also claimed to have taken a few lessons from Hudson Whittaker, the legendary blues singer and guitarist known as Tampa Red.)

But what most impressed the eager adolescent were the shouting, ecstatic crowds and blaring brass bands that, every Sunday, filled the "sanctified" churches like Bishop "Daddy" Grace's House of Prayer in Augusta. Back at Aunt Honey's house, James and his cousin Willie "Junior" Glenn, along with other friends, would try to imitate the singing of such popular male gospel groups as the Five Trumpets and the Golden Gate Quartet.

In his eponymous 1986 autobiography, James recalled attending revival services where the preacher "was just screaming and yelling and stomping his foot, and then he dropped to his knees. The people got into it with him, answering him and shouting and clapping time. After that . . . I watched the preachers real close. Then I'd go home and imitate them, because *I* wanted to preach."

Brown continued, "Audience participation in church is something the darker race of people has going [sic] because of a lot of trials and tribulations, because of things that we understand about human nature. It's something I can't explain, but I can bring it out of people. I'm not the only person who has the ability, but I *work* at it, and I'm sure a lot of my stage show came out of the church" (Brown and Tucker, p. 18).

Before he reached the age of 12, James had dropped out of school and into the world of low-wage, unskilled labor. He picked cotton, cut sugarcane, and washed cars. After his day's work was done, he'd set up a shoeshine stand outside radio station WRDW; to attract customers, James would dance on the sidewalk, sometimes singing to accompany himself. That part of his earnings not contributed to his extended family was often spent at the local "colored" movie theater. James was thrilled by the performances of 1940s rhythm and blues star Louis Jordan, in such all-black-cast screen musicals as *Reet Petite & Gone* and *Look Out, Sister*.

The odd jobs mixed with small-time crimes and street hustles: "The reality of Black existence at this time, when Georgia vied with Mississippi for the national lynching championship, was that in any attempt to be something besides a subservient menial worker, one could hardly avoid breaking the law, and even that didn't make life easy" (Stanley Booth, "The Godfather's Blues," in *Rhythm Oil*, London: Jonathan Cape, 1992, p. 232). In 1949, 16-year-old James Brown was convicted on four counts of breaking and entering (into cars), and given 8–16 years in a state penitentiary. When this draconian sentence was reduced, James was transferred to the Alto Reform School in Toccoa, Georgia. He became popular among the inmates for his gospel singing in chapel and trained as a boxer although he was only five feet, six inches tall and weighed 137 pounds. James also played baseball and showed impressive pitching skills until injuries put an end to his dream of a career in the Negro Leagues.

When a young gospel singer-pianist named Bobby Byrd came to perform at Alto, the two teenagers struck up an acquaintance. On June 14, 1952, James was paroled after serving three years and went to live with the Byrd family temporarily while he looked for a place to stay in Toccoa. (As a condition of his parole, James could not return to the county where his family resided.) When not working a variety of low-paying jobs, he sang with Bobby in the Ever Ready Gospel Singers. This group was affiliated with the Mount Zion Baptist Church, where James met Velma Warren—the first of his four wives. They were wed in Toccoa on June 19, 1953, and settled down there; within five years, Velma had given birth to Teddy, Terry, and Larry, the couple's three sons.

James's local performances brought him to the attention of Clint Brantley, the manager of Little Richard (not yet nationally famous), who urged Brown to relocate to Richard's home base in Macon. Soon, Brown had moved into a room above the Two Spot nightclub in Macon and found a day job with the Lawson Motor Company. In his off hours, he sang with such locally popular groups as the Gospel Starlighters and the R&B-oriented Four Steps of Rhythm (James also played piano and drums).

Bobby Byrd also moved to Macon and formed a new gospel outfit with Nafloyd Scott and Sylvester Keels called the Three Swanees. When first Johnny Terry and then James Brown joined the group, it became the Swanee Quintet; after switching to secular music, over the next year their name was changed to the Flames and then again to the Famous Flames. Whatever the name or style, Brown seems destined to have become the de facto leader and on-stage focus of this group, as he eventually did. He may or may not have been the best pure singer in the Flames, but he was almost certainly the most distinctive. Even at this early stage, James combined raw talent with a determined work ethic and an outsized ego fueled in part by envy and insecurity.

"He has no real musical skills," trombonist Fred Wesley Jr. told Cynthia Rose, "yet he could hold his own onstage with any jazz virtuoso—because of his guts. Can you understand that? James Brown cannot play drums at all.

But he would sit down on drums and get that look on his face like he's playin' 'em, and you would just play along with him. . . . He doesn't understand losing and he *truly* understands surviving. It's not that James wants to win every time—it's that he will not *lose*" (Rose, p. 22).

THE FAMOUS FLAMES

Without a record contract, the Famous Flames worked hard to build up their reputation on a black club circuit that extended from Chattanooga, Tennessee, south to lower Florida and west from Savannah, Georgia, into Mississippi. Their career at this stage was characterized by long hours, low pay, and exhausting, sometimes dangerous travel conditions across the segregated South. Macon disc jockey Ray "Satellite Poppa" Brown sometimes traveled with James in these early days. "Finding a motel room—that was unheard of, man," he later recalled. "You'd sleep in your car or stay at the club until daybreak" (Scott Freeman, "James Brown: Soul Brother No. 1," *Atlanta Creative Loafing,* Jan. 11–17, 2007).

Mostly the group sang other people's hits, including "Please Don't Go," a Top 10 R&B entry for the Orioles in 1952. The Famous Flames' extended live version of this song became an audience favorite and gradually evolved into "Please, Please, Please," a hypnotically repetitive ballad credited to James Brown and Johnny Terry that pitted James's raspy, emotive lead vocal against the Flames' doo-wop background. In late 1955, the group recorded a rough version of the song at Macon radio station WIBB in a session overseen by disc jockey Hamp "King Bee" Swain: "I put it on the air and we got a tremendous reaction. *Immediately.* The phone lines just lit up" (Freeman).

In January 1956, A&R man Ralph Bass heard the song on an Atlanta station while traveling through the South on a talent-scouting trip for King Records of Cincinnati. He tracked down the Famous Flames at a small club near Milledgeville, Georgia, and promptly signed the group for an advance of $200, then brought them to the King studios to re-cut the song with professional studio players. King's rotund, cigar-smoking founder Syd Nathan declared "Please, Please, Please" to be one of the worst songs he'd ever heard and told Ralph Bass he was crazy to have even paid James's train fare from Macon to Cincinnati. But Nathan changed his tune when the record began to sell throughout the South.

"Brown was way ahead of his time," Ralph Bass later recalled. "He wasn't really singing R&B. He was singing gospel to an R&B combo with a real heavy feeling. . . . He wasn't singing or playing music—he was transmitting *feeling,* pure feeling" (Arnold Shaw, *Honkers and Shouters: The Golden Years of Rhythm & Blues,* New York: Collier Books, 1978, pp. 241–42).

"Please, Please, Please" was released in March 1956 on Federal Records (a King subsidiary) with label credit inscribed to "James Brown & the Famous Flames." The disc hung on the *Billboard* R&B Singles chart for 19 weeks, peaking at number five; over time, it sold more than a million copies. The group's success attracted the interest of Ben Bart, the white founder and head of the potent New York booking agency Universal Attractions. Previously, Bart had managed the careers of swing bandleader Jimmy Lunceford, singer Dinah Washington, and a pioneering vocal group the Ravens; it was a big step up for the Famous Flames when he agreed to become their booking agent. Ben Bart later became the singer's manager, business partner, and beloved father figure, and the only person ever to refer to James Brown as "Jimmy" (Brown called him "Pop"). Their close and complex relationship lasted until Bart's death in 1968.

Nine more single releases followed, yet not one reached the *Billboard* R&B chart—perhaps because most were overly derivative of recent hits by better-established performers, including Little Richard ("Chonnie-On-Chon") and Ray Charles ("That Dood It"). Syd Nathan's personal distaste for Brown's music and his tight-fisted attitude toward promotional expenditures on behalf of *any* King artist also may have been significant factors. This string of failures, combined with Ben Bart's expressed desire to make James its front-and-center star, caused the original group to dissolve in 1957. Later, Bobby Byrd returned to Brown's organization for the long haul through the 1960s with the trio of male singer-dancers always billed as the Famous Flames—but always in a supporting role to Brown himself.

THE KING OF THE APOLLO

By the fall of 1958, Syd Nathan was ready to drop James Brown from the King/Federal roster when the singer came up with another slow, bluesy ballad, "Try Me." To the surprise of all concerned, the song shot to number one R&B in early 1959—and from that time until 1982, a year would not pass in which James Brown didn't place at least one song on the *Billboard* R&B chart. ("Try Me" also crossed over to the Hot 100, peaking at number 48.)

Brown became increasingly conscious of the need to maintain his own permanent road band. It was a bold and expensive move that harkened back to the big bands of Count Basie and Duke Ellington as well as Louis Jordan's Tympani Five. Many leading R&B performers of the period, including Sam Cooke and Jackie Wilson, traveled with just a guitarist and a drummer while recruiting other players as needed. But a James Brown *band* could be trained to play his music the James Brown way, night after night. It would also be available around the clock for spontaneous recording sessions in any studio convenient to the singer's never-ending tour itinerary. Among his first recruits (circa 1959) were bassist Bernard Odum, drummer Nat Kendrick, and saxophonists J.C. Davis and Albert Corley.

When James had regained his footing on the charts with "Try Me" and "Think" (number seven R&B), he moved from Federal to the parent King label. Now commanding a degree of grudging respect from Syd Nathan, he was free to write and produce his own material with his own musicians. Brown had no say over King's release schedule, however, and it was not unusual for six months or more to pass between the recording and the release of a new song like "Night Train." (In 1962, "Night Train" became James's eighth Top 10 R&B hit and his second Top 40 Pop entry.) When Brown suggested the idea of an instrumental based on a dance he called the mashed potatoes, Nathan told him to forget about it. James cut the track at his own expense (dubbing disc jockey King Coleman's voice over his own vocal interjections) and licensed the song to Henry Stone's Dade Records in Miami. Credited to Nat Kendrick and the Swans, "(Do The) Mashed Potatoes (Pt. 1 & 2)" reached number eight R&B in 1960.

Another, more significant confrontation between the artist and his label resulted in one of the key albums of James Brown's entire career. By 1962, his skin-tight, endlessly rehearsed live show was tearing up audiences across the country. Even James's best studio recordings couldn't capture the intensity of his on-stage delivery and the fervor of his fans' collective response. He needed a live album, and Ray Charles had shown the way with *Ray Charles in Person*, a Top 15 bestseller in 1960.

James proposed the idea to Syd Nathan—and was turned down flat. The label chief simply didn't believe that fans would buy an album of songs they'd already purchased in studio versions, and he was loath to pay the costs of location recording. In the fall of 1962, James opened the fifth extended engagement of his career at the Apollo Theater in Harlem—the premier showplace in "the Capital of Black America." On October 24, the performance was recorded at Brown's own expense for $5,700. The tapes were pared down to a 32-minute LP so carelessly edited that the break between the first and second sides came right in the middle of the climactic track, an intense 11-minute version of "Lost Someone." When the album was released in January 1963, King initially pressed just 5,000 copies.

Live at the Apollo was an immediate and unprecedented smash. It made no stylistic concessions to the pop mainstream, simply capturing a typically heated James Brown performance before an enraptured black audience. Yet *Live at the Apollo* rose all the way to number two among *Billboard* Top Pop Albums and hung on the chart for 66 weeks—in a year when the top-selling album artists included musical humorist Allan Sherman, folk trio Peter, Paul and Mary, and crooner Andy Williams. Reaction among black radio listeners was so intense that disc jockeys would often play both sides of the album in full, with commercial spots inserted in the break.

Forty years later, *Live at the Apollo* was ranked at number 24 on *Rolling Stone* magazine's list of the 500 Greatest Albums of All Time. In 2004, it was one of 50 recordings added to the National Recording Registry at the Library of Congress, alongside *Pet Sounds* by the Beach Boys and the Vladimir Horowitz/Arturo Toscanini recording of Tchaikovsky's *Piano Concerto No. 1, op. 23, B-flat minor*.

PLAY IT FUNKY

James Brown's music continued to evolve as new personnel came into his band. Among the key additions of the early 1960s were saxophonists Maceo Parker and St. Clair Pinckney, guitarist Jimmy Nolen, and the drummers Clyde Stubblefield and John "Jabo" Starks. Stubblefield is often credited with a crucial shift in emphasis from the second and fourth beats (as in traditional blues) to the first and third beats—"The One," as this rhythm dynamic became known in the lexicon of funk. Alfred "Pee Wee" Ellis, a saxophonist and arranger who joined Brown's revue in 1965, explained the importance of Clyde Stubblefield's "New Orleans beat" to Cynthia Rose:

"If, in a studio, you said 'Play it funky,' that could imply almost anything. But 'give me a New Orleans beat'—you got exactly what you wanted. And Clyde Stubblefield was just the epitome of this funky drumming. There was a way his beat was broken up—a combination of where the bass and the snare drums hit—which was topsy-turvy from what had been goin' on" (Rose, p. 47).

With the success of *Live at the Apollo*, James felt compelled to relocate to the center of the American music business; with Velma and their children, he moved into a 12-room Victorian house in Queens, New York. Brown and Ben Bart formed an independent company called Fair Deal Productions. The singer's attorney, Marty Machat, took the position that James's agreement with King had expired and signed him, through Fair Deal, to a lucrative new contract with Smash, a subsidiary of Mercury Records. Syd Nathan promptly filed suit, alleging breach of contract, but Brown recorded prolifically for Smash while the case wended its way through the legal system.

In the summer of 1964, his Smash recording "Out of Sight" became James's tenth Top 10 R&B hit and a number 24 Pop entry. On this track, "you can hear the band and me start to move in a whole other direction rhythmically," Brown later wrote. "The horns, the guitar, the vocals, everything was starting to be used to establish all kinds of rhythms at once. . . . I was trying to get every aspect of the production to contribute to the rhythmic patterns" (Brown and Tucker, p. 149).

In October 1964, he appeared at the Santa Monica Civic Auditorium in Los Angeles before a predominantly white audience as a part of a star-studded cast assembled to film *The T.A.M.I. [Teen Age Music International] Show*, a concert documentary that was released to theaters the following year. The bill included the Beach Boys, Marvin Gaye, the Supremes, and the Rolling Stones, but James pulled out all the stops in an explosion of song and dance.

"[I] hit the stage on fire, just because I was told by so many people not to push my heat button too hard. I mean, I torched those songs. . . . The minute we kicked in with our opening number, 'Out of Sight,' all those White kids in the audience went crazy!" It was, he recounted proudly, "the first time anybody in that neck of the woods had got a dose of real soul, James Brown style" (James Brown, *I Feel Good: A Memoir of a Life of Soul*, New York: New American Library, 2005, pp. 126–27).

The T.A.M.I. Show captured on film the so-called cape routine, a key ritual of James's live performance. "In a drama that would play itself out many times during the course of a single concert, Brown, supposedly overcome by torturous emotional and physical cravings, would drop prayerfully to his knees, unable to continue. Only when his seconds, the Famous Flames, draped a velvet cape across his shoulders and led the shambling singer from the stage would he again find the strength to continue" (Bob Merlis and Davin Seay, *Heart & Soul: A Celebration of Black Music Style in America 1930–1975*, New York: Stewart, Tabori & Chang, 1997, p. 51).

James's career took a curious turn when King obtained a court injunction which dictated that he release *instrumentals* on Smash and *vocals* on King. Mercury was forced to withdraw the *Out of Sight* album and instead put out instrumental sets like *Grits and Soul* and *James Brown Plays New Breed*, all featuring Brown on organ. Meanwhile, Syd Nathan delved into the King vaults and cobbled together "new" James Brown vocal releases from tapes recorded years earlier.

PAPA'S BRAND NEW BAG

Nineteen sixty-four, the year of the Beatles' American breakthrough, visited setbacks and tragedy upon a number of James's fellow soul stars. His friend and former King Records labelmate Little Willie John was charged with assault in Miami; he died in a Washington State prison in 1968. In October, Ray Charles was arrested for possession of marijuana and heroin in Boston. In December, Sam Cooke was shot and killed by a motel owner in Los Angeles. Jackie Wilson did not have one Top 10 R&B hit in 1964; Solomon Burke had several, mostly sung in a smooth ballad style. Wilson Pickett was between record contracts, and Otis Redding had not yet emerged as a national star from his Southern base.

All of these circumstances reinforced James Brown's position as the preeminent soul singer of the day. He criss-crossed the continent at the head of a troupe that now numbered nearly two dozen musicians and vocalists. When James's musical career began, the conditions of his parole prohibited him from remaining within the Augusta city limits for more than 24 hours. Now he could, by his insistence on playing to mixed audiences, effectively integrate first the Macon City Auditorium and then Bell Auditorium in Augusta—months before President Lyndon Johnson signed the Civil Rights Act into law on July 2, 1964.

Under a renegotiated contract with King, James was releasing a new single every few weeks. Two of these—"Papa's Got a Brand New Bag" and "It's a Man's Man's Man's World"—were among the best-selling and most influential songs of his entire career.

"Papa's Got a Brand New Bag" is a blues in form but with a sound far removed from the deliberate, Mississippi-bred style of Muddy Waters or Jimmy Reed. Brown's brusque vocal rides a taut, hard-hitting beat as he name-checks various dance crazes like the Twist, the Jerk, and the Boomerang. At the end of each verse, everything drops away for a few seconds of jazzy chicken-scratch chording by guitarist Jimmy Nolen and a blast of horns, signaling a repeat of the chord sequence. Like another massive hit from the summer of 1965, Bob Dylan's "Like a Rolling Stone," "Papa" feels like it could go on for a very long time. In fact, the complete original recording is over seven minutes in length; King's two-minute single edit was only part one of a three-part track.

"Papa" became the first James Brown single to reach the Top 10 of the *Billboard* Hot 100 and held the R&B number one position for eight weeks; it spawned a best-selling album of the same title that reached number 2 R&B and number 26 Pop. In 1999, "Papa's Got a Brand New Bag" was given a Grammy Hall of Fame Award as a recording "of lasting qualitative or historical significance."

"It's a Man's Man's Man's World" was the stylistic opposite, a slow minor-key ballad co-written by Brown and songwriter Betty Jean Newsome. James had produced an earlier version of the song for Tammi Terrell, a singer with his touring revue; it passed unnoticed when released under the title "I Cried." But Brown's own rendition is a moody masterpiece, with dark clouds of orchestration shadowing his lead vocal and the almost inaudible rhythm section. His tormented delivery, with its dramatic sobs and shouts, infused the lyrics with deeper, more universal emotions. Perhaps the depiction of "a man's world" that "would be nothing without a woman or a girl" reflected the pain of James's breakup with Velma from whom he separated in 1964 (they divorced in 1969).

Released in April 1966, "It's a Man's Man's Man's World" topped the R&B chart and cracked the Pop Top 10, peaking at number 8. The chord sequence and melody of "Fallin'," Alicia Keys's massive Grammy Award–winning hit of 2001, are startlingly similar to James's song—even though "Fallin'" is credited only to Keys.

BLACK POWER

Brown enjoyed his greatest crossover success in the period 1967–1968, when three of his number 1 R&B hits all reached the Pop Top 10. "Cold Sweat" and "I Got the Feelin'" were funk masterpieces, but "Say It Loud—I'm Black and I'm Proud" was that and something more. The song was released in September 1968, a year in which the United States was rocked by political assassinations, the Tet offensive in South Vietnam, widespread protests against the Vietnam War, and the violence that erupted during the Democratic National Convention in Chicago.

On April 4, Dr. Martin Luther King Jr. was assassinated in Memphis, Tennessee. The next night, Brown was scheduled to headline Boston Garden. At first, Mayor Kevin White wanted to cancel the show. Instead, a plan was formulated to broadcast the show live over Boston's public television station WGBH. A few thousand ticket-holders showed up that night; on stage, James paused several times in the course of his show to speak to the audience, cooling down tempers and heading off confrontations between young blacks and the police stationed inside the arena. His words were heard by a much larger audience that had stayed home to watch the show for free—and although civil disturbances broke out that night in nearly 100 cities across the nation, Boston remained calm.

In June, James flew overseas to entertain U.S. troops in Korea and Vietnam—an opportunity he'd been denied, despite his repeated requests to the USO, until Vice President Hubert Humphrey interceded on the singer's behalf. Brown and his band (stripped down to just five musicians for the trip) often played several shows in a day; they traveled in military helicopters that came under enemy fire on several frightening occasions.

James returned to the United States and in August recorded "Say It Loud" in Los Angeles. For the session, he recruited an amateur chorus of schoolchildren and adults to chant the title phrase. His lead vocal is quite literally a "rap," a string of spoken couplets, while the horn section and an unforgettable bass line provide the melodic content.

"Say It Loud—I'm Black and I'm Proud" became a rallying cry and a powerful expression of self-affirmation. Almost overnight, it seemed, terms like "colored" and "Negro" fell out of the African American lexicon. Through the expressive power of this song and its constant airing on black radio, James Brown "named an entire people: *Black* Americans," (Glen Ford, "James Brown: The Man Who Named a People," available online at www.countercurrents.org/ford090107.htm) wrote journalist Glen Ford, whose first full-time radio news job was on WRDW-Augusta, one of three radio stations owned by Brown in the late 1960s.

"The phenomenon built upon, but was more far-reaching than, Stokely Carmichael's popularization of 'Black Power' two years earlier. Carmichael's slogan called for—demanded—power for Black people. But James Brown's anthem actually empowered ordinary Black folks to signal to their leaders and oppressors—the whole world, in fact—the fundamental terms of any dialogue: how they were to be addressed" (Ford).

Brown's politics were complicated, contradictory, and rooted in personal experience. He was a member of the National Association for the Advancement of Colored People. In the summer of 1966, he performed in Tupelo, Mississippi, in support of James Meredith, who'd been shot in the back while making his March Against Fear from Memphis, Tennessee, to Jackson, Mississippi. But racial pride didn't prevent James from hiring white musicians or working with white managers and agents. Later in life, he even spoke of

George Wallace and Lester Maddox with admiration and forgiveness despite the fact that both men had bitterly opposed the civil rights movement when they served as the governors of, respectively, Alabama and Georgia.

The title of a 2006 book by business author Tyrone L. Cypress—*Say It Loud . . . I Sell and I'm Proud*—may have been a crude manipulation of the song's true historical meaning. But it was also consistent with the recurring theme of black capitalist uplift that ran through Brown's worldview and public rhetoric. For proof that America was indeed a land of opportunity in which hard work and determination could pay off beyond anyone's wildest dreams, James Brown needed to look no further than the nearest mirror. His economic philosophy might have been summed up by the title of his number 3 R&B/number 20 Pop hit of 1969: "I Don't Want Nobody to Give Me Nothing (Open Up the Door, I'll Get It Myself)."

In a real-life demonstration of the song's credo, Brown faced down a local campaign to prevent his realtor from closing on a large house that the singer intended to purchase in Walton Way, an upscale white section of Augusta. In October 1969, following his divorce from Velma, James married Deidre "Deedee" Jenkins and moved into the new home with his new wife, who later gave birth to their daughters Deanna and Yamma.

TOUGH LOVE

Republican President Richard Nixon "made Brown feel he was a key example of black capitalism at work, which appealed to the singer's gigantic ego," wrote Nelson George. "Brown didn't understand the nuances of Nixon's plan—reach out to showcase some black business efforts while dismantling [Lyndon] Johnson's Great Society programs, which for all their reputed mismanagement had helped a generation of blacks begin the process of upward mobility" (Nelson George, *The Death of Rhythm & Blues*, New York: Pantheon Books, 1988, pp. 103–104). James endorsed Nixon in his 1972 re-election campaign—one of the few black entertainers to do so, besides Lionel Hampton and Sammy Davis Jr. In May 1973, during a return engagement at the Apollo Theater, black demonstrators picketed the theater with signs that read "James Brown, Nixon Clown" and "Get That Clown Out of Town."

James was a temperamental and often vindictive employer of musicians and other personnel. Underlying nearly all his actions was, as Arthur Kempton noted, "his conviction that every inch of his way up had been bought and paid for by his own unreasonably hard effort" (Arthur Kempton, *Boogaloo: The Quintessence of American Popular Music*, New York: Pantheon Books, 2003, p. 145) as well as "the classic Napoleonic little man's disposition to take any subordinate's challenge as a towering affront" (Kempton, p. 394).

When trombonist Fred Wesley Jr. joined James's organization in early 1968, he was grateful to receive a salary of $350 per week regardless of whether

"Mr. Brown" (as he demanded to be addressed by everyone, at all times) was working or not. Wesley soon found out that this system was stacked in favor of the boss, who regularly worked 300 days of the year. The same weekly salary could cover multiple shows in the same venue or gigs in two cities in the same day; the musicians received nothing extra for recording sessions or television appearances. The payroll remained at about $6,000 a week, a paltry sum given Brown's earning power, "and he acted like he didn't want to give you that" (Fred Wesley Jr., *Hit Me, Fred: Recollections of a Sideman*, Durham: Duke University Press, 2002, p. 95).

In addition, band members were forced to endure "horror rehearsals" during which James would harangue and insult them for hours on end. He also imposed fines for on-stage offenses ranging from wrong notes to unshined shoes. Fred felt deeply that such manipulation was "unnecessary to the creation of an act as exciting as the James Brown Show. But, on the real side, there has never been a show that exciting, that tight, that completely entertaining. There also has never been a man so dedicated, so determined, so focused" (Wesley, p. 99).

In 1970, just hours before a show in Columbus, Georgia, the musicians threatened to quit unless Brown promised to change his ways. Instead, he summarily fired most of them including Maceo Parker, Clyde Stubblefield, and Jabo Starks. James then dispatched his Lear jet to Cincinnati to pick up a local group called the Pacesetters, led by 18-year-old William "Bootsy" Collins on bass and his brother Phelps "Catfish" Collins on guitar. They arrived in Columbus, were driven directly to the venue, and carried their equipment on stage as the other musicians were removing their own. Despite a few hours' delay, the James Brown Show went on as scheduled.

James changed the Pacesetters' name to the JB's. It was this group—later rejoined by Parker, Starks, and Fred Wesley Jr.—that provided the backing for many of his best and biggest funk hits of the 1970s. This series of inspired singles included "Get Up—I Feel Like Being Like a Sex Machine," "Super Bad," "I'm a Greedy Man," "Soul Power," and "Get On the Good Foot—Part 1." In 1974 alone, James scored three R&B number one hits with "The Payback—Part 1," "My Thang," and "Papa Don't Take No Mess—Part 1." The relentless repetition of beats, riffs, and vocal phrases, over tracks that (in their album versions) sometimes ran for 10 minutes or more, was not a drawback but an essential element of the James Brown sound. The individual songs seemed to form a non-stop and continuously evolving jam, with the leader verbally cuing one of the tightest and most versatile bands in all of popular music through the chord changes, horn solos, and drum breaks.

After nearly 20 years on the road, James remained a galvanizing live performer whose volcanic intensity and spontaneous eruptions could provoke near-hysterical reaction from audiences throughout Europe, Africa, and North America. In 1970, at a huge outdoor sports arena in Dakar, Senegal, "James demonstrated his endurance . . . by jumping off the ten-foot-high stage and running a lap around the stadium, wearing his 'Please, Please, Please' robe, after singing and dancing for two hours" (Wesley, p. 175). In Lagos, Nigeria, James communed with Nigerian superstar Fela Kuti. In the fall of 1974, the singer performed in Kinshasa, Zaire, as part of an African American music festival attached to the heavyweight title fight between Muhammad Ali and George Foreman.

Syd Nathan, the founder of King Records, died March 5, 1968, and in October his company was sold to Starday Records of Nashville. Starday itself was then sold to Lin Broadcasting, which sold James Brown's contract and catalog to Polydor Records of Germany in July 1971. James was a vital addition to the Polydor roster as the company sought to establish itself in the all-important U.S. market. In addition to Brown's own unending flow of singles and albums (including the two-LP sets *Revolution of the Mind*, *The Payback*, and *Get On the Good Foot*), he founded a new label, People Records, to distribute his productions of other artists: Hank Ballard, Bobby Byrd, Lyn Collins, and assorted instrumental configurations of the JBs.

TRAGEDY

In his off-stage life, however, the singer was under increasing personal strain. Beginning in 1968, he became embroiled in protracted disputes with the IRS, which claimed that he owed millions in back taxes. Eventually, Brown lost ownership of his three radio stations, his two private planes, and even his Augusta home to the agency. At times, he felt certain he was under government surveillance.

In August 1973, James's eldest son Teddy, age 19, was killed in a car accident in upstate New York, leaving his father "on my knees with grief." In his darkest moments, Teddy's death felt like "a kind of punishment for me that I could never be pardoned or paroled from, or a sin I could never properly atone for" (Brown, pp. 178–79). His marriage to Deedee began to disintegrate, although they were not legally divorced until 1981.

But the greatest threat to Brown's career was the advent of a kind of music—disco—that could never have existed without him. His complex polyrhythms were smoothed out into one metronomic dance beat; his jazzy horn riffs were replaced by sweeping string arrangements. In general, the new style was more adaptable to the melodic voices of female singers like Donna Summer and vocal groups such as the O'Jays. James derided disco as "a very small part of funk, like a vamp. The difference is that in funk you dig into a groove, you don't stay on the surface. Disco stayed on the surface" (Brown and Tucker, pp. 242–43).

Competition arose on another front from Parliament-Funkadelic, the extravagant "funk mob" led by George Clinton and featuring such former JBs as Bootsy Collins and Fred Wesley Jr. P-Funk's sprawling, wildly costumed live shows were filling the sports arenas and municipal auditoriums that had been Brown's live domain a few years earlier. Meanwhile, Stevie Wonder and Marvin Gaye were selling millions of copies of their progressive soul masterpieces like *Talking Book* and *What's Going On*. In contrast, James's albums seemed to be assembled from a stockpile of recordings while he was on tour or otherwise engaged; the paintings that adorned some of his LP covers had the weirdly sincere look of what later became known as "outsider art." In the course of his career, Brown placed 49 releases on the *Billboard* Top 200 Albums chart but only one—*The Payback*, from 1974—has been certified gold by the Recording Industry Association of America.

THE GODFATHER

Toward the end of the 1970s, the singer began to encounter a new and enthusiastic audience in "new wave" rock clubs, where hip young whites hailed him as influence and innovator. In 1980, diehard James Brown fans John Belushi and Dan Aykroyd cast him in the role of a singing sanctified preacher in their hit movie *The Blues Brothers* (which also featured appearances by Aretha Franklin and Ray Charles). That same year Brown recorded "Rapp Payback (Where Iz Moses)," one of his best late-career tracks. With his Polydor deal now expired, James licensed the song to T.K. Records, a label run by Henry Stone—the same Miami music entrepreneur who'd picked up "(Do The) Mashed Potatoes (Pt. 1 & 2)" two decades earlier. "Rapp Payback" only reached number 45 among *Billboard* R&B Singles but it would be a long time before James Brown again attained even this modest level of chart success.

Two years later, the singer met makeup artist Adrienne Rodriguez on the set of the TV show *Solid Gold*. She moved into James's new South Carolina home a few months later and they were married in 1984. In the same year, Brown released "Unity," a new single and video performed with Afrika Bambaataa—a Bronx DJ and rapper whose position in New York's hip-hop nation was comparable to Brown's role in traditional R&B.

In 1985, James's career was revitalized temporarily by his recording of "Living in America," the theme song from the movie *Rocky IV*. He had no hand in writing or arranging the song, which others had completed by the time James cut his lead vocal. Nonetheless, "Living in America" went all the way to number 4 to become the highest-charting Pop hit of his career as well as a number 10 R&B entry, and won the Grammy Award for Best Rhythm and Blues Recording.

As the song climbed the Hot 100, James Brown was among the inaugural group of musicians to be inducted into the Rock and Roll Hall of Fame. He attended the black-tie ceremony at the Waldorf-Astoria in New York on January 23, 1986, and later "spoke of it as the culmination of his career" (Booth, pp. 236–37). On the morning of January 28, the space shuttle *Challenger* exploded, killing the seven astronauts on board. Twelve hours later, James's first headlining appearance at New York's prestigious Radio City Music Hall began with a solemn invocation offered by Reverend Al Sharpton, the New York political activist who'd become the singer's close friend and confidant after Teddy Brown's death. James Brown then went through the motions of his performance in a manner that suggested either deep despair over the *Challenger* disaster or the fogged-in condition of drug use. Rather than a celebration of a triumphant comeback, the Radio City show was a harbinger of worse things to come.

Nonetheless, the *Rocky IV* soundtrack sold over a million copies and led to a new recording contract with Scotti Brothers Records. *Gravity* (1986), produced by pop hit maker Dan Hartman, was described by critic Robert Christgau as "not a James Brown album—a James Brown–influenced Dan Hartman record, with James Brown on vocals" (see www.robertchristgau.com/get_artist.php?id=631&name=James+Brown). *I'm Real* (1988) was a more artistically successful collaboration with the producer/performers of New York hip-hop group Full Force. The album yielded Brown's final number 1 R&B hit ("I'm Real") and a number 5 follow up ("Static") but only reached number 96 on the *Billboard* Pop Albums chart. If contemporary listeners were no longer receptive to new James Brown songs, perhaps it was because *old* James Brown songs were saturating the radio and MTV airwaves in the form of JB samples on innumerable rap hits.

James Brown: The Godfather of Soul, the first and best of the singer's two memoirs, appeared in 1986. Even if some of the reconstructed conversations didn't ring true, Brown's capacious memory created a richly detailed narrative that blended personal history with philosophical musings on poverty, politics, racism, marriage, and stardom.

PRISON BLUES

Financial pressures, career decline, marital strife, and drug use all came to a head for James Brown in 1988. He was arrested repeatedly on charges ranging from leaving the scene of an accident to domestic violence involving Adrienne. In September, attendees at an insurance seminar in Augusta were confronted by a shotgun-wielding James Brown who demanded to know if anyone had used his office's private restroom on the same floor. He then fled the building and a high-speed police chase ensued, back and forth across the Georgia/South Carolina state line. James's arrest resulted in multiple charges including assault on a police officer, possession of PCP, and carrying an unlicensed pistol.

The singer later insisted that "I never did anything the police said I did. It was simply a vengeance sentence, made worse by my celebrity. Because I was a famous Black performer, busted roadside in the South, I had to pay the price" (Brown, p. 209). Refusing to plead guilty, Brown was sentenced to a total of 6 years but served only 15 months in a South Carolina prison. Even as he protested his innocence, James admitted that his incarceration was "a much-needed break from the crazy merry-go-round of booze and drugs . . . I was tired, my resistance was low, and I needed a place to get myself together" (Brown, p. 210).

After 10 more months in a work-release program, Brown was paroled in February 1991. (Later the singer was arrested a few more times—for drug possession and domestic violence—but never re-incarcerated.) In June, he returned to public performance with a show at the Wiltern Theater in Los Angeles. Still on board were such longtime allies as manager Charles Bobbitt and MC Danny Ray, whose immortal line "Are you ready for star time?" had kicked off the first *Live at the Apollo* in 1963. The James Brown Show was now a slicker, more Las Vegas–style affair that incorporated, among other bits of razzle-dazzle, a troupe of female singer-dancers. One of them, Tomi Rae Hynie, became the fourth Mrs. James Brown—and the mother of his son James Brown Jr.—after Adrienne died in 1996 while undergoing cosmetic surgery.

Novelist Jonathan Lethem witnessed the spectacle in the course of writing a lengthy, revealing, and often hilarious profile of the artist for *Rolling Stone* magazine. A James Brown performance, he wrote, is

> the ritual celebration of an enshrined historical victory, a battle won long ago, against forces difficult to name—funklessness?—yet whose vanquishing seems to have been so utterly crucial that it requires incessant restaging in a triumphalist ceremony. The show exists on a continuum, the link between ebullient big-band "clown" jazz showmen like Cab Calloway and Louis Jordan and the pornographic parade of a full-bore Prince concert. (Jonathan Lethem, "Being James Brown," available online at www.rollingstone.com/news/story/10533775/being_James_Brown, June 12, 2006)

In 1991, James's recording career was surveyed on *Star Time*, a carefully compiled and critically acclaimed four-CD box set; new albums such as *Universal James* (1992) and a fourth *Live at the Apollo* set (1995) came and went without much media attention or commercial impact. But at this point—45 years after "Please, Please, Please" first hit the charts—it really didn't matter. A Kennedy Center honoree, the winner of a Grammy Lifetime Achievement Award, with his own star on the Hollywood Walk of Fame, the ragged boy from Twiggs Street was now an icon of global pop culture—and the show would go on. "We could work for a hundred years," one member of his Soul Generals band told Jonathan Lethem. "Because he's James Brown. It's like we're up there with Bugs Bunny, Mickey Mouse. There's no other comparison" (Lethem).

When not on the road, the singer—diabetic and in remission after a bout with prostate cancer—retreated to his home in Beech Island, South Carolina.

It was just across the Savannah River from Augusta, where Ninth Street was now James Brown Boulevard and where the civic center was renamed the James Brown Arena in August 2006.

LAST CALL

Brown's final tour was a two-week trek across Eastern Europe that included a private 50th birthday party in Moscow (the other "entertainment" was Jennifer Lopez). The concluding show, in Croatia, was the last he ever played with his own band. The musicians flew home to the United States, but James traveled to London. On November 14, 2006, he was honored by the U.K. Music Hall of Fame in a televised ceremony; backed by a stage band, he sang "I Got You (I Feel Good)." Four decades earlier, in 1965, the song had topped the *Billboard* R&B Singles chart for six straight weeks. No one could have predicted that it would be James Brown's last live performance.

On the Friday before Christmas, James Brown participated in his 15th annual holiday toy giveaway, at the Imperial Theatre in Atlanta. On Sunday, he was admitted to Emory Crawford Long Hospital in Atlanta with a diagnosis of pneumonia. A show in Connecticut was canceled, but the singer told associates that he looked forward to performing at B.B. King's Club in New York on New Year's Eve, as he'd done annually for several years. At 1:45 A.M. on Monday, December 26, 2006, James Brown died of congestive heart failure.

The Brown Burial Debate

On December 28, 2006, thousands of fans lined the block around 125th Street, to pay final respects to Brown. His body arrived at 1 P.M. in a white carriage drawn by two white horses. The casket, gold and shining, left a Georgia funeral parlor Wednesday for an all-night drive to New York. It arrived at the Rev. Al Sharpton's Harlem headquarters just before noon Thursday, and was transferred to the carriage for a 20-block procession to the Apollo Theater where Brown had ignited so many audiences. Brown's body lay in an open casket at the Apollo while mourners paid their last respects. Helicopters hovered overhead, police officers struggled to corral attendees, a horde of television cameras jostled for better views. Fans sang James Brown songs and reminisced about James Brown concerts.

But as it did in life, controversy dogged Brown after his death. Following the public and private memorial services, his body remained in its casket for a time in a temperature-controlled room at his estate. It was later moved to an undisclosed location, while his children, legal representatives, and fourth wife, Tomi Rae Hynie, became embroiled in disputes about Brown's final resting place. Over two months after his death, Brown's children and Hynie finally agreed upon a temporary burial site, in a crypt at the home of one of Brown's daughters,

Deanna Brown Thomas. According to Brown's family, the singer's body will remain buried there until the completion of a public mausoleum. His family wants to turn Brown's estate into a visitor attraction, à la Graceland, and they've been in talks with the Presley estate about how to do just that.

Albert "Buddy" Dallas, Brown's longtime attorney and one of the trustees for Brown's estate, expressed his intense disapproval over the situation. According an interview with the *Associated Press*, Dallas said that "Mr. Brown's not deserving of anyone's backyard" and that the trustees for Brown's estate "had made arrangements for Brown to be laid to rest at no cost at a 'very prominent memorial garden in Augusta.'"

Bob Gulla

LEGACY

The news of James Brown's death prompted a flood of tributes from his contemporaries and admirers. Soul queen Aretha Franklin said, "He was an original, [like] a Rembrandt or a Picasso" ("James Brown, 1933–2006," *Entertainment Weekly,* January 12, 2007). "For oppressed people," rap star Common declared, Brown's music "was the light at the end of the tunnel" ("James Brown, 1933–2006"). In the *Village Voice*, writer/musician Greg Tate hailed James Brown as "the embodiment of all the working-class African blood that got us through . . . all our collective love, joy, ingenuity, and indefatigability, all our spirited and spiritual survivalist complexity, all our freedom jazz dance. . . . In a nutshell, JB was our grand Black unifier" (Greg Tate, www.VillageVoice.com, January 2, 2007).

At a time when even such soul music pioneers as Ray Charles were moving toward a smoother, more pop-oriented sound, James Brown brought American black music back to its African-derived polyrhythmic roots even as he pushed it forward into the future. Although he never scored a number 1 Pop hit, Brown is one of an elite group of artists to have placed a song in the Top 10 of the *Billboard* Hot 100 and/or Top R&B Singles chart in each of four decades from the 1950s through the 1980s. He holds the *Billboard* R&B Singles record for Most Chart Hits (118), Most Top 40 Hits (100), Most Top 10 Hits (60), and Most Crossover Hits (88), that is, songs that "crossed over" from the R&B chart to the Hot 100.

Traces of James Brown's sound can be heard in the music of Sly and the Family Stone, Talking Heads, Parliament-Funkadelic, Fela Ransome-Kuti, Miles Davis, and Public Enemy, to name but a few. Hip-hop producers and MCs have sampled his recordings countless times, creating new contemporary hits from his classic beats, horn lines, and vocal refrains.

"Funky Drummer," one of Brown's lesser hit singles from 1970, contains a drum break played by Clyde Stubblefield that is probably the most sampled beat in hip-hop history. It has been used in songs by A Tribe Called Quest, the

Beastie Boys, George Michael, Public Enemy, and Sinead O'Connor, among others. Additional James Brown samples were used by Biz Markie on "Vapors" ("Papa Don't Take No Mess"), by Gang Starr on "Words I Manifest" ("Bring It Up"), and by Rob Base and D.J. E-Z Rock on "It Takes Two," which sampled James's production of "Think (About It)" by Lyn Collins.

"He was dramatic to the end—dying on Christmas Day," the Reverend Jesse Jackson told the Associated Press. "Almost a dramatic, poetic moment. He'll be all over the news, all over the world today. He would have it no other way" (see chronicle.augusta.com/stories/122606/met_109964.shtml).

SELECTED DISCOGRAPHY

Live at the Apollo (Polydor, 1963)

Roots of a Revolution (Polydor, 1984)

Messin' with the Blues (Polydor, 1990)

Star Time (Polydor, 1991)

Soul Pride: The Instrumentals (1960–69) (Polydor, 1993)

Foundations of Funk: A Brand New Bag, 1964–1969 (Polydor, 1996)

Funk Power 1970: A Brand New Thang (Polydor, 1996)

Make It Funky—The Big Payback: 1971–1975 (Polydor, 1996)

Say It Live and Loud: Live in Dallas 08.26.68 (Polygram, 1998)

FURTHER READING

Booth, Stanley. "The Godfather's Blues." *Rhythm Oil*. London: Jonathan Cape, 1992.

Brown, James. *I Feel Good: A Memoir of a Life of Soul*. New York: New American Library, 2005.

Brown, James, with Bruce Tucker. *James Brown:The Godfather of Soul*. New York: Macmillan, 1986.

Hirshey, Gerri. "Superbull, Superbad." *Nowhere to Run: The Story of Soul Music*. New York: Times Books, 1984.

Palmer, Robert. "James Brown." *The Rolling Stone Illustrated History of Rock & Roll*. New York: Random House, 1992.

Rose, Cynthia. *Living in America:The Soul Saga of James Brown*. London: Serpent's Tail, 1990.

Wesley, Fred Jr. *Hit Me, Fred: Recollections of a Sideman*. Durham: Duke University Press, 2002.

AP Photo/Curtom Records.

Curtis Mayfield

SUPER BAAAD!

During a career that spanned five decades, from the late 1950s to the late 1990s, Curtis Mayfield established himself as one of the few genuine innovators of modern soul music, high on the genre's short list of towering figures and a man who in the pantheon of pop music icons deserves a seat next to James Brown and John Lennon, no questions asked. In his first two decades of recording and performing, it would be difficult, in fact, to find an artist who made more of an impact on the landscape of popular music.

    Not only did he bridge the gaps between R&B and soul, then between soul and funk, he captured the optimism of the civil rights movement with a vibrant, fully unique sound that earned him an endless string of hits, both with his star-making group the Impressions and under his own name. So bright was his star during his lifetime that he has been inducted into the Rock and Roll Hall of Fame as an Impression and as a solo artist. Few in the history of popular music—Paul McCartney, Eric Clapton, Michael Jackson, and Paul Simon come to mind—have earned that accolade. Like many of these artists,

Mayfield excelled by redefining himself stylistically, something very few artists in the history of popular music have been able to do.

Short in stature and far from flashy, Mayfield made contributions to music as a writer, a producer, an arranger, a label owner, a record executive, and guitar player. As a tenor in the Impressions and the group's principal songwriter, Mayfield was finely attuned to the lives and challenges of the African American community, and his songs nailed that experience with the skill of a professional archer. In the mid- to late 1960s, when Smokey Robinson and the Motown stable were singing about "Doing the Monkey," essentially ignoring the struggles of this same community, and selling millions of records in the process, Curtis bucked the trend and spoke directly to that struggle. "It was always my way," he told an unidentified *Rolling Stone* interviewer in 1974. "I always believed that whatever I should speak or sing about should have some value. So while you're shakin' your leg [laughs], you can leave through that exit door with something in your head as well. I'm not totally about being just an entertainer, making people grin. It means a little bit more to me than that."

Even before the pioneering work of James Brown, Mayfield's compositions like "Gypsy Woman" in 1961 presaged songs of protest and racial unity, on his way to notching a seemingly endless string of hits, right up through his epic funk and blaxploitation work of the 1970s: "Superfly," "The Other Side of Town," and "Freddie's Dead." This later work exerted a profound and lasting impression on the styles and substance of virtually all soul and R&B musicians to come, an impact whose ripples are still felt through the popular music of today. His "Superfly"-era work in the early 1970s was embraced by the nascent rap community; his funky bass lines and urban motifs helped to form the bedrock of that sound as well.

Not exclusive to songs of social concern, Mayfield also brought a new dimension to the ballad, especially early on in his career, writing and singing some of the greatest love songs in pop by adding modern sentiment and instrumentation to the otherwise old-fashioned vocal group staple. He did most of this ballad work with the Impressions, a group he helped form in Chicago when he just 13. At the time, a man named Jerry Butler, who'd go on to an illustrious solo career himself, headed up the group. Mayfield took over lead responsibilities after Butler's departure in 1961, and didn't look back. In 1963 Mayfield and the Impressions hit their stride. They revitalized and updated their sound with moody gospel harmonizing, and made Mayfield's spare guitar tremolo (the springboard for a number of Jimi Hendrix ballads) an integral element. The group became a dominant force in fledgling soul music, helping to define the very idiom. Often exuding a potent, yet quiet majesty, his songs moved a generation of Americans.

Within three years of taking the reins of the Impressions, and barely into his twenties, Mayfield became increasingly focused on the subjects of racial harmony and justice. It was the dawn of the civil rights movement and Mayfield was there. In 1964, "Keep on Pushing" went to number 10 on the pop charts, and through the remainder of that decade he would consistently land songs in the upper reaches of the pop charts, higher on the R&B lists, based on his ability to express the frustrations and hopes of his audience.

His song titles would tell the story: "People Get Ready," "We're a Winner," "This Is My Country." Mayfield pushed his artistry; he was consistently at the vanguard, driving the crest of black music, helping popularize Afro-Cuban rhythms and forging new ground with big bands and complex orchestrations. When the hits became less frequent, he made the transition to producing other artists and composing film soundtracks. The latter projects became his 1970s signature. In the 1980s, when many older stars were unable to find labels to release their albums, Mayfield continued to reach his audience through Curtom Records, a label he founded in the late 1960s. Like his hero Ray Charles, Curtis maintained ownership of his own publishing rights, and the move sustained him through lean periods, the kind of periods in which most other artists would certainly have died off or disappeared.

Before he died in 2000, Mayfield laid down a life's work equal to few pop stars before or since. To this day, and perhaps for the unforeseeable future, black artists will pay tribute to his work, directly or indirectly, with their quiet storm ballads, urban funk, and literate lyrical matter. For four decades nothing could stop Curtis and his work. Only a poorly secured stage-lighting platform, blown over in a strong gust of wind as he was about to take the stage in Brooklyn, could take him off his feet. Even then, he'd still work, and work effectively. As he exhorted others to do, he kept pushing until his final days.

EARLY YEARS

Curtis Mayfield was born on June 3, 1942, in Chicago, and, after moving frequently, finally settled in the now-notorious Cabrini Green projects located on the city's North Side.

Growing up in an impoverished family, Curtis came of age under the watchful eye of two powerful women: his grandmother, who as he remembers was studying to achieve ministry in the church when Curtis was a child, and his mother, herself a poet and dedicated caregiver. The words of these women—and their ability to speak of matters important to people—resonated with Curtis and he often credited them with planting the seeds of his lyrics.

"[My grandmother] was also a healer who used the power of the spirit to cure physical ills. I saw music as an expression of the spirit, and I tried to use it to address social ills. Now, I'm not a preacher, but I figured a good use of music would be to lift people up and provide food for thought" (Ben Edmonds, "Curtis Mayfield and Superfly: No Exit," *Mojo*, June, 2002).

As a young boy, he had a strong church background that would, like so many black artists during this time, serve his musical interests directly. Unlike many children in Chicago at this time, Curtis never took to the musical idiom that saturated the city during this time: the blues. "I definitely appreciated the blues," he remembers. "During those early years all you heard was John Lee Hooker, Muddy Waters, Little Walter. . . . I came up with that, and I did admire them. But it just looked like my thing was to be a little different" (Chris Salewicz, "Keep on Pushing," *Face*, February 1985).

But in addition to the blues, Chicago was a pivotal location for both gospel and soul music. Thanks to the presence of Sam Cooke and icon Lou Rawls, Chicago had earned the identity as at least one of the earliest birthplaces of soul.

Gospel, though, was the style that spoke specifically to Mayfield and his family loudest. Their church, the Traveling Soul Spiritualist Church, had a choral group, the Northern Jubilee Gospel Singers, which included three of Mayfield's cousins in its membership. Spirituals formed the backbone of his artistry and his home, especially during his formative years, was steeped in it.

When he was 10, one of his cousins returned from a stint in the army with a guitar. He gave it to Curtis, and the young boy learned it with expedience. Though he knew nothing about how to play it, he taught himself. For as long as he played his guitar, which was right up until his accident in 1990, he never took a professional lesson. Despite that, he had become known in his lifetime as a consensus choice as one of the instrument's primary innovators.

As a young boy he had talked about becoming a scientist, but noted that he had no skills in math, and quickly gave it up. Soon, excitement about his music distracted Curtis from excelling in any schoolwork at all and he eventually dropped out to focus on writing, playing, and performing. A few years later, at 13, he started a secular vocal group, the Alphatones.

In 1956, a band called the Roosters, with roots in Chattanooga, Tennessee, decided to move to Chicago. When they did, the members met and enlisted Jerry Butler, a Mississippi-born talent who at the time was in the Northern Jubilee group with Curtis's cousins. When the Roosters were looking to recruit another member, Butler asked Mayfield to join. It was 1958 and Curtis had just turned 16. The vocal ensemble had been seeking an instrumentalist to help tie their melodies together.

At the time, the band included Butler, Sam Gooden, Emanuel Thomas, Fred Cash, and the Brooks Brothers, Richard and Arthur. Butler, and the others in the Roosters, came from the old school of church harmony. So rather than falling into doo-wop, which was incredibly popular at the time, the Roosters adopted a slightly different singing style, separate from the blues and the era's radio pop, with a gospel feel. Though at the time they didn't realize it, Mayfield and Butler were on the cusp of ushering in a new era of R&B and soul.

The Roosters hired a manager, Eddie Thomas, and changed their name to Jerry Butler and the Impressions. The name change had created some tension within the ranks, but the group, still young, was eager to make an impact on the pop scene in any way they could.

In early 1958, they signed with an affiliate of seminal R&B label Vee-Jay, purely by chance. According to Curtis, the story goes like this:

> The snow was about five feet to walk through when we went to Chess Records and knocked on the door. I guess there was a secretary in there but no one would let us in. So we turned around and what's across the street: Vee-Jay Records. We just went right across through the snow, dragging our amplifier and guitar. [Ewart] Abner was upstairs and the A&R man, Calvin Carter—they let us in. It must have been a weekend, no one was really working, and we sang this particular song, "For Your Precious Love," for Calvin right on the steps. He loved it. About a week later, I was in the studio for the first time. And that's really how we got off. (Alan Warner, *People Get Ready: The Curtis Mayfield Story*, liner notes, Rhino, 1996, p. 41)

That summer they scored a debut hit with the same smoldering ballad, "For Your Precious Love." The response was immediate and overwhelming. So overwhelming in fact that within the year, at the urging of Vee-Jay, Butler left the group to focus on a solo career. Mayfield rose up to occupy the space Butler vacated as lead vocalist and chief composer. But with the chemistry of the band changed, follow-up hits proved elusive. Their next few attempts never took off, and in 1959 Vee-Jay dropped the act from their roster.

Undaunted, Mayfield never stopped working. He continued to write. He and the Impressions gigged, if not with the frequency they would have had things gone well. And he played guitar in Butler's touring band, maintaining close association with the singer, whose star was now ascending. In an interview in 1972 Butler said, "Curtis and I always inspired each other writing and singing. Sometimes we'd fight about this or that, but when it came together it was beautiful" (Peter Burns, *Curtis Mayfield*, London: Sanctuary Press, 2003, p. 20).

About this time, Mayfield with Impressions' manager Thomas, took a rather unusual step. They formed a publishing company, Curtom Publishing. Perhaps this was in response to what Sam Cooke had done the previous year with his partner, J.W. Alexander. For black artists at the time, this was unprecedented. Instinctively, Mayfield knew what was best in terms of handling his own business. Too often he had seen R&B artists write songs, then share bylines with label owners or other unconnected parties eager to take illicit advantage. Artists were often told that publishing wouldn't make them any money. Only record sales and touring would put the big bucks in their pocket. This was, of course, bad advice. The reverse was actually true. Setting up Curtom, behind his decision to join the Impressions, would be the second best decision the young Mayfield would make in his career.

In 1960, Mayfield supplied Butler with a song, "He Will Break Your Heart," a tune that would become Butler's first number one hit on the R&B chart. Mayfield put the money from that success into a New York City studio session with the Impressions in early 1961.

A song from the session, "Gypsy Woman," a gorgeous, flamenco-flavored song Curtis had written a few years earlier, led to a five-year contract with the ABC-Paramount label, home to Ray Charles and Paul Anka, among other luminaries. For the first time since Butler departed, their career had taken a turn for the better.

The success resulted in the Impressions plunging into a hectic schedule of touring and other public appearances, including gigs at the Apollo and on Dick Clark's television show *American Bandstand*. With Curtis's career taking off and his reputation as a songwriter growing, he began to pick up studio and songwriting work.

> This somewhat unlikely figure, with his horn-rimmed glasses, gap-toothed smile and ever-present guitar, resembled a black Buddy Holly. And like Holly before him, Mayfield was a gentle revolutionary, a pop music *auteur* who personally imprinted every level of the process, from the writing and arranging to the singing, playing and production of his recordings—an example that was inspirational to Sly Stone, Stevie Wonder, Marvin Gaye and other soul giants that followed. (Ben Edmonds, "Curtis Mayfield" Obituary, *Mojo*, March 2000)

After signing with ABC-Paramount, the Impressions again experienced a couple of near misses and it seemed like Curtis, while successful in collaborating with outside arrangers and other artists, had lost his hit-making touch. The disappointment prompted the departure of the Brooks brothers and left the Impressions as a trio, with Mayfield, Gooden, and Cash.

Back in Chicago, the band entered the studio again, this time with local big band arranger and producer Johnny Pate. A veteran of the city's jazz scene in the 1940s, Pate had developed a signature sound involving heavy horn sounds and a percussive rhythm base. When he incorporated his own signature production techniques with the core style of the Impressions, great things began to happen.

With Mayfield singing lead, but pulling back to allow Gooden and Cash the spotlight as well with their more gospel-powered voices, the formula of the Impressions began to gel. Equally important, the team began to formulate what would come to be known as the Chicago Soul Sound. The vibe fused big band brass with heavy bass lines and occasional strings. Pate and Mayfield created lightning in a bottle, and many Windy City artists—Major Lance, Rufus—would imitate or co-opt that sound on their way to becoming hit makers themselves.

For their part, Pate and Mayfield teamed up to produce 10 Top 40 singles and 9 charting LPs in just five years. This sustained success had a remarkable effect on Curtis's confidence. In late 1963, he had another smash with the Impressions an anthemic, inspirational tune called "It's All Right." Coming as it did following the assassination of John F. Kennedy, the song helped ease the tension of a grieving nation. Not that Curtis had written it to be a message song. He wasn't there yet as an artist. But it did serve as a musical balm to a troubled time. That kind of societal impact sent the Impressions on a hit-making tear as budding superstars. It also got Mayfield thinking about the changing world around him, and his lyrical approach to it.

KEEP ON PUSHIN'

When Curtis composed "Keep on Pushin'" the world was indeed changing. The assassination of President Kennedy opened a wound, and society began to bleed. To help staunch the bleeding, Dr. Martin Luther King Jr. emerged, and his words did wonders to ease and empower black America. A milestone in the lyrical evolution of Mayfield, "Keep on Pushin'" provided spiritual support to King and the civil rights movement. But the song, the first of his true message songs, also managed to appeal to a wider audience, one locked in any kind of struggle. The universality helped Mayfield strike a chord, and its success encouraged him to pursue this vast avenue of expression more deeply.

Not that Mayfield left every other aspect of his writing style behind. The Impressions continued to record love songs and great ballads, including a record often mentioned as their masterpiece, Mayfield's "I've Been Trying." He had originally written it for Butler, and many artists have covered it since. It is a soul music masterpiece, and certainly near the top of Mayfield's best work.

In 1965, the Impressions enjoyed a watershed year. The seeds that had been planted in 1964 all reaped fruit the next year, and the group became familiar to fans of the pop charts. They'd place eight different songs on the Pop and R&B lists in 1965, including another classic, "People Get Ready."

"It is a completely open invitation to all [listeners] with no conditions, no religious or racial barriers. Mayfield had again added his social voice to the poetry of his love sonnets, cautiously at first, but also with growing confidence and self-assurance" (Burns, p. 30).

Curtis delivered messages promoting black pride in a clear-headed manner that only occasionally gave skittish white radio programmers pause. The breakthrough opened Mayfield's songwriting floodgates and material came pouring out. They addressed both sides of his composing persona: the ballads and the songs of social conscience. And his legend began to grow. The album *People Get Ready*, with all 12 songs Mayfield compositions, hit the Top 40 on the album chart. His tracks, particularly the message songs, spread to places outside America, especially in oppressed areas like Jamaica, where he was considered a visionary, a powerful voice of civil rights. Young music enthusiasts in Jamaica would filter Mayfield's soul through their own prism, in the process creating reggae. Bob Marley and Jimmy Cliff, for example, had followed Mayfield in their own early years as artists.

One of Curtis's role models, Ray Charles, had established a business template that Curtis admired. After Charles terminated his early contract with

Atlantic and signed with ABC, he retained the rights to his own masters, and set up Tangerine, his own publishing company. In a sense, Charles had become the president of his own music business. Mayfield wanted to do the same, so in addition to setting up Curtom, his publishing firm with manager Eddie Thomas, he established his own label, or in this case, labels: Windy C and Mayfield Records, to which he would sign, record, and produce young artists in hopes of developing them.

In time, these imprints would cede to another, more successful label venture, also called Curtom. This expansion was necessary for a number of reasons. During this time, Mayfield had boundless energy, created perhaps by the adrenaline of success. He could not stem the flow of material pouring out; it was too much for the Impressions to record, so he began looking for outside talent to record this overflow. He also had an eye for promise, and wanted to give opportunities to artists he felt had potential.

One of the more notable, but short-lived projects Curtis released came from the Mayfield label. They were called the Mayfield Singers, and included, among others, Donny Hathaway and Leroy Hutson. Mayfield also featured on their first single, a version of "I've Been Tryin'," on voice and guitar. In a testimony to Mayfield's discerning ear, both Hutson and Hathaway would go on to successful solo careers.

About this time, in the fall of 1966, the Impressions began focusing less on hits and more on albums. Without stemming the flow of songs coming from his pen, Curtis churned out material with little care of what would be a hit and what would serve as an album track. During this period in music, the R&B and rock and roll scenes were singles-driven, as had been true in popular music since its inception. But Mayfield couldn't be bothered with focusing on writing hits, so the Impressions became one of the first R&B/soul acts, just like Curtis's hero Ray Charles, to create music with the album concept in mind.

In 1967, at the tail end of their ABC contract, Mayfield with Gooden and Cash hit the studio for two days and emerged with their next big hit album and radio single of the same name, *We're a Winner*. Aimed at his core black audience, the song also, in inimitable Mayfield fashion, reached a much wider audience as well.

"Many of the songs I was writing were so different. 'We're a Winner' had a social conscience; it was about a mass of people during a time of struggle, and when it broke, it was so much out of the ordinary. It wouldn't be what you'd call a crossover record during those times, but the demand of the people kept it struggling and happening, and it's still one of my favorite tunes" (Warner, p. 44).

It's another slice of his pop social philosophy, this one coming just three months after the assassination of Dr. King. But while the song's success proved unstoppable, it failed to calm the violent fallout brought about by King's death.

In the end, the Impressions' tenure with ABC was unparalleled, both in terms of hits and in terms of how it fostered Mayfield's brilliance. They scored

22 hit singles, and charted a dozen records in just five years. Their departure from the label marked the end of one era and the beginning of another.

THE MESSAGE OF CURTOM RECORDS

> Curtom was more than a record label and music publishing company—it became Mayfield's creative home base, a magnet to which he could draw many more talents to add to his own. The production company became a conduit of creative influences some of which came and went and others that used the opportunity to create a body of work with the label. It was a compact sphere of creative talent with Mayfield at the hub. (Burns, p. 50)

Mayfield imagined when he conceived it that Curtom would become to Chicago what Motown was to Detroit. The label, formed by Mayfield and associate Eddie Thomas, set to work immediately. They engineered an alliance with Buddah Records, a hot pop label at the time, and began inking acts. They signed the Five Stairsteps, a family vocal group who'd go on to record a handful of hits, and they brought in talent like songwriter and singer Donny Hathaway, who logged some valuable creative time at Curtom before heading to Atlantic.

The Impressions recorded the first Curtom album release, *This Is My Country*, and it sold well in the winter of 1968. Composed in the aftermath of the King and Bobby Kennedy murders, Mayfield's songs—"Choice of Colors," "Mighty, Mighty (Spade and Whitey)"—became overtly political, direct in their messages. In place of mild urgings like "We're a Winner" came declamatory exhortations, articulating the outrage and frustration of millions following those hope-shattering assassinations. To Mayfield's credit, his writing is as relative today as it was nearly 40 years ago, a real credit to its timelessness. The struggle surrounding equal rights now became the subject at the epicenter of Mayfield's work.

At the end of 1969, Curtis made a momentous decision. His road with the Impressions would come to an end. He'd wrap up his work with the group and focus on his future as a solo artist. He wanted to focus on his label, and the Impressions ate up much of his time and energy with touring and recording. At the time, he admitted that the split wasn't permanent, that he simply needed to dedicate more of himself to Curtom. As a replacement for himself in the group, he hired the talented Leroy Hutson. The Impressions continued recording for Mayfield, and Mayfield's touch could be heard on much of their future output, especially their 1969 disc, *Check Out Your Mind*.

Unfortunately, the album didn't get the attention it deserved. But it wasn't because of the quality of the work. Just a few months after it came out, Mayfield's own solo debut was released and its release demanded greater notice, not just for what it represented—Curtis's solo debut—but for what it contained in its grooves.

CURTIS, ALONE

Curtis, issued in September 1970, instantly validated his decision to go it alone. It broke the Top 20 in *Billboard*'s album chart in the States, caught fire in Europe, and became Curtom's best-selling release to date. Demand for Mayfield in both time and in-person performances increased substantially, and soon the studio guru was making plans for a worldwide tour.

The material on *Curtis* would be his most potent and message-oriented to date. The disc opened with "(Don't Worry) If There's a Hell Below We're All Going to Go," a bold opening salvo that became the album's first single. The set also included the anthemic "Move on Up," and the influential "We the People Who Are Darker Than Blue," a rallying cry for the African American community to band together.

A live album followed less than a year later and it too cracked the Top 20, in the process bolstering the chart presence of its predecessor, which benefited from all the renewed interest. Another album, *Roots*, surfaced by Christmas of 1971.

At the same time all this activity was going on for Curtis, an artist over at Motown, Marvin Gaye, had written and recorded *What's Going On?* Plainly, the artist had been influenced by Curtis's message songs, and his attempt at a concept album pulling together the many elements already introduced by Mayfield proved to be a huge success. But far from being resentful, Curtis had simply admitted that Marvin "had said all there needed to be said," about the subject of social injustice and the political strife in America. He even had the Impressions tackle Gaye's "Inner City Blues."

Admiring the achievement, Mayfield masterminded the Impressions' *Times Have Changed* partly in response to Gaye's album. On it, the producer made his opinions clear at least with his song choices. "Stop the War" was his boldest political statement yet, and the Gaye cover bolstered that candor. The Impressions were back on the map, and business at Curtom began booming.

In early 1972, after a performance at Lincoln Center in New York City, producer Sig Shore and writer Philip Fenty approached Curtis to compose the score for a movie they were producing. The film, titled *Superfly*, presented the story of a Harlem drug dealer looking to make one last lucrative deal that would earn him enough cash to quit the drug trade. It would become the third of the so-called blaxploitation classics (behind *Sweet Sweetback's Baadasssss Song* and *Shaft*) but the only one that would have an indispensable soundtrack.

Blaxploitation Films

Blaxploitation films first cropped up in the early 1970s, led by Melvin Van Peebles original, and very angry, independent film *Sweet Sweetback's Baadasssss Song*. This was the work that would come to serve as the blueprint for indie African American films, most of which were, like Peebles's film, heady doses of violence, drugs, sex, and attitude. The storytelling was relatively simple; the plots were shells, holding within it as much grisly action and sex as possible. The characters—outlaws, pimps, marauders, prostitutes, and the muscular detectives that pursued them—were vividly wrought, though, and the music, generally hard-charging funk, enhanced the overall experience, more so than in most mainstream Hollywood films.

Ironically, most of these films, while boasting an all-black cast, were conceived and produced by white film execs. They essentially followed Peebles's lead, exploiting the genre, and make off with the profits, which in some cases, was considerable. *Shaft* escaped from the box office with over $12 million gross receipts.

The soundtracks of these films were generated by some of black music's most talented songwriters: James Brown, Isaac Hayes, Marvin Gaye, and Curtis Mayfield. Mayfield's *Superfly* is perhaps the best-known and best executed of all the blaxploitation soundtracks. In fact, *Superfly* made an immediate impact at the box office not only because the film was highly anticipated but because the soundtrack was as well. At the time, Mayfield was perhaps the hottest R&B star of the early 1970s and audiences clamored for his latest work, whatever it was. *Superfly* sold millions of copies upon its release, and has since outlived its short-term reputation as a blaxploitation score to become one of funk's finest hours. Isaac Hayes's epic, Oscar-winning "Theme from Shaft" has done the same, transcending its humble roots to become a classic. Some other notable but less known blaxploitation soundtracks include Willie Hutch's *The Mack*, James Brown's *Black Caesar*, and Rudy Ray Moore's *Eat Out More Often*.

These soundtracks contained many of the same musical elements, including wah-wah effects on electric guitar (best heard on "Theme from Shaft," but also in many of Mayfield's tracks at this time, like "Pusherman" and "Freddie's Dead," one of the best examples of the style. This material also had booming bass lines and funky rhythmic drum shuffles.

After the first wave of films were issued, this particular school of filmmaking debilitated into hokum, parodies of itself. Peebles's *Revenge* was violent and serious. But by the time *Shaft* and the nearly 400 other films followed, the genre was so diluted that it measured little of its original impact, cinematically or musically. As the movie genre died out in the late 1970s, so did the music, but both the films and the soundtracks have remained cult favorites well into the next century.

Mayfield, with his prophetic, street-smart style, urban cachet, and track record with the sort of raw material the film called for, was a natural candidate for the project, even though he hadn't done any film scoring to this point.

Rather than address the film in terms of feel and atmosphere, with ambient instrumental music, he composed themes for each character, real songs that were essentially character sketches. The effect vaulted a rather ordinary, and in many cases cheesy flick, into legendary status. In fact, many say that attendance figures rose at theaters simply because viewing the film provided an opportunity to hear Curtis's soundtrack.

Songs like "Pusherman," "Freddie's Dead," and "Little Child Runnin' Wild" captured the seedy ghetto truisms with startling accuracy and the film, along with the soundtrack, became huge hits. The film even gave Curtis some valuable screen time, when the scriptwriters wrote in a scene featuring him performing one of the score's songs, "Pusherman." One of the results of collaborating on *Superfly* was that it brought the songwriter into the fabric of the film, right alongside the actor and the director. It would become another of Mayfield's profound musical milestones.

The chart impact of *Superfly* was enormous and the album went on to sell over a million copies. The momentum carried well into Curtis's next album, 1973's *Back to the World*, which went gold, propelled by songs like "Future Shock," "If I Were Only a Child Again," and "Can't Say Nothin'."

As the success of black-oriented film carried on, so did Curtis's involvement in composing musical scores for them. Next up was the film *Claudine*, in which he served as musical director and composer. This time he recruited Gladys Knight and the Pips for a collaboration, "On and On." It also included a gorgeous reading of one of his best ballads, "To Be Invisible."

In 1975, the landscape of the music business was experiencing a sea change stylistically. Funk, thanks to artists like Gaye, Mayfield, Sly Stone, the Ohio Players, War, and Parliament, was in full swing, but about to give way to the more dance-oriented disco. This would render many of the R&B bands at the time insignificant. Fans wanted hooks to dance to, not complicated and substantive social criticism or contemplative storylines. Many had already lived through the turbulence of the late 1960s and early 1970s, what with its protests and political turmoil. It was time, to, well *party*. Thankfully, this attitude didn't reel Curtis in the way it did many other artists. He did make a change, swapping distributors, opting to go with the bigger, wider-reaching Warner Bros. over his smaller distributor Buddah. This wouldn't serve him as well as he'd anticipated.

He made a handful of records as a solo artist between 1975 and 1978, all of which failed to sell with any consistency. During this time, he worked with Aretha Franklin on *Sparkle* and with the Staple Singers on the soundtrack to the film *Let's Do It Again*, both of which demonstrated that Mayfield hadn't lost his touch.

He had stopped touring for the second half of the 1970s, given all the studio production work he'd slated for himself and a handful of film scores he had in progress. One soundtrack he had high hopes for, *Short Eyes,* based on a play by Miguel Pinero, fell flat. With its strong subject matter—"short eyes" is a prison term for child molesters—Curtis perhaps didn't fully anticipate disco's party mood. The *Short Eyes* soundtrack had the dubious distinction of being the first Curtis Mayfield (solo artist) album not to chart.

From the end of the 1970s through much of the 1980s, Curtis's Curtom label had struggled to find an act that would take it out of financial disrepair. The Impressions and Hutson were long gone, and a few other attempts at star-making failed as well. Curtis decided to close the label in 1981 and fold it into Neil Bogart's new imprint, Boardwalk. Bogart, the former president of Buddah, had made a killing with Casablanca, a label that experienced success with acts like Donna Summer and KISS. Boardwalk put out the next two Mayfield albums, but neither one made an impression on the charts. Bogart and Boardwalk pressured Mayfield to stay away from the kind of weighty substance he'd been partial to throughout his career. Rather, by teaming him with dance and disco talent, they compelled him to stray from his soul roots.

The lack of results and paucity of sales didn't support that decision and Mayfield considered the experience to be entirely unfulfilling. He made a permanent move to Atlanta from Chicago and decided to recommence activities with Curtom. Under a new distribution agreement with Ichiban he recorded the much more characteristic *We Come in Peace with a Message of Love*, a welcome return in both heart and soul.

To further reconnect with his early roots, Mayfield reunited with the Impressions intermittently beginning in 1983. He also contributed to the soundtrack of *I'm Gonna Git You Sucka*, a 1989 flick with Jim Brown and Isaac Hayes.

At the outset of 1990, Mayfield was as busy as ever. He had committed to making *The Return of Superfly*, a sequel to his epic soundtrack and a second solo album through Ichiban, *Take It to the Streets*.

In August, Curtis was laying the groundwork for another tour of Europe when the accident occurred. He told Steven R. Rosen, a journalist from the *Denver Post*, what he remembered of that day.

> "The stage was like the back end of a truck platform. It had all the lighting and everything," he recalls. "My band was up there playing 'Superfly' as an intro and I had been called, so I had my guitar on. I'm walking up the ladder steps from the rear and as I take maybe three steps toward the front of the stage, that's all I remember."
>
> The stage-lighting scaffolding had fallen on him. "Next thing I was on the floor totally sprawled out. No guitar, my glasses were off and I found my hands and feet were not where I thought they were. And of course it didn't take but a second to find I could not get up or move.
>
> "However, I could move my head and move my neck. So upon looking from one side to the other, I saw my body just totally spread out on the floor. And then it began to rain." (Steven R. Rosen, "No Sad Songs," *Denver Post*, March 6, 1994)

After the accident, which happened when he was 48, and until his death, Mayfield remained paralyzed from the neck down. Dependent on the support of his family, he endured expensive medical attention. Fortunately, royalties from his success as a songwriter and artist managed to cover most of the cost. He even managed to donate proceeds from a fundraiser benefit, *All Men Are Brothers*, featuring artists like Aretha Franklin, Bruce Springsteen, Elton John, and Whitney Houston, to the Miami Project, which researches potential cures for spinal injuries.

Another benefit in Mayfield's honor, *People Get Ready: A Tribute to Curtis Mayfield*, went down in 1993. That one spawned a hit, a cover of Curtis's "It's All Right" by Huey Lewis and the News.

"I feel the world is all we got," he told the *Detroit News* in 1997. "And in spite of all the hardship and struggle, to live, to breathe, to sleep, all the many earthly things and some godly things, and to be a human being, there's nothing really yet comparable. While there are hardships, every day you want to laugh some, you want to learn to cry. It's really simple: being here on Earth is just a powerful thing."

LEGACY

Curtis Mayfield died on December 26, 1999, after a 10-year struggle with near total paralysis. He died at the North Fulton Regional Hospital in Roswell, Georgia. At his funeral, Jerry Butler, Fred Cash, and Sam Gooden sang "Amen," one of the Impressions' early hits. Obituaries poured in, all of which attempted in so many words to encapsulate such a monumental career. Martin Weil of the *Washington Post* said, "He was known as a man who expanded the horizons of black popular song, to speak not only of the matters of the heart but also the issues of the street. . . . Black music as we hear it today simply would not exist without him" (Martin Weil, The *Washington Post*, December 27, 1999).

In retrospect, Curtis Mayfield was a terrifically independent artist. Despite growing up in an underprivileged home, without the aid of music schooling or any sort of formal training, Mayfield learned to sing, write, and play guitar completely on his own. Racism and poverty could not contain him. Curtis was fortunate enough to be at the crossroads of soul, in a city whose musicians saw to it to meld the gospel and blues of their childhoods with a smoother, easier, and more elegant sound. He was there, and he fully participated in its development, along with Chicago icons like Lou Rawls and Sam Cooke.

Mayfield's early work with the Impressions introduced the pop scene to an exquisite talent, whose ability grew with each passing record. Each recording session it seemed put forth another feather in his cap, a brighter jewel in his crown, from polishing his vocal and guitar techniques, to writing songs that had an impact not only on music fans but society in general.

But rather than pour his lyrical sensibility through a filter of bitterness and delusion, he implored his listeners for improvement. Instead of criticizing, he merely proposed possible solutions, earthy, feel-good possibilities like unity and love. Destruction for Mayfield was not an option. Freedom, he sang, should be available to everybody regardless of race and creed. Everybody within earshot, he seemed to sing, should demand that these freedoms be available. No one should be left on the margins. We are all one.

Oddly enough, Curtis was seen as a renegade when he first issued these opinions. That's how unexpected and unique they were. To that point, we'd not heard much in the way of political substance from black artists. But the civil rights movement was a call to action not only for social reformers and activists, but for musicians as well. Curtis Mayfield led the charge for so many fine artists who'd choose to follow in his footsteps, including Sly Stone, George Clinton, the Temptations, Marvin Gaye, and Stevie Wonder.

Of course, Mayfield was anything but a threat or a renegade. He was a facilitator, a uniter, and a poet whose words were written to bring togetherness to fractious communities. He just happened to write and play music better than nearly anyone else who tried doing the same.

SELECTED DISCOGRAPHY

Curtis (Rhino, 1970/2000)
Superfly (Rhino, 1972/1999)
Curtis in Chicago (Curtom, 1973/2005)
People Get Ready! The Curtis Mayfield Story (Rhino, 1996)

The Impressions

The Impressions (Universal, 1963/2007)
People Get Ready (Universal, 1965/2007)
This Is My Country (1968/2006)

FURTHER READING

Burns, Peter. *Curtis Mayfield: People Never Give Up*. London: Sanctuary Publishing, 2001.
Edwards, Wayne, David Nathan, and Alan Warner. *People Get Ready! The Curtis Mayfield Story*. Liner notes. Rhino, 1996.
Werner, Craig. *Higher Ground: Stevie Wonder, Aretha Franklin, Curtis Mayfield, and the Rise and Fall of American Soul*. New York: Three Rivers Press, 2005.